Studies in
Chinese
Literary
Genres

Studies in Chinese Literary Genres

edited by
Cyril Birch

University
of California Press
Berkeley,
Los Angeles,
and London

University of California Press
Berkeley and Los Angeles
University of California Press, Ltd.
London, England
© 1974 by The Regents of the University of
   California
ISBN 0-520-02037-5
Library of Congress Catalog Card No. 77-157825
Designed by Steve Reoutt
Printed in the United States of America
Type set by Cathay Press Limited, Hong Kong

In Memoriam,
Shih-Hsiang Chen,
1912–1971

Shih-Hsiang Chen, whose study of the *Book of Songs* opens this symposium, died suddenly on May 23rd, 1971. His fellow-contributors dedicate this volume to the memory of a distinguished man of letters who was also the warmest of friends.

Contents

Acknowledgments

This volume is the outgrowth of a research conference on Chinese literary genres held in Bermuda in January 1967, under the chairmanship of Harold Shadick. The conference was sponsored by the Committee on Studies of Chinese Civilization (Chairman, Arthur F. Wright) of the American Council of Learned Societies. The support and encouragement of the Council are hereby acknowledged. Thanks are due also to A. C. Graham for his contribution to the conference discussions.

Of the eleven papers here assembled, six are reprinted, with some revisions, from the following journals:

"The *Shih-ching:* its Generic Significance in Chinese Literary History and Poetics," from *Bulletin of History and Philology,* Academia Sinica, Vol. xxxix, Part 1, Jan. 1969;

"The Quest of the Goddess," from *Asia Major,* New Series, Vol. xiii, Parts 1–2, 1967;

"Wu Wen-ying's *Tz'u:* A Modern View," from *Harvard Journal of Asiatic Studies,* Vol. 29, 1969. A somewhat expanded Chinese version appeared in the journal *Hsin ch'ao* 新潮 (Vols. 14–15, 1967) published by the Chinese Literature Society of National Taiwan University;

"The Conventions and Craft of Yuan Drama," from *Journal of the American Oriental Society,* Vol. 91, No. 1, Jan.–March 1971;

"Urban Centers—the Cradle of Popular Fiction," from *Archiv Orientálni,* Vol. 36, 1968;

"The Early Chinese Short Story: A Critical Theory in Outline," from *Harvard Journal of Asiatic Studies*, Vol. 27, 1967.

A Chinese translation of "The Military Romance" appeared in *Ch'un wen-hsüeh* 純文學, No. 13 (Vol. 3, no. 1), Taipei, Jan. 1968.

Editorial thanks are due to Mrs. Hua-yuan Li Mowry for her meticulous assistance, and to Professor Shadick for his wise guidance at all stages.

Mischances of one kind and another have delayed by years the appearance of these papers in symposium form. It would be tiresome to recount the sad story in picayune detail. Let it suffice to affirm here the gallant attempt of the University of California Press to transform a difficult manuscript into a volume of model grace and clarity without imposing a price to shrivel the student's pocketbook. The aid of a Hong Kong printer in this endeavor proved all but disastrous. Total collapse was avoided in the end only by resort to the photographic offset process. To the contributors, each of whom responded to requests with exemplary swiftness and skill, and to interested scholars whose patience has been so sorely tried, apology is hereby tendered.

Introduction

A literary genre is a comfortable saddle. The writer-rider once installed has the assurance that he will be in full control of his mount; the reader-rider who follows need not fear being bounced and shaken beyond endurance. With line fourteen we shall reach the end of the sonnet. Line four of the *lü-shih,* "regulated verse," will present a syntactic and semantic parallel to line three, as line six will to line five. In the Chinese "lawsuit story" we shall see the upright magistrate trace evidence already known to the reader but ignored or rejected by the stupid official who first mistried the case. Expectations of form fulfilled leave us freer to contemplate the total meaning.

Happiest of all will be the literary critic-historian, for he will be able to determine where the work "belongs." All will canter smoothly along, in fact, until the genre itself changes, or splits, or falls to pieces and is replaced as new original talents make new demands of it. Then literary history is made as genres form, grow, dominate their day, and decline.

A possible sub-title for this book might have been "Essays Toward a History of Chinese Literature." For if the eleven contributing scholars are agreed on one point it is that no satisfactory history of Chinese literature has yet been written. Perhaps the time is not yet ripe: too many problems remain unsolved, too many areas underexplored. But when the history is written, it will need to pay the closest attention to the nature of the literary genre, its definition, evolution, scope, and effects. Only in this way shall we advance beyond the level of the existing histories, whose concerns too often are limited to biographical data and the brief characterization of "representative works."

Each of the papers collected in this symposium limits itself to the consideration of the whole or a part of a single genre. The body of literature here reviewed begins with the earliest poetry in the *Book of Songs* and ends with certain novels of the nineteenth century. Representation is of course highly selective: gaps yawn especially wide for poetry (except for *tz'u* and dramatic verse) from T'ang onwards, and for prose genres other than some fiction. Furthermore, in approaching a body of literary works none of the present writers felt obliged to attempt comprehensive treatment, but each concentrated on those generic features in which he chanced to be most actively interested.

The symposium may serve, then, to illustrate certain current trends in the scholarly study of Chinese literature. Literary criticism and literary history blend as mutually supportive disciplines. The essays by Hans H. Frankel and James J. Y. Liu offer the most comprehensive treatments of genres, the first by defining the corpus of *yüeh-fu* poetry and analyzing its subdivisions, the second by the inclusive characterization of the subject matter of the *tz'u* lyric and of the techniques peculiar to its practice. In contrast, James R. Hightower concentrates on the nature of a single poetic device, that of allusion, as practiced by T'ao Ch'ien, whilst Chia-ying Yeh Chao essays the re-evaluation of a single author, Wu Wen-ying, in terms of his place in the lyric tradition. James I. Crump and Cyril Birch both make descriptive presentations of selected features from the corpus of drama, the metrical and musical conventions of Yuan *tsa-chü* in the first instance, the narrative themes and modes of Ming *ch'uan-ch'i* in the second. S. H. Chen explores the origins of the earliest poetry by redefining and reinterpreting the *hsing* "refrain" or "incremental repetition"; origins are again very much the concern of Jaroslav Průšek who presents an exhaustive survey of the known milieu of the early storytellers. Each of the remaining three essays suggests a further refinement of our definitions. David Hawkes establishes archetypes in the *Ch'u-tz'u*, the "itineraria" and the "tristia," which throw light not only on the total meaning of these early poems themselves but on the *fu* of Han and later times. Patrick Hanan in similar fashion applies new critical criteria to an old problem, and by analysis of the formal aspects of early *hua-pen* stories suggests new possibilities of tracing the evolution of the art of fiction in China. C. T. Hsia, finally, identifies a category of "military romances" which facilitates the more just evaluation of an entire genre of Chinese heroic fiction.

Advances in our knowledge of literature may result from many factors. Precious new sources of information come to light as rare texts turn up in private collections and are made public. Recent decades have been productive of such materials especially in the spheres of Chinese fiction and drama; an example is the reappearance of Lo Yeh's *Tsui-weng t'an-lu,* a work virtually lost to scholars for centuries but from which Jaroslav Průšek is now able to cull precious new information on the popular fiction of Sung times.

New materials may be brought into play from a different kind of source when scholars engage in cross-cultural studies. The effectiveness of the comparative approach judiciously applied is demonstrated by Hans Frankel's study of *yüeh-fu* poetry. From the scholarship on European balladry he draws criteria and critical approaches which at times corroborate and at other times call for a revision of traditional interpretations and distinctions.

In a somewhat different sense, Patrick Hanan takes advantage of new resources by applying in the Chinese context methodologies devised by scholars working entirely within their own Western tradition. If the author-reader relationships defined by Wayne C. Booth or the mimetic levels postulated by Northrop Frye can be of value in the analysis of Western literature then there is a good case for their application beyond their initial bounds.

In fact, the course of Chinese literary criticism in this century has been a history of precisely this kind of advance, at least since Wang Kuo-wei re-examined the *Dream of the Red Chamber* from the standpoint of Schopenhauer's theory of tragedy. But the situation varies from one major branch of literature to another, just as the very definition of literature in China differed from that of the Western tradition. Fiction and drama especially were regarded by traditional Chinese men of letters as entertainments, and were the object of serious study only by certain unconventional, even eccentric men. The critical writings of these men are often fragmentary, unsystematic, and excessively "technical." Although they can be acutely perceptive they provide only a partial foundation for the history or systematic analysis of these genres. Methods derived from Western practice have therefore tended to dominate these fields throughout the recent decades of growing interest.

The situation is exactly reversed when we consider modes such as memorials, eulogies, or even many forms of historical and philosophical writing. These were highly regarded by traditional critics, carefully distinguished and painstakingly preserved, yet they would be excluded from the domain of creative literature, or at best regarded as peripheral by most modern critics and historians. It is no accident that such modes as these are absent from consideration in the present symposium, although certainly the glaring omission of prose writings other than fiction was less a matter of design than a reflection of the current reduced interest in these genres.

Lyrical verse was the flower of the classical literature and the object of the most substantial and sophisticated body of criticism. As the essay by S. H. Chen amply demonstrates, the modern scholar must take account of a tradition of *Shih-ching* scholarship unbroken through two millennia. He may reject, restate, revise, but he cannot disregard it.

In sum, then, these essays may serve to demonstrate the relative fruitfulness of different critical approaches applied to different bodies of literary artifacts. Depending on the genre under consideration, they lean variously on the native critical tradition or on parallel types of material from other cultures, on comparativist methodology or on previously untried modes of analysis. Critical treatments of different genres must be expected to show wide variations in level of sophistication. The long unbroken tradition of scholarship in relation to the corpus of early poetry, the *Book of Songs* and *Ch'u-tz'u*, has already been alluded to; in contrast, study of the ideological or moral content of dramatic works (as distinct from formal prosodic analysis) is only beginning.

The essays are arranged in approximate chronological order. Accordingly the first two papers show much concern with the origins of poetry in China. From signs preserved in the canonical *Songs* S. H. Chen takes us back to song and dance in the fertility rites of the earliest age. David Hawkes suggests a progression from religious to secular as we move from the world of the shaman "summoning back the departing soul" *(Chao hun)* to the poet of the *Li sao* (although the order of dating might be reversed for the actual surviving specimens of these two generic types). Religious elements still more clearly observable in the *Nine Songs* are transformed, personalized, secularized in the *Li sao*. This extraordinary poem originates in the ritual journey, the undertaking of which by the ruler confers on him power over the material world symbolically traversed. From this source certain thematic materials enter poetry: the orderly enumeration of objects, the observance of spatial sequence. Carried on into the *fu* of later centuries these features once identified enable us to appreciate the *fu* as something less static than we would at first suspect, but rather as a mode of presentation of a universe dynamically perceived. It is a clear illustration of generic evolution, the kind of statement without which we can reach no satisfactory understanding of the history of Chinese poetry.

Hans Frankel in his treatment of *yüeh-fu* folk-poetry indicates some of the problems of genre definition. He describes a scale which extends in provenance from religious hymns to worldly ballads, in diction from the oral to the strongly literary, in mode from the lyric to the narrative. Subgroupings and necessary distinctions are very much his concern as he re-examines traditional classifications of the *yüeh-fu* corpus. Vastly more extensive is the later genre of *tz'u* or "lyric." Despite the size and chronological span of the body of surviving *tz'u*, James Liu demonstrates the usefulness of the generic definition. The "lyric" is most readily identified by its established metrical pattern with the lines of irregular though prescribed length. But at least for the early period, before Su Shih and his Sung contemporaries and successors extended the thematic scope of the lyric, the formal distinction is accompanied by highly characteristic matter, mood, and tone. There is a distinctive world of the lyric, feminine and miniature in scale, almost claustrophobic in its feeling. The *tz'u* poet sits in close, even oppressive proximity to his incense burner, his painted screen—or, more properly, to "her" bed-curtains or gauze-covered window, since the author, real or implied, is so often a woman. The natural world is seen from the inside looking out, and it is usually a melancholy confrontation.

In the identification of generic types, probably more work remains to be done in the field of Chinese fiction than in any other branch of literature. The late-Ming novel *Feng-shen yen-yi* is labeled *ling-kuai,* "spirits and monsters," by the eminent bibliographer Sun K'ai-ti, yet once C. T. Hsia has established his category of "military romance" he is able clearly to show that this is where the book belongs, and that it may be more effectively understood when viewed in this light. Subject matter, diction, narrative devices and rhetoric, authorial persona and attitude, all will conspire to place a given work in its proper tradition and to render more precise its total meaning. Patrick Hanan's essay shows us something of the illumination we can expect when these features have been carefully distinguished through the large and so far undifferentiated corpus of "promptbook" fiction.

We shall need to look very carefully, also, at generic links or transfers. Themes are shared, for example, by the *ch'uan-ch'i* stories of the T'ang literati and the promptbooks of the Sung storytellers. What is the exact line of advance here? Did *Li Wa chuan* first appear as an oral performance, a good story to tell in the pleasure quarters? Or was it narrated there only after it had been conceived and established in written form by an individual scholar-author? How closely can we follow the process by which (as a tentative reconstruction) folk stories were "discovered" and recast by literary men—and then recirculated among the people? As genres reflect social levels, the study of this kind of generic interchange will necessitate more of the cross-cultural analysis, as between élite and popular, which is a feature of Jaroslav Průšek's contribution.

No genre has exclusive rights to a particular literary endeavor. A story may be told in narrative and presented more or less "dramatically" there; or it may be formally dramatized and offered as an exceptionally "narrative" kind of drama. Cyril Birch in his study of selected Ming *ch'uan-ch'i* plays makes conspicuous reference to the values of fiction achieved in the plays themselves.

This book results from the conviction that we must take careful stock of generic conventions as they have evolved in Chinese literary practice. Critics and historians of past ages drew precise distinctions and established fixed rules for literary composition. We are free, of course, to accept or reject, as we should certainly reject the principles on which the dramatist Shen Ching gratuitously revised the "unorthodox" work of his more gifted confrère T'ang Hsien-tsu. But our recognition of generic characteristics is of prime importance. These are the restrictions within which the writer chose to work, or against which he found himself struggling in his act of creation. If it is true that any new art involves breaking through old restrictions, then our understanding of Chinese literature must depend heavily on those genre studies which can more clearly illuminate this process as it was repeated over and over again by the great creators of the past.

The *Shih-ching:*
Its Generic
Significance
in Chinese Literary
History and Poetics

by Shih-Hsiang Chen

It is inevitable that the search for the beginnings of Chinese poetry should focus on the *Shih-ching,* or *Book of Songs.* And since poetry marks the beginning of the creative literature of any nation, it is the concern of literary history to seek in the *Songs* such embryonic features as may typify much of later Chinese literary genres, in so far as they can be said to have a "national character." If one pauses to ask the question, in very general terms, of readers who are conscious of other literatures as well, what the most striking quality of Chinese literature would be, one of the possible answers might be that it is the combination or fusion of technical niceties, high sophistication and refinement of sensibilities with keen, direct, simple, and perhaps sometimes naive observations of man and nature. This quality should become evident in our discussion of the *Songs,* a quality that foreshadowed much in later Chinese literature, from the Han *yüeh-fu* to the *wu-yen shih,* from the T'ang *shih,* especially the *chüeh-chü,* to the Sung *tz'u* and from the drama to the novel. We know well the processes of the development of each of these later genres, which in every case can be traced from folk origins to the polish and refinement of courtly circles or the intelligentsia, and which would suggest a cause of the quality we have noted. Consequently, in the whole body of works of any great writer, from Ch'ü Yüan to Ts'ao Chih and thence to Li Po, Su Shih and Huang T'ing-chien, not to mention the dramatists and novelists, we find the blending of folk motifs and the distinctive creation of individual genius.

In the light of this estimation this study attempts to reveal the process of the formation of the corpus of the *Songs*, its artistic achievement, and its contribution to traditional criteria of Chinese criticism. We want, in stricter terms of literary history, to confirm and justify the claim that, in Professor Karlgren's words: "Throughout the history of Chinese literature there is no document which in importance and influence over later ages can compete with the *Shi*."[1]

The three hundred and five surviving Songs, gathered and reverently preserved in one Book, with the pious title *Shih-ching* "Classic of Songs" formulated to honor it since the Sung dynasty,[2] may seem too diversified to be called a literary genre, if by genre is meant such perfect metrical or thematic unity as would be applicable to later literary forms. But genre, as a term applied to ancient literature, despite the legion of conflicting theories about its definition and function, whether prescriptive or descriptive, has hardly ever meant such neat apparent unity. It is remarkable that Plato should first hint at literary genre distinctions only in such general terms as "narration" and "mimesis," referring the former to the narrative part of the epic and the latter to the dramatic. These two great categories were so all-embracing for Plato that a third type was merely called "mixed," or "union of the two."[3] Aristotle's *Poetics* elaborates on epic and drama as if they were the only two recognized archetypal genres. A third category of "melic" poetry is barely mentioned. Two modes of reproduction of the object seemed to be the concern. In the first the artist imitated and personified, or in Plato's terms, "assimilated himself" into the object; in the other the artist as an impersonal bystander depicted the object in "simple narrative."[4] Thus in the ancient Greek classification, as some Western literary historians even today still complain, "no room was left" for a third great category, "for the genre of self-expression or the lyric, in which the poet expresses directly his own feelings and thoughts."[5] We know that

---

[1] Bernhard Karlgren, "Glosses on the Kuo Feng Odes," *Bulletin of the Museum of Far Eastern Antiquities*, no. 14, p. 71.

[2] The earliest use of the term *Shih-ching* as a formal label of the book appears to be in the work *Shih-ching chiang-yi*, 詩經講義, by Liao Kang 廖剛 (1070-1143). Cf. 屈萬里, 詩經釋義, 叙論, Taipei, 1952.

[3] Plato, *Republic* III, p.392.

[4] *Ibid.*, p. 393.

[5] G. N. G. Orsini, article on "Genre," in *Encyclopedia of Poetry and Poetics*, Princeton, 1956.

lyrical poetry abounded in ancient Greece. But it was evidently not given critical attention when the sense of literary genres first awakened. It was, at best, subsumed under miscellanea, and, as in Plato, casually noted to be among "other styles of poetry."[6]

But imagine for a moment that the Confucian and Attic Ages of Chinese and Greek civilization had been fused into one, and we can be sure that a great trinity of the three primary genres would have been readily established. The third member of this trinity would no doubt have been the "lyric."[7] And the lyric genre would have referred mainly to the *Shih*, these songs which the Chinese treated as their major kind of poetry. There was, moreover, a definition in classical China of the middle Chou age that circumscribed for the lyric its rightful province. Juxtaposed against the Platonic declaration that "all mythology and poetry is a narration of events, either past, present, or to come,"[8] would have been the contemporary Chinese phrase, *shih yen chih* 詩言志, serving as a counterstatement, that "poetry," as a generic term, "speaks the heart's desire." *Shih* by nominalistic definition is a "song-word," hence "lyric" in the fullest sense as a working term for our modern criticism. And whenever the Chou people spoke of *shih*, they meant the *Songs* and those works that were like them and formed with them a literary category or kind.

It was not because lyrics were not available to the ancient Greeks that they did not recognize and treat them as a genre. There must have been cultural and philosophical reasons for their concentration on epic and dramatic verse in their poetics. Suffice it to say for the moment that the dominant position of the *Songs* in Chinese literary valuation as well as creation, in contradistinction to that of ancient Greek epic and drama, is a thought-provoking phenomenon. We believe, however, that the recognition of a genre as a distinctive kind of literature, which the *Book of Songs* certainly is, has the advantage of setting up a frame of reference whereby we can discuss coherently a common body of works of a given period in regard to its source,

[6] Plato, *op. cit.*, p. 393.

[7] Recognition has been given to the lyric in the study of Egyptian pyramid texts (*ca* 2600 B.C.) as consisting of eulogies to the kings, hymns to the gods, working songs, laments and festive songs. Cf. A. Erman, *The Literature of the Ancient Egyptians* (tr. by A. M. Blackman, 1927). The songs of the *Shih-ching* consist of almost exactly identical counterparts.

[8] Plato, *op. cit.*, p. 392.

growth, achievements, and, finally, its aesthetics. And by a generic approach to the *Songs* as "lyric"—that is lyric in accordance with the ideal of the term in modern critical usage as we shall be able to evince later in this paper—we may hope to retain this literary, aesthetic essence in our mind throughout our discussion. To speak of the *Songs* as lyric is to find for our discussion of them a common language in modern criticism, as well as to distinguish them as a prototype characterizing the first accomplishment of Chinese literary creation and fathering a native tradition as truly as the ancient Greek drama and epic fathered the European.

The Chinese word for poetry, *shih*, seems to have made its first appearance in the *Book of Songs* itself. It is found in neither the earlier bronze nor the oracle bone inscriptions. In demonstrably ancient sections of another time-honored tome of the Confucian canon, the *Book of Historical Documents* or *Shang shu*, it is notable that the word *shih* appears in the chapter "Gold-bound Coffer," *Chin t'eng*, where the word has reference to a quotation of one of the *Songs*, no. 155.[9] In the *Songs* themselves, the word was employed only three times (nos. 200, 252, 259), significantly all in the *Ya* 雅 or "Elegantiae" Sections, where a greater consciousness of the art of poetry-making, of polish and refinement of style, becomes evident. The production of at least two (nos. 252, 259) of these can be firmly dated by material evidence, internal as well as circumstantial, to be of the late ninth century B.C., during the heyday of Early Chou civilization, and no sufficient argument has been advanced to disprove the well-established tradition that the third, 巷伯 (no. 200), belongs to the same era.[10] Considering the context and the burden of meaning[11] in which the Chinese word for poetry, *shih*, made its debut, we may fairly say that a general conception of poetry as a *literary* art, definable by name and nature, had already begun to develop at an early stage of Chinese civilization.

To say that there is no Chinese word for poetry[12] means as much or

---

[9] References to numbers for the *Songs* henceforth are according to the Harvard-Yenching *Concordance to Shih-ching* and Karlgren's translations of the *Book of Odes*.

[10] Cf. my article, 詩字原始觀念試論, in *Bulletin of the Institute of History and Philology*, Academia Sinica, Ext. vol. 4, 1961.

[11] *Ibid.*

[12] Arthur Waley, "The Forms of Chinese Poetry," in *The Temple and Other Poems*, 1923, p. 137.

little as to say there is no word for *shih* in Greek, or indeed any non-Chinese language. No word so pregnant with meaning as "poetry" can be identical in semantic range in all its occurrences in any two languages. Even *Poésie* and *Dichtung* are not exactly identical. But *shih* for the ancient Chinese stood for the general concept of the art of words, as "songwords" but with emphasis on "words," as ποίησιS did for Aristotle, defined by him as that "art which imitates with language alone, but . . . has hitherto been without a name."[13] Not much later the use of the Chinese word *shih*, like the English word poetry, as a general term for poetic compositions whether accompanied by music or not became evident in the early *Ch'u Elegies* themselves.[14] And in still later and wider usage, *shih*, like "poetry," clearly indicated an essence or abstract quality transcending the boundaries of all arts, as in *shih chung yu hua, hua chung yu shih* 詩中有畫, 畫中有詩, "there is painting in poetry *(shih)*, and poetry in painting,"[15] a saying in art criticism current about the 11th century.

But *shih* and "poetry" are widely different in etymology. ποίησιS, which Aristotle used for an "art hitherto without a name" as late as the fourth century B.C.,[16] holding to the basic idea of "making," indicated the master critic's consciousness of poetry as a craft. Hence his *Poetics* advances many analytical, finely differentiated technical considerations concerning the art of poetry which were to form the basis of western literary criticism. The term for "poetry" in Aristotle, conceived as an abstract notion of "making," could therefore accommodate both of the two major Greek genres, epic and drama, whose complexity drew the Greek attention to abstract principles of construction and design. But the Chinese term *shih* signified an essence, a representation of the property and nature of an art, evidenced by the dominant, if not the sole, genre that was then current in ancient Chinese creative literature, the *Songs*. There the term *shih* was a natural-born entity, not constructed for the purpose

[13] Aristotle, *Poetics*, 1. 6.

[14] As in *Nine Songs*: "展詩兮會舞," where *shih* of course was accompanied by music; but in *Chiu chang*, 悲回風: "竊賦詩之所明," the intent of the word-meaning is emphasized, hence the least reference to music. In either case there is evidence that the same word *shih* as a general term is used for different kinds of verse as early as Late Chou.

[15] Su Shih's 蘇軾 (1036–1101) tribute to Wang Wei 王維, in his 題王維藍關煙雨圖.

[16] The *Poetics* is known to have been composed between 335 and 322 B.C.

of critical terminology but put forth as a manifestation of the early creative consciousness of the poetic art, with a keen sense of its origin, character, and content as lyric.

The fact that the *Songs* gave rise to, and was in ancient times identified with, the generic name *shih* affords a revelation of the *Songs'* early roots, their process of development, and fundamental traits for aesthetic appreciation. We can say without doubt that the *Songs* attained during Confucius' lifetime in the sixth century B.C. a scope similar to their present one.[17] Later transmission occasioned textual variations and corruptions, with perhaps greatest damage to the last section, the *Sung* 頌 or "Eulogia."[18] But to a very large extent, the *Songs* as we see them today have retained the original shape in which they were popular and familiar to the educated class of the Confucian age.

We have overwhelming evidence, according to ancient works such as the *Kuo yü* 國語 and the *Tso chuan* 左傳, of their popularity in high society at courtly or diplomatic gatherings. To quote from the *Songs*, often out of context, to suit an occasion of diplomatic negotiation among the states, or to put across a point in some court intrigue was a common practice. There was a cultural aura about them, so much so that Confucius admonished his son that "Without studying the *Songs*, one would not know how to speak."[19] And he asserted that the cultivation of one's character should be "inspired by the *Songs*, established according to ritual, and accomplished through music."[20]

The Mohists said of their Confucian contemporaries that "They recite the three hundred *Songs*, play the three hundred on strings, sing the three hundred and dance to the three hundred."[21] All these assertions in Chou works since the sixth century B.C., including Confucius' own frequent references to the "three hundred *Songs*,"

[17] The *Tso chuan* record, never successfully refuted, of 季扎觀樂 in 544 B.C., shows the same scope and number of categories. A large majority recorded in *Tso chuan* and *Kuo yü* as having been quoted through seventh to sixth century are identifiable in our present Mao texts. Song no. 153 may be the latest of the *Songs*, referring to events of about 520–514 B.C., perhaps incorporated into the corpus after the scope had been established.

[18] Cf. 傅孟眞先生集, vol. II, 詩經講義稿: 周頌說.

[19] *Analects*, XVI, 13.

[20] *Ibid.*, VIII, 8. About "inspired" 興, we shall soon have much more to say. We believe Confucius was using this word here in the vernacular sense of his day.

[21] *Mo-tzu*, Kung Meng Chapter 墨子公孟篇.

point to one fact: a whole, fairly standardized and integrated collection existed at that time, circulated among the upper classes, and was spoken of by the leading philosophic minds, as if with a uniform sense of value, despite the *Songs'* great internal prosodic and thematic diversity. They were all called *shih,* connoting a unified impression of a great category.

We ask, is there a common denominator shared among them, other than their common social status which was established by the middle Chou period for both political and educational purposes? By that time, as we shall see, the long refining process of the versions had been completed. In their now polished, well-adapted and regulated form, we are told that they were not only all "recited, played on strings and sung," but "danced to." This description would not only satisfy the definition of the *Shih* as lyric, but would allude to something more. The fact that the *Songs* in their final forms in courtly possession were *all* sung to musical accompaniments has been fairly well established.[22] We must, however, examine more carefully than the rest the last part of the Mohist assertion, that all the three hundred *Shih* or *Songs* were danced to by the Confucian scholars. Even though this Mohist statement, made in antipathy to the Confucian valuation of the arts, may be an exaggeration of the tradition, still the fact that when the *Shih* was spoken of, recital, music, and dance were all mentioned in one breath suggests a notion from which we may trace back to the primordial origination of the *Shih* and find a rudimentary factor that had given the *Songs* a common basis, prior to the many fissiparous developments of high culture, down to the sixth century B.C. This will be important both for our historical study of the *Songs'* development from a pristine generic form and for our appreciation of their aesthetics.

We have only two slender clues to follow: first, the true implication of the word *shih,* by which the *Songs* have come to be called, traced to its primary etymon; and, second, an old term in the critical nomenclature of the *Songs,* long remembered and talked of, but much the worse for wear and tarnished in meaning. This second term is *hsing* 興, of which we feel the best workable translation for our latter-day purpose of aesthetic appreciation is "motif"; it is evidenced prosodically in "burden," or "refrain," and, more importantly, in

---

[22] Cf. important articles by Ku Hsieh-kang 顧頡剛 in 古史辨, vol. III.

"incremental repetitions." By unravelling these two clues and finally tying them together we may discover a common embryonic feature of the *Songs* which gives them a fundamental generic unity beneath the many overlaid strands that make them so widely disparate.

Elsewhere, by observing the primary etymon for *shih* in the archaic word *tjəg, graphed 㞢 or 㞢 [23] as agreed on by modern scholarship, [24] I have established by detailed arguments that the root meaning of the Chinese word for poetry 䚯 (詩) ś*jəg, *shih*, derived from and remained closely associated with the concept of beating rhythm with the foot on the ground, as graphically represented by the archaic character 㞢. [25] The beating of rhythm with the foot clearly indicates the primordial art of dance, with which both music and song were embryonically at one. Western studies of the primitive origination of the medieval ballad and carol have amply proved this and will greatly help us in our examination of the development of the songs of the *Shih-ching* from their antique origin into such a rich variety of lyrics. The fact that all the songs in the "Eulogia" or *Sung* 頌 section, which has been proved to have preserved the oldest datable hymns in our extant texts, were danced to in solemn ceremonies in the ancestral temples of royalty of early Chou time has been well ascertained, not only by long tradition but by modern philological identification of *sung* with *jung* 容, i.e. "formal manners" of dance. [26] And it goes without saying that ancient traces of song, music, and dance performed in unity can often be sensed conspicuously in the lines or stanzas in both the "Elegantiae" or *Ya* 雅 and the "Airs" or *Feng* 風 sections. [27] But we need to keep in mind two important distinctions before we proceed further to find the true common factor in the origination of these *Songs* as lyrics. First, while there are, as we have seen, strong elements of the dance retained in the *Songs*, which are called *Shih* as if in remote reminiscence of those elements, we must distinguish between textual accounts of the dance in the contents of

[23] Oracle-bone script and late bronze inscription, respectively.

[24] Cf. Yang Shu-ta 楊樹達, 積微居小學金石論叢, vol. 1. pp. 21–22; and Wen Yi-to 聞一多, *Complete Works*: article 詩與歌.

[25] Cf. my article, "In Search of the Beginnings of Chinese Literary Criticism," in *University of California Publications in Semitic and Oriental Philology*, vol. XI, 1951.

[26] Well established by Juan Yüan 阮元 (1764–1849) in 揅經集室, vol. I, "釋頌"; later approved by Chang Ping-lin 章炳麟 and Wang Kuo-wei 王國維.

[27] Striking examples: songs nos. 220, 136, 137, 165.

the *Songs* portraying contemporary life on the one hand; and on the other the rhetorical devices evolved from dance rhythms that affect the structure of the songs regardless of the contents. We believe that these latter devices derived from a more primitive origin which the *Songs* generally share in the texture of their composition. Secondly, the distinction should be made between later formalized ceremonial dance-song performances, such as all the "Eulogia" had come to represent, and more primitive acts of dance accompanied by spontaneous emotional utterances, perhaps mere ejaculations at first, that gave rise to the most primordial elements of the *Songs*. Here we are faced with an apparent paradox. In our present extant texts of the *Songs*, so far as they are severally datable according to content, the "Eulogia of Chou" have proved to be the oldest, mostly being of the founding period of the dynasty during the tenth century B.C. With their later pretentious imitations in the "Eulogia of Shang" and the "Eulogia of Lu," they form one traditional category.[28] The Elegantiae" are mostly of the middle era of Early Chou, identified with events of the ninth to the eighth century B.C. The "Airs" apparently joined the corpus last, with some from as late as the sixth century B.C. But despite the later evolution of their entire composition, the "Airs", preserving more of the pristine folk quality, have retained most of the primordial elements of the *Songs*.

We postulate that the term *hsing* 興, in its archaic Chinese pronunciation *xi̯əng, is one of the slender and intricate clues crucial to tracing these primordial elements. We shall understand it as "motif," but we shall find it largely evolved in the extant textual materials into burdens, refrains, or "incremental repetitions"[29] which bear upon the structure of the *Songs*. The *Mao Annotations* 毛傳 to the *Songs*, as the highest traditional exegetical authority that has survived since the Han age,[30] may seem to have provided us with enough convenient pointers by having marked off, with apparently meticulous care, hundreds of lines and phrases (predominantly in the

---

[28] The *Shang Eulogia* are of Duke Hsiang's reign (651–635 B.C.); the Lu Eulogia, of Duke Hsi's (659–627 B.C.). Cf. Fu Meng-chen 傅孟眞, *op. cit.*

[29] Term used by F. B. Gummere in *The Popular Ballad*.

[30] We accept Wang Kuo-wei's 王國維 calculation (書毛詩故訓傳後, in 觀堂別集 vol. I) that the *Annotations* carry a pre-Han tradition transmitted by Mao Heng 毛亨 but have thence been elaborated on by Mao Ch'ang 毛萇 with early Han lore. We shall, however, refer the authorship of the extant corpus generally to the latter.

"Airs" and "Minor Elegantiae" sections) and called our attention to them as *hsing*.

But still, so many inconsistencies and obscurities of referent were felt by later scholars in Mao's identification of *hsing* that Chu Hsi 朱熹 (1130–1200), who may be said to have established a second milestone after Mao in traditional Chinese *Shih-ching* scholarship, found it necessary to readjust the scope of *hsing* as a critical exegetical term in his *Shih chi-chuan* 詩集傳, or *Comprehensive Annotations to Shih-ching*. Mao's *Annotations* had marked off phrases, lines, and sometimes whole stanzas in as many as 116 songs out of the total 305, as *hsing*. Now the result of Chu's new effort was to reassign a large number of Mao's *hsing* passages to two other categories in the traditional critical terminology of the *Songs* handed down along with the Mao text in the *Ta hsü* 大序 or "Great preface," whose authorship is still under debate.[31] Chu therefore reinterpreted a good part of Mao's *hsing* entities as either *pi* 比, "similes," or *fu* 賦, "narrations." But while on the one hand he reduced the old *hsing* identifications somewhat, on the other he expanded the *hsing* category in new directions by placing under the *hsing* rubric many passages which Mao had not noted as such. Between Mao and Chu, of course, came Cheng Hsuan (A.D. 117–200), who composed the *Cheng ch'ien* 鄭箋, known as the "Cheng Commentaries," which has since the second century A.D. become an inseparable addendum to the extant Mao text. The "Cheng Commentaries," by superimposing Cheng Hsüan's allegorical interpretations on the *Mao Annotations,* literally or by implication multiplied the *hsing* items to a great extent.[32] If Cheng has been justly criticized for his latter-day political and moralistic rationalizations and strenuous allegorical interpretations, Chu, in his not very successful attempt to free himself from these, by recasting the *hsing* category and commingling it with "similes" and "narratives" in a process of contraction and expansion, showed the bias of a latter-day poetic and rhetoric developed during the Six Dynasties and the T'ang age, and was thus even further removed from the original meaning of *hsing.*

[31] Modern scholarship tends to accept Wei Hung 衛宏 of Later Han as the author, but the issue is not entirely settled.

[32] Cheng included many items which, though not noted by Mao, were said to be "really *hsing* with senses self-evident, hence unnoted." See *Cheng Chih* 鄭志, Answer to *Chang Yi* 答張逸.

We are not minimizing the contribution to Chinese poetic criticism made in terms of the latter-day understanding of *hsing*. If the designation of *hsing* in the *Ta hsü* or "Great Preface" (final version possibly by the first century A.D.) as one of the *liu yi* 六義 or "Six Principles" was a pious attempt at scriptural interpretation, it was also the beginning of an act of literary criticism that showed a sense of more general textual classification as to the contents, in terms of *feng, ya,* and *sung*. There was as yet but a glimmering notion of compositional technique, as distinct from contents or subject matter, in terms of *fu, pi* and *hsing*, stated in that order.[33] The "Preface" expatiated at great length on the former three categories but seemed oblivious to the latter three, simply separating them and laying them aside. It is therefore most noteworthy that when what may be called truly specialized or pure literary criticism first rose to its height in China in the fifth century, the articulate voice of the great poetic critic of the age, Chung Hung 鍾嶸 (469–518) should, in bold contradistinction to the laconism of the "Great Preface," have spoken *only* of the latter three terming them the *san yi* 三義, the "Three Principles," and have given prominence to *hsing* by listing it ahead of *pi* and *fu*. He explicated the *hsing* as sense beyond words: "Where the letter (or *wen* 文) has ended, meaning goes on";[34] hence as connotative, associative power, overtones and undertones. But we can observe that he was speaking of the effects of poetry in the abstract with explicit reference to the quadrasyllabic and pentasyllabic verse known to have been practiced in his own time, and with but a vague genuflection, if any, to the *Songs*.

A century later K'ung Ying-ta 孔穎達 (574–648), following Cheng Hsüan's authority, reiterated the "Six Principles"[35] put forth by the "Great Preface" and, with clearer formal balance, divided them into

---

[33] It should be noted that the *feng, fu, pi, hsiang, ya, sung,* 風 賦 比, 興, 雅, 頌, stated in that order, had been called in *Chou li* 周禮 the *liu shih* 六詩 the instruction of which being the function of the "Grand Master" (*ta shih* 大師) of court musicians, hence understood as six ways of presenting or performing the *Songs*. The *Chou li* is consistent in warranting this sense in both citations in vol. IV, under "Grand Master" and "Lesser Master" (hsiao shih 小師). Especially in the "Lesser Master" section is the mention of *liu shih chih ke* 六詩之歌 clearly indicative that the six terms were originally *all* in reference to "song-tunes." To call them *liu yi*, "six principles," is a later invention in the "Great Preface" to suit a latter day canonical-literary concept in disregard of the original meaning.

[34] "Preface" to *Shih p'in* 詩品序.

[35] In *Mao-shih cheng-yi* 毛詩正義.

two equal sets and treated them on equal terms, the one set as
"poetic corporality,"[36] hence substance, in terms of *feng, ya* and
sung; and the other as "poetic usages,"[37] hence technique, in terms of
fu, pi, and *hsing.* This was the canonical interpretation of the "Six
Principles" authoritatively established for the study of the *Songs* in
the T'ang age, and has since been conveniently accepted by posterity.
But K'ung's work, despite its claim to *"Rectification of the Orthodoxy
in the Mao Texts of the Songs",* as its name *Mao-shih cheng-yi* suggests,
gave no more critical heed to the prominence of *hsing* which Mao had
so painstakingly pointed out, than to call it "arcane of reason" or
li yin 理隱. K'ung's "Rectification" only reinforced the trend in
Chinese literary criticism of separating technique from substance, or
form from content, which, when carried to extremes, became a pitfall
not unique to Chinese literary thought. Henceforth the meaning of
hsing, technically regarded, became either rarified or mystical. Chu
Hsi, with his fidelity to the texts of the *Songs* themselves, saw in them
more *hsing* elements even than Mao, and sometimes with flashes of
fresh insight. But preoccupied with contemporary literary vogue, he
made two most important statements that left unfortunate influences.
For him *hsing* was either just a way of starting a poem, which has
given encouragement to even some modern Chinese scholars to
dismiss it as meaningless,[38] or it was something like an "inspiration to
the poet from what he saw,"[39] that prompted his allegorical fancy.
This might be true enough of Chu's own or any other sophisticated
age. But the individual poet Chu seems to propose here looks too
anachronistic a figure for high antiquity. Later terms were derived
from *hsing* at the final fruition of Sung poetics with such rarified and
intangible senses as *"hsing chih* 興致*"* and *"hsing ch'ü* 興趣*",* translatable as "inspirational gusto" and "zest," which were advocated
with almost mystical ecstasy by Yen Yü 嚴羽[40] (fl. 1225–1264).
These became immensely popular not only in later poetic criticism,
but as current colloquial idioms. We have been using these phrases

---

[36] *Shih chih ch'eng hsing* 詩之成形.

[37] *Shih chih so yung* 詩之所用.

[38] Chu, in his 詩傳綱領, speaks of *hsing* as "starting a composition by resorting to
some objects, basically without regard for meaning": 託物興辭, 初不取義.

[39] Chu, in annotation to song no. 23.

[40] Cf. 滄浪詩話, especially chap. 1, sect. 5.

for centuries in works on poetic appreciation and in daily life, comfortably oblivious of the *hsing* of the *Songs,* and with typical unconsciousness of the atavism in linguistic history.

So from Chung Hung to Chu Hsi and thence through the ages the interpretation and appreciation of *hsing* found accommodation with contemporary fashions of literary criticism and creation. But the most observant of all literary historians in the fifth century, the peerless researcher Liu Hsieh 劉勰 (ca. 465–522), a contemporary of Chung Hung, declared with penetrating insight, "The (true) meaning of *hsing* had been lost!" or *"hsing yi hsiao wang* 興義銷亡.[41] To prove his point Liu went on to cite authors from Chia Yi 賈誼 (201–169 B.C.) to those close to his own time and complained that because "the *hsing* was forgotten", their "literary qualities became inferior to those of the Chou people", to those qualities exemplified by the *Songs.* We may not share Liu's idealization of a "golden past", but we do recognize the difference. In fairness to these later writers, we would rather say that the difference lies in the fact that the *Songs* as *shih* formed a genre from an antique origin, identifiable in the usages of the *hsing* in its primary sense, which later writings no longer shared. The "loss" was on account of the change of a generic practice as well as the change of poetic concepts.

We believe that a genre, while it may signify in its full development a complex set of recognizable literary fashions and conventions in a society at a given age, can and should be traced back to its pristine origin as a simpler common mode of expression of the emotional and imaginative life of a human community. On close examination, the "Mao Annotations" that uniformly mark off many phrases and lines as *hsing* reveal a set of conventions spreading through all parts of the texts of the *Songs.* The *hsing* elements bear up the structure of each poem where they appear, as they start or reinforce the rhythm, establish the sound pattern, and set the mood. They do this in the form of refrains or burdens, but more often than not as subtly significant strophes, as "incremental repetitions." They are quintessential to the whole charm and success of the generic character of the *Songs* as their main technical aspect. We suggest that Mao's unfortunate inconsistencies and deficiencies, diligent as he was in noting these *hsing* elements for us, came about because he (and who knows if

---

[41] Liu Hsieh, 文心雕龍, chap. 36, 比興.

there were not many other hands of Han ideologues tampering with his texts?) was already too preoccupied with allegorical interpretations in accordance with current political and moral ideology, and would consequently appear to be making light of the *hsing's* basic technical importance. His allegorical interpretations would read like second thoughts, but so elaborated as to overshadow his primary concern with the *hsing,* each time after he cried out loudly *"hsing yeh* 興也", "this is hsing!" But certainly Mao knew that the *hsing* was an ancient song technique. For the *Chou li,* prior to Mao, had explicitly called the *hsing* one of the "Six Song-tunes."[42] Some reliable scholars[43] believe that the "Great Preface," despite the possible late date of its final version, represented a tradition forming the basis of *Mao's Annotations,* and that the "Preface" had taken over the term *hsing* verbatim from the *Rites of Chou* text to formulate its so-called "Six Principles": *feng, fu, pi, hsing, ya, sung.* (See note 33.) By verbal legerdemain, the "Preface" had pigeonholed the *hsing,* as it were, in its rigid formulation of the "Six Principles," thus obscuring the original vital link of *hsing* with "song." But if we look elsewhere in the *Chou li,* we often find that the *hsing* stands significantly alone, apart from the rest of these six terms, in singular eminence, and with a vibrant sense in relation to music. In its section on the "Great Minister of Music," *Ta ssu-yüeh* 大司樂, a more eminent office than that of the "Grand Music Master" (note 33), the *Chou li,* or *Rites of Chou,* cites *hsing* to head a list of descriptions of ways of *yüeh yü* 樂語 "musical elocution",[44] along with musical speech and declamation. And in its section on the "Dance Master," *Wu shih,* it laconically cites the term *hsing wu* 興舞, noting that it was "not for minor sacrifices,"[45] and so must have been for all major ones. Hence *hsing wu* with this solemn implication should not be taken merely to mean "rise to dance" as the later simplified sense of the word may seem to indicate, but should appropriately suggest memories of more ancient customs.

   Being a "primary ideogram," the word *hsing* is of itself illuminating by what is found to be its earliest archaic graph and sound, written

[42] For the term *liu shih chih ke* in *Chou li,* vol. IV, cf. above, note 33.
[43] Cf. 朱自清, 詩言志辨, p. 58 and footnote 16.
[44] *Chou li,* vol. VI, beginning of Section 1: 樂語 . . . . . 興道諷誦言語.
[45] *Chou li,* vol. III, under Wu shih 舞師 section.

舁 and pronounced *xiəng. When the word was first discovered in the oracle-bone inscriptions, it was misread by Lo Chen-yü 羅振玉 for a rather amusing reason. Unable as yet to shake off the *Shuo wen* 說文 tradition, Lo claimed the character to be *yü* 與, citing as its etymological cognate 舁 (𢍏) from the *Shuo wen*, read *yü* in the sense of "give."[46]

Lo's misinterpretation of 1914 was not corrected until Shang Ch'eng-tso 商承祚 and Kuo Mo-jo 郭沫若[47] both uncovered it in 1933. Now we have no doubt[48] that the word *hsing* had its antique origin in the oracle-bone inscriptions as 𢍏, identified by Shang Ch'eng-tso as "four hands each holding up the corner of a tray." The fact that the middle element in the graph. the object that is held, is *p'an* or a tray and not *chou* or a boat, has been reinforced by Kuo Mo-jo's forceful agrument.[49] Kuo pointed out the "corrupt deviations" (*o pien* 譌變) from *p'an* to *chou* in the bronze inscriptions, and, restoring the original significance of the graph *p'an* 片 as the pictograph of a tray, he stressed its essentially dynamic sense of "turning round" by identifying it as the primary graph for 肸, later written 般, 槃, or 盤, which had long since been accepted as meaning both "tray" and "turning round." The association of these two senses in ancient and later usage is too close to be dismissed as a case of mere phonetic loan. Shang Ch'eng-tso's convincing analysis of the early graphic components of *hsing*, combined with Kuo's dynamic interpretation, in fact suggests their vital relationship, which will establish

---

[46] Cf. Lo Chen-yü, 殷虛書契攷釋, 1914, p. 56. To force the identification Lo glossed over the fact that there are four hands around the graph 𢍏, and finally preferred to recognize only two hands to suit the cognate form. He could not quite make up his mind about the middle part of the graph, the element 片, which had long since been in a state of confusion in the history of the Chinese script, thought to be either *chou* 舟 for "boat," or *p'an* 盤 for "tray," despite both their great phonetic difference and semantic variance. He tried to reconcile these by adding as an afterthought that "*p'an* is also *chou*, for containing things," thus inadvertently, of course, suggesting the broad sense of "vessel," which could be either "boat" or "tray" or any container as we might accept it to be in English. But still *p'an* and *chou*, "boat" and "tray," phonetically and in their semantic usages cannot possibly be identical. For the etymonic graph of *hsing* in our concern, the case must be decided one way or other.

[47] Shang, 殷契佚存考釋, p. 62; and Kuo, 卜辭通纂攷釋, p. 34.

[48] I owe it to my friend Professor Kao Ch'ü-hsün 高去尋 of Academia Sinica to have reconfirmed the word's identity in our correspondences, March, 1967, where he supplied me with the most recent extensive data supporting Shang and Kuo's analysis, and refuting others. Especially appreciated are his citations of those relevant parts from Professor Li Hsiao-ting 李孝定, 甲骨文字集釋, vol. III, 1965.

[49] Kuo, *op. cit.*, p. 29.

the true etymology of the word. Having established the graph as a symbol of four hands each holding part of a tray, Shang went on to observe the variant forms of the graph with an additional element 曰, *k'ou* or "mouth," such as 簋 and 爨, in bronze inscriptions, and came to the conclusion that *hsing* < *$xi\partial ng$* was an ejaculation uttered when a group of people were lifting up a thing together. He decided that the sound of the word *hsing* was onomatopoeic, in the class of such Chinese interjectives as *ya hu* 邪許. In English we may find as its equivalent something like "heave-ho." The ejaculation thus uttered, however, may not, as Shang suggested, be only caused by the weight lifted together. The central object being depicted in the 月 shape of a tray, how much weight could it really have? As Kuo Mo-jo saw in it and in its cognates the dynamic sense of "turning round," or the movement "around," it may not be simple upward lifting but a group circling as well. Hence the indication of the sense of dancing. And the heave-ho was likely as well an expression of joy and excitement in the playful cavorting of the group as in co-operative labor. By but a slight semantic extension, the central element *p'an* in the word *hsing* soon came to generate such cognate compounds in very early classical texts as *p'an yu* 盤游, "dallying,"[50] and *p'an huan* 盤桓, "hovering about (blissfully)."[51] And in texts of the *Songs* themselves, we see it either means "joy"[52] or signifies dance.[53]

Thus the premise can be established that the *hsing* < *$xi\partial ng$*, which was to become so mercurial in meaning yet to remain such a crucial key concept in traditional Chinese poetics as well as in the study of the *Songs*, was a primitive "heave-ho" or "hurrah," ejaculated in joy and high spirits. This was probably done with a feeling of emotional and physical uplift by a group turning round a central object while joining hands in a dancing circle. We believe that herein lies the primeval origin of the *Songs* as *shih*, which was to be the name for all later Chinese poetry. We shall see *hsing* as the essence of the *Songs*'

[50] In *Shang Shu*: 尚書, 五子之歌: *p'an yu wu tu* 盤游無度, "to dally without temperance"; 逸周書, V: *p'an yu an chü* 盤游安居, "to dally in secure living."

[51] In 易經: 屯卦初九: *p'an huan li chü chen* 盤桓利居貞, "hovering about, omen good for making home."

[52] Song no. 296: 般 glossed as "joy".

[53] Song no. 56: *K'ao p'an* 考槃; song no. 137: 婆娑 *p'o so* = *p'an so* 槃娑, with 婆 *p'o* given as *p'an* according to text in *Shuo wen* 說文. Waley's superior translation of *K'ao p'an* is greatly helped by this textual emendation.

generic character, concerning both their social functions, however idealized and formalized later in Chou time, and their intrinsic poetic distinction, even though the texts were evolved after long civilizing processes through many centuries. The primitive voices, transformed and refined into prosodic devices and conventions in their texts, still strike us, despite their great diversity, as a general "tonality," to which Mao, with perhaps very imperfect remembrance, gave prominence by reminding us of the common term *hsing*.

Let our discovery of the primeval sense of the word *hsing* first help us solve a few rather basic general problems of the *Songs*. In order to do so, we may greatly profit by introducing an analogy from western scholarship in the study of the medieval European carols and ballads, with which the *Songs* are in many ways comparable, though not entirely similar, in their course of development, their later involvement with a social, official, and courtly life,[54] and their sometimes striking resemblance in formal features. As the modern tendency to treat many of the *Songs* largely as anonymous "folk songs" has been violently opposed to the earlier Chinese tradition of attributing them to individual ancient worthies, kings, queens, dukes, and wise sages, so has opposition arisen among western scholars studying the ballad and the carol, who either insist on their being communal folk products, or individual creations.[55] The question needs to be clarified before it is solved. No one reading a so-called "folk-song," be it a ballad, carol, or a *Shih-ching* song of even the most naive primitive charm, can help but feel that some individual talent, however natural-born and anonymous, is responsible for the current version. One cannot accept with ease that all were uniformly collective impromptu compositions. Field studies in surviving customs of ballad production today have again and again reported discoveries of individual talents in backward communities. And reading the *Shih-ching,* even those of the *Kuo-feng* or "Airs" section, one more often than not feels the heart's cry of an individual, a self-expression which is the soul of the lyric, though spoken anonymously and without

---

[54] A revealing parallel can be found in A. B. Friedman, *The Ballad Revival*, 1961, treating the relations of ballads to official poetry from 1100 to the present.

[55] Salient examples are arguments between F. B. Gummere, *The Popular Ballad* (1907) and Louise Pound, *Poetic Origins and the Ballad* (1921).

clear personal identity. But, on the other hand, one cannot help being struck by such distinctive elements in the *Shih-ching* as those in the burdens, refrains, and especially the "incremental repetitions," sometimes vivid or odd and often "arcane of reason," but nevertheless stock figures that must have come from earlier convention long before the accomplished versions of the *Songs*. So the question of the "folk" origin of the *Songs,* as of the carol and the ballad, has reference not to the complete composition of the current versions, but to the more primitive elements, still generically shared by them, yet traceable to far more remote antiquity if we possess a clue. And the word *hsing,* as we have analyzed it, is such a clue. The case becomes clear beside its western parallel.

Sir Edmund K. Chambers, upon whom we can rely as an up-to-date authority who takes a moderate position, would be the last to accept the "communal" folk production theory to account for current versions of the ballads and carols transmitted since the medieval ages. In good humor he derided the "communalists," from Lang to Gummere, by alluding to "the quiet irony of George Meredith in *The Amazing Marriage,* where Dame Gossip's 'notion of the ballad is, that it grows like mushrooms from a scuffle of feet on grass overnight.' "[56] In his learned and witty book, however, Sir Edmund saw fit to trace the origin of the popular medieval carol to a common primitive central element through philology. For the Greco-Latin root *chorus* is suggested to derive from a "round-dance," or in perhaps a lesser, derivative sense from *choraules,* the "flute accompanist" of such a dance, and finally, from *corolla,* a little crown or garland, a concrete central object around which the dance was performed, or which implies the round movement. Sir Edmund comes to the conclusion that "in either case, the sense of a 'ring' is there."[57] For a graphic illustration of the "ring" dance around a circle, he cites a medieval miniature showing "a group of men and women dancers with raised arms and joined hands."[58] Chambers visualizes the scene in the primeval folk community, where under stimulation the "feet of the chorus (round-dancers) break into the

[56] *English Literature at the Close of the Middle Ages,* Oxford University Press, 1947, p. 174.
[57] *Ibid.,* p. 66.
[58] *Ibid.,* p. 68.

*uplifting*⁵⁹ (italics mine) of the dance." And with the dance came "originally the song . . . which may have been no more than an inarticulate outcry."⁶⁰

This "song," indeed this "inarticulate cry," is what we hear in the long-drawn interjection, the ejaculation of "*Xiəng*!", the archaic Chinese "heave-ho," spontaneously uttered in high spirits in a primitive communal gathering. At first it perhaps had been on happy occasions when the joy of joint labor transcended physical exertion and rose to the spirit of play. Or, again, it could have been from the sheer delight in the joint movement of limbs and bodies in the most primitive festivities. In either case, joyous labor or festive play, the "heave-ho" or its like was to grow and develop with the rhythmic repetition and variation which must have been of the essence in any collective movement that gave pleasure and uplift.

On this assumption we feel safe in saying that the primal embryonic element of the "folk song," be it a "*Xiəng*!", a "heave-ho," a "hurrah" or what not, was "communal" in origin, stemming from the collective impulse and group feeling of "uplift." But "communalism" for the origination of the "folk song" can prevail in the strictest sense only up to this point. For after the practice of the joint rhythmic "inarticulate cry," or even perhaps during it, an individual "leader" would soon emerge who grasped the meaning of the occasion, imparted his personal insight, was inspired by immediate objects or contingent events symbolic of the feeling of the whole occasion, and became articulate with more words. Thus he would trace the theme, as it were, and utter inspired rhythmic and expressive phrases which would form "motifs" to "start" the song and set the pattern of the sound as well as the mood. Such was the *hsing* as it developed among the *Songs*. There had been the time when the uplifting "inarticulate cry" of the primordial "*Xiəng*!" soon grew into inspired phrases, iterated by the group to the accompaniment of uncouth music and the round dance, while the "leader" continually traced and expanded the theme into the prototypes of primitive folk songs. Between this time, however, and the time of the composition of the highly elaborated songs of the *Shih-ching* with their adaptation to

⁵⁹ In a conversation with Professor Peter Boodberg on the *hsing* in our present concern, the word "uplift" spontaneously and simultaneously came to both our minds.

⁶⁰ *Op. cit.*, p. 69.

solemn courtly music and royal temple dances, as well as to lesser social ceremonies, many centuries must have elapsed. But it is remarkable how the *hsing* element has remained recognizable in the extant texts of the *Songs.*

To the extent that the *hsing* element spread through all the sections of the texts, we see it as a guideline for establishing the general generic character of the *Songs.* And once it has been traced to its original sense, concept, and significance, it leads us to presuppose a very long and much earlier tradition behind the composition of the songs, which can in themselves no longer properly be called primitive folk songs. But the primitive folk origin, carried over through long processes of refinement and sifting, is still clearly discernible in the *hsing* elements. In these elements the songs retain traces of the pristine beauty of the poetry of an innocent fresh world, where music, dance, and song lent magic power to each other. This is why the songs were ever to be emulated though not equalled in the later Chinese poetic tradition.

Let us go further to deal with some other perennial problems about the *Songs* in the light of our discovery. These have to do with certain dominant themes and their treatment, and a surmise, if possible, concerning the historical-social genesis and evolution of their texts into a collected corpus. First we take all the sections, the *Feng, Ya,* and *Sung,* or "Airs," "Elegantiae," and "Eulogia," as a whole. The themes that stand out most distinctly are always those somehow related either to agricultural or to human fertility in the broad sense, the latter including, of course, love. These are treated either with a ceremonial attitude or otherwise, but most often with motifs derived from natural or man-made objects observed in agricultural activities and, to a lesser degree, in the herdsmen's or hunters' life and labor. Or, in the case of love songs, there are objects that smack of the open fields that were cultivated on plains, in the hills, or by the streams. And especially remarkable in the love or courtship songs is the prominent position of woman, a theme that is relatively frequent.

We think we have sufficiently suggested the long tradition behind the composition of the *Songs.* These themes and motifs cannot therefore be entirely explained by contemporary Chou cultural conditions. Neither a political analysis of the Chou mode of agricultural production, whether slave-based or feudal, nor sociological knowledge of the position of the Chou women can give us a satisfactory answer. But by projecting these themes and motifs, and tracing them back to their generic origin, we may venture to produce the reason. The clue discovered in the *hsing* has given us graphic and semantic illustrations which both point to the scene as dance and song were born in Chinese high antiquity and maintain for us the possibilities of appreciating the traces of the pristine poetic qualities still manifest in the contents as well as in the formal features of the *Songs*. We can assume the growing importance of agriculture to Chinese life even before the Shang dynasty.[61] In investigating the origin of the carol and the ballad, the importance of the same elements has been assumed for ancient Europe. Gummere, in fact, found that the "agricultural community," even "in its crudest stages," was perhaps the primary and certainly the most prolific source that "fosters the communal song"[62] in its origin. The "uplifting dance" and with it the simultaneous high-spirited cry that was to grow into song, as the basic meaning of *hsing* compositely suggested, must have arisen on occasions of vital concern to the community such as bounteous harvests and high human productivity. Ritualistic and festive in mood as they gathered, the communal groups would be moved to feel that the essence of natural and human fertility was all in one. "And," in Chambers' words about the origin of the carol, "as the spirit presided over human as well as other fertility, it was natural that women should take a leading part, and that the impulse of the dance should be amorous."[63] So the prominence of women's position in the *Songs* was not so much the result of contemporary Chou life as a sustained generic convention from antiquity. The convention had grown and was now elaborated and refined to produce many of the exquisite *Songs*, which we can even better appreciate, however, by gaining a greater psychic distance from contemporary Chou social history and turning back to the primary source of the genre.[64] So too

[61] Witness the highly developed knowledge of farming seasons and work, and the vital concern with them recorded in the Shang oracle bones.

[62] F. B. Gummere, *Origins of Poetry*, MacMillan, 1901, p. 279.

[63] *Op. cit.*, p. 89.

[64] For the support of this view we would venture to suggest that when Confucius so often spoke of the *Songs* as if they were a whole, he must have sensed in them a long-established generic unity. Furthermore, when he discoursed on the *Songs*, including the love songs, with so much reverence, aesthetically as well as morally, he was not reading out

must the objects invoked from nature or the crafts have been laden with older traditional beliefs, primitive perceptions fashioned by convention into poetic usages, which should be appreciated for their generic artistic effects rather than as mere realistic reportage.

These are generally to be recognized in the distinctive *hsing* elements, which still "uplift" us as they did the song-makers of Chou, who adopted them as the generic properties that established and characterized the *Songs* as a fully developed artistic genre. Even though the inspiration might now have been personalized and drawn from real life experiences, yet an established genre deriving from old traditions would continue to favor the treatment of certain themes and the use of certain motifs in such ways as had developed since olden times. Thus the prominent position of women in the love songs and the invocation of natural or other concrete objects can all be ultimately traced back to the first exuberant cries of "*Xiang!*" that went with the "uplifting dance," when in felicitous moments the bounty of nature and the fruition of enamoured maidens seemed to be a single phenomenon, just as song, music, and dance comprised a single art to express this joy.

Now we can attempt to view the general contents of the *Shih-ching* more closely, first in broad categories and then more in aesthetic detail. Among the contents of the *Shih-ching*, the *Sung* or "Eulogia" section of course had the most elevated position in the court. Of these the *Chou sung* are the oldest, the *Shang sung*[65] and *Lu sung*[66] following as well known imitations from the middle seventh century B.C. We have been assured of one fact about the *Sung* or "Eulogia" songs. It is that they were each danced to on the most solemn occasions of sacrifice in royal ancestral temples. The *Chou sung*, as the oldest pieces, perhaps of the tenth century B.C. when the Chou dynasty was first founded, typify this solemn spirit. Even though the parts we

---

of them realistic depictions of contemporary social customs, which, we know, he in fact censured if not detested. Indeed, some of the *Songs*, at least in the "Airs" section, are found to have been composed near his own lamentable time. But he accorded them all, including the amorous love songs, equal appreciation and respect, for no other reason we can see than that he, even as a moral philosopher, recognized in them more ancient surviving conventions, which he wanted in idealistic retrospection to restore and reunite with meaningful rituals of a golden bygone age.

[65] In the time of Duke Hsiang of Sung 宋襄公 (r. 650–636 B.C.)

[66] Time of Duke Hsi of Lu 魯僖公 (r. 659–633 B.C.).

possess of them in our extant texts are known to have suffered the worst damage of the whole corpus, the *Chou sung* songs, even in their fragmentary version, are clearly marked with two main concerns. They are either devoted to praising ancestors as progenitors identified with a bounteous or protective heaven[67] that propagated as well as nourished man with "wheat and barley";[68] or to invoke a sacred religious feeling for farming labor and productivity.[69] There is a third important concern admixed with these in the *Chou sung*, namely, festive conviviality, the offering of wine and food, not only to the spirits of male and female ancestors,[70] but among the sacrificers themselves, who would on these "spirited" occasions "have drunk and eaten our fill," *chi tsui ch'ieh pao* 既醉且飽.[71] Songs nos. 290 and 291 are especially full of explicit expressions of the joyous excitement of agricultural work and fecundity, with women's part played in it, women who were "lovely," and were productive of children. We remember that all these were for the solemn occasions of the royal temple sacrifices. But they are all clearly reminiscent of the primordial fertility rites that began with "uplifting dance."

The point of special interest here is the revelation of generic character from origination to full development. We believe this knowledge would add a fresh look to even these "Eulogia" songs which in the traditional as well as modern appreciation of the *Songs* as a whole used to put the readers off, either as being at too great a distance because of the religious awe traditionally taught about them, or as being too formalized and therefore mummified. To exhibit the generic elements in them is, we hope, to stir up a sense of life and revive some of the original lyricism which pervades all the *Songs*. Furthermore, we think that the "Eulogia" section was perhaps more instrumental than the popular "Airs" in establishing firmly the genre concept of the *Songs*, called *shih* since early Chou times. The importance of the idea of dance in the formation of the term *shih* we have decided earlier. We have also seen that dance was inseparable from the performance of these *Sung* or "Eulogia Songs," and was in

[67] Most notably songs nos. 273, 275, 294 in the Mao text.
[68] Song no. 275.
[69] Songs nos. 276, 277.
[70] Songs nos. 279, 290.
[71] Song no. 275.

fact the fundamental meaning of *Sung,* as revealed by the latter's etymological identity with *jung* 容, "formal manners" of dance. But we further note that the "Eulogia," being the oldest in the corpus of the *Songs,* were also among the earliest to be quoted currently in courtly and diplomatic circles of the states known since at least the eighth century B.C., although quoting from the "Airs" was not a practice until 635, according to the *Kuo yü* and *Tso chuan* records.[72] It is a very notable fact that when the songs of the *Sung* were quoted at that early date, they were often mentioned just as *shih.* Certainly when they were so mentioned, the quoters, mostly court officials or nobility, were very much aware that these songs were by implication all part and parcel of the formalized temple dances. Their use of the term *shih* applied to the "Eulogia" songs would therefore carry that implication. But on the other hand, when used in conversation the songs were no longer sung, and the impact of the meaning of words became prominent. This was perhaps, we suspect, the way in which the word *shih,* with its primary etymon 𡳿 *chih* **ț̣iag* signifying dance, and its later "determinal" 丝 (言) *yen* "word" element added, became a felicitous term gaining wide currency. Thus it came to denominate, or "glamorize" so to say, all the rest of the *Songs* of the other sections as a generic term. But we surmise it was primarily because the songs in the *Sung,* of such elevated position, had made precedents among courtly circles and the intelligentsia who, in appreciation of the fact that they were both *danced* to with music, and spoken as polite quotations for the value of their *words* in polished conversation, sanctioned and circulated the term *shih* as carrying both senses.

Now since the *Sung* section has such a special significance for the *shih* genre, let us examine it a little more. We find that in the *Sung* both of these senses, of "dance" and of "word," were distinctly present, but in a way bifurcated, each growing in a grand manner in its own direction. Danced to they must be, but now in grand processions of the Chou royal temples with forms of religion and elaborate rituals far advanced over the primitive. So the words in the composition of the songs, to suit the occasions, must be of such import, that most often they, too, sublimated the primordial devices of the "uplifting" *hsing* prototype of burdens or refrains. The effects of the

---

[72] Cf. Lao Hsiao-yü 勞孝興, 春秋詩話, vol. II. A *Tso chuan* record of an early quoting of the "Airs" has been dismissed by authorities as spurious.

motifs remained, as we have seen, but the patterns shifted. Reading the "Eulogia" texts, we should therefore, while savoring the words, visualize the pomp and circumstance of the solemn dance and music that were to go with them, to obtain the total uplifting effect. And in analyzing the structure of all the *Songs*, it will be in the *Ya* and *Feng*, or "Elegantiae" and "Airs" sections, that we encounter more fully the *hsing* element.

Whether or not all the "Airs" and the "Elegantiae," as if in full reminiscence of the generic origin, having stemmed from the high-spirited, uplifting "*Xiǎng!*" were danced as well as sung to music, we cannot be sure. But they have certainly retained many of the motifs in the ancient pattern of refrains and incremental repetitions, which are clearly recognizable, and were marked off, however haphazardly, in the *Mao Annotations*. They were given prominence by Mao, mainly in the "Airs" and "Minor Elegantiae," *Hsiao Ya* 小雅, sections with four additional instances in the "Major Elegantiae," *Ta Ya* 大雅, which next to the "Eulogia" are the most courtly and solemn in subject matter. And Mao did indicate two instances of the *hsing* in the "Eulogia" section as well. We think we have now suggested strongly enough the importance of *hsing* for appreciating the *Songs* with a fair sense of generic criteria.

For the moment, looking closely at the *hsing* elements just as Mao noted them, we find that they are all invocations of either natural objects large and small: the sun, the moon, hills, and rivers and the fields, birds, plants, fishes, and insects; or objects of primitive crafts: boat, fishing rod, farming implements; plus a good portion inspired by work in the farm: picking herbs, cutting timber, or such activities in the fields as catching birds and animals; and a small amount having to do with clothing and weaving. Having traced the significance of *hsing* < *Xiǎng to its primeval origin, we can now appreciate its pristine quality, as manifested in these evocations of objects, natural or human. Compare Professor H. W. Garrod: "Once upon a time the world was fresh, to speak was to be a poet, to name objects an inspiration; and metaphor dropped from the inventive mouths of men like some natural exudation of the vivified senses."[73]

The *hsing* elements in the *Songs* are of the quality inherited from that "fresh world." They carry with them, in terms of formal

[73] As quoted in C. Day Lewis, *The Poetic Image*, p. 25.

distinction, the ancient integrity, the oneness or the unity of the musical speech and the rhythm of the spontaneous and simultaneous primeval "uplifting dance." Their appeal is therefore instantaneous, even kinesthetic as well as imagistic. By observing the frequent doublets and rich onomatopoeia we hear the keynote and are tuned to the whole rhythm of any one of the *Songs* in which the *hsing* element is recognized. By recalling how in the rest of the song a host of alliterations as well as rhymes or pararhymes grow as if in response to its spirit to make the whole poem vibrant with it we realize how the *hsing* element is the soul of the *lyric*.

To this extent, the hsing elements deserve the name, in the modern formal sense, of "motif" to the *Songs*. But they also set the mood and atmosphere of the whole song, or rise of a sudden to control and govern them. On this point we want to be specific rather than leaving such experiences of mood or atmosphere barely stated in the fashion of traditional as well as some modern appreciative critics, though we have no doubt that they genuinely and deeply felt these. First we may look at some almost too obvious examples. Too obvious, that is, when we approach them with full alertness to their sensuousness and all-evocative powers, and are ready for the uplifted feeling taught by the "*Xiəng!*" rather than vivisecting them ratiocinatively or following the allegorical arguments taught by scholastic tradition. Most often the *hsing* element begins a song. An example is song no. 1, 關雎, "Quacks the Osprey." Not only do the starting lines:

關關雎鳩　　*Kwan kwan ts'io kiôg
在河之洲　　*Dȝ'əg g'â t̂iəg t̂iôg

set the basic rhyming scheme, generating a host of alliteratives, assonances, and pararhymes which echo these syllables, but the sympathy of a whole range of sounds bears upon the dominant emotional tone of the song, which the *hsing* lines at the beginning have already announced. We can speak of the mood and atmosphere as being "obvious" when sound and sense are realized to be so fused that we feel the overtones and the conjured light and color in their interplay inform and deepen our emotional experience of the whole poem. It is only after going beyond the ratiocinative sense of the song, to feel the total impact of the *sensation* in the words in their interrelationship that we can speak of "meaning beyond words." Such "meaning" now is actually a feeling, genuinely felt but not entirely expressible in words. As such it may be called the spiritual or emotional "sensation" of the song, readily experienced as pervading it. Hence we recognize it as "atmosphere," and as we feel it, we say we share the whole "mood." It comes from the intricate, rich yet naturally harmonized sound relations, and the distinct yet spontaneous rhythm, as well as the striking, untrammelled, naked images like living things in their natural state. The *hsing* element, retaining the primordial efficacy of the unity of song, music, and dance is its core.

In song no. 143, 月出, "The Moon Rises," the *hsing* or "motif" lines:

月出皎兮　　*Ngi̯wăt t'i̯wət kiog ɣiei
佼人僚兮　　*Kiog ńi̯ěn liog ɣiei

generate three stanzas of incremental repetitions which constitute the whole song, and each and every line is an exclamatory construction ending with *hsi* 兮. The total sympathetic sound relationships are even more readily felt than in Song no. 1, suffusing the whole song as does the light of the rising moon, which is the dominant image introduced by the *hsing* lines of this song. Thus when we speak of the "mood" and "atmosphere" of the poem we are referring to tangible things that have effected them: echoing syllables of sounds and pervading light or color evoked, which produce the "sensation" together with the simple regular beats of the tapping rhythm. We believe that the high lyricism of this song is inspired by dance, and that this is evidenced by its content.

Our next example will illustrate the use of *hsing* in a poem of much greater complexity. It will show that the *hsing* is not just a way of "beginning a poem," as Chu Hsi, for example, thought, for here it does not even appear at the beginning. It will show further that its function and significance are of direct poetic concern, and not at all allegorical. Song no. 168. 出車, "Out Goes the Chariot" belongs to the *Hsiao Ya* or "Minor Elegantiae" section. The *hsing* lines are:

喓喓草蟲　　*Iôg iôg ts'og d'i̯ông
趯趯阜螽　　*T'i̯ok t'i̯ok b'i̯ôg t'i̯ông

followed by

未見君子　*Mǐwəd kian kǐwən tsǐəg
憂心忡忡　*Iôg sǐəm t'ǐông t'ǐông

The two *hsing* lines do not appear until after four long stanzas of the song. That they had stemmed from a common source of old generic convention, and not "what the poet saw" at the moment of individual inspiration is clearly indicated by their recurrence elsewhere as stock phrases. Not only are the same lines, identical word for word, found marked by Mao as "This is *hsing*" in song no. 14, in *Shao nan* 召南 of the "Airs" category; but the two lines that follow are also identical word for word, with more lines of similar sense and emotive impact in both songs.

The "Elegantiae" Songs are not necessarily more attractive than the "Airs," but there is no denying their greater artistry. Not so bound up as the "Eulogia" with solemn, formalized royal temple rituals on the one hand, yet having risen farther above the "folk song" level than the "Airs," these "Elegantiae" songs allow more room for individual ingenuity. We do still think, for reasons already indicated, that it was the elevated, grand position of the "Eulogia" that, sharing the generic character of the *Songs,* lent dignity to the whole corpus, embraced as it was by the nobility and intelligentsia before middle Chou and accepted as the prestigious *shih.* But we think the song-makers of the "Elegantiae," though bards rather than poets in the modern sense, still were, in their observation of the *hsing* convention, more nearly individual artists.

The use of *hsing,* as well as the structure and intent, of song no. 168, bears remarkable evidence of this. It is a song of six long stanzas, doubling the normal three of those in the "Airs," but with a clear shift and development of senses observable in two parts with three stanzas to each. The two *hsing* lines, which we may mimic in translation,

Iog, iog, sing the cicadae,[74]
Tip, dip, go the grasshoppers,

[74] Waley took this, originally 草蟲, to be cicadae, and interpreted the line as "Dolefully cry the cicadae." The entomological accuracy may still be in question. But the effect of the sense is clear here for our purpose.

appearing in the beginning of the fifth stanza, thus stand out right in the middle of the concluding part. We hear in them a new crescendo of sounds, drawing resonance out of syllables of the foregoing stanzas from their alliterative and rhyming effects and foreshadowing those to come. We also see these *hsing* lines introduce the stanza that constitutes a new focus in the sense of the song, and thus as its central image reveal the real intent of the poem. All the three stanzas in the first part of the song speak of a military expedition. The individual status, though not the individual personality, of the song-maker (who was an officer of the army of trek) is clear. In the first three stanzas, through his "song-words," we hear the rumbling, the *pwang-pwang 彭彭, of the chariots; we see and also hear the fluttering, the *b'wad-b'wad 旆旆, of the banners and flags, out on the long roads and open fields. But the tenor of the poem ("poem" we are calling it now, with emphasis on the song-*words*) is not that of military triumph, nor is the whole emotional tone one of triumph.

The hardship, anxiety, and forlorn existence of the officer and his soldiers separated from their wives are the poem's concern and set its emotional tone, rather than martial spirit or victory, though victory and reunion do finally come. The whole picture from the beginning is that of small, desolate human beings who go helplessly *"tip, dip"* on vast plains and endless roads. Their stature in that threadbare existence is even further dwarfed by contrast with that of the Commanding General named Nam D'iông, 南仲, alluded to with only a cryptic phrase as *xǎk-xǎk* 赫赫, "awesome," "terrible," or "overpowering," who finally brought them victory. But while in the description of the whole expedition in the first three stanzas the dominant emotion is the "worry," the iôg 憂 in heart that was "anxious-anxious", ts'iog-ts'iog 悄悄, it is also the seeking of relief in the hope of a successful campaign and homecoming, thus foreshadowing the efficacious use of the *hsing* convention here to express a changed but further developed and more complex, uplifting emotion.

In the *hsing* lines which stand out in the central stanza of the concluding part of the poem, we hear the "iôg, iôg" 喓喓 of the cicada and see the *"tip, dip"* of grasshoppers, and feel in a flash that things in nature are at last again what they ought to be, and men are reuniting with their wives in joy. But these *hsing* lines, in their total organic relationship to the three stanzas of the first part, play more parts than just to change the mood. The mood pervades the whole poem, but not until we reach these *hsing* lines is it so epitomized and highlighted. The tiny insects with their small movements and sounds recall the smallness and insignificance of men erstwhile in the wilds, but now by transmutation back to normal stature, as husbands with their wives. And the insects, which the wives as grasswidows would have often forlornly heard and watched would now be heard and seen together in peace and quiet. Their "worries," so "anxious-anxious," that is, their *ʾịôg, so *ts'ịog-ts'ịog, now began in the transformation into joyful feeling to be echoed and refracted, as it were, in the *ʾịôg ịôg of the "singing cicada" as the *hsing* lines begin. Thus alerted by these *hsing* lines, if we read the poem again, we may realize that many of the rest of the sounds in the six stanzas cohere into vibrant senses, mutually related by parallel or contrast. The *ʾịôg sound with its assonance ịô, as if it were the excited cry that gave the keynote to the primeval dance-song from its generic origin, dominates much of the poem. We have observed the ịôg that expresses the worry and "anxiety" as the basic emotion of the poem, and the *ʾịôg-ịôg as relief and uplift of it. No doubt in the first three stanzas of the poem the "fluttering" and "rumbling" of the military emblems and equipment are also tinged with the same emotion. But the "banners" and "flags" that are the sources for the "fluttering" sounds are the *d'ịog 旟 and the *mog 旄; the "chariots" that go "rumbling" are the *kịo 車, and what caused the greatest "fear" and "anxiety," the "King's tablet of Command," is the *sịo 書. The two insects in the *hsing* lines are the cicadae, the *d'ịông 蟲, and furthermore, the grasshopper, the *t'ịông 螽. We have observed that their sounds and movements signify a state of agitation to begin with, but are utterly sympathetic and benign. And we find them in the same stanza rhymed with the "agitation," *t'ịông 忡, of the heart, and then the blissful "calm," g'ông 降. The name of the "awesome" Commanding General was mentioned once and singularly unfitted to the rest of the sounds among the first three stanzas of the poem. Now in the concluding part the name Nam D'ịông is brought into sonorous rhyme with the *hsing* lines and the rest of this central stanza. So rhymed, the name is now invoked and thus harmonized with the context of the human scene in peace and victory, where families are at last reunited, "the spring days are long-drawn, the plants and trees flourishing," the insects jump and sing *i̯ôg-i̯ôg, while the bumpings and rumblings of the war chariots are memories fainter perhaps than even the cicada song, and all is right with the world. And the "awesome" general who in the end obtained the peace and victory for them is back in harmony with nature and his fellowmen, too.

The examples we have so far cited are strictly in accordance with the *Mao Annotation* which have distinctly marked as *hsing* those lines we have just analyzed. If we keep well in mind the efficacy and significance of the *hsing* as it developed from its generic origin, such as we have been at pains to discover and analyze, then we can properly follow Chu Hsi's more liberal spirit in recognizing more *hsing* elements than those indicated in the Mao texts, and treat them fruitfully.

We well realize Chu Hsi's inability to free himself from the moral allegorical tradition, and therefore cannot expect him to go much further beyond it. He did indicate the meaning, too, of the "incremental repetitions" which he reidentified as *hsing*. But this "meaning" was derived by him rather from his ethical concern than from the poetic essence, as regards structure and emotional and psychological logicality within the context of the poem. He was also trammeled by the Han formula of the "Six Principles" set down in the "Great Preface," and moved narrowly within the stringent categories of "metaphor," "simile," and "narration." He therefore tended to recognize a large number of "incremental repetitions" as being *hsing* only when they seemed to him allusive, metaphorically suited to his moral allegorical interest. He would dismiss those more direct ones and call them "narration," even though they were distinctly "incremental repetitions" with the simplest pattern of recurring sounds and rhythm throughout, and therefore reminiscent of the most primitive high-spirited song and dance. These in fact represent the most revealing features of the pristine *hsing* usage such as we have found and studied. The outstanding example is the familiar song no. 8:

采采芣苢　　*Ts'əg ts'əg b'i̯ŭg zi̯əg
薄言采之　　*B'âk ngiăn ts'əg ti̯əg
采采芣苢　　*Ts'əg ts'əg b'i̯ŭg zi̯əg
薄言有之　　*b'âk ngiăn gi̯ŭg ti̯əg.

Our mimicry of a translation would be:

> Pick, pick, we pick the plaintain,
> Hurrah, we pick it!
> Pick, pick, we pick the plaintain,
> Hurrah, we have it!

The rest of the "incremental repetitions" throughout the song continue with small variations of a word or two, in the same tapping-clapping rhythm and rhyme, to depict various movements of the picking, such as "plucking," "culling," or "putting in lapel." The belief that the plaintain fruit is "good for pregnancy," as Mao recorded it, has had a long Chinese tradition decisively authenticated by modern *Shih-ching* scholarship.[75] So the "picking" of the plaintain here is undoubtedly a symbolic action derived from primitive fertility rites uniting human objectives with natural objects. Both the theme and the structure of this song clearly signify the primary origin and function of *hsing*, we are certain. The "incremental repetitions" here which carry forward the motif throughout the song evince the essence of the *hsing*, exhibited in a large number of the other songs, where Mao noted "This is *hsing*." If Mao's failure to indicate the the *hsing* in this song can be explained by such negligence and inconsistency as criticized by later commentators of his whole *Annotations*, Chu's regarding it as *fu* or "narration" is because of its great simplicity and directness.

Of course in some of the *Songs*, the "incremental repetitions," having clearly stemmed from the ancient *hsing* convention, had in the development of rhetorical devices become an integral part of a song's straightforward statement. Perhaps because of this, Chu recognized in song no. 76 a "narration." The first stanza begins with:

> 將仲子兮　*Tsi̯ang d'i̯ông tsi̯əg γiei
> 無踰我里　*Mi̯wo di̯u ngâ li̯əg

All the eight lines of the first stanza develop into two more stanzas of "incremental repetitions," line for line, to complete the whole poem. The tenor of the poem is clear, that of a girl's trepidation about

---

[75] See Wen Yi-to 聞一多, 詩經通義 and 匡齊尺牘 in Wen's *Complete Works*, 1948.

others' concern with the relation between her and her lover. As the
stanzas progress by repetition, with changes of a few essential words,
the concerns develop and subtly vary, from "parents' words" to
"brothers' talk" and finally "people's gossip." The concerns according to the contexts range from perhaps light scolding or even
solicitous care of the closest and next of kin to a public scandal, from
just "words" or "talk," *yen* 言, of parents and then of brothers, to *to
yen* 多言, the "busy gossip" of everyone in village or town. She sees
the three situations develop as if her lover's movements toward her
were watched. And the psychological truth of the poem is cogently
presented in clear order. When the young lover just "clambered"
into the "hamlet" or "small village," the *liəg 里,[76] and broke some
village trees,[77] the parents being closest to her would already with
natural solicitousness begin to worry and speak up. When he came
closer, clambering over the "wall" of the house, and broke some trees
there, the brothers, initially less concerned than the parents, would
now "talk." It is finally only when he came closest to her, clambering
into the "garden" 園, as the tryst was nearly to happen, that she was
palpitating with the greatest trepidation, as well as with love, that a
public scandal would be abroad among all the village people who
might not have hitherto much cared. A "narration" Chu Hsi
preferred to call this song. It is not our intention to quibble about the
stringent categories of the unrealistic aspects of the old "Six Principles." But this song is obviously not a simple narrative. It is not a
story of any great interest. It is its psychological and emotional
logic that attracts us. But we further observe that it is the sound-and-
meaning pattern subtly wrought into a song with total "incremental
repetitions" derived from the original *hsing* convention that enhances
its generic character and makes it one of the most popular and loved
pieces of the *Songs*.[78] It is the haunting, lilting rhythm throughout and
the delicately varied, echoed, and repeated sounds congruous with
the images that uplift us with the effect of such an appealing *lyric*
true to its genre.

[76] Mao notes 里 as a community of 25 families.
[77] These trees are explained by Ma Jui-ch'en 馬瑞辰 as (傳) 社木, 其社所宜木, "village
trees specially suited to the community," in 毛詩傳箋通釋.
[78] This song is one of the most favored among Chinese and Western anthologists.

Enough linguists and philologists have noted the extraordinary richness of sound patterns of the *Songs* in their profusion of rhymes, pararhymes, and consonance and assonance in complex internal oblique and slant relationships as well as line-endings. K'ung Kuang-sen,[79] for instance, recognized these relationships by categories, and analyzed them according to 130 formulae. Modern efforts of phonologists suggest even greater possibilities of recognizing more elements of euphony.[80] We are grateful for the meticulous works of such scholars in exhibiting the immense riches in the *Shih-ching* of sounds interacting with sounds. We also appreciate Arthur Waley's remark that when he first read the *Songs* in 1913, without quite understanding the sense, even as mere "incantations," he found a "succession of fresh and lovely tunes," the sounds of "the texts sang."[81] Our present hope, however, is to have further exemplified the possibility of reintegrating the richness of sounds with the richness of sense and imagery, by the aid of a proven hypothesis of the generic origin where the sounds and senses of words were integrated with musical melodies and even with the rhythm of the "high-spirited" dance. This the primal meaning of *hsing* has now confirmed; and we have seen that even the meaning of the word *shih* still had, however covertly, such implications when it was first adopted to name the *Songs* in early Chou time.

[79] K'ung Kuang-sen 孔廣森, 詩聲分類.

[80] Cf. Tung T'ung-ho 董同龢, 上古音韻表稿, *The Bulletin of the Institute of History and Philology*, XVIII, Academia Sinica, 1948.

[81] Waley, *Book of Songs*, 1937, p. 326.

The Quest of the Goddess

by David Hawkes

Bereft of dates, the literary critic flounders in aestheticism. This, rather than any desire to rehabilitate a patriot poet,[1] must be the Occidental's motive in seeking some sort of chronology for the *Ch'u-tz'u* poems. Whether much is to be expected from the mechanical application of linguistic criteria—statistical researches into the use of vocabulary, rhyme, characteristic structural features, and so forth—is questionable. Reconsideration of my own attempts with these methods[2] suggests that they can indeed supply valid data, but that the precise evaluation of these data is impossible. At best they can but point up common features or distinctive usages as between one work and another. Their conversion into an exact chronology is, it must be confessed, no less intuitive and divinatory than conclusions based on less respectable methods lacking their pseudo-scientific allure.

[1] The modern cult of Ch'ü Yüan as China's first patriotic poet seems to date from the war years. Cf. Wen Yi-to's article "Ch'ü Yüan—the People's Poet" 聞一多: 人民的詩人— 屈原 in 神話與詩. The article ends with these words: "Although Ch'ü Yüan did not write about the life of the people or voice their sufferings, he may truthfully be said to have acted as the leader of a people's revolution and to have struck a blow to avenge them. Ch'ü Yüan is the only person in the whole of Chinese history who is fully entitled to be called 'the people's poet'." Kuo Mo-jo's play *Ch'ü Yüan*, written during ten days in January 1942 and compared by his enthusiastic friends with *Hamlet* and *King Lear*, accords his subject a similar treatment. Under the People's Republic this view of Ch'ü Yüan became *de rigueur*. A little book for high school students published in 1957 opens with the words "Ch'ü Yüan is the first great patriotic poet in the history of our country's literature" (張縱逸: 屈原與楚辭.吉林人民出版社, Ch'ang-ch'un, 1957). Reluctance to see the number of his works diminished and a revulsion from the highly skeptical attitude which many scholars formerly entertained towards the authenticity of the "works of Ch'ü Yüan" have been an inevitable consequence of the cult.

[2] *The Problem of Date and Authorship in Ch'u-tz'u*, unpublished thesis, Oxford, 1956.

In the earliest form in which it has come down to us—the seven-teen-*chüan* book of the second-century exegete Wang Yi—the *Ch'u-tz'u* collection, if we ignore Wang Yi's own appended effusions, essentially represents a first century B.C. codification of a still extant but neglected literary tradition felt to be in need of restoration and revival. Liu Hsiang and Wang Pao, whose contributions (again excepting Wang Yi's much later addendum) are the latest material in the book, began their careers at the court of the emperor Hsüan, the literary patron who summoned to his court an aged Mr. P'i from Kiukiang, a *Ch'u-tz'u* expert who, it is quite clear from Liu Hsiang's own account of the matter,[3] was sought out by the emperor not with entertainment in view, but for purposes of preservation and revival, in the same way that a modern folk-song collector will cherish and pursue with tape-recorder and notebook some aged inhabitant of the Hebrides, Galway, or Tennessee to capture from his quavering accents what would otherwise not survive the extinction of his capacious memory.

Ch'u-tz'u, then, is the name of a literary tradition, already suffi-ciently antiquated to be in need of revival by the second half of the first century B.C., but still apparently flourishing at the beginning of emperor Wu's reign in 140 B.C.[4] The advent of Ssu-ma Hsiang-ju on the literary scene at about that time had, we may suppose, something to do with its eclipse.

I do not believe that *tz'u* was originally thought of as a genre. *Tz'u* means "words": the words of artistic composition, whether in verse

[3] The biography of Wang Pao in *Han Shu* 64B contains the following statement on this subject: "Under Emperor Hsüan there was a revival of the literary enthusiasms of Emperor Wu's reign. The writings of the Six Disciplines were expounded and discussed and the Emperor displayed an inexhaustible avidity for every kind of curious and interesting learning. He summoned to his court a Mr. P'i of Kiukiang who was an authority on the *Ch'u tz'u* and commanded him to appear before him and recite them. He also invited a number of men of outstanding talent, like Liu Hsiang, Chang Tzu-ch'iao, Hua Lung, and Liu Pao, to reside at his court as pensioners of the Gate of the Brazen Horse." *T'ai-p'ing yü-lan* 879 (a section devoted to the subject of "Porridge") quotes from Liu Hsiang's *Ch'i lüeh*: "Emperor Hsüan summoned a Mr. P'i to his court to appear before him and recite *Ch'u-tz'u*. Mr. P'i was very old and feeble, and had to be given gruel every time he recited."

[4] Chu Mai-ch'en, who found favor with Emperor Wu in the middle years of his reign, was a *Ch'u-tz'u* expert. His fellow-countryman Yen Chu, who first recommended him to the Emperor's notice, was the son of Yen Chi, author of *Ai shih ming* and member of a group of Wu poets who lived at the provincial courts of Wu and Liang. *Ch'i chien*, whether or not it is by Tung-fang Shuo, probably belongs to the same period.

or prose and whether oral or written. This proposition must be self-evident to anyone who reflects that *Li sao, Chiu ko, T'ien wen, Pu chü* and *Chao hun* are all indisputably *Ch'u-tz'u,* but cannot in any sense of the word be thought of as belonging to a single genre. *Ch'u-tz'u,* as a vague collective title, may be compared with the *"Matière de Bretagne"* which in medieval times designated the whole vast corpus of prose and verse romance woven around the legend of King Arthur and his knights and the quest of the Grail. *Ch'u-tz'u* is the *"Matière de Ch'u."*

If, then, there is no formal consistency between the different parts of this *"Matière de Ch'u,"* what is it that they all have in common? The answer to this, I believe, is that all of them represent the cannibalization by a new secular, literary tradition of an earlier religious, oral one. As an alternative to this it might be suggested that all of them are in one way or another associated with the name of Ch'ü Yüan: that the *"Matière de Ch'u"* is really the *"Matière de Ch'ü Yüan"*—or in other words, that *Ch'u-tz'u* may be defined as the writings of Ch'ü Yüan and his School. In fact this is merely to restate the first definition in different terms, since the secularization of a religious tradition is precisely what Ch'ü Yüan is supposed to have done.

I am referring, of course, to Wang Yi's statement that *Chiu ko* is a literary recasting of traditional religious material.[5] He makes no such statement about any other work in the corpus, and what he says about *Chiu ko* is notoriously suspect. Nevertheless I believe that this statement was an inspired and fruitful guess which might well prove the key to a better understanding of the whole collection. If we could analyze the use which Ch'u poets made of an existing religious tradition, we should, I believe, be well on the way to understanding the nature of poetic inspiration and the workings of poetic imagination in that remote and formative era of Chinese literary art.

[5] "In former times the people living in the area lying between the Yüan and Hsiang rivers south of Nan-ying were superstitious and much given to the worship of spirits. In their service of the gods they would sing, play, drum, and dance to do them pleasure. It was in this area that Ch'ü Yüan concealed himself after his banishment. Full of grief and bitterness and in a greatly disturbed state of mind, he would go out to watch the sacrificial rites of the local inhabitants and witness the singing and dancing which accompanied them. Finding the words of their songs crude and barbarous, he composed the *Nine Songs* to replace them. In this work he both sings the praises of the gods and at the same time uses the hymns as a vehicle for expressing his own resentments." (From Wang Yi's introduction to *Chiu ko.*)

I should like to begin an attempt at such an analysis by re-examining what must surely be one of the most variously interpreted poems in the Chinese language: *Hsiang chün*. The following is a greatly altered version of the translation I published in 1959:[6]

The goddess comes not, she holds back shyly.	君不行兮夷猶
Who keeps her delaying within the island,	蹇誰留兮中洲
Lady of the lovely eyes and the winning smile?	美要眇兮宜修
Skimming the water in my cassia boat,	沛吾乘兮桂舟
I bid the Yüan and Hsiang still their waves	令沅湘兮無波
And the Great River make its stream flow softly.	使江水兮安流
I look for the goddess, but she does not come yet.	望夫君兮未來
Of whom does she think as she plays her reed-pipes?	吹參差兮誰思
North I go, drawn by my flying dragon,	駕飛龍兮北征
Steering my course to the Tung-t'ing lake:	邅吾道兮洞庭
My sail is of fig-leaves, melilotus my rigging,	薜荔拍兮蕙綢
An iris my flag-pole, my banner of orchids.	蓀橈兮蘭旌
Gazing at the distant Ts'en-yang mooring	望涔陽兮極浦
I waft my magic across the Great River.	橫大江兮揚靈
I waft my magic, but it does not reach her.	揚靈兮未極
The lady is sad, and sighs for me;	女嬋媛兮爲余太息
And my tears run down over cheek and chin:	橫流涕兮潺湲
I am choked with longing for my lady.	隱思君兮陫側
My cassia oars and orchid sweep	桂櫂兮蘭枻
Chip all in vain at ice and snow.	斲冰兮積雪
I am gathering wild figs in the water!	采薜荔兮水中
I am looking for lotuses in the tree-tops!	搴芙蓉兮木末
The wooing is useless if hearts are divided;	心不同兮媒勞
The love that is not deep is quickly broken.	恩不甚兮輕絕
The stream runs fast through the stony shallows,	石瀨兮淺淺
And my flying dragon wings swiftly above it.	飛龍兮翩翩
The pain is more lasting if loving is faithless:	交不忠兮怨長
She broke her tryst; she told me she had not time.	期不信兮告余以不閒
In the morning I race by the bank of the river;	鼂騁騖兮江皋
At evening I halt at this north island.	夕弭節兮北渚
The birds are roosting on the roof-top;	鳥次兮屋上
The water laps at the foot of the hall.	水周兮堂下
I throw my thumb-ring into the River.	捐余玦兮江中
I leave my girdle in the bay of the Li.	遺余佩兮澧浦

[6] Hawkes, *Ch'u tz'u, the Songs of the South*, Clarendon Press, 1959, 37–38.

Pollia I've plucked in the scent-laden islet	采芳洲兮杜若
To give to the lady in the depths below.	將以遺兮下女
Time once gone cannot be recovered.	告不可兮再得
I should like to enjoy myself at leisure.	聊逍遙兮容與

This translation assumes a single speaker throughout: the male shaman who seeks, but fails to make contact with, the river goddess. He has hopes of her appearing. He even hears the music of her pipes; but it is not for him that she plays. For one reason or another she fails to emerge; and the shaman leaves disconsolately, after first casting jade offerings into the waters of the river.

The singer's appearing to be sometimes in a boat, which he describes in considerable detail, and sometimes on a flying dragon is not a difficulty. Ts'ao Hsü, the Chekiang shaman who was drowned in A.D. 143 while going out in a boat to seek the river god,[7] met his

---

[7] *Hou Han shu* 84 (列女傳): "The filial daughter, Ts'ao O, was a native of Shang-yü in Kuei-chi. Her father, Ts'ao Hsü, was a skilled musician and shaman. On the fifth day of the fifth month of the year Han-an he was drowned while rowing out towards the oncoming bore to meet the god with dancing in the Shang-yü river, and his body was never recovered."

Waley (*The Nine Songs: A Study of Shamanism in Ancient China*, Allen and Unwin, 1955) says that Ts'ao Hsü (he calls him "Ts'ao Yü") was going out to meet "the Dancing Goddess," following the 沂濤迎婆娑神 of the received text. However, 困學紀聞 13 (攷史) makes it quite clear that the received text has the character in the wrong order: "曹娥碑云「盱能撫節安歌，婆娑樂神，以五月時迎伍君」。傳云「迎婆娑神」誤也." 伍君 is 伍子胥, whose spirit became the god of the tidal bore and who was, in fact, the local river god at Shang-yü in Ts'ao Hsü's day; whereas the "Dancing Goddess" is, to the best of my knowledge, unheard of outside this text.

For the Han cult of Wu Tzu-hsü as a river god, see *Lun heng* 4 (書虛): "The history books say that when King Fu-ch'a of Wu killed Wu Tzu-hsü, he boiled him in a cauldron, put his body in a wineskin, and threw it into the river. But Tzu-hsü's hate was so powerful that it drove the waters before it and made the rushing tidal bore in which people are drowned. Today in the Kuei-chi area there are temples to Tzu-hsü on the Yangtze at Tan-t'u and on the R. Chekiang at Ch'ien-t'ang. These have been founded to mollify his hatred and assuage the violence of the tide . . . . The Chekiang river, the Shan-yin river, and the Shang-yü river all have this tidal bore."

There are other but less revealing references to this Han superstition in *Wu-yüeh ch'un-ch'iu* and *Pao-p'u-tzu*.

I suggest that what Ts'ao Hsü did in his boat was to attitudinize (婆娑) while singing to his own accompaniment on the castanets (撫節安歌). Alternatively, 撫節 may imply that he beat out the stroke for the rowers on a drum. He could still sing and posture while doing this. Han art contains many representations of people drumming and dancing simultaneously and there is at least one pre-Han representation of a drummer in a boat beating out the stroke for rowers. The expression 撫節安歌 may be compared with 疏緩節兮安歌 in *Tung-huang t'ai-yi* l. 10. 曹娥碑 is, of course, the inscription immortalized in Ts'ai Yung's riddling commendation (黃絹幼婦外孫齏臼).

death on the fifth day of the fifth month, the day of the Dragon Boat
Festival, whose great antiquity has been demonstrated by Wen
Yi-to.[8] It seems highly probable that Ts'ao Hsü's craft was a dragon
boat, and equally probable that the "cassia boat" and "flying
dragon" of this poem both refer to one and the same vessel.

That the poem was designed to be sung by a shaman actually in
motion on the water is perhaps questionable. The Hsiang Chün, we
know, had an island shrine in lake Tung-t'ing, and it is true that the
poem contains references to the goddess's failure to appear from her
island, to the shaman's journey to Tung-t'ing, and the water which
laps beneath the goddess's hall. Nevertheless the journeys indicated
in the poem must be purely imaginary ones. This becomes evident
when we try to map out Ts'en-yang, the Yangtze, the rivers Yüan,
Hsiang, and Li, and lake Tung-t'ing—all mentioned in this poem—
and find ourselves unable to fit them into an area of much less than
one hundred miles square; or when we reflect that a whole day is
supposed to elapse during the course of two lines of the poem. We
may therefore suppose as a first possibility that the poem was
intended to be sung and mimed on a stationary boat moored at the
foot of a waterside temple. In that case we must probably imagine a
whole flotilla of boats, of which the leading one was occupied by the
shaman and his rowers and the others by spectators and worshippers
arriving for a seasonal or perhaps annual rite at an island shrine,
probably with its back to the jungle and approachable only by water.
Alternatively we may suppose that the poem was to be used in a
performance on dry land with the shaman standing in a grounded
boat, or symbolic representation of a boat, or even, perhaps, holding
a toy boat—a dragon-headed stick with a miniature paddle tied
across its neck,[9] or something of the sort. It is impossible to be sure,
and we are, it seems to me, entitled to choose whichever it amuses us
most to believe.

If we do opt for the view that the poem implies a water-borne
shaman, there is ample evidence to show that shamans did on
occasion take to the water for their ceremonies, from the unfortunate

---

[8] 聞一多, 端午考 in 神話與詩, Peking, 1956, 221–38.

[9] A Siberian shaman in the museum at Copenhagen holds a stick in one of his hands
with a tiny horse's head carved on the upper end of it, which I take to be the shaman's
"mount."

case of Ts'ao Hsü already mentioned, to the numerous instances cited
by Mr. Wen Ch'ung-yi in his invaluable study of these matters.[10] Of
course, it is still open to us to accept Wang Yi's thesis that the poem
is a literary improvement, and therefore not written for performance
at all, but for reading and recitation. But even if we do, the problem
of how the oral originals were performed still remains to be solved.

However, none of these details of performance is very important.
The point I wish to establish is that by far the best sense is made of
this poem—and incidentally also of the companion-piece *Hsiang fu-
jen* which follows it—if we assume that the whole of it is sung by the
questing shaman, who, for the benefit of an audience of worshippers,
describes the extroardinary difficulties of his journey in pursuit of the
goddess, the extremely evasive nature of her behavior when at last he
draws near her, and finally his quite understandable failure to do
much more than, as it were, leave his visiting-card at her doorway
before departing. For the goddess, it is hinted, is already closeted with
a Very Important Person—none other, we are given to understand,
than her male consort.[11] Under the circumstances the shaman, who
has done his level best, could hardly be expected to achieve more.
Everyone feels sorry for him. He feels sorry for himself. Though,

---

[10] 文崇一, 九歌中的水神與華南的龍舟賽神 *Bulletin of the Institute of Ethnology,*
Academia Sinica, Taiwan, (中央研究院民族學研究所集刊) 11 (1961), 51–124.

[11] For a similar reference by the shaman to a divine rival, see *Shao ssu-ming* 18.
The person who detains the goddess in her island in 1, 2 is presumably Shun. His
presence is even more clearly indicated by the reference to his burial-place, Doubting
Mountain 九疑山 in the *Hsiang fu-jen* poem. That Shun, under the name Ch'ung-
hua, was the object of a popular cult in Ch'u may be deduced from the references to
him in *Li sao* and *Chiu chang*. The legend of his death on an expedition to the south
and of the search of his two sorrowing queens seems like a folk memory of the southward movement of the cult, comparable with the legend of the westward journey of
Dionysus. Since the object of the expedition was the chastisement of the Miao tribes,
it would seem highly probable that the ruling class of Ch'u brought the cult with
them, so that Shun's southern expedition symbolizes their own southward movement,
and his chastisement of the Miao their own displacement of local tribes.
I believe that my earlier skepticism about the identification of the Hsiang goddesses
and their consort with Shun and his two queens was misplaced. Certainly the cult of
the Hsiang goddesses (or goddess) may well have existed long before the Shun cult
arrived on the scene, and it would only be after the latter event that they became
identified with Shun's queens. (*Shan hai ching* calls them the daughters of the god of
heaven.) But my guess is that the author of *Li sao* would have given the same answer
as the learned doctors of Ch'in Shih-huang's court if asked to name the goddesses and
their male consort. Wang Yi, curiously enough, appears to give the wives of Shun an
adulterous liaison with an anonymous river god. He could be right. The identity of
the shaman's divine rival does not affect my point.

curiously, the phrases which round off the poem seem to imply that his outing has been successful and enjoyable. I shall say more of them presently.

There is no question but that this poem, even though it may have been subjected to literary improvement by a poet whose preoccupations were other than religious ones, embodies a religious rite whose pattern has been evolved and hallowed by long tradition; whose very words, we may confidently assert, if we compare this with the other poems of *Chiu ko*, contain time-honored formulae, the use of which was dictated more by ritual appropriateness than by logical necessity. Thus the shaman will convey some sense of the great length of his journey by conventional reference to the passage of time: "In the morning I do such-and-such; in the evening I do so-and-so." His route is described in conventional phraseology: "Now I bend my course towards so-and-so";[12] "Now I halt my pace at such-and-such."[13] He will, either in his own person or that of a god whom he represents, praise the entertainment provided as being so delightful that he "forgets to return."[14] The excuses he makes in order to explain the nonappearance of the goddess—somewhat reminiscent of the reasons sarcastically suggested by Elijah to the priests of Baal to explain the nonappearance of *their* deity—are couched in conventional language.[15] And finally, the parting words, "I wish I could stay and enjoy myself a little longer"[16] are a set formula used, as we have just observed, even in contexts where they do not seem strictly appropriate.

If the songs of *Chiu ko* are essentially religious in intent, *Li sao* is unquestionably a secular poem. Magic and the supernatural are among the themes it makes use of; but in general intent it is the personal statement of a secular poet. The traces of shamanistic influence in the poem have seemed so obvious that the mere statement of their existence is usually felt to be sufficient. In much the

[12] 遭吾道: *Hsiang chün* 10, *Li sao* 172.

[13] 弭節: *Hsiang chün* 30, *Li sao* 96, *Li sao* 182.

[14] 忘歸: *Tung chün* 10, *Ho po* 7, *Shan kuei* 15.

[15] I Kings 18: "Cry aloud: for he is a god; either he is talking, or he is pursuing, or he is in a journey, or peradventure he sleepeth, and must be awaked."
The goddesses in *Chiu ko* are "busy." See *Hsiang chün* 28 and *Shan kuei* 20.

[16] *Hsiang chün* 38, *Hsiang fu-jen* 40, *Li sao* 99.

same way the linguistic similarities of *Li sao* and *Chiu ko* are so evident
that little attempt has been made to analyze and interpret them.[17]
I believe, however, that a more careful study of these influences and
similarities might be rewarding, and shall attempt to justify this
belief by examining the section of *Li sao* that begins at l. 94:

94.	In the morning I start my journey from Ts'ang-wu;	朝發軔於蒼梧兮
	In the evening I arrive at the Garden of Paradise.	夕余至乎縣圃
95.	I should like to stay a while in *these* divine precincts,	欲少留此靈瑣兮
	But the day is swiftly drawing towards evening.	日忽忽其將暮
96.	So I order Hsi-ho to halt the pace	吾令羲和弭節兮
	And overlook Yen-tzu mountain without going in.	望崦嵫而勿迫
97.	The road is very long and far:	路曼曼其脩遠兮
	I shall go up and down in it seeking a mate.	吾將上下而求索

At this point the poet's quest of the goddess has just begun. Observe
that he uses the language not of narration but of dramatic performance: *"these* divine precincts." A whole day is made to elapse in the
space of a single line, and explicit reference is made to the great
length of the journey. The phrase "halt the pace" is used by the
questing shaman in *Hsiang chŭn* in lines which also incorporate the
"morning-evening" formula:

29.	*In the morning* I gallop beside the river;	朝馳余馬兮江皋
30.	*In the evening* I *halt the pace* at the northern island.	夕弭節兮北渚

---

[17] To take the two most obvious and striking ones, there is the characteristic use of 予 as
pronoun object, perhaps representing a different realization of 余 in specific syntactic
contexts—as if we were to distinguish orthographically between the pronouns in "Give'em
hell" and "Give it to them." This usage is only found in *Li sao* and *Chiu ko* and no other
Chinese text:

Li sao	66	申申其詈予
	71	夫何煢獨而不予聽
	105	倚閶闔而望予
	177	召西皇使涉予
Chiu ko, Hsiang fu-jen	17	聞佳人兮召予
Ta ssu ming	8	何壽天兮在予
Shao ssu ming	4	芳菲菲兮襲予
Ho po	18	魚鱗鱗兮媵予
Shan kuei	4	子慕予兮善窈窕
	16	歲既晏兮執華予

(I follow various modern editors in treating what appears to be an example of this
in *Hsiang fu-jen* 2 as a case of textual corruption). The other is the expression 靈脩,
used (apart from very late imitations) only in *Li sao* (22, 25, 44) and *Chiu ko* (*Shan
kuei* 15).

Passing over a few lines descriptive of the poet's brilliant cortège and the aerial journey which he makes with it, we come to l. 110:

110.	Now I am going to visit *this* Palace of the Spring.	溘吾遊此春宮兮
	I break a jasper branch to tie to my girdle.	折瓊枝以繼佩
111.	Before its lustrous petals drop off,	及榮華之未落兮
	I look for a woman below to whom I can offer it.	相下女之可詒
112.	I command Feng Lung to mount on a cloud	吾令豐隆乘雲兮
	And look for the place where Fu-fei lives.	求宓妃之所在
113.	I unfasten my girdle as a pledge of my good faith,	解佩纕以結言兮
	And order Chien Hsiu to plead my suit.	吾令蹇脩以爲理

Observe once more the dramatic language: "*this* Palace of the Spring." Note that Fu-fei, like Hsiang chün, is a river goddess. In *Hsiang chün* the questing shaman drops his *p'ei* into the water as an offering to the goddess. In this passage the poet uses his *p'ei-hsiang*, his girdle, as a pledge. Most remarkable of all, the expression *hsia nü*, which I believe has its quite literal sense of "the woman who is down below" (i.e. the goddess in the depths of the river, not, as some commentators have thought,[18] "serving-woman") is used only here and in *Hsiang chün*, l. 36. In the *Li sao* passage the poet seeks a *hsia nü* to whom he can give the jade flowers he has plucked from the paradise tree; in *Hsiang chün* the shaman states his intention of offering to the *hsia nü* the flowers he has plucked in a river islet.

The shamanistic quest of the goddess lent itself well to the poet's allegorical theme, since the allegory *required* that the poet's quest of a mate should be unsuccessful, and the shaman's quest of the goddess was, as we have seen, invariably and inevitably unsuccessful.

I do not mean to imply that the pattern of failure was uniform throughout all the shaman's transactions with the gods. It was the female deities of rivers and mountains who persistently eluded him. The heavenly gods were willing to oblige with their presence, albeit only in hurried and perfunctory visits. According to ancient custom,

---

[18] E.g. Hung Hsing-tsu, 楚辭補注 and Chu Hsi, 楚辭集注. Wang Yi's comments on *Chiu ko* are best passed over in decent silence. Chu Hsi refers back to *Li sao* III, on which he has the comment 下女謂神女之侍女也. In modern times Chiang Liang-fu follows this interpretation (姜亮夫, 屈原賦校註, 人民文學出版社, Peking, 1957, p. 220). The only commentator, as far as I can see, who has firmly and explicitly identified 下女 with the goddess and adduced full and convincing arguments for doing so is the Japanese scholar Hoshikawa Kiyotake. Cf. 星川清孝, 楚辭の研究, Nara, 1961, pp. 531-532.

river deities were sacrificed to with offerings dropped into the water.[19] Dwelling in the silent depths below, they were little likely to manifest themselves to the worshipper. The heavenly gods, on the other hand, were worshipped with great roaring bonfires,[20] and it needed little imagination to see the effulgence of the descending deity in the blaze and sparkle of the oblatory fire.

The god has no sooner descended in a blaze of glory,	靈皇皇兮既降
Than off in a whirl he soars again, far into the clouds	猋遠舉兮雲中

sings the shaman in *Yün-chung chün*. Compare those lines of *Yün-chung chün* with *Li sao* 141–3:

I heard that Wu Hsien was descending in the evening	巫咸將夕降兮
So I lay in wait with offerings of peppered rice-balls.	懷椒糈而要之
The spirits come thronging down in a dense cloud,	百神翳其備降兮
And the host of Chiu-i mountain come crowding to meet him.	九疑繽其並迎
His godhead was manifested in a blaze of radiance,	皇剡剡其揚靈兮
And he addressed me in these auspicious words.	告余以吉故

Wu Hsien, like the cloud god, is said to *descend*. In each case a similar term is used to describe the brightness in which the god's descent is

---

[19] This method of sacrificing to the River God is extremely well attested. From the Shang period to the Later Han there must be hundreds of references to the sacrifice of animals, objects, or humans by throwing or sinking them in the water (a custom still to be observed in the English superstition of throwing pennies into wells). To cite only two examples: 沈郊 (i.e. 妾) 于河 occurs in the oracle bone inscriptions; whilst in 108 B.C., on the occasion of the breach of the Yellow River dyke at Hu-tzu-k'ou, Emperor Wu sacrificed a white horse and jade *pi* by throwing them into the water. (Cf. *Shih chi* 7.) For an exhaustive study of the River God cult, see 文崇一, 九歌中河伯之研究, 中央研究院民族學研究所集刊 9 (1960), 139–162.

[20] 周禮, 大宗伯:

以禋祀祀昊天上帝
以實柴祀日月星辰
以橊燎祀司中司命飄師雨師
以血祭祭社稷五祀五嶽
以貍沈祭山林川澤
以疈辜祭四方百物

Note that there is even a different verb used to distinguish between the fiery sacrifices made to the heavenly gods and the various other sorts of sacrifices made to earthly deities. 禋 was a smoke offering. 實柴 and 橊燎, made to the sun, moon, stars, *ssu-chung*, Master of Fate, Wind God, and Rain God, were various sorts of bonfire. Four of our *Chiu ko* deities would have qualified for the "sacrifices by burial or drowning" prescribed for the worship of mountain and river gods.

manifested. Moreover we may note that the curious term *yang ling,* to emit or radiate one's divinity, or one's magical powers, is used both of Wu Hsien in the *Li sao* passage and of the questing shaman in *Hsiang chün.* And we may observe in passing that the half-line in the *Li sao* passage about the spirits of Chiu-yi mountain is identical with l. 33 of the *Hsiang fu-jen,* where the questing shaman is joined by the spirit host just at the moment when he makes his offerings to the river goddess.

It is by no means fanciful to suppose that these recurring phrases were among the liturgical formulae of shamanistic ritual which the secular poet appropriated for his own use. The nineteen *Hymns for the Suburban Sacrifices,* dating from the early Han period, contain a number of such formulae strongly reminiscent of ones found in *Chiu ko.*[21]

Combined with the theme of quest in *Li sao,* and sometimes even displacing it, is the theme of the magic-making journey, a sort of royal progress through the sky in which the poet, riding in a chariot drawn by flying dragons, is attended by a dazzling retinue of gods and spirits. Strangely enough this theme—for which the poet was equally indebted to his shaman predecessors—proved a far more productive influence on the Chinese literary imagination than the seemingly more poetical, more inspiring Quest of the Goddess.

[21] 漢郊祀歌十九首 (樂府詩集, 1)

  For example, note the following lines:

    九重開 (兮) 靈之游
    靈之車 (兮) 結玄雲
    駕飛龍 (兮) 羽旄紛
    靈之下 (兮) 若風馬
  . . . 澹容與 (兮) 獻嘉觴

               (From No. 1 練時日)

    華爗爗 (兮) 固靈根
    神之游 (兮) 過天門
  . . . 神之楡 (兮) 臨壇宇
    九疑賓 (兮) 夔龍舞
  . . . 沛施祐 (兮) 汾之阿
    揚金光 (兮) 太橫河

             (From No. 16 華爗爗)

    靈殷殷 (兮) 爛揚光
    延壽命 (兮) 永未央

            (From No. 19 赤蛟)

  Probably the "九夷賓" in No. 7 (惟秦之) ought to be 九疑賓, in which case we can add these lines:

    鐘鼓竽笙 (兮) 靈舞翔翔
    招搖靈旗 (兮) 九疑賓將

Apart from the explicitly shamanistic poems (*Chiu ko,* the "Summons" poems, and the unclassifiable *T'ien wen*) the content of the *Ch'u-tz'u* poems is classifiable into two main categories: one, which I shall designate *tristia,* expresses the poet's sorrows, his resentments, his complaints against a deluded prince, a cruel fate, a corrupt, malicious and uncomprehending society; the other, which I shall designate *itineraria,* describes the poet's journeys, occasionally real ones, but more often the imaginary, supernatural journeys to which I have just referred.

It is possible that the plaintive tone of the *tristia* element in Ch'u poetry derives from the characteristic note of melancholy and frustration which shamanistic tradition prescribed for the hymns which they addressed to their fickle and elusive deities. But so many other ingredients of a purely secular and literary kind have gone into the make-up of *tristia*—to name only one, the conventional listing of historical analogues—that the quest theme can almost be discounted as a source of inspiration in later literature, always excepting the beautiful "Goddess" *fu* by the pseudo-Sung Yü and its imitation by Ts'ao Chih, which can be thought of as offshoots of the tradition embodied in *Hsiang chün, Hsiang fu-jen, Shan kuei,* and the Quest passages of *Li sao.*

The idea of the *progress,* the ritual journey—usually a ritual circuit—made for the purpose of affirming or acquiring, or both affirming and acquiring, power appears in Chinese tradition in many contexts and at many levels. It is always essentially magical; but its travel may be real or imaginary, and the traveler may be a wizard, a mystic, or a king. It postulates a symmetrical cosmos whose various parts are presided over by various powers. These powers can be induced to give either their submission or their support to the traveler who approaches them with the correct ritual. A complete and successful circuit of the whole cosmos will therefore make him a lord of the universe, able to command any of its powers at will, if he is a wizard; to move in it with utter freedom, if he is a mystic; to rule by divine right and title with the allegiance of both temporal and spiritual powers, if he is an emperor.

In China the first recorded attempt to comprehend the entire space-time universe in a single closed system was made by Tsou Yen, a philosopher roughly contemporaneous with the author of *Li sao.*

But Tsou Yen's ideas, though representing the tendency towards synthesis and integration in the advanced thought of his day, are obviously no guide to the accepted cosmological, geographical, and religious beliefs of the majority of his contemporaries. Among the latter we observe a number of related but inconsistent ideas, some perhaps of alien origin, which were later formalized and coordinated in the all-embracing cosmology elaborated and perfected, to a large extent by anonymous thinkers, during the two succeeding centuries. But we shall search in vain for any *summa* or all-inclusive system in the literature produced by writers of Tsou Yen's own day.

Mu t'ien-tzu chuan records the imaginary progress to the far west of an ancient king, and the offerings which he made to various powers in the course of it. And *Shan hai ching*, or rather the earliest stratum of that many-layered book, by assuming that every mountain and river of the known world has its guardian power and by naming the offerings appropriate to their propitiation, implies the existence of power-seeking travelers—kings or wizards—who might feel disposed to make use of the information it supplies.

The colored guardians of the quarters also begin to appear in this period. We may presumably assign to approximately the same date as the last two writings that remarkable passage in *Mo-tzu* in which Mo-tzu himself is made to refer to the views of the astrologers:

God kills the green dragon in the east on the day *chia-yi*;
he kills the red dragon in the south on the day *ping-ting*;
he kills the white dragon in the west on the day *keng-hsin*;
and he kills the black dragon in the north on the day *jen-kuei*.[22]

This superstition would seem to have some bearing on a portentous incident in the early life of Han Kao-tsu recorded by Ssu-ma Ch'ien.[23] Kao-tsu had killed a large snake in the marshes, and an old woman who claimed to be the snake's mother was later found weeping beside it. The snake was the son of the White *Ti*, she said, and had been slain by the son of the Red *Ti*.

---

[22] 墨子, 貴義 (47).
[23] *Shih chi* 8 (*Kao-tsu pen-chi*).

The worship of the colored *Ti* was a state cult in Ch'in, if Ssu-ma Ch'ien's statement can be believed, as early as the fifth century B.C.[24] and must certainly have existed in Chin by the third, since shamans from Chin were settled in Ch'ang-an to maintain this cult at the beginning of the Han dynasty.[25] The Five *Ti* feature as part of a cosmological system in *Lü-shih ch'un-ch'iu*, written a century later than Tsou Yen and *Li sao* and on the very eve of imperial unification.[26]

Political integration not surprisingly had its intellectual counterpart in cosmological theory, which was, in turn, reflected back in the religious behavior of the governing class. Nowhere is this more apparent than in the emergence of that system of beliefs and practices which Ssu-ma Ch'ien designates by the term *feng-ch'an*. Let me demonstrate this by returning for a moment to the subject of *Hsiang-chün*. In seeking to identify the person of the deity who is the subject of this hymn, most commentators cite a well-known passage from Ssu-ma Ch'ien's *Annals of the First Ch'in Emperor* in which Hsiang-chün became the object of the emperor's vindictive ire:

> Traveling in a southwesterly direction he crossed over the R. Huai and came at length to Heng-shan. At Nan-chün he took boat and was sailing down the river to the Hsiang-shan shrine when a great wind arose and nearly prevented his getting to land. The emperor inquired of his wise men who Hsiang-chün was. They replied, "According to our information, Hsiang-chün are the daughters of Yao and wives of Shun who are buried in this place." At this the First Emperor was greatly enraged. He set three thousand convicts to work to cut down the trees of Hsiang-shan and to paint the mountain red. He then left Nan-chün and returned to Hsien-yang by way of the Wu-kuan pass.[27]

[24] *Shih chi* 28 *(Feng-ch'an shu)*: 其後百餘年靈公作吳陽上畤，祭黃帝，作下畤祭炎帝. Ssu-ma Ch'ien credits Ling's predecessors of much earlier date with having founded the cults of the White *Ti* (西畤) and the Green *Ti* (密畤); but probably the identification of the gods of these earlier cults belongs to the later period.

[25] 長安置祠祝官，女巫. 其 ... 晉巫祠五帝，東君，雲中君，司命 ... 之屬 ... *(Shih chi* 28).

[26] In point of fact *Lü-shih ch'un-ch'iu* gives the names of the *four Ti* who preside over the four seasons, and the names of their attendant spirits. The colors associated with them have to be matched by the earthly ruler in his costume and furnishings throughout the year. The same *Ti* and attendant spirits reappear in *Yüan yu*, however, as guardians of the four quarters. There is an almost total fusion of space and time in the *Lü-shih ch'un-ch'iu* cosmology.

[27] See *Ch'in Shih-huang pen-chi*, 28th year:

Let us look into this excursion of Ch'in Shih-huang's a little more
carefully. First of all "Nan-chün" here means not the whole com-
mandery of that name but its administrative center, the old city of
Ying, which in Ch'ü Yüan's day was the capital of the kings of Ch'u.
"Hsiang-shan" is another name for Chün-shan (the "Mountain of
the Goddess") or Tung-t'ing shan, as it was sometimes called—an
island in the northeast of lake Tung-t'ing, which *Shan hai ching* also
mentions as the site of the Hsiang goddesses' shrine.[28] Heng-shan, the
southernmost point of this journey, is the southernmost of the Five
Sacred Mountains, whose successive propitiation was an essential part
of the *feng-ch'an* ritual prescribed for a universal sovereign seeking
supernatural sanction for his rule.

This imperial progress took place in the twenty-eighth year of
Ch'in Shih-huang's reign. It began with a visit to the east, in the
course of which, after discussions about the *feng-ch'an* sacrifices with
various local *ju*, he ascended T'ai-shan, the eastern and most holy of
the Five Sacred Mountains, and performed the appropriate rituals
on its summit. There can be little doubt that the visit to Heng-shan
which followed was accompanied by similar offerings, although
Ssu-ma Ch'ien does not see fit to mention them, and that the subsequent journey to the island shrine of the Hsiang-chün was undertaken with the intention of making appropriate offerings to the
principal river deity of the Heng-shan area. The disagreeable outcome
of this well-intentioned trip was no doubt the reason for the emperor's
abandonment of the *feng-ch'an* circuit, which he had undertaken so
enthusiastically, after visiting only two of the Five Sacred Mountains.

He did, as a matter of fact, visit Chiu-yi mountain and make
offerings to Shun, who is buried there, in the last year of his reign;[29]
so presumably he had some time previously issued a royal pardon to

---

... 乃西南渡淮水，之衡山。南郡浮江，至湘山祠。逢大風，幾不得渡。上問博士曰
：「湘君何神？」博士對曰：「聞之，堯女，舜之妻，而葬此。」於此始皇大怒，使
刑徒三千人皆伐湘山之樹，赭其山。上自南郡由武關歸。

[28] See *Shan hai ching* 5 *(Chung shan ching)*, Ssu-pu pei-yao ed., p. 41b seq.: 又東南一百
二十里曰洞庭之山 ... 帝之二女居之。是常遊于江淵澧沅之風交淵湘沅之淵。出入必以飄
風暴雨 ... (Ch'in Shih-huang ought to have been warned!)

The text is obviously corrupt. I think the middle part should read 常遊於澧沅之江, 瀟湘
之淵。

[29] *Ch'in shih-huang pen-chi*, 37th year:
... 十一月，行至雲夢，望祀虞舜於九疑山 ...

the offending goddesses, and perhaps even planted a few trees on their bare red island. Shun was supposed to be the husband of the Hsiang goddesses, and could hardly be expected to extend a favorable reception to a visitor who was still treating his wives like convicts.

The ritual circuit of the cosmos, not in the shaman's airy flight or the mystic's imagination, but in actual earthly travel was thus really undertaken, though never concluded, by the Ch'in First Emperor. Emperor Wu's well-known predilection for magic and ceremonial also disposed him to give a favorable hearing to the *feng-ch'an* experts, particularly when all five of the Sacred Mountains were in territory which came under the imperial government's jurisdiction.[30] A weakness for more exotic kinds of religious practice deflected him, however, from completing what Ch'in Shih-huang had failed to accomplish before he had even achieved as much, and T'ai-shan was the only one of the Five Sacred Mountains which Wu-ti ever favored with a visit. Nevertheless, the mere fact that powerful rulers like Ch'in Shih-huang and Han Wu-ti were prepared even to contemplate a *feng-ch'an* progress shows the extent to which the new cosmology had gained ground, and helps to explain the great influence it was to have on literature and art.

We can obtain a very good idea of its literary influence if we compare *Li sao* with the much later *Yüan yu*. *Li sao* depicts, in unmistakable colors, a magic-making progress; but the cosmos in which it takes place is not defined. Even the route is uncertain. We are vaguely given to understand that it is westward, like the journey of the sun—whose progress the poet seems at times to be deliberately imitating—and K'un-lun and points west of it are mentioned; but the itinerary could in no sense be described as a circuit. *Yüan yu* precisely delineates a symmetrical, mandala-like cosmos—the same

---

[30] *Feng ch'an shu* (The date of the second event referred to in this passage was 113 B.C.):
   At this juncture the Prince of Chi-pei, believing that the Emperor was about to embark on the *feng-ch'an* sacrifices, sent him a letter offering him T'ai-shan and the adjacent towns. The Emperor thanked him, and bestowed some other towns on him in their stead. Also the Prince of Ch'ang-shan (i.e. Heng-shan, the northernmost of the Five Peaks, which had to change its name because of the taboo on Emperor Wen's name) was removed from his fief at about this time because of some offense, and the Emperor transferred the Prince's younger brother to maintain his family's sacrifices in Chen-ting, annexing the fief of Ch'ang-shan to the crown. By this last act all five of the Sacred Mountains now came within the imperial jurisdiction.

cosmos which embellishes the backs of contemporary mirrors[31]—and describes a circuit which approaches each of its guardian powers in due order before achieving climax in the center, which is the hub of power.

The mandala-like cosmos had its origin, needless to say, in psychical rather than in physical facts.[32] It could be said to have a physical basis in the sense that our equilibrium, which profoundly affects our psychosomatic well-being, can be effectively maintained by conscious self-orientation within an imaginary frame; and the mandala-cosmos is an archetype of all such frames. But it is without physical basis in the sense that it does not conform to discernible geographical or astronomical facts.

Yet the nature of the ancient system of thought of which this concept formed a part was such that transference from one plane to another was easy. What applied to the microcosm would apply also to the macrocosm, and *vice versa*.[33] The power-formulae employed by the mystic in his transcendental flights could equally well be employed by the ruler in his physical domain.

This ease of transference enabled the highly personal and seemingly unsuitable themes of the Ch'u poet to be adapted without difficulty to the taste of an imperial court. The *itineraria*, originally based on the

[31] The earliest 四神 mirrors are supposed to date from the latter half of the Western Han period. The expressions 左龍右虎，青龍在左白虎居右 found in mirror inscriptions and referring to the Green Dragon and White Tiger of the decoration are frequently echoed in the *itineraria* (e.g. *Hsi shih* 6: 蒼龍蚴虬於左驂兮，白虎騁而為右騑. Some of these inscriptions explicitly refer to cosmic travel: 上太山見神人食玉英飲澧泉駕交龍乘浮雲白虎引之直上天 (cf. Karlgren, *Early Chinese Mirror Inscriptions, Bulletin of the Museum of Far Eastern Antiquities* 6, No. 94); or the following: 鏡 上有仙人不知老渴飲玉泉飢食棗浮游天下敖四海 (No. 215). Komai Kazuchika has a section in his book about mirrors on the connection between mirror inscriptions and the *Ch'u-tz'u* literature. (駒井知愛, 中國古鏡の研究 Iwanami, 1953, 17–27).

[32] Tucci (*The Theory and Practice of Mandala*, Rider and Co., 1961) calls the mandalas "psycho-cosmogrammata."

[33] Cf. Tucci, *op. cit.*, 23: "A mandala is . . . above all a map of the cosmos (Ital.: *un cosmogramma*) . . . the universe not only in its inert spatial expanse, but as a temporal revolution and . . . a vital process which decays from an essential principle and rotates round a central axis, Mount Sumeru, the axis of the world on which the sky rests and which sinks its roots in the mysterious substratum . . . [it is] reflected in the plan of the Iranian rulers' imperial city, and . . . in the ideal image of the palace of the *cakravartin*."

See also Mircea Eliade, *Yoga and Freedom*, New York, 1958, p. 221: "In India and elsewhere, sovereignty is related to the sacred . . . . The disciple is assimilated to the sovereign because he rises above the play of cosmic forces; he is autonomous, wholly free. Spiritual freedom—and this is true not only of India—has always been expressed by sovereignty."

magic-making flight of the shaman and used by secular poets as part
of an allegorical representation of their flight from a corrupt society
and a foolish and faithless prince, could be made to appeal to a ruler
who was accustomed to associate travel with the performance of
magic-making rituals, and who aspired, as master of all men and
therefore entitled to the highest benefits attainable by man, to
procure for himself the powers and pleasures which normally could
be acquired only by the labors of the magician or the meditations of
the mystic. This is precisely what Ssu-ma Hsiang-ju, China's first and
greatest court poet, in fact did.

> Hsiang-ju, observing that the emperor had a liking for magic and
> mysticism, said, "What I wrote about the Shang-lin Park is not really
> very wonderful. I can do much better than that. I once wrote a
> '*Fu* on the Great Man' which I did not, however, finish. I should like
> to get it into shape and present it to Your Majesty." Hsiang-ju felt
> that the traditional picture of the Immortal living in the mountains
> or the marshes, his body emaciated with fasting, was not at all a suit-
> able model for mystically-inclined royalty, and his '*Fu* of the Great
> Man' was written to suit the requirements of the latter.[34]

In *Ta jen fu* the Great Man of the title, with whom the emperor is
invited to identify himself, seems to have as his only motive for travel
the fact that the sublunary world is too small for him.[35] The journey
on which Ssu-ma Hsiang-ju conducts him and his glittering cortège
is a sort of Cook's tour of the cosmos in which every god and godlet of
the Chinese pantheon is included. The guardians Hsüan-wu and the
Scarlet Bird, the Great Unity (a favorite deity of the emperor Wu),
the Five *Ti*, Hsi-wang-mu—all are there. The *tristia* element which
nearly always accompanies the *itineraria* in the more private and
personal expression of preceding poets is, for obvious reasons,
entirely excluded.

It is instructive to compare *Ta jen fu* with *Hsi shih*,[36] written by an
anonymous poet who may have been a somewhat older contemporary of Ssu-ma Hsiang-ju. Lines 2–16 of *Hsi shih* describe a
celestial journey in which, as in *Ta jen fu*, the Great Unity and the
guardians of the quarters (Scarlet Bird, Green Dragon, and so

[34] *Shih chi* 107 (p. 3056 in the 1959 Chung-hua shu-chü edition).
[35] 宅彌萬里兮曾不足以少留
[36] *Ch'u-tz'u* 11 (惜誓).

forth) are mentioned. What follows, from l. 17 to the end of the poem, is *tristia*. The motive for the magic flight, given in the opening couplet, was the poet's distress at the advance of age. The object of his flight is the prolongation of life and the perpetuation of youth. The hinge which joins the two very dissimilar halves of the poem is the sudden access of nostalgia perfunctorily mentioned in l. 17 and obviously an imitation of *Li sao*, 184–185.[37] This wave of regret for what he has left behind causes the poet to break off in the middle of his hitherto successful life-prolonging experiment. *Ai shih ming*, another of the later *Ch'u-tz'u* poems written by the generation of poets who were still alive in Ssu-ma Hsiang-ju's youth, consists almost entirely of *tristia*, but contains one brief passage (ll.21–23)[38] in which the poet describes himself as a Great Man who, like the Great Man of *Ta jen fu*, finds the confines of the sublunary world too narrow to contain him.

As a study in thematic development the development from *Li sao* to *Ta jen fu* is clearly unconvincing. The celestial journey of the Great Man, with which Ssu-ma Hsiang-ju entertained his imperial patron, is more like a regression to the ancient theme of the shaman's flight— a theme which formed only one of several ingredients in the complicated allegories of secularizing Ch'u poets more than a century earlier. Thematically *Li sao* is a far more complex and sophisticated poem than *Ta jen fu*. Indeed, the highest and most elaborate development of the flight theme, Chang Heng's *Ssu hsüan fu*, written in the second century A.D., is thematically a mirror image of *Li sao*[39] and

[37] *Hsi shih*   17   念我長生而久僊兮
                        不如反余之故鄉
    Li sao   184   陟陞皇之赫戲兮
                        忽臨睨夫舊鄉
            185   僕夫悲余馬懷兮
                        蜷局顧而不行

[38] *Ch'u-tz'u* 14   (哀時命).
            21   冠崔嵬而切雲兮劍淋灕而從衡
            22   衣攝葉以儲與兮左袪挂於搏桑
            23   右袵拂於不周兮六合不足以肆行

[39] For example, where Ch'ü Yüan goes to Ts'ang-wu to tell his griefs to the spirit of Shun, Chang Heng goes to Ch'i-shan and consults Wen Wang. Where Ch'ü Yüan has unsatisfactory experiences with various goddesses, Chang Heng is graciously entertained by Hsi-wang-mu and a lady called the Jade Maid of T'ai-hua mountain, but considers their characters unstable. Like Ch'ü Yüan, Chang Heng consults Wu Hsien. Like Ch'ü Yüan, he encounters the Heavenly Porter who, however, treats him with more respect, admitting him to the Heavenly City where he listens to a celestial orchestra playing edifying music. The *fu* ends, like *Li sao*, with an envoi. Chang Heng calls his a 系.

stands in no sort of relationship to *Ta jen fu*. In dwelling on the exploitation of the flight theme for the purposes of court poetry, it was not my intention to suggest that the main development of *fu* lay in that direction, but merely to draw attention to the seeming paradox that a kind of poetry which evolved as a medium for the allegorical expression of seditious thoughts could, with very little modification, be adapted for the flattery and delectation of princes.

The development of *fu* is an extremely complicated phenomenon which cannot be conveniently disposed of in a single formula. Indeed, in literary theory simplifications have a way of increasing the confusions and complexities which they set out to resolve. For example, it would be necessary, in accounting for the various elements which entered into the evolution of this genre, to mention the rhetorical exercises of the sophists, whose debates and set pieces are clearly mirrored in the dialogue structure of so many *fu* of the Han period.[40] We find it, for example, in several of the *fu* by the pseudo-Sung Yü, in the greatest of Ssu-ma Hsiang-ju's *fu*, and in the masterpieces of Pan Ku and Chang Heng. Yet this undeniably important element is totally unconnected with those shamanistic elements which equally clearly played an important part in the development of the medium, and could not be accounted for in a monolithic theory which sought to trace the unmixed descent of *fu* from the chants of the medicine men.

However, there is one important respect in which I think the influence of the Ch'u *itineraria*, which *were* of shamanistic origin, was crucial in the *fu*'s development. If we apply the word "narrative" to the *itineraria*, its absurd inappropriateness is at once apparent. Yet *Li sao, Yüan yu, Ssu hsüan fu* do in fact record movement, and events taking place in some sort of time. The reason why the term "narrative" is so immediately unacceptable is that the development in these poems is conceived of as a spatial squence. In the ritual circuit whose object is the accumulation of magic power, the actual passage

---

[40] See J. I. Crump, *Intrigues, Studies of the Chan-kuo Ts'e*, Ann Arbor, 1964, p. 76: "It is certainly not by chance that the *fu* of late Warring States and early Han times have for their particular province much the same territory encompassed by the term rhetoric. Arthur Waley sees a close similarity between the word-magic of early *fu* and the prose of the *Intrigues*. Hellmut Wilhelm sees a connection between 'persuasion by indirection' and the 'School of Politics', and concludes that Han era *fu 'matured* [persuasion] from a technique into an art'," etc.

between one power-nucleus and the next, though indispensable, is not of intrinsic interest.

> In the morning I started my journey from Ts'ang-wu;
> In the evening I arrived at the Garden of Paradise

—this is not the narrative of a journey. The journey might have been a long and interesting one; but the poet's business is with the enumeration of significant places, not with the experience of reaching them. This becomes more evident as the poet's cosmology becomes more defined. The perfunctory verbal expressions denoting transit between one point and another in the celestial circuit become mere connectives linking one passage and another. The all-important structural element is not temporal sequence but spatial order: the enumeration in correct order of fixed points in the cosmos. The movement could just as well be that of a pointing finger as of a dragon-powered chariot.[41]

This orderly enumeration of the parts of a cosmos is already found in early examples of shamanistic literature. The Summons poems contain examples of it when they list the dangers lurking in different quarters of the universe which threaten the wandering soul. The book *Shan hai ching*, which lists the mountains of the earth in due sequence and with ritual-religious intent, consists exclusively of such orderly enumeration. Both *Shan hai ching* and the Summons poems are examples of literature conditioned by magical and ritual patterns of thought. As a literary archetype, if we can call it that, this "orderly enumeration" can appear in many guises. All kinds of litanies and invocations are examples of it, including the invocation, one after

---

[41] Conversely, and for the same evolutionary reason, description of a static scene tends to become dramatized and filled with movement. A *fu* writer does not say, "Across the lake is a little hill, at the top of which is a garden containing a high terrace with a stone staircase leading up to it" but "Rowing over the lake, climbing up a little hill, one passes through a garden. Reeling giddily, one ascends the stone steps of a lofty terrace." This may seem no more than is achieved nowadays by the writers of guidebooks, and can indeed be partly accounted for by the exigencies of Chinese idiom. Yet I doubt whether that can account for the inveterate habit of dramatization as observable, for example, in Chang Heng's *Chou-t'ien ta-hsiang fu*, a poem half as long again as *Li sao*, whose topic is a straightforward enumeration of the constellations. A perfectly static description would seem indicated; yet Chang Heng treats his subject in such a way that if all the nouns were blotted out one would gain an impression of violent and continuous motion. Unconsciously the poet envisages himself not as a static observer but as a tourist.

another, of the three persons of the Trinity which rounds off the prayers of the Christian church.

The archetype is in origin essentially magical and religious. The nature of its origin, however, by no means precludes its successful employment in secular literature. When we are asked to illustrate the highest achievement of the *fu* writers of the Han period with one or two examples, most of us would unhesitatingly point to Ssu-ma Hsiang-ju's *fu* on the hunting parks and to the "Capitals" *fu* of Pan Ku and Chang Heng. The sheer magnitude of conception and design of these majestic panoramas compels us, as it did the great anthologist Hsiao T'ung, to assign them a leading place in any assessment. They stand as symbols of a supremely self-confident age—an age confident that it could explain and control everything: man and nature, heaven and earth, human society and the human heart, the whole cosmos in fact.

It would be easy to dismiss as fanciful an attempt to link the ordered enumeration, which is found in a most extreme and highly developed form in these panoramic *fu*, with the magician's enumeration of the quarters of his divine cosmos, on the grounds that the nature of the material must itself have imposed on the poet the necessity of creating for it some such structure as we find in these *fu*. In topographical description the use of orientations is, after all, a rather obvious way of classifying and ordering a heterogeneous mass of material. To the north we find so-and-so, to the south such-and-such; in front is this, behind is that; and so on. But I am unconvinced by this commonsense view, for a number of reasons.

In the first place, the *fu* is not truly descriptive any more than it is truly narrative. The genre would never have been exposed to the attacks of moralists[42] if it were merely descriptive. The ancient, no doubt highly dubious derivation of *"fu"* from a word meaning "spread," "unfold"[43] comes quite close to our "enumerate" and is still serviceable to the extent that it can warn us away from definitions like "narrative" and "descriptive."

[42] The *fu* writers deliberately aimed to "carry you away," and even if they did thereafter attempt some sort of moral edification, you would be too far gone to profit from it. This seems to be the gist of Yang Hsiung's later-life objections to the *fu*. For a discussion of Han critics' attitudes to the *fu* cf. 郭紹虞,中國文學批評史, Commercial Press, 1942, 51 *seq.*

[43] 賦之言鋪, 直鋪陳今之政教善惡. This etymology appears in several texts. The earliest appears to be Cheng Hsüan's commentary on *Chou li,* 5 (s.v. 大師).

   In the enumeration of the *fu* there always lurks a residuum of
name-magic. It should be observed that Ssu-ma Hsiang-ju, who
virtually invented the panoramic *fu*, does not aim to provide us with
an accurate impression of any of the palaces, lodges, parks, lakes,
and the like which he introduces into his account. His aim is to
knock us back reeling and gasping with wonder at their magnitude,
majesty, and magnificence. There is moreover a constant confusion
of scales and levels, of the smaller with the greater cosmos in these
poems. At first glance the dimensions of the Shang-lin park appear
almost commensurate with China itself. Partly this is occasioned by
the historical fact that emperors reproduced on a small scale in their
parks and gardens the mountains and lakes of their far-flung empire.
(Traces of this tradition survive to our own day. The Summer Palace
at Peking has a K'un-ming lake and a Soochow canal.) But this
circumstance is deliberately exploited by Ssu-ma Hsiang-ju, and
throughout the whole *fu* no opportunity is lost of exalting us above
the mundane level of bricks and trees to a higher world of gods and
phoenixes. Nowhere is this more apparent than in the section which
describes the chase. This is treated in such a way as forcibly to remind
us of the god-attended celestial journeys of poet-magicians in the
itineraria. Consider this (from *Shang-lin fu*) :

Next, with aspiring steps, aloft he soars,	
Treads the wind's startling blast,	
Cleaves through the whirlwind's shock,	然後揚節而上浮
Rides in the empty void	陵驚風，歷駭飆，
Companion of the gods:	乘虛無，與神俱，
Tramples the ancient crane,	轔玄鶴，亂昆雞，
Confounds the jungle fowl,	遒孔雀，促鵕鸃，
Spurns peacocks underfoot,	拂鷖鳥 . . . .
Affrights the golden pheasant,	
Grasps at the rainbow bird	

As a description of what actually takes place on a grouse moor this is
positively misleading. And it is not enough to say that this is hyperbole. It is a special kind of hyperbole deliberately slanted to exalt its
subject out of a mundane into a supernatural environment.
   Consider the beginning of this section on the royal hunt, where the
emperor's train is described:

When the year turns its back on autumn
  and edges into winter
The Son of Heaven goes forth to hunt the
  driven game.
Mounted on ivory drawn by six jade-
  scaled dragons,
Fluttering with rainbow flags, with cloud
  banner outspread . . . .

於是乎
背秋涉冬，天子校獵
乘鏤象，六玉虯
拖蜺旌，靡雲旗 . . .

The chariot and team of the emperor is quite deliberately made to
seem like the divine equipage which carries gods and magicians in
their flights across the sky.

Nor is Ssu-ma Hsiang-ju, that great master of hyperbole, the only
writer to accord the theme this sort of treatment. In Chang Heng's
Fu on the Royal Hunt, two centuries later, the emperor's cortège is
described in the following terms:

Then, the phoenix having presented a lucky day,
The Master of Horse made ready horses and carriage,
Ch'ih Yu rides at the head of the procession,
And the Rain God with sprinklings clears the road
  ahead.
The mountain spirits form a protective guard;
The Guardians of the Quarters make up the royal train,
Hsi-ho holds the reins, and with slow pace drives to
  westward . . . .

於是

鳳皇獻歷
太僕駕具
蚩尤先驅
雨師清路
山靈護陣
方神蹕御
羲和捧轡
弭節西征

The expression in this last line which I have translated "with slow
pace" is the curious one occurring in *Li sao* and *Hsiang chün* which I
have discussed earlier in this paper. The Royal Hunt is, of course, a
feature not only of those *fu* which the anthologists and encyclopedists
classify as "hunting *fu*" but also of the "capitals *fu*". The passage just
quoted is, as a matter of fact, in part borrowed from Pan Ku's
account of the imperial procession setting out for the hunt in his *Fu
on the Eastern Capital.*

The Royal Hunt is only a comparatively small part of these
panoramic *fu*. Even in the *fu* on the Shang-lin park, for example, only
a quarter of the poem is devoted to the hunt itself and the entertainment following it. By far the largest section is an account of the park.
But I think it is significant that in all of these panoramic poems the

progress of the emperor comes as a climax. We are made to feel that
the purpose and function of the enormously elaborate account of
palaces, gardens, parks, lodges, and so forth is merely to provide a
setting in which the Great Man, the emperor, who is the heroic
protagonist of this little cosmos, may be revealed in power and
splendor. Essentially this kind of *fu* is not the description of a place
but the epiphany of a person.

What relevance have these observations to the great majority of *fu*
—even, one might add, the great majority of Han *fu*—which are *not*
panoramic studies of cities or hunting parks, which do *not* have the
emperor as their central figure and his exaltation as their principal
aim? The point I have been laboring to make is that the patterns of
thought associated with what one might call the cosmological
approach to art became so ingrained that they affected all literature,
not only those kinds whose themes suggested it. It seems to me, for
example, that we find our archetype even in so sophisticated a
product as the *Fu on Literature* by Lu Chi, dating from the latter part
of the third century A.D.

This is how Lu Chi begins his *fu* after the preliminary lines of
introduction:

Taking his position at the hub of things, the writer   佇中區以玄覽
contemplates the mystery of the universe . . . .[44]

Then after a few lines on the writer's contemplation of the works of
nature and of art, he continues as follows:

His spirit gallops to the eight ends of the universe;   精騖八極
    his mind wanders along vast distances.   心遊萬仞
In the end, as his mood dawns clearer and clearer, objects,   其致也 / 情瞳矓而彌鮮
    clean-cut now in outline, shove one another forward,   物昭晰而互進
He sips the essence of letters; he rinses his mouth with   傾群言之瀝液
    the extract of the Six Arts.   漱六藝之芳潤
Floating on the heavenly lake, he swims along; plunging   浮天淵以安流
    into the nether spring he immerses himself.   濯下泉而潛浸

The metaphor which is sustained throughout the whole of the
opening passage of which these are the last four lines treats the

[44] Cf. Achilles Fang, "Rhymeprose on Literature: The *Wen-fu* of Lu Chi (A.D. 261–303)," *Harvard Journal of Asiatic Studies* 14 (1951), 531–532.

creative writer as a magician who moves through the universe like the mystics and shamans of old in their celestial journeys.[45] Lu Chi's approach to his subject, literature, is unhesitatingly cosmological. The poet in the cosmos. Out of the systematic exploration of that cosmos power is engendered, in this case the power of literary creation —just as power of a different kind is gained by the magician through his peregrination of the quarters of the sky.

The study of archetypes in literature must to some extent involve the study of other disciplines such as anthropology and psychology, and the student of Chinese literature, exhausted with laboring in his already overextended domain, may justifiably shrink back from those borderlands in which misleading sprites can all too easily beguile the traveler into swamps of facile generalization and crackpot theory. Nevertheless, formal description can never by itself be enough to satisfy the inquiring mind, and where new theories are lacking, old doctrine will push in. It seems to me important to use what material there is to hand for the elucidation of observable archetypes, and I present these observations on *Ch'u-tz'u* and *fu* not with much confidence that they will survive intact when submitted to intensive critical scrutiny, but in the hope that other, more qualified scholars will feel stimulated to pursue the same theme to more permanently satisfying conclusions.

[45] The "spirit man" in *Chuang-tzu* 1 *(Hsiao-yao-yu)* "inhaled the wind and drank the dew and, riding on a chariot of cloud vapor drawn by flying dragons, traveled beyond the confines of the four seas." The last line of the *Wen fu* passage may be compared with Wei Mou's description of Chuang Chou in *Chuang-tzu* 17 *(Ch'iu-shui)*: "One moment he will be paddling in the Yellow Springs, the next mounting up into the height of heaven."

Yùeh-fŭ Poetry

by Hans H. Frankel

Definition and Range of the term "*Yùeh-fŭ* Poetry"

Yùeh-fŭ was the name of the Music Bureau established by the Hàn emperor Wŭ-tì around 120 B.C. In Chinese literature, the term *yùeh-fŭ shīh* 樂府詩 ("Music Bureau Poems"), or simply *yùeh-fŭ*, has been applied to an ever widening sector of poems, as follows.

First, *yùeh-fŭ* referred to the hymns (texts and tunes) composed at the Music Bureau for ritual purposes.

Second, the term included texts selected by the Music Bureau from the works of known authors and provided with music at the Bureau, also to be used at state ceremonies.

Third, it meant anonymous songs collected by the Music Bureau from various parts of China (the Ch'ŭ region was the richest source) and from abroad. Most of these already had tunes; for those that did not, music was composed at the Bureau.

Fourth, after the abolition of the Music Bureau in 6 B.C. (most of its functions were taken over by other government offices), the name *yùeh-fŭ* continued to be applied to hymns and popular songs of the three categories just listed. These new song words were either fitted to existing tunes or created with new music; their titles were sometimes traditional, sometimes new. Hence there are four kinds in this category: (1) old titles, old tunes, new words; (2) old titles, new tunes, new words; (3) new titles, old tunes, new words; (4) new titles, new tunes, new words.

Fifth, numerous men of letters from late Hàn times down to the modern period wrote poems in the style of anonymous *yùeh-fǔ* poems. These imitations, which were not necessarily set to music, often bore the same titles as their anonymous models but were apt to differ considerably from their models in meter and content. Some literati, rather than using traditional *yùeh-fǔ* titles, created new titles for their *yùch-fǔ* poems. Such new titles were often taken from old *yùeh-fǔ* texts.

Sixth, some T'áng poets of the eighth and ninth century, such as Yúan Chíeh, Pó Chǔ-yì, and Yúan Chēn, used the term *hsīn yùeh-fǔ* ("new *yùeh-fǔ* poems") for their poems of social criticism. These were written, like some of the oldest *yùeh-fǔ* poems, in lines of uneven length; otherwise they were rather different from earlier *yùeh-fǔ* poetry in their titles, content, and style. They were not set to music.

Seventh, the term *yùeh-fǔ* is sometimes used in a very broad sense to include all poetic genres that were originally accompanied by music, notably *ch'áng-tǔan chù* 長短句 (*tz'ú* 詞) and *ch'ǔ* 曲.

The present study is limited to the first five categories.

Classifications of *Yùeh-fǔ* Poetry

Even with this limitation, there is so much diversity in *yùeh-fǔ* poetry that we cannot conceive of it as a single literary genre. Let us distinguish, then, two separate genres, as suggested by James Robert Hightower: *yùeh-fǔ* hymns and *yùeh-fǔ* ballads.[1] True, there are a few *yùeh-fǔ* forms which combine characteristics of both genres, for example a special class of ritual hymns from the Southern Dynasties, to be discussed below. But the existence of such poems does not invalidate the distinctness of the two genres, just as the existence of gray does not invalidate the distinction between black and white.

Despite this dichotomy, the term "*yùeh-fǔ* poetry" is so well established in Chinese literary history that it cannot be abolished. Also firmly established is the traditional classification, embodied in the *Yùeh-fǔ shīh chí* 府府詩集 (hereafter *YFSC*). This is the main repository of *yùeh-fǔ* poetry, comprising nearly all extant examples from the end of the third century B.C. (a few older ones are also included) down to the tenth century of our era. It was compiled by

---

[1] Hightower, *Topics in Chinese Literature*, Ch. VIII, especially pp. 50–51.

Kūo Mào-ch'ien 郭茂倩 in the twelfth century. Kūo divides the entire corpus of *yüeh-fü* poetry into twelve categories:

(1) *chīao-mìao kō tz'ú* 郊廟歌辭, "hymns for suburban and ancestral temple rituals" (*chüan* 1–12 in *YFSC*);

(2) *yèn-shè kō tz'ú* 燕射歌辭, "state banquet songs" (*ch.* 13–15);

(3) *kǔ-ch'ūi ch'ǔ tz'ú* 鼓吹曲辭, "songs accompanied by drums and wind instruments" (*ch.* 16–20);

(4) *héng-ch'ūi ch'ǔ tz'ú* 橫吹曲辭, "songs accompanied by horizontal flutes" (*ch.* 21–25);

(5) *hsīang-hò kō tz'ú* 相和歌辭, "matching (?) songs" (*ch.* 26–43);

(6) *ch'īng-shāng ch'ǔ-tz'ú* 清商曲辭, "songs in the tunes *ch'īng* and *shāng*" (*ch.* 44–51);

(7) *wǔ-ch'ǔ kō tz'ú* 舞曲歌辭, "dance songs" (*ch.* 52–56);

(8) *ch'ín-ch'ǔ kō tz'ú* 琴曲歌辭, "songs for the lute" (*ch.* 57–60);

(9) *tsá-ch'ǔ kō tz'ú* 雜曲歌辭, "miscellaneous songs" (*ch.* 61–78);

(10) *chìn-tài ch'ǔ tz'ú* 近代曲辭, "songs of recent times" (*ch.* 79–82);

(11) *tsá kō-yáo tz'ú* 雜歌謠辭, "miscellaneous songs and airs" (*ch.* 83–89);

(12) *hsīn yüeh-fü tz'ú* 新樂府辭, "new *yüeh-fü* poems" (*ch.* 90–100).

Kūo's classification scheme, derived and elaborated from the works of his predecessors, has been adopted, with some modifications, by most subsequent writers on the subject, down to the most recent studies. For our present purposes, however, its usefulness is limited since nearly all his terms have to do with the musical setting rather than the literary aspects of the *yüeh-fü* songs. As the music has long been lost, the situation is about the same as if we had a collection of paintings, preserved only in black-and-white copies but classified on the basis of the original color schemes. Kūo's classifying headings cannot be ignored, of course, for they do convey precious information about the origin and background of the songs. But for a workable classification of the *poems*, one should seek a different approach. In classifying the poems treated in this short paper, I make the following distinctions: first, the difference between the oral and the literary tradition; second, the dichotomy of hymns and ballads; third, regional differences; and fourth, differences of period. On the basis of these distinctions, I will treat the *yüeh-fú* poems under five headings:

(1) ritual hymns of the Hàn dynasty,

(2) a special class of ritual hymns from the Southern Dynasties,

(3) anonymous ballads of the Hàn period,

(4) anonymous ballads of the Southern and Northern Dynasties,

(5) ballads in *yüeh-fú* style by men of letters.

Ritual Hymns of the Hàn Dynasty

We have a corpus of ritual hymns from every dynasty, beginning with the Hàn. As may be expected, their literary merits are generally slight, but they are of great interest to students of institutional and cultural history and, to a lesser extent, to students of literary history. From the Hàn Dynasty we possess two groups of hymns, called *ān-shìh fáng-chūng kō* 安世房中歌 and *chīao-ssù kō* 郊祀歌.

Ān-shìh fáng-chūng kō probably means "songs to set the world at ease, for inside performance." The name was changed to *ān-shìh yüeh* ("music to set the world at ease") in 194 B.C. The seventeen extant hymns of this group are all said to have been composed around 206 B.C. by one of Hàn Kāo-tsǔ's consorts, known as Lady T'áng-shān 唐山夫人. They were performed at sacrificial rites in the ancestral temple of the imperial house (*tsǔ mìao* 祖廟). In addition, they were also used to entertain guests at official state banquets. The term *fáng-chūng yüeh* ("music for inside performance") was used in Hàn times synonymously with *yèn yüeh* 燕樂 ("banquet music") as a technical term for music played to entertain either ancestors or guests at official functions.[2] As for contents, the *ān-shìh fáng-chūng kō* extol the Confucian virtues, particularly filial devotion. As for their form, thirteen of the seventeen hymns are in the four-syllable meter familiar from the *Shīh chīng,* three are in three-syllable lines, and one contains both seven-syllable and three-syllable lines. Since the last-mentioned hymn is of some literary as well as metrical interest, it may be translated and discussed here.

[2] Cf. Hsīao, p. 42.

	The great sea is vast, vast, the waters come to it.	大海蕩蕩水所歸
2	The noble sages are kind, kind, the people cherish them.	高賢愉愉民所懷
	The Great Mountain is lofty,	大山崔
4	The hundred plants grow there.	百卉殖
	Whom do the people hold dear?	民何貴
6	They hold dear the virtuous.[3]	貴有德

In six short lines, this hymn manages to convey a good deal of Confucian morality and of the world view that goes with it. It does this by means of devices that are appropriate to religious poetry— devices of association, juxtaposition, and emotional appeal. The catchy rhythm has an ingratiating quality, and the question-and-answer sequence in the final couplet has a catechizing flavor. The first four lines work with two grand analogies between the natural world and human relationships. These analogies forcefully and succinctly drive home the moral lesson without any recourse to reasoning or preaching, simply by juxtaposing natural and human phenomena. The juxtapositions suggest four cardinal points of the Confucian doctrine:

(1) Human society is ordered according to the same principles as the world of nature.

(2) It is proper for the members of the upper classes of human society to be virtuous and benevolent, and for the common people to obey their superiors.

(3) These proper modes of behavior come about naturally, like the flow of rivers to the sea, and like the growth of plants in a favorable environment.

(4) Whenever the proper order is upset, it will correct itself "naturally," as the people will turn their backs on unworthy masters and flock to those who treat them well.

The meter of this hymn shows variety and unity: variety in the change from the seven-syllable to the three-syllable meter, and unity in that each couplet of three-syllable lines (with a pause at the end of every line) is the equivalent of a seven-syllable line followed by a pause. Thus we have here an early instance of the seven-syllable line

[3] *YFSC*, 8. 2a; Shěn, p. 37; Uchida, p. 69.

with the caesura between the fourth and the fifth syllable. (Other early instances are the poems "Chāo hún" 招魂, "Tà chāo" 大招, and "Chú sùng" 橘頌 in the *Ch'ŭ-tz'ú* 楚辭. Later instances are found in the *Hàn chīao-ssù kō*.)

The other group of Hàn ritual hymns, the *chīao-ssù kō* ("songs for suburban sacrifices"), were performed at the suburban sacrifices to Heaven, Earth, and other deities. They were also performed sometimes in the ancestral temple of the imperial house. These nineteen hymns, unlike the *Hàn ān-shìh fáng-chūng kō*, were not written by a single author, nor were they all composed at the same time. The earliest, "Chāo lŭng shŏu" 朝隴首, was written in 122 B.C. to celebrate the capture of a "white unicorn."[4] The latest, "Hsìang tsài yú" 象載瑜, was composed in 94 B.C. to commemorate another auspicious catch, namely, a "red wild goose."[5] The authors of these nineteen hymns are not known with certainty. It is recorded that some of them were written by Ssū-mă Hsìang-jú and other poets of Wŭ-tì's court. Some are attributed to "Master Tsōu" 鄒子 (i.e., Tsōu Yáng 鄒陽?). The hymn "Jìh ch'ū-jù" 日出入 is perhaps by Lĭ Yén-níen 李延年.[6]

The individual hymns were destined for specific festivals, deities, or celebrations of auspicious events. There was, for example, a hymn to welcome each of the four seasons at the appropriate suburban altar: the hymn "Ch'īng yáng" 青陽 was performed in the Eastern Suburb on the day *lì ch'ūn* 立春 to welcome spring; "Chū míng" 朱明 in the Southern Suburb on the day *lì hsìa* to welcome summer; "Hsī hào" 西顥 in the Western Suburb on the day *lì ch'īu* to welcome autumn; and "Hsúan míng" 亥冥 in the Northern Suburb on the day *lì tūng* to welcome winter. The hymn "Tì lín" 帝臨 is devoted to Húang-tì, the Yellow Emperor, and "Jìh ch'ū-jù" 日出入 to Jìh-shén 日神, the Sun God.

As far as form is concerned, the meters most commonly used in the *Hàn chīao-ssù kō* are four-syllable and three-syllable lines. Eight of the nineteen hymns are entirely in four-syllable lines, seven in three-syllable lines, and four in mixed meters of lines from three to seven syllables. Parallelism is used occasionally.

[4] *YFSC*, 1. 7a.
[5] *YFSC*, 1. 7b.
[6] Cf. Hsīao, p. 52.

A Special Class of Ritual Hymns from the Southern Dynasties

The many ritual hymns of the dynasties following the Hàn are, generally speaking, of less interest than the ones just discussed. They are usually written in stilted, archaic, monotonous language and deal with a limited range of constantly repeated moral precepts. This goes for the hymns of all dynasties, no matter whether the rulers governed all China, the North, the South, or other sections of the divided country. A refreshing exception is a small group of songs from the Southern Dynasties, known as *shén-hsíen kō* 神弦歌 ("songs for gods, with string accompaniment").[7] There are seventeen of them. Unlike the bulk of *yüeh-fǔ* hymns, they do not bear the stamp of orthodox Confucianism, of court officials and literati. They are rather in the nature of simple folk songs, and recall the *Chǐu kō* ("Nine Songs") of the *Ch'ǔ-tz'ǔ* in that they are sung by shamans and shamanesses preparing to receive the gods. But they differ from the *Chǐu kō* not only in being shorter and simpler but also in that the gods appearing in them are lesser deities whose cult is generally restricted to a small region. From the localities mentioned in the songs, we know that they belong to the region around Chìen-yèh (modern Nanking), the capital of the Southern Dynasties. They seem to date from the third, fourth, or fifth century. Along with local deities of the Nanking region, some Taoist worthies appear, as popular Taoism is intermingled with shamanism and other local cults in these songs. An abundance of popular religious practices far removed from the state cult of Confucianism (and often censured by Confucian scholars and government officials) must have flourished in this area during the Southern Dynasties, as attested in the historical and narrative literature of the time. The rituals of which these hymns formed a part obviously included dancing as well as singing. Some of the songs imply amorous relations between gods and human beings.

As to form, the songs are all short, running from two to six lines, the four-line form being most common. The lines are of three, four, five, and six syllables, but the five-syllable line is favored.

---

[7] Wáng Yǔn-hsí has a good special study on these songs, "Shén-hsíen kō k'ǎo," in his *Lìu-ch'áo*, pp. 167–181.

I will give three examples of *shén-hsien kō*

Song of the Sacred Lord 聖郎曲

No more mimicking on the left,	左亦不佯佯
2 No more flapping on the right.	右亦不翼翼
The Immortal is at the Lord's flank,	仙人在郎傍
4 The Jade Maiden is at the Lord's side.	玉女在郎側
The wine lacks the taste of sugar	酒無沙糖味
6 To bring him contact and color.[8]	爲他通顏色

The first two lines apparently speak of a mime and dance just performed by the shamans. The Immortal and the Jade Maiden of lines 3 and 4 may either be deities whose appearance is expected or (as suggested by Wáng Yùn-hsī) roles played by the shamans. The wine mentioned in the last two lines may be offered to the gods, or consumed by the shamans, or both.

Song of the Lord of White Rock 白石郎曲

The Lord of White Rock	白石郎
Dwells above the river.	臨江居
The River God leads the way, the fish bring up the rear.[9]	前導江伯後從魚

Song of the Little Maiden of Blue Stream 青溪小姑曲

Her gate opens on the bright water,	開門白水
2 Nearby there is a bridge,	側近橋梁
That's where the Little Maiden dwells,	小姑所居
4 All alone without a man.[10]	獨處無郎

"Blue Stream", according to one interpretation, is the name of a canal dug in the winter of 241–242 east of Chìen-yèh.[11] About this "Little Maiden" many legends are recorded.[12] The last line of our song makes her very human, and suggests the erotic aspect of these cults.

Anonymous Ballads of the Hàn Period

I said earlier that *yùeh-fǔ* poetry comprises two distinct genres: hymns and ballads. As we turn now from the former to the latter, we are doing more than progressing from one form of poetry to another

---

[8] *YFSC*, 47. 4b–5a; Yǔ, *Yùeh-fǔ*, pp. 93–94; Wáng, *Liu-ch'áo*, pp. 173–174.

[9] *YFSC*, 47. 5a; Yǔ, *Yùeh-fǔ*, pp. 94–95; Wáng, *Liu-ch'áo*, pp. 174–175.

[10] *YFSC*, 47. 5a–6a; Yǔ, *Yùeh-fǔ*, p. 95; Wáng, *Liu-ch'áo*, pp. 175–177.

[11] Cf. Wáng, *Liu-ch'áo*, p. 175.

[12] Cf. Wáng, *Liu-ch'áo*, pp. 175–177.

—we are entering a completely different domain of literature. The ballads we are about to consider, though preserved in written form, must originally have belonged to the *oral* tradition. For a full understanding of the anonymous Chinese ballads, it is necessary to view them in the light of the oral tradition that created surprisingly similar ballads in other parts of the world, under conditions which exclude any genetic relationship. I have used for comparative purposes some European ballads and modern studies of them.

One of the striking facts about the art of balladry both in China and in Europe is that it oscillates between two poles, the narrative and the lyric. Most ballads—European as well as Chinese—tend to be an uneven mixture of both. Another important polarity is the tendency to pare everything down to essentials, to be so concise as to appear abrupt and at times fragmentary, and the opposite tendency to elaborate, to linger, to dwell on details. To illustrate these conflicting trends, and to provide a concrete basis for the subsequent discussion of the anonymous Hàn ballads, I will now cite three poems. The first will be a concise narrative ballad, the second a short lyric, and the third a more elaborate narrative poem. Each translation will be followed by a few comments on matters pertaining to that ballad alone. Features which these poems have in common with other poems will be discussed thereafter.

> East of the P'íng-líng Tomb　平陵東
> East of the P'íng-líng tomb,　平陵東
> 2 Among the pines, the cypresses, the *wú-t'úng* trees,　松柏桐
> I don't know who abducted the Honorable Lord.　不知何人刦義公
> 4 They abducted the Honorable .Lord　刦義公
> To the Magistracy　在高堂下
> 6 For a ransom of a million cash and two swift steeds.　交錢百萬兩走馬
> Two swift steeds　兩走馬
> 8 Are hard indeed to get.　亦誠難
> I look at the extorting constables, my heart is full
>　　of pain.　顧見追吏心中惻
> 10 My heart is full of pain,　心中惻
> My blood is draining out.　血出漉
> 12 Now back to tell my family to sell the brown calves.[13] 歸告我家賣黃犢

---

[13] *YFSC*, 28, 3a–b; Húang, *Hàn Wèi, ch.* 1. pp. 9–10; Wén, p. 19; Yǔ, *Yüeh-fü*, pp. 12–13; *Liang Hàn*, pp. 514–515.

Metrically, the poem is typical of early *yüeh-fü* poetry in consisting of lines of uneven length. But the structure of this poem is unusual for a Chinese ballad in that it is neatly divided into stanzas. Each stanza consists of two three-syllable lines balanced by one seven-syllable line.[14] (We have encountered the same sequence in the "Song of the Lord of White Rock," and the combination of three-syllable and seven-syllable lines had already been used in the hymn "The great sea is vast . . . ."). There are three slight irregularities—but irregularities are to be expected in *yüeh-fü* prosody: (1) line 5 is one syllable too long; (2) line 8 is the only line which lacks a rhyme; (3) the last stanza does not introduce a new rhyme but continues the rhyme of the preceding stanza.

Our poem displays another interesting structural and rhetorical feature: the last three words of each stanza are repeated to form the opening line of the following stanza. This feature, common in *yüeh-fü* poetry but seldom employed as consistently as here, is known technically as *ting-chēn t,ǐ* 頂眞體; it is also called *lien-chū kó* 聯珠格, *chū-ssū chieh-fǎ* 蛛絲接法, or *ch'án-lien chū-ssū* 蟬聯珠絲. It serves here to mark the division of the poem into stanzas, and at the same time to join the stanzas together. Beyond that, the overlapping wording (and rhyme scheme) corresponds to overlapping stages in the gradual revelation of the situation. As each stanza first resumes the conclusion reached in the preceding stanza and then goes on to new matters, so each stage uncovers a new aspect that had been hidden before. We are reminded of a similar rhetorical device in English and German ballads that has been called "incremental repetition."[15] A well-known example is the British ballad "Lord Randal."[16]

P'íng-líng in the first line of our poem (literally "flat mound") was the name given to the tomb of the Hàn emperor Chāo-tì, who died in 74 B.C. So we know that the ballad must have originated later than that year—but how much later it is impossible to say. The P'íng-líng tomb was located northwest of Ch'áng-ān, the capital of Former Hàn.

---

[14] Húang (see preceding note) has a different line division, but I prefer the one offered by Wén, Yǔ, and the editors of *Liang Hàn*.

[15] The term was coined by Gummere, p. 177. Cf. also Gerould, pp. 93, 107, 108; Friedman, Introduction, p. xvii; Kayser, p. 4.

[16] Child, No. 12.

A Song of Grief 悲歌

	A song of grief may take the place of weeping	悲歌可以當泣
2	A look into the distance may take the place of homegoing.	遠望可以當歸
	The thoughts of longing for home	思念故鄉
4	Crowd together, pile up high.	鬱鬱纍纍
	I want to go home—but no one is there;	欲歸家無人
6	I want to cross the river—but there's no boat.	欲渡河無船
	The thoughts in my mind can not be spoken,	心思不能言
8	In my entrails cart wheels are going around.[17]	腸中車輪轉

The turning wheels in the last line graphically express the physical pain felt by the homesick man in his belly. At the same time, the revolving movement may stand for the frustration of never reaching the goal, and the notion of the cart may be connected with the desired journey, or with the hardships of travelling far from home. Twice in the poem (lines 1–2 and 5–6), the parallelistic structure serves to conceal sharp differences beneath the appearance of similarity. Line 6 speaks of the *means* of returning, while line 5 is concerned with the *purpose* of returning. In the opening couplet, the repetition—so common in the ballad style—has a lulling effect and purposely misleads the audience into expecting the second line to have the same import as the first line. This expectation enhances the impact of the sarcasm inherent in the second line.

The Mulberry Trees on the Field Path 陌上桑

	The sun rises at the southeast corner	日出東南隅
2	And shines on our Ch'ín family's house.	照我秦氏樓
	The Ch'ín family has a fair daughter,	秦氏有好女
4	She calls herself Ló-fū.	自名為羅敷
	Ló-fū likes to work with silk worms and mulberry leaves;	羅敷喜蠶桑
6	She picks mulberry leaves at the wall's south corner.	採桑城南隅
	Green silk strands form the basket cord,	青絲為籠係
8	A cassia twig forms the basket handle;	桂枝為籠鉤
	On her head the "horse mane" (?) coiffure,	頭上倭墮髻
10	On her pierced ears the "bright moon" pearls;	耳中明月珠
	Of yellow silk her skirt below,	緗綺為下裙
12	Of purple silk her jacket above.	紫綺為上襦
	The passers-by who see Ló-fū	行者見羅敷

[17] *YFSC*, 62. 1b–2a; Yú, *Yüeh-fü*, p. 52; Hsü, p. 40; *Liang Hàn*, p. 536; Uchida, pp. 167–168.

14 Put down their loads and stroke their beards. 下擔捋髭鬚

The young fellows who see Ló-fū 少年見羅敷

16 Take off their caps and adjust their headcloths. 脫帽著悄頭

The tillers forget their ploughs, 耕者忘其犁

18 Those who hoe forget their hoes. 鋤者忘其鋤

When they go home they find fault and are wroth 歸來相怒怨

20 Just because they've looked at Ló-fū. 但坐觀羅敷

The Prefect comes from the South, 使君從南來

22 His five steeds stop and hesitate. 五馬立踟躕

The Prefect sends his men to ask, 使君遣吏往

24 Who is this pretty woman? 問是誰家姝

The Ch'ín family has a fair daughter, 秦氏有好女

26 She calls herself Ló-fū. 自名爲羅敷

What is Ló-fū's age? 羅敷年幾何

28 Not quite twenty yet, 二十尚不足

A little more than fifteen. 十五頗有餘

30 The Prefect asks Ló-fū, 使君謝羅敷

Would she ride with him? 寧可共載不

32 Ló-fū steps forward and replies: 羅敷前置辭

How stupid is the Prefect! 使君一何愚

34 The Prefect has his own wife, 使君自有婦

Ló-fū has her own husband. 羅敷自有夫

36 In the East, among more than a thousand horsemen, 東方千餘騎

My husband holds the top position. 夫婿居上頭

38 How can you recognize my husband? 何用識夫婿

A white horse walks behind (?) a black colt. 白馬從驪駒

40 Green silk strands are tied to the horse's tail, 青絲繫馬尾

Of yellow gold the halter on the horse's head. 黃金絡馬頭

42 At his hip a sword with the "pulley" design, 腰中鹿盧劍

Worth more than a million. 可值千萬餘

44 At fifteen he was county clerk, 十五府小吏

At twenty, provincial court councilor, 二十朝大夫

46 At thirty, palace attendant, 三十侍中郎

At forty, lord governor. 四十專城居

48 His personal appearance: a pure white complexion, 爲人潔白皙

Fine hair and a slight beard. 鬑鬑頗有鬚

50 Slow is his pace, as becomes a dignitary, 盈盈公府步

With stately, graceful steps he moves around the office. 冉冉府中趨

52 The thousands of men assembled there   坐中數千人
    All say my husband looks distinguished.[18]   皆言夫壻殊

The consistent use of the five-syllable line distinguishes the late phase of the Hàn ballad from the earlier phase where lines of uneven length were commonly used. There is other internal evidence to show that this poem dates from the Later Hàn period, notably the appellation *shǐh-chǔn* (line 21) for a prefect *(t'ài-shǒu)*[19] and the career outlined in lines 44–47.

The story of the virtuous and resourceful young woman who successfully resists the advances of the mighty official has something in common with a certain type of medieval European *pastourelle,* where a shepherdess thwarts a philandering gentleman. But I have not found any European counterparts for this particular Chinese ballad.

One of the facts emerging from the investigations of European balladry is that oral ballads have no fixed texts. They are created anew in each performance, and subject to constant changes. There is never a definitive version. This is important for the textual criticism of ballads preserved in written form. When more than one version has come down to us (as is the case, for instance, with the anonymous ballad "Tūng-mén hsíng" 東門行 ("Song of the East Gate"),[20] we need not assume that one version is correct and the other corrupt; both may be equally authentic.

Another basic fact that can be learned from European studies is that ballads tend to get shorter, not longer, in the refining and polishing process of oral transmission. The ballad style is characterized by brevity, which may go to the point of abruptness. Many ballads start when the action is already under way or past ("East of the P'íng-líng Tomb" is an example), and they tend to break off without finishing the story. The fragmentary nature of ballads is often misunderstood. Though it can sometimes be accounted for

---

[18] *YFSC,* 28. 3b–4b; Shěn, pp. 60–61; Húang, *Hàn Wèi,* ch. 1, pp. 10–13; Yú, *Yüeh-fü,* pp. 13–16; Yú, *Hàn Wèi Liu-ch'ao shìh hsuan,* pp. 32–34; Hsǔ, pp. 42–44; *Liang Hàn,* pp. 515–516; Kūng, pp. 22–26; Uchida, pp. 147–151; Iritani, pp. 63–71. Translated by Arthur Waley, "The Song of Lo-fu," in *Chinese Poems* (London, 1946), pp. 65–67. Cf. also five essays on this poem in *Yüeh-fü shìh yén-chīu lùn-wén chi,* pp. 60–83.

[19] Cf. *Liang Hàn,* p. 518, n. 13.

[20] *YFSC,* 37. 6a–7a.

historically—some Spanish ballads, for instance, originated as fragments of long epic poems, others were mutilated by Renaissance editors[21]—it is important to realize that abruptness is a characteristic of the genre.

Brevity and abruptness go together with directness and immediacy. The ballad singer instinctively follows the precept which modern apprentice writers of fiction learn in Lesson One: show, don't tell. Events are acted out rather than narrated. That is one reason why direct speech plays such an important part in balladry. (Speech and dialogue will be discussed below.) The illusion of immediacy may also be created by an eyewitness report, as for example in "East of the P'íng-líng Tomb." A favorite formula in Spanish ballads is "Helo, helo, por do viene" ("Behold, behold, there he comes"). A French ballad begins: "Av'-ous point vu la péronnelle, que les gens d'arm' ont emmené?" (Haven't you seen Péronnelle, whom the constables have taken away?")[22] This comes very close to Chinese *yüeh-fù* formulas *chün pú chìen* 君不見 ("Haven't you seen ...?") and *chün pù wén* 君不聞 ("Haven't you heard ...?").[23]

Such questions addressed to the audience serve the additional purpose of involving the listener in the action. This may go so far as to blame the listening public for not having intervened to avert the tragedy:

> Ye Highlands, and ye Lawlands,
>   Oh where have you been?
> They have slain the Earl of Murray,
>   And they layd him on the green ....[24]

A similar device is the use of the first-person possessive in "The Mulberry Trees on the Field Path," line 2: by speaking of "*our* Ch'ín family," the singer sets up a we-group which includes himself, the heroine, and the audience.[25]

---

[21] Cf. Alatorre, Prólogo, pp. xxxvi-xxxvii.

[22] "La Péronnelle," Doncieux, p. 44.

[23] *Chün pú chìen* was the standard opening for the old ballads—not extant today—titled "Hsíng lú nán" ("The Hardships of Travelling"), according to the eighth-century work *Yüeh-fù chìeh t'í*, cited *YFSC* 70. 1a.

[24] "The Bonny Earl of Murray," Child, No. 181A.

[25] This interpretation is suggested in part by Lǐ Hsíang 李翔, see *Liang Hàn*, pp. 516–517, n. 2.

Akin to the penchant for brevity and abruptness is another characteristic of the genre: understatement. Listen to the mortally wounded hero in a Scottish ballad:

> "Ffight on my men," sayes Sir Andrew Barton,
>   "I am hurt, but I am not slaine;
> I'le lay mee downe and bleed a-while,
>   And then I'le rise and ffight againe . . . . "[26]

Understatement may be coupled with sarcasm or irony, as in "East of the P'íng-líng Tomb," line 3, and in the opening couplet of "A Song of Grief." In the latter instance, the sense of sarcasm is enhanced by the elaborate pattern of substitution and parallelism.

One of the basic features of oral narrative poetry is the use of formulas and formulaic expressions, as demonstrated convincingly in the monumental fieldwork done among illiterate epic singers in Yugoslavia.[27] To be sure, the preponderance of formulaic language is not, as asserted by Albert B. Lord and others, clear proof of orality.[28] But when there are other reasons for assuming a corpus of poetry to belong to the oral tradition, we may expect to find formulaic language as one of its features. Unfortunately the bulk of Hàn ballads is too small to reveal the full extent of this phenomenon, but despite this limitation, a considerable number of formulas can be found. I have made a study of the longest of the extant Hàn *yùeh-fŭ* poems, "Southeast Fly the Peacocks" (355 lines long), and found more than half of it to consist of formulas and formulaic expressions.[29]

Here are some formulas and formulaic expressions in the Hàn ballads cited above:

(1) The last two lines of "A Song of Grief" are identical with the last two lines of the "Kŭ kō" 古歌 ("Ancient Song") which

---

[26] "Sir Andrew Barton," Child, No. 167A, st. 65.

[27] Cf. Lord, passim. He defines formulas and formulaic expressions on pp. 30 and 44–48.

[28] Benson has shown that Anglo-Saxon poems which meet Lord's test for being formulaic were nevertheless composed in writing.

[29] "The Formulaic Language of the Chinese Ballad 'Southeast Fly the Peacocks'," in *Bulletin of the Institute of History and Philology*, Academia Sinica, Taipei, Volume XXXIX (in honor of Lĭ Fāng-kùei on his sixty-fifth birthday), part 1, January 1969.

begins "The autumn wind goes *hsiao hsiao,* so sad it kills people."[30]
Within the same couplet, the phrase *pù néng yén* ("cannot speak" or
"cannot be spoken") also occurs in the *yǔeh-fǔ* "Yèn-kō hó-ch'áng
hsíng" 豔歌何嘗行,[31] line 18.

(2) Lines 3–4 of "The Mulberry Trees on the Field Path" recur
not only in the same poem (lines 25–26) but also, adapted to a
different context, in "Southeast Fly the Peacocks,"[32] lines 37–38:

> Our eastern neighbors have a virtuous daughter,
> She calls herself Ch'ín Ló-fū.

In the latter poem, line 37 is repeated again as line 321.

(3) Line 41 of "The Mulberry Trees on the Field Path" is
identical with line 23 of "Chī míng" 雞鳴 ("The Cocks Crow")[33] and
with line 17 of "Hsīang féng hsíng" 相逢行 ("Song of an Encounter").[34]

Formulaic language represents a kind of patterning that is not
restricted to ready-made phrases, lines, couplets, and even larger
units, but also reveals itself in fixed attributes, qualities, human types,
and situations. In "The Mulberry Trees on the Field Path," silk
strands are invariably green (lines 7, 40), as steeds are "milk-white"
and maids "nut-brown" in British ballads. A fine house as fancied by
the Hàn *yǔeh-fǔ* singers has a door of gold, a hall of jade, and a pool
with seventy-two mandarin ducks, arranged in orderly rows.[35]

Such unrealistic accumulations of wealth belong to the dream
world of common people who enjoy in their literature the luxuries
denied them in real life. Thus they invent improbably luxurious
wedding gifts in "Southeast Fly the Peacocks" (lines 236–249). A
formula current in British ballads says of a horse:

[30] Yú, *Yǔeh-fǔ,* pp. 60–61. Not in *YFSC.*

[31] *YFSC,* 39. 6a–b.

[32] *YFSC,* 73. 2a–5a.

[33] *YFSC,* 28. 1a–b.

[34] *YFSC,* 34. 6a–b.

[35] "Chī míng," lines 7–8, 13–16; and, in almost the same words, in "Hsīang féng hsíng,"
lines 7–8, 20–22.

With silver he was shod before,
With burning gold behind.[36]

This hyperbolical trend also accounts, I believe, for Ló-fū's fancy dress and ornaments in "The Mulberry Trees on the Field Path." The humble folk like to dress up their heroes and heroines, with the same disregard for verisimilitude that is often found in theatrical costuming.

As for fixed human types, we have already met the beautiful girl bearing the type name Ch'ín Ló-fū in "The Mulberry Trees on the Field Path," and again, in a different context, in "Southeast Fly the Peacocks." The stock surname Ch'ín also occurs in the ballad "Wū shēng" 烏生 ("The Crow Gives Birth"),[37] and again in the poem "Ch'ín Nǔ-hsīu hsíng" 秦女休行 ("Song of Ch'ín Nǔ-hsīu") by Tsǒ Yén-níen 左延年 (early third century A.D.).[38] The latter poem—which is not anonymous, to be sure—employs the same formula as "The Mulberry Trees on the Field Path," but the girl has a different name this time:

The Ch'ín family has a fair daughter,
She calls herself Nǔ-hsīu.

Types in the Spanish ballads include the Christian king, who is usually despotic, arbitrary, timorous, and wrathful; the Moorish king, who tends to be generous, chivalrous toward friend and foe, weak, and complaining; the messenger; the page boy; the old man; knights; prelates; and noble ladies.[39] In the Hàn ballads, the human typology is less developed. We have seen the ideal husband figure in "The Mulberry Trees on the Field Path." He is a composite picture,

---

[36] "Tam Lin" (Child, No. 39A), st. 16; "Lord Thomas and Fair Annet" (Child, No. 73A), st. 16; and with variations of the formula: "Child Maurice" (Child, No. 83 B), st. 1; "Fair Mary of Wallington" (Child, No. 91 E), st. 5; "Young Waters" (Child, No. 94), st. 4. The lavish use of gold, silver, and other precious materials is widespread in world balladry and may originally have been connected with magic and fairies. Cf. Wimberly, pp. 180–188.

[37] *YFSC*, 28. 2a–b.

[38] *YFSC*, 61. 3a.

[39] Cf. Alatorre, Prólogo, pp. xxxi-xxxii.

looking first like a military leader (lines 36–43) and later like a civil official (lines 50–53).

Typical situations in the Chinese ballads are two people meeting on a road which is often narrow (to make the encounter seem inevitable);[40] a lone man going out through a gate;[41] the homesick traveler, who may be a soldier;[42] and a lady longing for her absent husband or lover.[43]

When stock situations or themes are woven into a ballad, the resulting poem does not always achieve perfect consistency between the component parts. We must bear in mind that oral ballads are improvised, without any opportunity for checking and revising, and that the critical standards by which the audience judges them are different from the standards governing literary productions.

We pass on to another basic principle of ballad style, the principle of repetition. This principle stems from the association with music. Phrases which would occur only once in an ordinary poem are repeated when the poem is rendered as a song. For example, the first two lines of a French ballad read as follows:

> N'an son très fraires,
> N'an una suer a maridar.

(There are three brothers,/They have a sister to marry off.) But in the actual singing performance of the ballad, the two lines become five:

> N'an son très fraires,
> N'an son très fraires,
> N'an una suer a maridar,

[40] For example, "Hsīang féng hsíng," *YFSC*, 34. 6a–b; "Ch'áng-ān yǔ hsía-hsíeh hsíng" 長安有狹斜行, *YFSC*, 35. 1a; "Shàng-shān ts'ǎi mí-wú" 上山採蘼蕪, Yú, *Yüeh-fǔ*, pp. 58–59 (not in *YFSC*).

[41] Examples: "Tūng-mén hsíng" ("Song of the East Gate"), *YFSC*, 37. 6a–7a; "Hsī-mén hsíng," ("Song of the West Gate"), *YFSC*, 37. 5b–6a; "Pù ch'ū hsìa-mén hsíng" 步出夏門行, *YFSC*, 37. 3a; "Líang-fǔ yín" 梁甫吟, *YFSC*, 41. 5b–6a. This is an anonymous ballad, the attribution to Chū-kó Lìang is erroneous, see *Liang Hàn*, p. 534, n. 1.

[42] Examples: "A Song of Grief," quoted and discussed above; "Tūng kūang"東光, *YFSC*, 27. 3a.

[43] "Yǐn-mǎ ch'áng-ch'éng k'ū hsíng" 飲馬長城窟行 ("Song of Watering Horses at the Great Wall Waterhole"), *YFSC*, 38. 1a–2a; "Yǔ sǒ ssū" 有所思 ("There is One of Whom I Think"), *YFSC*, 16. 6b–7a; the last part of "Yèn-kō hó-ch'áng hsíng" 豔歌何嘗行, *YFSC*, 39. 6a–b.

> N'an son très fraires,
> N'an una suer a maridar.[44]

In the Chinese *yüeh-fü,* as in the ballads of other countries, there must have been many more of these repetitions than are visible today, for they tend to be omitted when the text is written down without the music. But there are some instances in our printed texts, e.g., in the ballad "Yǔ sǒ ssū" 有所思 ("There is One of Whom I Think"):[45]

. . . I tear [the gift] to bits, crush it, burn it,	拉雜摧燒之
Crush it, burn it	摧燒之 · · · ·
No more thought of you, thought of you	勿復相思相思

A special form of repetition is the *tǐng-chèn t'ǐ,* of which we saw an instance in "East of the P'íng-líng Tomb." A related device is the repetition with slight variations, building up a descriptive or narrative series. This device may be compared with similar techniques in musical composition. Here are some examples:

(1) The fish play among the lotus leaves.	魚戲蓮葉間
The fish play east of the lotus leaves.	魚戲蓮葉東
The fish play west of the lotus leaves.	魚戲蓮葉西
The fish play south of the lotus leaves.	魚戲蓮葉南
The fish play north of the lotus leaves.[46]	魚戲蓮葉北

(2) "The Mulberry Trees on the Field Path," lines 7–8, 11–12, 13–18.

(3) A Scottish example:

> Word's gane to the kitchen,
>   And word's gane to the ha,
> That Marie Hamilton gangs wi bairn
>   To the hichest Stewart of a'.
>
> He's courted her in the kitchen,
>   He's courted her in the ha,
> He's courted her in the laigh cellar,
>   And that was warst of a'.[47]

[44] "La Maumariée vengée par ses frères," st. 1, Doncieux, p. 489.
[45] *YFSC,* 16. 6b–7a.
[46] "Chǐang nán" 江南 ("South of the River"), *YFSC,* 26. 9a–b.
[47] "Mary Hamilton," Child, No. 173 A, st. 1–2.

(4) A Catalan example:

"Valga 'm Deu, quin jovenet! llástima que siga frare!"
Per sentir milló 'l sermó, sota la trona 's posava.

Al primer mot del sermó, dintre del cor ya li entrava;
Al segon mot del sermó, Magdalena suspirava;

Al tercer mot del sermó, Magdalena cau en basca.
Acabat qu'es lo sermó, Magdalena se'n va á casa.[48]

("So help me God, what a youth! A pity he's a monk!"
To hear the sermon better, she placed herself beneath the pulpit.

At the first word of the sermon, it got inside her heart;
At the second word of the sermon, Magdalena sighed;

At the third word of the sermon, Magdalena fell in a swoon.
When the sermon was finished, Magdalena went home.)

Yet another form of repetition is the refrain. Common in British ballads, it is comparatively rare in Spanish and Chinese ballads. I suspect that it may have been more frequent in the Hàn ballads than we can now know, for it is likely that early Chinese recorders, like their European counterparts, tended to leave out the refrains.[49] We do have a few of them. In the ballad "Tǔng T'áo" 董桃[50] every line ends with the refrain *Tǔng T'áo*, which was probably the name of a Taoist immortal. Later, when the warlord Tǔng Chó was taking over the country in the late second century of our era, the refrain was reinterpreted to mean "Tǔng is on the way out" (substituting the homonym *t'áo* 逃 "to flee" for the name T'áo.) In the ballad "Wū shēng" ("The Crow Gives Birth") the refrain *chà-wǒ* 嘈我 appears five times at fairly regular intervals. *Chà wǒ* is onomatopoeic, representing both the crow's call and a sigh. Refrains are also to be found in the *yüeh-fǔ* poems of the literati, e.g., in Ts'áo P'ēi's 曹丕 (187–226) "Shàng-líu-t'íen hsíng" 上留田行,[51] where every even-numbered line is the refrain *Shàng-líu-t'íen* (a place name).

Refrains are significant not only as a repetitive, structural feature but also because they are often "irrelevant" in their context. They should therefore be considered together with other "meaningless"

---

[48] "La Pénitence de Marie-Madeleine," st. 8–10, Doncieux, p. 147.

[49] Cf. Friedman, Introduction, p. xxii.

[50] *YFSC*, 34. 3b–4a, quoting the "Treatise on the Five Elements" of the Hòu-Hàn shū; Wén, pp. 31–32.

[51] *YFSC*, 38. 6b; Húang, *Wèi Wǔ-tì*, p. 53.

sounds in the ballads. Some British ballads are interspersed with lines whose function is almost exclusively musical, for example:

> There were three rauens sat on a tree,
> *Downe a downe, hay downe, hay downe*
> There were three rauens sat on a tree,
> *With a downe*
> There were three rauens sat on a tree,
> They were as blacke as they might be.
> *With a downe derrie, derrie, derrie, downe, downe.*[52]

A similar combination of repetitions and nonsense syllables can be seen in this French ballad:

> La Pernette se liève
> *La tra la la la la, la tra la la, londeri ra,*
> Treis ores davant jor,
> Treis ores davant jor,
> Treis ores davant jor.[53]

(Pernette gets up/Three hours before daybreak.)

Here are a few examples of what may be filler words without meaning in Hàn ballads.

(1) *K'āi líu lí lán* 開留離蘭, being the last four syllables of the ballad "Shíh líu" 石留 (variant 石流).[54]

(2) The syllables *chíh* 之 (occurring three times) and *nú* 奴 (occurring once) in the ballad "Tíeh-tíeh hsíng" 蜨蝶行 ("Song of the Butterfly").[55]

(3) The sequence *lù tzǔ hsíeh* 路訾邪 in the ballad "Chū lù" 朱鷺[56]

One cannot be quite certain whether or not these syllables are really meaningless, because our texts are sometimes corrupt, and even where they are not, their meaning is at times unintelligible. Besides, the musical notation which used to accompany some song words may have got mixed up with the text in a few places.[57]

---

[52] "The Three Ravens," Child, No. 26 a, st. 1.

[53] "La Pernette," st. 1, Doncieux, p. 475.

[54] *YFSC*, 16. 8b. They are taken to be meaningless filler words by Hsü, p. 38.

[55] *YFSC*, 61. 2b. They are proposed as possible filler words by Yü, *Yüeh-fü*, p. 51.

[56] *YFSC*, 16. 3b–4a. They are assumed to be meaningless by Yü, *Yüeh-fü*, p. 3.

[57] Cf. Yü, *Yüeh-fü*, Introduction, p. 7.

A related category of words favored in *yùeh-fù* poetry is ejaculations. These are not entirely meaningless, but neither do they carry a full semantic load. Thus we have exclamations in oaths such as *yéh* 邪 in "Shàng yéh" 上邪,[58] curses like *tó* 咄 in "Tūng-mén hsíng" ("Song of the East Gate"), and a great many sighs, such as *féi hū hsí* 妃呼豨 in "Yǔ sǒ ssū" ("There Is One of Whom I Think").

There also are onomatopoeic words, e.g., *sù sù* 肅肅 for the sound of wind in "Yǔ sǒ ssū." Onomatopoeia, however, is less common in the Hàn ballads than in those of the Southern and Northern Dynasties.

Next, I want to make a few observations about openings and conclusions. We have already seen certain stereotyped openings, such as going out through a gate or meeting on a narrow road. A great many openings indicate the location where the action is going to take place. This is a natural procedure for a beginning, and commonly found in European as well as Chinese ballads. But the Chinese often add to this a refinement that is peculiarly theirs: they make the orientation relative, placing the scene of action north, south, east, or west of another definite or vague place. I will give a few examples, to be added to those that have already been mentioned.

(1) They fought *south* of the walls,   戰城南
     They died *north* of the ramparts . . . .[59]   死郭北

(2) There is one of whom I think,   有所思
     He lives *south* of the great sea . . . .[60]   乃在大海南

(3) The pairs of white swans that come aflying,   飛來雙白鵠
     From the *Northwest* they come . . . .[61]   乃從西北來

(4) The butterfly roams in the *East* Garden . . . .[62] 蛺蝶之遨遊東園

These relative terms of reference create the illusion of a precise locus and maintain at the same time that characteristic vagueness which is one of the charms of the ballad genre.

As far as conclusions are concerned, we have already observed that ballads tend to break off without finishing the story. This means

[58] *YFSC*, 16. 7b.
[59] "Chàn ch'éng-nán," *YFSC*, 16. 5a.
[60] "Yǔ sǒ ssū," *YFSC*, 16. 6b–7a.
[61] "Yèn-kō hó-ch'áng hsíng," *YFSC*, 39. 6a–b.
[62] "Tíeh-tíeh hsíng," *YFSC*, 61. 2b.

that in many poems there is no conclusion. Abruptness is most conspicuous when it occurs at the very end. But this is not always the case. To cushion the shock of an abrupt or tragic ending, Chinese singers would sometimes conclude by invoking a blessing on the audience, as in the ballad "Yèn-kō hó-ch'áng hsíng" 豔歌何嘗行:

Here we are today, enjoying mutual bliss,	今日樂相樂
May our lives be stretched to last ten thousand years.[63]	延年萬歲期

Such a final blessing can also be found in the English ballad tradition:

Thus endys the talkyng of the munke
And Robyn Hode i-wysse;
God, that is euer a crowned kyng,
Bryng vs all to his blisse![64]

Direct speech and dialogue are, as we have already seen, favorite modes of discourse in the ballad, both in China and elsewhere. Directness and immediacy are achieved by letting the action unfold itself and the characters speak for themselves as far as possible without the narrator's intervention. A whole ballad may be spoken by a single person, usually one of the principal characters or an eyewitness. ("East of the P'íng-líng Tomb" is an example of the latter type.) Some ballads shift back and forth between the first and the third person when they refer to the hero. Thus in "Kū-érh hsíng" 孤兒行 ("Song of the Orphan Boy")[65] the orphan boy is referred to alternately in the third person (lines 1–2, 19) and in the first person (lines 8, 20, 42, 44). In the rest of the poem, there is no indication of whether the narrator or the boy is speaking, since the Chinese language does not require the grammatical subject to be specified in every statement. Such shifts are also found in English ballads:

[63] *YFSC*, 39. 6a–b. There are similar final blessings in "Ch'áng-kō hsíng" 長歌行, *YFSC*, 30. 3a (the poem ends with the words *Yén nien shòu-mìng ch'áng*, "May the years be stretched and life prolonged"; what follows is another poem, cf. Yú, *Yüeh-fü*, pp. 16–17); in "T'áng-shàng hsíng" 堂上行, *YFSC*, 35. 6a–7a (attributed to Wèi Wǔ-tì [Ts'áo Ts'āo] and others but actually an anonymous Hàn ballad, see Yú, *Yüeh-fü*, p. 22); and in "Pó-t'óu yín") "Song of the Whitehead," first of two poems), *YFSC*, 41. 2a.

[64] "Robin Hood and the Monk," Child, No. 119.

[65] *YFSC*, 38. 9a–b.

> Down in London where *I* was raised,
> Down where *I* got my learning,
> *I* fell in love with a pretty little girl;
> Her name was Barbara Ellen.
>
> *He* courted her for seven long years,
> She said she would not have *him*.
> *Pretty William* went home and took down sick
> And sent for Barbara Ellen . . . .[66]

and in German ballads:

> Als *ich* ein kleines Kindelein war,
> Legt man *mich* in die Wiege;
> Man streicht *mir* das Mus mit den Fingern ein,
> Man verbindet *mir* alle die viere.
>
> Und da *ich* ein klein bissle grösser war,
> Da lehrt *mich* mein Vaterle's Geigen:
> 's wär besser, er liess *mich* z'Acker fahrn,
> Dene Bäurlen ihre Ochselein treiben.
>
> Und da *er* ein bessle grösser war,
> So geiget *er* auf der Gasse;
> 's braun Annele am Lädle stand
> Und tät auf *das Geigerlein* passen . . . .[67]

Such shifts of viewpoint are connected with the general indefiniteness and vagueness that characterize much of the ballad style. Even the identity of the speaker is not always made clear.

The frequent use of dialogue, on the other hand, has to do with the trends toward directness and confrontation which bestow on the genre a certain dramatic quality. But ballad dialogue is not the same as dramatic dialogue, nor is it the language of everyday speech. One of its peculiarities is that it contains formulas, repetitions, and other familiar features of the ballad style. Thus, the words "The Ch'ín family has a fair daughter,/She calls herself Ló-fū" ("The Mulberry Trees on the Field Path," lines 25–26) are not, strictly speaking, a fitting answer to the Prefect's question. Rather, they are

---

[66] "Barbara Allen," st. 1–2, Hodgart, p. 235, after Campbell and Sharp (eds.), *English Folksongs from the Southern Appalachians*. This is a seventeenth century English ballad (Child, No. 84) which became popular in the U.S.

[67] "Der Spielmannsohn," st. 1–3, Meier, *1*, 94, after E. Meier, *Schwäbische Volkslieder* (1855), No. 202.

a repetition of lines 3–4 of the same poem, and also, as we have seen, a formula of Hàn balladry. Ló-fū's account of her husband's career in the same poem (lines 44–47) is identical in pattern with the young wife's account of her training and career in "Southeast Fly the Peacocks" (lines 3–7). This enumeration, in turn, is repeated later, with some variations, in a speech by her mother (lines 154–158).

One more aspect of the Hàn ballads that is worthy of attention is the frequent appearance of animals and plants. Symbolic and magic relationships between the human and the natural world play an important role in popular religion and literature. In European ballads, animals are sometimes the sole actors in a "human" drama. Thus the turtledove is a widow in mourning in the Spanish ballad "Fontefrida";[68] the "treacherous" nightingale proposes to her, but she rejects him in a violent speech. In other ballads, there are relations between animals and human beings. In a German folk song of around 1550, for example, a bird has a love affair with a lady:

> Es flog ein kleines Waldvögelein
> Der Lieben vors Fensterlein . . . .[69]

Still another type of ballad deals with animals transformed into human beings, and vice versa. In the German ballad "Der Nacht-jäger,"[70] a hunter catches a deer who then becomes a woman and sleeps with the hunter. In the English ballad "Young Hunting,"[71] the slain hero is metamorphosed into a bird that denounces the woman who killed him. In "The Three Ravens,"[72] the doe is obviously the mistress of the dead knight.

There are many Hàn ballads in which animals play human roles. The fish in "K'ū yú kùo hó ch'ì" 枯魚過河泣 ("The Withering Fish Weeps As He Passes the River")[73] writes a letter to his fish friends in order that they may learn from his misfortune. "Tíeh-tíeh hsíng" ("Song of the Butterfly") tells of a butterfly being caught by a

---

[68] Smith, No. 61.

[69] "Waldvögelein," Theodor Echtermeyer and Benno von Wiese (eds.), *Deutsche Gedichte* (Düsseldorf, 1960), pp. 66–67.

[70] Meier, *2*, 234–244 (seven versions).

[71] Child, No. 68.

[72] Child, No. 26.

[73] *YFSC*, 74. 1a.

swallow, from the butterfly's viewpoint. In "Yèn-kō hó-ch'áng hsíng" the white swan couple shows at first a mixture of human and animal behavior, but in the last part the animal metaphor is entirely abandoned as the wife addresses her husband. Of the various animals, birds appear more frequently in the Hàn *yùeh-fŭ* than other kinds of animals—another interesting parallel to the European ballads.[74]

In the symbolic references to plants there are also points of similarity between Chinese and European ballads. For example, the two plants growing and entwining on the graves of two lovers is an international folk motif. We find it at the end of "Southeast Fly the Peacocks" and in many ballads from all over the world.[75]

Anonymous Ballads of the Southern and Northern Dynasties

The anonymous ballads of the Southern and Northern Dynasties differ from those of the Hàn period chiefly in two respects: they tend to become standardized in form, and their mode is predominantly lyrical rather than narrative. The prevailing prosodic pattern achieved or approximated in most of the songs is four lines of five syllables each—a forerunner of the *chúeh-chù* 絕句 of T'áng. Truly narrative ballads are rare. The only full-fledged narrative poem from the oral tradition of this period is the "Mù-lán shīh" 木蘭詩,[76] composed in North China between the mid-fifth and the mid-sixth century, and then transmitted to Southern China.

The ballads of the Southern Dynasties, in particular, are intensely lyric in nature.[77] They consist of two principal groups, *Wú-shēng kō* 吳聲歌 and *hsī-ch'ǔ kō* 西曲歌. The *Wú-shēng kō* were sung around Chìen-k'āng (modern Nanking), while the *hsī-ch'ǔ kō* were composed

---

[74] Cf. Child, Index of Matters and Literature, s.v. "Birds."

[75] Child, "Plants from Graves"; Wimberly, pp. 37–43.

[76] *YFSC*, 25. 10a–11a; translated by Arthur Waley, "The Ballad of Mulan," in *Chinese Poems* (London, 1946), pp. 113–115; translated by Evans. pp. 127–128. Cf., among other studies, Lǐ Ch'ún-shèng 李純勝 "Mù-lán shīh k'ǎo" [木蘭詩] 考, *Tà-lù tsá-chih* 大陸雜誌, *31* (1965), 369–371; Chíang Wèi-lú 江慰廬, "T'án-t'án tsěn-yàng yén-chiu 'Mù-lán shīh' "談談怎樣研究 [木蘭詩]" *Wén-hsúeh yí-ch'ǎn tsěng-k'ān* 文學遺產增刊, No. 1 (Peking, 1955), pp. 109–120. There is another version, generally ignored but possibly older, *YFSC*, 25. 11a–b.

[77] Two excellent recent studies of the Southern Dynasties *yùeh-fŭ* are Wáng, *Liù-ch'áo* and Evans.

farther up the Yangtze, around Chīang-líng (in modern Hupei). Both groups of songs are rooted in an urban milieu. They reflect the life of traveling traders and their women who are often engaged in sericulture. The favorite theme is love. Parting, leavetaking, and separation are typical situations. We have about 330 *Wú-shēng kō*, with 45 different titles. The *hsī-c'hǔ kō* number about 140, with 35 titles. The differences between the two groups are well brought out in Mrs. Evans's monograph. According to her, the *hsī-ch'ǔ kō* "tend to be a bit more straightforward in their diction and a little less apt to draw upon figurative language than the Wú-shēng."[78] Homely details of everyday life, especially the life of the traveling merchant, are more prominent in the *hsī-ch'ǔ kō*, while the *Wú-shēng kō* often display an idealized landscape or an intimate boudoir furnished with "silk curtains, lattice screens, jeweled vanity cases, and embroidered robes."[79] Whereas the *Wú-shēng kō* are predominantly feminine in spirit, we find in the *hsī-ch'ǔ kō* both the man's and the woman's point of view. Comparing the two groups of songs with other Chinese lyric poetry, Jane Evans aptly characterizes them as "lighter and more informal in tone, livelier and more playful in feeling, and very obviously more sharply personal in focus than conventional Chinese verse."[80] She also notes their "momentary quality" and the pervading "feeling that all is always now."[81] I will now give two examples of *Wú-shēng kō*.

Tzǔ-yèh Song　子夜歌

When my love is sorry I'm sad too,	歡愁儂亦慘
2 When he laughs I'm also glad.	郎笑我便喜
Haven't you seen the twining trees,	不見連理樹
4 Rising from different roots with branches joined?[82]	異根同條起

The Slope of Mt. Húa　華山畿

I dare not accept your proposal,	未敢便相許
2 At night I heard my family discuss it,	夜聞儂家論
They won't give me to you.[83]	不持儂與汝

[78] Evans, p. 18.
[79] Evans, ibid.
[80] Evans, p. 116.
[81] Evans, p. 117.
[82] *YFSC*, 44. 4b.
[83] *YFSC*, 46. 3a; *Wèi Chin*, p. 363.

The pronoun *núng* 儂 ("I, me") of the second and third line, belongs to the Wú dialect of the time. Its frequent occurrence in the *Wú-shēng kō* attests to their lively colloquial style and gives them a regional flavor. Now a *hsī-ch'ǔ kō*:

Song of Shíh-ch'éng　石城樂

I heard my love was going far away,	聞歡遠行去
2 I saw him off at the pavilion of Mt. Fāng.	相送方山亭
The wind blew on the phellodendron hedge,	風吹黃蘗藩
4 I hate to hear the bitter sound of parting.[84]	惡聞苦離聲

This poem contains two puns. The phellodendron has a bitter taste, and the mention of the hedge (line 3) suggests a synonym, *lí*, whose homonym, *lí* "parting," appears in the last line.

Punning is indeed an important poetic device in both the *Wú-shēng kō* and the *hsī-ch'ǔ kō*.[85] The prevalence of this device is another indication that these songs belonged, at least initially, to the oral tradition. Here is another *Wú-shēng kō* that works with puns:

Tzǔ-yèh Song　子夜歌

When I was first about to know you,	始欲識郎時
2 I hoped our two hearts would be as one.	兩心望如一
When I straightened out the silk thread and put it on the broken loom	理絲入殘機
4 How was I to know it wouldn't make a piece![86]	何悟不成匹

My translation fails to convey the puns: *ssū* "silk thread" is homonymous with *ssū* 思 "love thoughts," and *p'ǐ* "piece of cloth" simultaneously means "mate, pair."

To what extent these highly personal lyric songs are really part of the oral tradition, and to what extent the printed versions extant today have been worked over by men of letters is a difficult problem on which experts do not agree.[87] I find a strong indication of their oral nature in the widespread occurrence of formulas, though this is not conclusive evidence, as mentioned above (see n. 28).

[84] *ȲFSC*, 47. 9a; Yǔ, *Yùeh-fǔ*, pp. 96–97.
[85] Cf. the detailed discussion of puns in both groups in Wáng, *Liù-ch'áo*, pp. 121–166.
[86] *ȲFSC*, 44. 4a; *Wèi Chin*, pp. 359–360.
[87] Cf. Wáng, *Liù-ch'áo* and Yǔ, *Yùeh-fǔ*, passim.

The ballads of the Northern Dynasties,[88] smaller in number than the Southern songs, take up the greater part of the section titled "Líang kǔ chǔeh héng-ch'ūi ch'ǔ" 梁鼓角橫吹曲 ("Líang Dynasty songs accompanied by drums, horns, and horizontal flutes") in *YFSC* (*ch.* 25). Less intimate and less concerned with the momentary aspects of life, they are distinguished by a sensitive appreciation of nature, including its grandeur and wildness. They contain striking juxtapositions of natural scenes and human situations. In their nature imagery, animals play an important part. The parallel between the natural and human situation is not always clear to the modern reader. This may be because we are not sufficiently familiar with the poetic language of the period and the genre; it may also be because the connection is vague on purpose, conforming to a tenet of the *yüeh-fü* genre, as noted earlier in this essay.

One of the basic historic facts shaping the culture of the Northern Dynasties was the symbiosis of Chinese farmers and city dwellers with nomadic peoples of alien origin. It is therefore not surprising that some of the Northern *yüeh-fü* poems are said to be Chinese translations of foreign originals. It is universally true that songs are translated from one language into another more easily than other forms of poetry. Music, which is not restricted by language barriers, provides a convenient link between different cultures. In the following Northern song, the singer is a foreigner—or plays the role of a foreigner in the fictitious world of the song:

> Breaking Off a Willow Branch   折楊柳歌辭
>   In the distance I see the River at Meng Ford,   遙看孟津河
> 2 The willows grow thickly together and sway.   楊柳鬱婆娑
>   I am a barbarian,   我是虜家兒
> 4 I don't understand the songs of the Chinese.[89]   不解漢兒歌

I will conclude this section with two more examples of Northern *yüeh-fü* poems.

> Song of the Prince of Lāng-yéh   瑯琊王歌
>   At East Mountain I see West River,[90]   東山看西水

---

[88] Lǐ Ch'ún-shèng has a recent essay on them.

[89] *YFSC*, 25. 7a; Yú, *Yüeh-fü*, p. 115; *Wèi Chin*, p. 377.

[90] Or: East Mountain looks at West River.

2 The river flows among huge rocks.   水流盤石間
His father died, his mother remarried,   公死姥更嫁
4 Poor little orphan boy![91]   孤兒甚可憐

    The Flowing Stream at the Top of Mt. Lǔng   隴頭流水歌
The flowing stream at the top of Mt. Lǔng   隴頭流水
2 Drips down on the West side.   流離西下
I think of myself, drifting all my life in the wilderness.[92] 念吾一身飄曠野

Ballads in *Yüeh-fú* Style by Men of Letters

The anonymous *yüeh-fú* ballads of the Hàn and subsequent periods
have exerted a tremendous influence on the poetry of the literati. So
widespread has been this influence that to trace it would amount
to writing a large portion of the history of Chinese poetry from the
end of Hàn down to modern times. This absorption of the oral
ballad tradition by the literati is paralleled by the wealth of literary
ballads, modeled on the anonymous prototypes, in English, German,
and especially Spanish literature. The Chinese literati blended the
elements received from the *yüeh-fú* tradition with their own personal
styles in many different ways. But we can observe some general
manifestations of the literary *yüeh-fú* style in diction, syntax, imagery,
structural and rhetorical devices, in the scarcity of learned allusions,
and in the absence of orthodox Confucian attitudes, as well as in
such external phenomena as traditional *yüeh-fú* titles and lines of
uneven length. To illustrate a few of these features, I will cite two
poems, one written when the literary *yüeh-fú* genre was just beginning
to bud, and the other when it had reached maturity.

    Ts'áo Ts'āo (155–220), "Variation of the   曹操，卻東西門行
Songs of the East and West Gates"
The wild geese are born north of the passes,   鴻雁出塞北
2 In a land without men.   乃在無人鄉
Raising their wings, they fly a myriad miles,   舉翅萬餘里
4 Traveling and stopping in regular formation.   行止自成行
In winter they eat the rice of the South,   冬節食南稻
6 In spring they fly back to the North.   春日復北翔

[91] *YFSC*, 25. 3a; Yú, *Yüeh-fú*, p. 108.

[92] *YFSC* 25. 5b; a variant version in which the meter is regularized in a pattern of 4
lines of 4 syllables each is "Lǔng-t'óu kō-tz'ú," *YFSC*, 25. 8a.

In the field there is the tumbleweed,   田中有轉蓬
8 Borne by the wind, it drifts far and high,   隨風遠飄揚
Forever out off from its native roots,   長與故根絕
10 Never to meet them again in a myriad years.   萬歲不相當

What help is there for him, this soldier on the march?   奈何此征夫
12 How can he ever get back from the earth's four corners?   安得去四方
His war horse is never without a saddle,   戎馬不解鞍
14 His armor never leaves his side.   鎧甲不離傍
Little by little, old age comes upon him,   冉冉老將至
16 When can he ever go home?   何時反故鄉

The holy dragon stays in the water's depth,   神龍藏深淵
18 The fierce tiger paces his lofty ridge.   猛虎步高岡
The dying fox turns his head toward his native hill.   狐死歸首丘
20 How can one forget his home?[93]   故鄉安可忘

The poem begins with a directional opening and an animal metaphor that is sustained for six lines; animals appear again in lines 13 and 17–19. A plant metaphor (lines 7–10) matches the preceding animal metaphor. The nature metaphors illuminate the human theme from two sides: the animals represent the ideal which man cannot attain, while the tumbleweed shows up the stark reality that oppresses the eternal soldier. The cumulative effect of these metaphors is to reduce the soldier to a vegetating status below the level of animals.

The war horse (line 13) plays a different role: it *represents* the warrior rather than being a foil to him. A similar use of horse imagery occurs in an anonymous Han *yüeh-fü* to convey the idea that the best men have died in the war, with useless men surviving:

The brave war steeds have died in battle,
The worthless nags neigh, running hither and thither.[94]

We may also recall the Prefect's horses in "The Mulberry Trees on the Field Path" (line 22), which "stop and hesitate" when the Prefect is struck by the sight of Ló-fū. Similarly, the husband's

[93] *YFSC*, 37. 8a; Húang, Wèi Wǔ-tì, p. 30; Yú Kùan-yīng 余冠英, *Ts'áo Ts'āo Ts'áo P'èi Ts'ác Chíh shih hsǔan* ("Selected Poems by Ts'áo Ts'áo, Ts'áo P'èi, and Ts'áo Chíh") (Hong Kong, 1966), p. 8 (text), pp. 62–63 (commentary); *Wèi Chìn*, pp. 8–10.

[94] "Chàn ch'éng-nàn" ("They Fought South of the Walls"), *YFSC*, 16. 5a.

horse in "Southeast Fly the Peacocks" (line 269) expresses his master's mood when he rushes to his wife at a critical moment.

In putting together the four sections of his poem, Ts'áo Ts'āo takes advantage of the option inherent in the *yüeh-fŭ* genre which allows the combination of disparate elements in a single poem, without any need for smooth transitions. Thus the poem shifts abruptly from wild geese to tumbleweed, to soldier, to dragon, tiger, and fox, and back to man. But the combination also reveals the literary craftsman in the calculated relevance of the various images to the central theme. Such a well-integrated composition would hardly be possible in the oral tradition. The mark of literary craftsmanship may also be seen in the balanced length of the four parts: 6+4+6+4 lines. The human figure makes its appearance at the very center of the poem. Prior to this, there is a nice balance between the wild geese living in a non-human environment (line 2) and the humanizing touch applied to the tumbleweed by the striking term *kù kēn* "native roots" (line 9), analogous to *kù hsīang* "native home," which appears in lines 16 and 20.

Formulaic language is used deliberately but sparingly in the *yüeh-fŭ* of the literati. What had been a basic structural phenomenon in the oral tradition becomes now a conscious literary device, to be used selectively in conjunction with other devices. I find only one unquestionable instance of a *yüeh-fŭ* formula in Ts'áo Ts'āo's poem, namely, *tzù ch'éng háng* ("in regular formation") in line 4.[95] Other devices characteristic of the *yüeh-fŭ* style in this poem are three rhetorical questions (lines 12, 16, 20) and an exclamation (line 11). Then there is the demonstrative adjective *tz'ŭ* "this" in line 11, bestowing a sense of immediacy on the introduction of the central human figure.

Lǐ Pó (701–762), "The Hardships of the Road to Shŭ"[96] 李白，蜀道難

---

[95] This formula occurs in the anonymous *yüeh-fŭ* poems "Chī míng" ("The Cocks Crow," *YFSC*, 28. 1a–b), line 16, and "Hsīang féng hsíng" ("Song of an Encounter," *YFSC*, 34. 6a–b), line 22.

[96] Shŭ is the western part of modern Szechuan Province, with Ch'éng-tū (the "Brocade City" of line 41) as its center. For this poem I follow the Sùng edition of Lǐ Pó's Works in the possession of the Seikadō Bunko, Tokyo, as reproduced by Hiraoka Takeō, *Works of Li T'ai-po: Texts* (T'ang Civilization Reference Series, No. 9, Kyoto, 1958), p. 28.

Other texts of the poem, with commentary: *Fēn-lèi pŭ-chù Lǐ T'ai-pó shīh* (Ssù-pù ts'úng-k'ān ed.), 3. 4b–9a; Shū Wú 舒蕪, *Lǐ Pó shīh hsüan* (Hong Kong, 1959) pp. 15–17;

Yü-hsü-hsī! Ah, so perilous! Oh, so high! 噫吁戲危乎高哉

2 The hardships of the road to Shǔ are harder
  than ascending blue heaven. 蜀道之難難於上青天

Ts'àn Ts'úng and Yǔ Fú 蠶叢及魚鳧

4 Founded the state of Shǔ way back—how dim! 開國何茫然

The next forty-eight thousand years 爾來四萬八千歲

6 No human smoke linked up with it across the
  passes of Ch'ín. 不與秦塞通人煙

In the West, at Great White Mountain, there's
  the Bird Road, 西當太白有鳥道

8 How get across from there to Mt. O-méi's peak? 何以橫絕峨眉巔

The earth collapsed, the mountain fell,
  the stalwart warriors died.[97] 地崩山摧壯士死

10 Thereafter sky ladders and cliff planks made
  connection at last. 然後天梯石棧相鉤連

Above is the high top where the six dragons
  pulling the sun turn back, 上有六龍回日之高標

12 Below is the river turning back with colliding
  waves clashing and breaking. 下有衝波逆折之回川

The yellow crane in its flight can't make it, 黃鶴之飛尚不得過

14 The monkey wanting to pass is afraid of the climb. 猿猱欲度愁攀援

Chīang Shǎng-hsíen 姜尚賢, *T'áng Sùng míng-chīa shīh hsīn hsüan* 唐宋名家詩新選 (Tainan, Taiwan, 1964), pp. 180-184; Takebe Toshio 武部利男, *Ri Haku* 李白 (Tokyo: Iwanami Shoten 岩波書店, 1957-1958), 2, 23-30; Aoki Masaru 青木正兒 *Ri Haku* (Tokyo: Shūeisha 集英社 (1965), pp. 304-309.

English translations: Witter Bynner and Kiang Kang-hu, *The Jade Mountain* (New York: Knopf, 1929), pp. 67-68; Arthur Waley, *The Poetry and Career of Li Po* (London, (1950), pp. 38-40. French translation: Chang Fu-jui and Jean-Pierre Diény in Paul Demiéville (ed.), *Anthologie de la poésie chinoise classique* (Paris, 1962), pp. 223-225. Japanese translations: Takebe and Aoki.

Editors disagree on the complex prosodic structure of the poem. For the line division and rhyme scheme I follow Aoki, with one unimportant exception: my lines 33-34 are a single line in Aoki. I have divided the poem into four sections on the basis of the five rhyme groups. (Since the third rhyme group—lines 26-27—is so short I have combined it with the fourth rhyme group into a single section.)

[97] Lǐ Pó refers here to local legends concerning early contacts between the states of Ch'ín and Shǔ. His source may have been Yáng Hsíung's (53 B.C.-A.D. 18) *Shǔ wáng běn-chì* ("Basic Annals of the Kings of Shǔ"); cf. the extant fragments of this work in *Ch'üan Hàn wén* ("Complete Prose of the Former Han"), 53. 4b-7a. The commentators and translators have not convincingly identified the myth or myths involved at this point. Whatever they are, they may be connected with the conquest of Shǔ by Ch'ín in the late fourth century B.C., as suggested by Shū Wú. The historical kernel of the legend, we may speculate, could have been either a battle or a road-building accident.

How curling is Green Mud Road!   青泥何盤盤

16 Nine bends for every hundred paces twine among
    the crags.   百步九折縈巖巒

Touching Orion and passing Gemini,
    you look up and hold your breath.   捫參歷井仰脅息

18 You stroke your breast, sit down, and heave a long
    sigh.   以手撫膺坐長嘆

I ask you, Sir, traveling West, when will you return?   問君西遊何時還

20 The fearful road is so steep it can't be climbed.   畏途巉巖不可攀

You only see sad birds calling in old trees,   但見悲鳥號古木

22 The male flies, the female follows, winding through
    the forest.   雄飛雌從繞林間

You also hear the cuckoo cry to the night moon,
    melancholy empty mountain.   又聞子規啼夜月愁空山

24 The hardships of the road to Shu are harder
    than ascending blue heaven,   蜀道之難難於上青天

They make men who hear this lose their rosy color.   使人聽此凋朱顏

26 Linked peaks are less than a foot away from heaven;   連峯去天不盈尺

Withering pines hang upside down,
    leaning on sheer precipices.   枯松倒掛倚絕壁

28 Flying torrents and waterfalls vie in clamor,   飛湍瀑流爭喧豗

They strike cliffs, they circle pebbles, a myriad
    valleys thunder.   砯崖轉石萬壑雷

30 Such are the dangers,   其險也若此

So, O traveler from afar, why do you come?   嗟爾遠道之人胡為乎來哉

32 The Sword Mountain Walkway is lofty and steep,   劍閣崢嶸而崔嵬

With one man at the barrier   一夫當關

34 Ten thousand cannot force it open.   萬夫莫開

Unless you are his kin   所守敎匪親

36 The guard will turn into a wolf and jackal.   化為狼與豺

In the morning shun fierce tigers,   朝避猛虎

38 In the evening shun long snakes.   夕避長蛇

They whet their teeth, they suck blood,   磨牙吮血

40 They kill people like hemp.   殺人如麻

Though they say Brocade City is gay,   錦城雖云樂

42 It's better to return home early.   不如早還家

The hardships of the road to Shu are harder
    than ascending blue heaven.   蜀道之難難於上青天

44 You twist your body, look west, and utter a long
    moan.   側身西望長咨嗟

Lĭ Pó's poem has a number of features marking it as belonging to the literary *yüeh-fŭ* tradition. I will take up eight of these features.

First, "The Hardships of the Road to Shŭ" is a traditional *yüeh-fŭ* title, going back at least to the fifth century of our era. Though no anonymous poems bearing this title are extant today, we do have six literary antecedents for Lĭ Pó's poem, dating from the sixth and seventh centuries.[98]

Second, the meter is irregular. While most of the lines consists of five or seven syllables, there are also lines of four, six, eight, nine, ten, and eleven syllables.

Third, there is a refrain in lines 2, 24, and 43.

Fourth, three lines are headed by traditional *yüeh-fŭ* formulas: "I ask you, Sir" (line 19), "You only see" (line 21), and "You also hear" (line 23). We note, incidentally, that these three formulas are placed close together, in alternate lines, near the middle of the poem. The poet has carefully plotted his rhetorical devices.

Fifth, certain syntactic patterns are avoided in standard T'áng poetry *(shīh)* but freely used in *yüeh-fŭ* and other poetic forms that were in vogue during the T'áng period. Our poem employs several such patterns. One is the use of the genitive particle *chīh* (in the refrain and in lines 11, 12, 13, and 31). Other particles seldom seen in standard T'áng poetry are *yĕh*, indicating a break within the sentence (line 30); *érh* "and" (line 32); and *yŭ* "and" (line 36). All these particles could be dispensed with as far as the "sense" is concerned. In fact, the genitive particle *chīh* is present in the refrain but absent in the title.

Sixth, the poet deliberately departs from standard language at the very opening. The phrase read *yŭ-hsŭ-hsī* in modern Mandarin is said to be an exclamation of bewilderment in the Szechuan dialect.[99]

Seventh, in addition to this opening touch of local color, the poem alludes throughout to local myths and legends rather than to standard Confucian literature. True, Lĭ Pó did not get his information on local "history" and mythology from the mouths of the people but from books. Yet such allusions, bookish or not, show a

[98] *YFSC*, 40. 4b–5a.
[99] The authority for this statement is Sùng Ch'í 宋祁 (998–1061), cited by Chīang and Aoki.

conscious effort to link the poem to the regional and popular *yüeh-fü* tradition.

Eighth, the poem is far from the normal posture of lyric poetry *(shih)* in being completely impersonal, thus following the mainstream of the *yüeh-fü* tradition. As I read the poem, at any rate, there is no indication that the speaker himself is traveling the road to Shŭ. Nor are we justified in assuming that the poem is addressed as a warning to any specific individual.[100]

Despite these and other *yüeh-fü* features, Lĭ Pó's poem—like Ts'áo Ts'āo's—displays a deft literary craftsmanship which would hardly be found in the anonymous, popular tradition. Note for instance the sustained emphasis on the motif of turning back, with direct verbal repetitions *(húan* "return," lines 19 and 42; *huí* "turn back," lines 11 and 12) and numerous indirect hints, of which I will mention one. The crying cuckoo (line 23) refers not merely to the legend of a king of Shŭ who had to give up his throne and was metamorphosed into a cuckoo. More significant in this context is the tradition (noted by Takebe) that the cuckoo, as heard by Chinese ears, cries *Pù jú kūei-ch'ü* 不如歸去, "Better go back home!"

These examples may suffice to show the *yüeh-fü* of the literati to be a separate art form, distinct from the anonymous *yüeh-fü* on the one hand, and standard poetry on the other.

---

[100] Cf. Aoki for a concise, comprehensive demonstration that the specific warning interpretations are groundless.

Bibliography

(See also "Hàn Wèi liù-ch'áo yǔeh-fǔ shīh yén-chīu shū-mù t'í-yào" 漢魏六朝樂府詩研究書目提要 in Wáng, *Yǔeh-fǔ*, p. 123–157.)

Alatorre, Margit Frenk (ed.). *Cancionero de romances viejos.* México, 1961.

Benson, Larry D., "The Literary Character of Anglo-Saxon Formulaic Poetry," *PMLA, 81* (1966), 334–341.

Chāng Shòu-p'íng 張壽平, "Yǔeh-fǔ kō-tz'ú lèi-píeh k'ǎo-tìng" 樂府歌辭類別考訂, Tà-lù tsá-chìh 大陸雜誌, *31* (1965), 364–368.

Child, Francis James (ed.). *The English and Scottish Popular Ballads.* 5 vols. New York: Dover, 1965. (First published Boston, 1882–1898.)

Doncieux, Georges (ed.). *Le Romancéro populaire de la France.* Paris, 1904.

Entwistle, William J. *European Balladry.* Oxford, 1939.

Evans, Marilyn Jane Coutant. *Popular Songs of the Southern Dynasties: A Study in Chinese Poetic Style.* (Yale Ph.D. dissertation, 1966.) Ann Arbor: University Microfilms, 1966.

Friedman, Albert B. (ed). *The Viking Book of Folk-Ballads of the English-speaking World.* New York: Viking Press, 1956.

Gerould, Gordon Hall. *The Ballad of Tradition.* New York, 1957. (First published 1932.)

Gummere, Francis Barton. *The Popular Ballad.* Boston, 1907.

Hightower, James Robert. *Topics in Chinese Literature.* Rev. ed. Cambridge, Mass., 1953.

Hodgart, Matthew (ed.). *The Faber Book of Ballads.* London: Faber and Faber, 1965.

Hsiāo Tí-fēi 蕭滌非. *Hàn Wèi liù-ch'áo yǔeh-fǔ wén-hsǔeh shǐh* 漢魏六朝樂府文學史. Chungking, 1944.

Hsú Ch'éng-yǔ 徐澄宇 (ed.). *Yǔeh-fǔ kǔ-shīh* 樂府古詩. Hong Kong. Chīn-tài t'ú-shū kūng-ssū 今代圖書公司, n.d. (His preface dated Shanghai, 1955.)

Húang Chíeh 黃節 (ed.). *Hàn Wèi yùeh-fù fēng chìen* 漢魏樂府風箋. Hong Kong: Commercial Press, 1961. (His preface dated 1923.)

Húang Chíeh (ed.). *Wèi Wǔ-tì Wèi Wén-tì shīh chù* 魏武帝魏文帝詩註. Hong Kong: Commercial Press, 1961.

Iritani Sensuke 入谷仙介 (ed.). *Koshisen* 古詩選. Tokyo: Asahi Shimbunsha 朝日新聞社, 1966. (Shintei Chūgoku kotensen 新訂中國古典選, Vol. 13.)

Kayser, Wolfgang. *Geschichte der deutschen Ballade*. Berlin, 1936.

Kūng Mù-lán 龔慕蘭 (ed.). *Yùeh-fù shīh hsǔan chù* 樂府詩選註. Taipei, 1961.

Kūo Mào-ch'ìen 郭茂倩 (12th century) (ed.). *Yùeh-fù shīh chí* 樂府詩集 (abbreviated *YFSC*). Edition used: *Sùng-pěn yùeh-fù shīh chí* 宋本樂府詩集, 3 vols., Taipei: Shìh-chìeh shū-chú 世界書局, 1961. For corrections to names of authors, see "Yùeh-fù shīh chí tsò-chīa hsìng-shìh k'ǎo-yì" 樂府詩集作家姓氏考異 (completed 1926), in Yǔ, *Hàn Wèi lìu-ch'áo shīh lùn-ts'úng*, pp. 108-126.

Lǐ Ch'ún-shèng 李純勝, "Líang kǔ chúeh héng-ch'ūi ch'ǔ" 梁鼓角橫吹曲 *Tà-lù tsá-chìh* 大陸雜誌, *28* (1964), 392-395.

Lǐang Hàn wén-hsúeh shǐh ts'ān-k'ǎo tzū-lìao 兩漢文學史參攷資料 Prepared by Department of Chinese Literature of Peking University. Shanghai, 1960.

Ló Kēn-tsé 羅根澤. *Yùeh-fù wén-hsúeh shǐh* 樂府文學史. Peiping,1931.

Lord, Albert B. *The Singer of Tales*. New York: Atheneum, 1965. (First published Cambridge, Mass., 1960.)

Lù K'ǎn-jú 陸侃如 *Yùeh-fù kǔ-tz'ú k'ǎo* 樂府古辭攷. Shanghai: Commercial Press, 1926. (Kúo-hsùeh hsǐao ts'úng-shū 國學小叢書.)

Meier, John (ed.). *Balladen*. 2 vols. Leipzig, 1935-1936.

Menéndez Pidal, Ramón. *Romancero hispánico (hispano-portugués, americano y nefardí): Teoría e historia*. 2 vols. Madrid, 1953. (Obras compíetas de Ramón Menéndez Pidal, Vols. 9-10.)

Menéndez Pidal, Ramón, and others (ed.). *Romancero tradicional de las lenguas hispánicas*. 2 vols. published so far. Madrid, 1957-1963.

P'ān Ch'úng-kūei 潘重規 (ed.). *Yùeh-fù shīh ts'ùi-chìen* 樂府詩粹箋 Hong Kong, 1963.

Shěn Té-ch'íen 沈德潛 (1673–1769) (ed.). *Kŭ-shīh yűan* 古詩源. Hong Kong: Shàng-hǎi yìn-shū kǔan 上海印書館, 1962. (First published 1725.)

Smith, C. Colin (ed.). *Spanish Ballads*. Oxford, 1964.

Uchida Sennosuke 內田泉之助 (ed.). *Koshi gen, jō* 古詩源, 上. Tokyo: Shūeisha 集英社, 1964. (Kanshi taisei 漢詩大系, vol. 4.)

Wáng Yùn-hsī 王運熙. *Lìu-ch'áo yǔeh-fǔ yǔ mín-kō* 六朝樂府與民歌 Shanghai, 1961.

Wáng Yùn-hsī. *Yǔeh-fǔ shīh lùn-ts'úng* 樂府詩論叢. Shanghai, 1962.

Wèi Chìn nán-pěi-ch'áo wén-hsűeh shìh ts'ān-k'ǎo tzū-lìao 魏晉南北朝 文學史參攷資料. Prepared by Department of Chinese Literature of Peking University. Peking, 1962.

Wén Yì-tō 聞一多 (ed.). *Yǔeh-fǔ chìen* 樂府箋. Printed as appendix to *Sùng-pěn yǔeh-fǔ shīh chí* (see under Kūo Mào-ch'ìen).

Wimberly, Lowry Charles. *Folklore in the English and Scottish Ballads*. New York: Dover, 1965. (First published Chicago, 1928.)

YFSC: see Kūo Mào-ch'ìen.

Yú Kùan-yīng 余冠英 (ed.). *Hàn Wèi lìu-ch'áo shīh hsǔan* 漢魏六朝詩 選. Peking, 1961.

Yú Kùan-yīng. *Hàn Wèi lìu-ch'áo shīh lùn-ts'úng* 漢魏六朝詩論叢 Shanghai, 1962.

Yú Kùan-yīng (ed.). *Yǔeh-fǔ shīh hsǔan* 樂府詩選. Hong Kong: Shìh-chìeh ch'ū-pǎn shè 世界出版社, n.d. (His preface to first ed. dated 1950; his postface to revised ed. dated 1954.)

Yǔeh-fǔ shīh yén-chīu lùn-wén chí 樂府詩研究論文集. Edited by Tsò-chīa ch'ū-pǎn shè pīen-chì pù 作家出版社編輯部, Peking, 1957.

Allusion in the Poetry of T'ao Ch'ien

by James R. Hightower

I cannot supply accurate statistics for T'ao Ch'ien's use of allusion, neither the total number of allusions in his poems nor their distribution among the commoner Classical texts. The real difficulty in making such a count is not so much to identify the allusions in the first place (though this is not always easy), as to decide what constitutes an allusion. This problem could be approached in various ways: from the nature of the materials alluded to ("an allusion should be to an identifiable written source"), from the writer's technique of manipulating those materials ("an allusion should contribute to the paraphrasable content of the poem"), from the reader's reaction to occurrences of allusion ("he should be aware of an occurrence of allusion even where he fails to identify it"). I shall not attempt a formal definition of allusion, but I hope that the dimensions of the problem will be clearer after this investigation of T'ao Ch'ien. Ultimately I am interested in how the device functions in poetry, what it contributes to the density and complexity of a poem, and this concern has led me to examine specific instances of allusion in terms of the role each plays in a given poem. I have made no attempt to treat allusion in perspective as only one of the many resources of an artist in language. It is certainly not an indispensable one, and it is more subject than most to abuse. In fact, poetry that relies heavily on allusion and allied devices is suspect nowadays—in China at least—of being mannered and decadent, if not merely affected.

It is often assumed that T'ao Ch'ien's poetry, unlike that of

Hsieh Ling-yün and other Six Dynasties contemporaries, is pretty much free from blemishes of this sort: the Prophet of the Natural wrote poetry which is simple, spontaneous, plain. The Farmer Poet got his materials as well as his inspiration from nature and did not need to deck out his poems with learned phrases from books. Didn't he say of himself (in the transparent disguise of the Gentlemen of the Five Willows) "He liked to read, but did not care about an exact understanding of what he read"?[1]

You do not have to read beyond the first chapter of T'ao Ch'ien's *Collected Works* to discover that his poetry can be as mannered, erudite, and allusion-laden as that of any Six Dynasties poet, but this in a way is cheating, for the first chapter contains only four-word poems, an archaic form in which you would expect to find allusions, and these are precisely the poems of T'ao Ch'ien that no one reads. I shall take only a couple of my examples from them, and I am excluding from consideration here his *fu*, another form that normally uses many allusions.

As a framework to fit my materials into, I have devised a sort of spectrum of degrees of allusion, ranging from the allusion which is the subject of or an excuse for the whole poem to the wholly fortuitous resemblance which is only a trap for the too conscientious exegete or the too learned reader. The spectrum, not surprisingly, yields seven varieties. To be consistent, each should be described in terms of its quantitative contribution to the sense of a passage, and the series should be in ascending order of difficulty of noticing that an allusion is involved. The two criteria do not always coincide, and both involve a judgment that is bound to be occasionally subjective, but the arrangement does focus attention on the thing I am interested in, namely, the contribution of the allusion to the poem.

These are the Seven Varieties:

1. The allusion is the subject of the poem. Unless it is identified you do not know what the poem is about.

2. The allusion is the key to a line; you cannot understand the line without knowing the allusion.

---

[1] *Works* 6.9b (T'ao Shu 陶澍, *Ching-chieh Hsien-sheng chi* 靖節先生集. Chiang-su shu-chü woodblock edition of 1883. References to poems are to Ting Fu-pao 丁福保, *T'ao Yüan-ming shih chien chu* 陶淵明詩箋注, Yi-wen Yin-shu-kuan, 1964 photographic reprint of original typeset edition of 1927).

3. The line makes sense, but not in context; the allusion provides another reading which makes the line meaningful as a part of the poem.

4. The line makes perfect sense; the allusion, when identified, adds overtones that reinforce the literal meaning.

5. An expression or phrase in the line also occurs in a text undoubtedly familiar to the poet, but it makes no contribution to the reader's appreciation of the line, and it is impossible to say whether the poet's adaptation of it was conscious or not.

6. A word is used in a sense familiar from a Classical text. It makes no difference whether you (or the poet) learned the meaning of the word from a dictionary or from its source.

7. The resemblance is fortuitous, and misleading if pressed.

I will begin with the most obvious kind of allusion, where the whole poem is written around a familiar story in a well-known recension. It may recount episodes, but in elliptical form, intended to remind the reader of something he already knows; it is not like a ballad which tells the story, if only in outline. In the anthologies these poems are often placed together in a special category, *yung shih shih* "Poems celebrating historical persons."[2] T'ao Ch'ien wrote eight such poems, all with the word "Celebrating" in the title: "Celebrating the Two Tutors Surnamed Shu," "Celebrating the Three Good Men," "Celebrating Ching K'o," and five short poems of the group entitled "Celebrating Impoverished Gentlemen."[3] The three long poems are similar in style, and they are also alike in not being the first poems on their subjects. This is one reason why T'ao Ch'ien could expect his readers to be equally familiar with the story of Ching K'o and with that of the two tutors surnamed Shu. However, it is not enough to know the story, you must also have in mind the language of the story if you are to understand the language of the poem. In the Ching K'o poem, when you read "The map came to an end and the thing

---

[2] 詠史詩 as in *Wen hsüan* 文選 21 (Yi-wen Yin-shu-kuan, 1955 reprint of Hu K'o-chia edition).

[3] All in Ting 4.9a–14b. There are seven poems in the "Impoverished Gentlemen" series, but the first two are not devoted to individuals.

was there"[4] you must remember that Ssu-ma Ch'ien wrote "The King of Ch'in unrolled the map. When the map came to an end the dagger came into view."[5]

That is all right for Ching K'o, but the Two Shu have given even the commentators trouble, and this is the poem I propose to examine in more detail to demonstrate the first variety of allusion. I quote the poem first, then one by Chang Hsieh on the same theme, and finally the relevant parts of the *Han shu* biography.

In Praise of the Two Tutors Surnamed Shu[6]   詠二疏

As the firmament turns, the seasons pass,	大象轉四時
When its task is done, each takes its leave.	功成者自去
One might well ask, since the Chou declined	借問衰周來
How many men have ever grasped this point?	幾人得其趣
Look there in the archives of the Han—	游目漢廷中
The two tutors Shu restored the practice.	二疏復此舉
With a high-pitched whistle they went back home,	高嘯返舊居
Taking final leave of the prince they tutored.	長揖儲君傅
The whole court came to see them on their way,	餞送傾皇朝
The road was blocked with coaches of the great.	華軒盈道路
It was this parting gave them cause for grief,	離別情所悲
Not, surely, the honor they renounced.	餘榮何足顧
The rare event affected passersby—	事勝感行人
"True Sage" is no everyday praise.	賢哉豈常譽
Content to enjoy village pleasures	厭厭閭里歡
With no pressing duties to tend to;	所營非近務
For feasts they would invite old friends	促席延故老
And with raised cups discuss the past.	揮觴道平素
They asked about the gold, and then explained,	問金終寄心
Their pure words instructing the unenlightened.	清言曉未悟
Devoted to pleasure for their remaining years	放意樂餘年
They had no time to think of cares after death.	遑恤身後慮
And who will say these men are dead and gone?	誰云其人亡
With time their example shines the brighter.	久而道彌著

It is most likely that T'ao Ch'ien knew Chang Hsieh's poem on

[4] 圖窮事自至.

[5] 秦王發圖, 圖窮而匕首見.

[6] Ting 4.12a–b, J. R. Hightower, *The Poetry of T'ao Ch'ien* (Clarendon Press, Oxford, 1970), p. 216.

the Two Tutors Shu and expected his own to be read as a variation (and perhaps improvement) on the theme:[7]

Long ago in the Western Capital	昔在西京時
City and country greatly rejoiced.	朝野多歡娛
In crowds they gathered by the Eastern Gate	藹藹東都門
As all the lords came to see the Two Shu off.	羣公祖二疏
Vermilion coaches shone by the metal wall	朱軒曜金城
Service tents lined the long thoroughfare.	供帳臨長衢
Men of understanding, they knew when to quit,	達人知止足
Abandoned glory as though it were nothing.	遺榮忽如無
They pulled out cap pins, took off court robes,	抽簪解朝衣
Let their hair fall free and went to the seacoast.	散髮歸海隅
Onlookers shed tears at the sight	行人爲隕涕
And exclaimed, "What sages, these men!"	賢哉此丈夫
They scattered their gold, rejoicing in the present,	揮金樂當年
In their declining years, they kept no hoard.	歲暮不留儲
To their guests on all sides they said,	顧謂四坐賓
"Much property is a trap for the stupid."	多財爲累愚
Their pure example inspires ten thousand ages	清風激萬代
Their names joined with Heaven and Earth.	名與天壤俱
Ah, you guests with cicada-emblem caps,	咄此蟬冕客
This should be inscribed on your sashes!	君紳宜見書

This poem depends less on a knowledge of the *Han shu* biography of the Two Shu than T'ao Ch'ien's, which almost certainly borrowed from Chang Hsieh. Still, it is to the *Han shu*[8] one must go to be prepared to understand the details of both poems. I shall paraphrase in part, translating where there are direct borrowings.

Shu Kuang and his nephew Shu Shou were respectively Senior Tutor and Junior Tutor to the Heir Apparent of the Han Emperor Hsüan (reigned 73–48 B.C.). They discharged their duties in an exemplary manner, and when the Heir Apparent was twelve years old he had mastered the *Classic of Filial Piety* and the *Conversations of Confucius*. Whereupon Shu Kuang said to his nephew, "I have heard that knowing when you have enough will spare you disgrace, knowing when to stop saves jeopardizing your achievements, and

---

[7] 張協, 詠史詩, *Wen hsüan* 21. 5a–b.

[8] *Han-shu pu-chu* 漢書補注 71. 3b–5a. (Yi-wen Yin-shu-kuan photographic reprint).

retiring when you are successful is the Way of Heaven. Now we
hold offices with the highest salaries, and we have made a name as
public servants. If we don't get out now, I am afraid we will regret
it. Would it not be a good idea if the two of us, uncle and nephew,
resigned and went back home to live out our lives in peace?"
Shou knocked his head on the ground and said, "I follow your
instructions, Sir."

They were permitted to resign on grounds of illness and were
given a bonus of twenty catties of gold by the Emperor and fifty
catties by the Heir Apparent. All the court nobles and officials
came with over a hundred carriages to the east gate of Ch'ang-an to
see them off. Onlookers exclaimed, "What sages these Tutors are!"
And some sighed and shed tears.

When they got back to their hometown, Kuang had his family
prepare a feast every day, and invited friends and relatives to enjoy
it with him. He often asked the family how much gold was left and
kept selling it to provide for his expenses. After a year of this, his
heirs were worried that he would spend it all. They got someone
to suggest to the old man that he invest his money in land so as to
provide for his descendants. He said, "I am not so senile that I do
not think of my descendants. But we have the old house and land.
If they work hard here, they can provide food and clothing as well
as commoners. If I add to it to make a superfluity, it will only
make them lazy. If a man is virtuous and has too much property,
he loses his ambition. If he is stupid and has too much property,
it just increases his misdeeds. What's more, the rich are envied by the
masses. I have no way to teach my descendants to be good, but
at least I do not want to increase their misdeeds and make them
envied. Besides, this gold was given by a sage ruler to keep me in
my old age. It makes me happy to finish my remaining days by
sharing the enjoyment of this gift with my fellow villagers and their
relatives. Isn't this all right?"

Let us consider how T'ao Ch'ien's poem is related to the *Han shu*
story. The first two lines of the poem state the moral, an idea
discoverable in the *Tao te ching* and reflected in Shu Kuang's speech
to his nephew, but the closest parallel is in the *Shih chi,*[9] "Each of

---

[9] *Shih chi* 史記 79.37 (Takigawa edition).

the four seasons leaves in turn as its task is done." Lines 5–6 identify the "Two Shu in the Court of Han" as the subject of the poem more clearly than the title itself and name them as illustrations of the moral. Notice that the bare identification is supposed to be enough: T'ao Ch'ien tells us nothing about their early life or court career, only that they gave up their position as Tutors to the Heir Apparent to go back home.

Line 10 summarizes another passage in the biography, but intelligibly and with no use of its language. Here Chang Hsieh's poem relies more directly on the biography (lines 4–6), but introduces a term *chu hsüan* "vermilion coaches" not in it, of which T'ao Ch'ien's *hua hsüan* "ornamented coaches" is perhaps a reflection.

T'ao Ch'ien's line 11 is either a misreading of the text or a deliberate change to make a point, for neither the *Han shu* nor Chang Hsieh's poem says the Two Shu were grieved; it is rather the onlookers or passersby *(hsing jen)* who wept. In line 13 T'ao Ch'ien picks up the "passersby," probably from Chang Hsieh again, whose *yi jung* "lingering glory" (line 8) may have prompted T'ao's *yu jung* "remaining glory." (But the biography has "the court considered them glorious.") The exclamation "What sages!" *hsien tsai* in line 14 could hardly be understood in either poem without reference to the source.

Line 16 is another summary without verbal borrowing. It is continued in line 18, where the *hui* may have been suggested by Chang Hsieh's *hui chin* "to scatter gold" in line 14, but typically applied by T'ao to the winecup.[10]

Line 20 has caused trouble for both commentators and translators, and I will give an example of the kind of interpretation suggested. Chiang Hsün is most often quoted:[11]

> The two lines beginning "They asked about gold" are not easily explained. I suggest it is those urging Kuang to leave the gold to his descendants, which prompted Kuang to say, "If a man is virtuous and has too much property, he loses his ambition," etc. The sense of the poem seems to be that having asked about the gold, they are pre-

[10] E.g., 還舊居, Ting 3.8a; 雜詩, 2, Ting 4.4b.

[11] 蔣薰, 評陶淵明詩集, in *T'ao Yüan-ming shih wen hui-p'ing* 詩文彙評 p. 278 (Shih-chieh shu-chü photographic reprint of Peking original, cited as *Hui-p'ing*).

occupied with gold, and Kuang with pure words awakened his
unenlightened friends.

One trouble with this is that it makes T'ao Ch'ien's line either
inconsequential ("They ask because they want to ask") or contradictory—if they are preoccupied to the end with gold, those
pure words cannot do much for them. Ku Chih noticed this last
point without offering any alternative. "In the year and more
Kuang spent carousing with his friends, there must have been
lots of pure words and heartfelt talk. If they still urged him to buy
property to provide for his descendents, they really were preoccupied
with gold to the end and in the dark about his ideas."[12]

None of the other commentators does any better, but the solution
of the difficulty surely lies in the biography, where it is clearly
stated that the one who asked about the gold was Shu Kuang
himself, and though he asked frequently, he was not preoccupied
with it; he just wanted to know if there was some left that he might
sell for his present needs.

This poem is an example of one dominated by an allusion. It is
not a very good poem; in fact, in general this use of allusion does
not produce important poetry. Of course, I do not claim to have
treated even all the allusions in this poem, but have dealt only
with the ones derived from the Han shu. The necessary condition
for an allusion of the first type is that it underlies the whole poem
and that it refers back to a written text from which it makes verbal
borrowings. In my usage, a poem about Wang Chao-chün which
depends on no specific written version of the story does not constitute an example of allusion at all, however puzzling it might be
to a reader who never heard of that unfortunate lady.

The first category might be made clearer with an example that
does not belong. The fifth of the poems "On Reading the Seas
and Mountains Classic" is sandwiched between verses so allusion-
ridden as to be wholly unintelligible without an indexed copy
of the Shan hai ching within easy reach, but this one is remarkably
transparent, a charming personal lyric instead of an exercise in
versified mythology:[13]

---

[12] 古直, 陶靖節詩箋, 4.11a (Taipei Kuang-wen shu-chü photographic reprint of
original typeset edition).

[13] Ting 4.16a–b.

Flap, flap, the Three Blue Birds—
Delectable the rare colored plumes.
Mornings Hsi-wang-mu's messengers,
Evenings back to Three-Peak Hill.
Through these birds I should like
To send word to Hsi-wang-mu:
In this world all I want
Is wine, and length of years.

翩翩三青鳥
毛色奇可憐
朝爲王母使
暮歸三危山
我欲因此鳥
具向王母言
在世無所須
唯酒與長年

There is no text which supplies the reader with information needed to fill out the sense of the poem. The *Shan hai ching* (plus Kuo P'u's commentary) says that the Three Blue Birds are Hsi-wang-mu's messengers—but so does the poem. It also says that the birds' occupation is to bring food to Hsi-wang-mu, but that is not only irrelevant, it jars with the fact of her immortality, which does have something to do with the poem. *Shan hai ching* also says that the Three Blue Birds dwell on Three-Peak Mountain, another piece of information that can be inferred at least from the poem. It helps to know that Hsi-wang-mu has at her disposal the gift of immortality (here the legend is too widespread to tie to a single textual source, of which the *Shan hai ching* in any case is not one), and that she is generous of her wine (on the occasion of Emperor Mu's visit she was). These facts too can be inferred from the poem. Consequently, though the poem is written on mythological characters which appear in the *Shan hai ching* (and so properly belongs in a series of poems with that title), the allusion is not the subject of the poem.

My next category is nearly as obvious and hard to ignore as the first: the allusion is the key to the line, which you cannot understand without knowing the allusion. The easiest example of this kind of allusion is a proper name. In one sense a proper name can be regarded as only another lexical item. It "means" something, and you look it up in a dictionary if you don't recognize it. But what it means can be terribly complex. It "means" the one anecdote that everyone knows about Po Ya and Chung Tzu-ch'i, or it can mean what the poet feels about Confucius. In nearly every case it is used as a convenient shorthand to make one or two syllables carry information that it may take pages or volumes to spell out. Here is an example:[14]

[14] No. 11 of "Drinking Wine" 飲酒, Ting 3.16a.

Master Yen they praised for being good   顏生稱爲仁
And Old Man Jung was said to be a sage: 榮公言有道
The one was often empty—he died young,   屢空不獲年
The other always hungry—he lived long.   長飢至于老

It is not enough to know that Yen Hui was Confucius' favorite
disciple; to match the lines properly you need also to associate with
him the epithet "frequently empty," and to get the full impact of
the allusion you should recall a passage from the Po-yi Shu-ch'i
Biography in the *Shih chi*:[15] "Of the seventy disciples, Confucius
praised only Yen Hui for his love of learning. But 'Hui was often
empty,' not having his fill even of coarse fare, and he died young.
Is this the way Heaven rewards good men?" Jung Ch'i-ch'i as he
appears in *Lieh tzu*, is not an example of goodness unrewarded,
but that is the way T'ao Ch'ien thought of him and refers to him
elsewhere.[16] This is a complication not unrelated to the problem
of allusion. We are faced with the choice that *(a)* T'ao Ch'ien was
alluding to another story about Jung Ch'i-ch'i, one that is now
lost, or *(b)* T'ao Ch'ien was inaccurate in his recollection of the
Lieh tzu story. In either case the allusion as allusion fails of its
intended effect.[17]

This is not quite the same as the allusion which is not appropriate
in all its details, for most occurrences of allusion require the reader
to be selective in applying what he knows to the present situation.
Even an allusion so obvious and run-of-the-mill as this one calls
for some flexibility in interpretation:[18]

You are as kind as the washerwoman,   感子漂母惠
But to my shame I lack Han's talent.   愧我非韓才

This of course refers to Han Hsin, who became Han Kao Tsu's
great general.[19] As a young man he was generally despised and in

[15] *Shih chi* 61.11–12.

[16] No. 2 of "Drinking Wine," Ting 3.12b.

[17] No. 5 of "In Praise of Impoverished Gentlemen," for example, begins with a reference to the known anecdote about Yüan An snowbound, without explaining how he
belongs in the company of poverty-stricken worthies, and continues with a Master Juan
who can no longer be identified at all. The result is a poem in which the specific allusions
have no function.

[18] "On Begging for Food" 乞食, Ting 2.10a.

[19] The "Biography of the Marquis of Huai-yin," *Shih chi* 92, is translated by John De
Francis in *Harvard Journal of Asiatic Studies* 10 (1947) 179–215.

straitened circumstances, but a washerwoman took pity on him
and fed him for several weeks. When he promised to pay her back,
she indignantly denied that she expected any reward. In T'ao
Ch'ien's poem the allusion is appropriate only for the circumstances
of the favor: befriending someone completely down and out with no
expectation of reward. T'ao's patron was neither humble nor
a woman.

A somewhat more complicated example involving two proper
names is from one of the Imitations (No. 8):[20]

All I saw were the ancient mounds—	惟見古時丘
Two high graves by the side of the road,	路邊兩高墳
Po Ya in one, the other Chuang Chou.	伯牙與莊周
Men like these are hard to find,	此士難再得
If I went now, what would I seek?	吾行欲何求

Now here are two very familiar names being held up for our admiration, but by virtue of what quality? "Po Ya was reluctant to
play his cither for one who was not a connoisseur; Chuang Chou
retired from the world to speak his mind, unwilling to serve lightly.
If I could get these men for my companions, even though we could
not reform the world, at least we would be able to retire together."
This is Huang Wen-huan's contribution.[21] Ch'en Tso-ming says,
"Po Ya was a real musician, Chuang Chou a man of true understanding; it stands to reason they are not easily come by."[22] I quote
these two commentators to show that the answer is not obvious. It
is not Po Ya the musician and Chuang Chou the philosopher that
are being paired (to remind us that T'ao Ch'ien was both cither
player and Taoist), but the two men who were able to realize
themselves only through an understanding friend: "When Chung
Tzu-ch'i died, Po Ya broke the strings and smashed his cither,
knowing that in the whole world no one would appreciate him.
When Hui Shih died, Chuang Tzu ceased to speak, seeing that in
the whole world there was no one with whom he could converse."[23]
This *Huai nan tzu* passage associates the two names in the way

[20] No. 8 of the "Imitations" 擬古, Ting 4.3b.
[21] 黃文煥, *Hui-p'ing* 241.
[22] 陳祚明, *ibid.*
[23] *Huai-nan tzu* 准南子 19.11a (*SPTK* edition).

appropriate to the present poem, and another example spells it out:
"Yin Min was a close friend of Pan Piao. They considered their
relationship to be like that of Chung Tzu-ch'i and Po Ya or Chuang
Chou and Hui Shih."[24] So what T'ao Chien was saying was
that in the whole world there was no understanding friend with
whom to make common cause, though for the line to be wholly
appropriate he would have to refer to Chung Ch'i and Hui Shih.

With names as allusions there may be a more basic difficulty
than deciding what to associate with a given individual; you have
after all to identify the individual first. It may be that you simply
do not know anything about the person named:[25]

Of old there was Huang Tzu-lien	昔在黃子廉
Who dusted his cap to serve the state.	彈冠佐名州
He resigned one day and went back home:	一朝辭吏歸
For pure poverty he's hard to match.	清貧略難儔

The poem also says that his wife complained about his neglect of
their children, but that is all we know about him, for no one has
been able to find out who he was. As a result the poem remains
rather a puzzle.

Or the man may be alluded to in a way that leaves you in doubt
about his identity. When you read "Old Man Jung was said to
be a sage,"[26] you may remember Jung Ch'i-ch'i, but T'ao Ch'ien
also alludes to him in the line "At ninety he wore a rope for a belt,"
since Jung Ch'i-ch'i appears in *Lieh tzu*,[27] "dressed in deerskin,
wearing a rope for a belt, and playing the cither as he sang." In
either case there is no danger of identifying him with someone else.

Without help from the commentators no one is likely to guess who
is the subject of the lines:[28]

Chang-kung once served a term in office	長公曾一仕
And still was young when he saw the times were wrong.	壯節忽失時
He closed his gate and never more went forth,	杜門不復出
Renounced the world for all his remaining days.	終身與世辭

[24] *Hou-Han shu* 後漢書 79A. 10b (Yi-wen Yin-shu-kuan photographic reprint).
[25] No. 7 of "In Praise of Impoverished Gentlemen," Ting 4.11b.
[26] No. 11 of "Drinking Wine"; see above.
[27] *Lieh tzu* 列子 1.4b (*SPTK* edition).
[28] No 12 of "Drinking Wine," Ting 3.16b.

Chang Chih, *tzu* Chang-kung, is known from the two lines tacked on to his father's *Shih chi* biography,[29] which adds to the information in the poem only the fact that he reached the rank of Great Officer before retiring.

When a man is alluded to by his *tzu*, there is often the possibility of more than one historical person so called:[30]

Since there is no Meng-kung here   孟公不在茲
In the end I keep my feelings to myself.   終以翳吾情

A Sung dynasty commentator, Li Kung-huan, identified Meng-kung with Ch'en Tsun, a Han dynasty gentleman with a fondness for wine who always had a houseful of drinking guests. Since this was the only commentary on the line until the twentieth century, it must mean that the poem was misread by several generations of readers. For this poem is a rather bitter complaint about hardship and poverty, not a celebration of convivial drinking. The lines immediately preceding are

A dismal wind blows round my wretched shack   弊廬交悲風
And a waste of weeds engulfs the courtyard.   荒草沒前庭
In coat of felt I sit the long nights out   披褐守長夜
When morning cocks refuse to start to crow.   晨雞不肯鳴

The proper identification of Meng-kung, made by Ku Chih,[31] is certainly Liu Kung, who recognized the abilities of Chang Chung-wei, a poet living in poverty. The pair is celebrated by T'ao Ch'ien in No. 6 of his "Impoverished Gentlemen":[32]

Chung-wei was committed to his poverty—   仲蔚愛窮居
Around his house the weeds grew tall.   遶宅生蒿蓬
Retired, he gave up social ties   翳然絕交游
And wrote poems which were not bad.   賦詩頗能工
In all the world none knew his worth   舉世無知者
Save one man only, Liu Kung.   止有一劉龔

[29] *Shih chi* 102.11.
[30] No. 16 of "Drinking Wine," Ting 3.18a.
[31] Ku Chih 3.12a. Ting Fu-pao also quotes the passage.
[32] Ting 4.11a.

Hence, in the "Drinking Wine" poem the last line does not mean "I will conceal the fact that I want a drink (since there is no one around who will give me one)," but "I will keep to myself the feelings that I could express only to an understanding friend."

Of course this second type does not have to refer directly to a person at all; it could as well be to a place-name or a book or an event in history, but most often a person is involved. For example, two familiar episodes relating to Confucius are recalled in the lines[33]

> Although no phoenix came to nest 　　　　　　　鳳鳥雖不至
> Briefly Rites and Music were renewed. 　　　　禮樂暫得新

though the things named are the bird *feng-huang* and the books *Li* and *Yüeh*. Confucius has been identified in the preceding couplet as "the old man of Lu," so there could be no question but it is his work as editor of the Classics that is meant, even if the first line were not straight out of the *Conversations* ("The phoenix doesn't come, the River puts forth no map—it's all up with me."[34] Incidentally, of the ten couplets that make up this poem, all but the last two involve one or more allusions, mostly to Confucian texts or traditions, and each providing an example of allusion of the Second Type.

The third variety contains some of the most troublesome allusions. Here the allusion is buried in a line which makes perfectly good sense when taken at its face value, and it is possible to miss the allusion altogether unless you read carefully enough to discover that the "perfectly good sense" is limited to the one line (or couplet) and fails, in the context of the whole poem, to give an adequate reading. I will start with a simple example from the poem "Finding Fault with my Sons":[35]

> A-hsüan would be ambitious to learn 　　　　　阿宣行志學
> But love of letters is not in him. 　　　　　　而不愛文術

This seems like a nice touch of irony and fits in well enough with the unflattering comments allotted to the other sons. But something is lacking which is part of the structure of the poem—A-hsüan's age, a statistic supplied for all the others:

[33] No. 20 of "Drinking Wine," Ting 3.19b.
[34] *Lun yü* 論語 9/9.
[35] Ting 3.23b.

> Already Shu is twice times eight—   阿舒巳二八
> For laziness he has no match.   懶惰故無匹
>
> . . . .
>
> Both Yung and Tuan count thirteen years—   雍端年十三
> They cannot add up six and seven.   不識六與七
> T'ung-tzu is getting on toward nine   通子垂九齡
> And all he seeks are pears and chestnuts.   但覓梨與栗

So for A-hsüan we must add that he was going on fifteen, remembering that at fifteen Confucius had his mind bent on study. This reading is inescapable if we have noticed how often T'ao Ch'ien refers to this particular *Conversations* passage[36] in giving his own age. However, it leaves the translator in a quandary, for he has no easy way of combining the irony of the literal reading and the information conveyed by the allusion. "At A-hsüan's age Confucius studied" manages only to be enigmatic while smothering the irony.

Another straightforward example of a line that makes sense—but the wrong sense—when read literally occurs in the couplet[37]

> The Shang mode song is no affair of mine   商歌非吾事
> I yearn to plow in double harness.   依依在耦耕

The first line is an example of the Second Type and refers to the line "Ning Ch'i sang a Shang song below the carriage, and Duke Huan understood";[38] the implication is "I have no ambition to play the role of advisor to those in power." In the second line the words *ou keng* "plowing in pairs" do not mean he wants someone to join him in field work, but that he longs to be a recluse like Chang-chü and Chieh-ni, who were yoke-mates pulling a plow together when Confucius encountered them.[39] If you are going to translate the allusions you get something like this:

> I am not one to volunteer my services
> I only yearn to lead a farmer's life.

---

[36] *Lun yü* 2/4, "At fifteen my mind was bent on study, at thirty I was established, at forty I had no indecisions, at fifty I knew Heaven's ordinance," etc. In No. 19 of "Drinking Wine" he says, "At the time I was approaching the age of being established" 是時向立年, and in No. 16 of the same series, "I went on and on until now I am nearly without indecision" 行行向不惑.

[37] "At Tu-k'ou at Night during the Seventh Moon of the Year 401," Ting 3.4a.

[38] *Huai-nan tzu* 9.3b–4a.

[39] *Lun yü* 18/6.

A more complicated example is found in the opening couplet of
No. 4 of the "Untitled Poems":[40]

| The hero makes the world his goal: | 丈夫志四海 |
| May I never recognize old age. | 我願不知老 |

It is easy to identify the "I" of the poem with the hero of the first
line and to understand that the poet is begging for time to achieve
his own heroic deeds. You expect to hear more of his ambition in
the next line, or at any rate something about prolonging life, perhaps
through drugs or breathing exercises. But no, you find the poet
enjoying himself with his family, getting up late in the morning
to spend his days in song and wine. As if that were not enough,
he concludes with

Why be like the men of today	孰若當世士
Their breasts crammed with ice and fire.	冰炭滿懷抱
A hundred years and they go to the grave	百年歸丘壟
Following the road of empty fame.	用此空名道

Clearly, then, he is not the hero of the first line, and the second
line must say something that contrasts with the first. The phrase
"not recognize old age" *pu chih lao* provides the clue, again by way
of the *Conversations*:[41] "He is the sort of person who in his enthusiasm
forgets his meals and in his joy forgets his cares, unaware that old
age is coming on." Confucius so characterized himself, but here
T'ao Ch'ien is not so much saying "I would like to be like Confucius"
as "I want to be so taken up with the things that give me pleasure
that I forget everything else—like Confucius." So the lines could
be translated

A hero makes the whole world his goal
But I will lose myself in what I like.

My last example of a line that seems to make sense in isolation
but depends on an allusion to yield a satisfactory reading in context
is much less clear-cut than the preceding ones. In the first place,
it consists in two lines, adjacent but belonging to different couplets,

[40] Ting 4.5a.
[41] *Lun yü* 7/19.

and it does not rest firmly on a verbal borrowing from a text. The poem is "Drinking Alone in the Rainy Season," and I quote the first twelve lines to establish the context:[42]

Whatever lives comes to its end at last	運生會歸盡
From the beginning of time it has been so.	終古謂之然
If Immortals Sung and Ch'iao once lived	世間有松喬
Where do you suppose they are today?	於今定何間
The old fellow who sent this gift of wine	故老贈余酒
Said to drink it makes a man immortal.	乃言飲得仙
I try a cup, and all my cares are gone,	試酌百情遠
More, and all at once I forget Heaven.	重觴忽忘天
But is Heaven so far from this after all?	天豈去此哉
Nothing tops the one who trusts the true.	任眞無所先
The cloud-high crane with the wonderful wings	雲鶴有奇翼
Can reach the ends of the earth in a moment of time.	八表須臾還

In reading the poem you find, beginning with line 7, what seems to be the poet's report on the results of an experiment in drinking designed to test the validity of the claim in line 6, that to drink wine will make a man immortal. Each of the three following lines seems to make sense by itself, but the linkage between the statements is obscure, and one is driven to look for an allusion. In particular we would like to know just what is meant by "forgetting Heaven." Is it hyperbole? If you forget even Heaven, how much the more will you have ceased to worry about ordinary mundane things. If "Heaven" means God or fate, forgetting it could amount to taking your mind off your worries, if you happen to be overly concerned with such things ("I try a cup, and all my cares are gone"). Either way of taking the phrase makes forgetting Heaven a good thing, and leaves no room for the readmission of Heaven in the next line, except by making it mean something else there.

The clue to the transition is provided by a passage in *Chuang tzu*:[43] "To forget things of this world and to forget Heaven, the name for this is 'forgetting oneself.' Of the man who forgets himself we say that he has entered into Heaven." In these terms T'ao Ch'ien's line 9 is a part of a logical sequence. He drinks to see if this really

---

[42] Ting 2.13b–14a.
[43] *Chuang tzu* 莊子 5.10b (*SPTK* edition).

is a way of becoming a Taoist immortal. The first effect of the wine is to make him forget his cares. Then he forgets Heaven—perhaps the very thing he was seeking—only to realize that (according to Chuang Tzu) in forgetting the world and Heaven he was forgetting himself, and that this amounts to actually entering Heaven. How appropriate then the symbolical cloud-flight of the crane in the next couplet. Wine may not be the elixir of immortality, but it has helped him toward one of the reputed pleasures of the Immortals.

My fourth and fifth categories are two rather than one because my examples are too far apart to put under a single heading. However, the two shade into one another, and there is a large area where the division is subjective and to a certain extent arbitrary. In both cases a line of a poem makes sense without the allusion. What a reader must decide is, did the poet write his line expecting him to recognize his source? And does the identification of his source add anything to the reading of his line? This is easier to answer affirmatively (a) where there is a high degree of verbal identity and (b) where the text in question is one often used by the poet for allusions belonging to the first three types.

I will start with a clear-cut example of the fourth type, where the line makes perfect sense, but where the literal sense is reinforced and extended by the allusion. The couplet reads[44]

If we do not enjoy ourselves today,	今我不爲樂
How do we know there will be another year?	知有來歲不

Behind this is the *Classic of Songs* couplet[45]

If we do not enjoy ourselves today	今我不樂
The days and months will pass us by.	日月其除

Now the *Classic of Songs* is one of T'ao Ch'ien's favorite texts, and there can be no doubt that his use here was deliberate (he has simply introduced an extra word to make the line fit his five-word meter). Both poems are about autumn and both urge enjoying present pleasures. The earlier poem also warns against excess ("The good gentleman is sedate"), and T'ao is certainly proposing nothing very immoderate when he concludes

[44] "To Liu, Prefect of Ch'ai-sang" 酬劉柴桑, Ting 2.16b.
[45] *Shih ching* 詩經 No. 114/1.

> I tell my wife to bring along the children—   命室攜童弱
> This is a perfect day to make an outing.   良日登遠遊

The total effect of referring T'ao's line to its source is to lend the
weight of classical authority to a proposition which otherwise might
be taken as a frivolous piece of Six Dynasties hedonism.

More debatable, but still examples of the Fourth Type, are the
two *Shih ching* borrowings here:[46]

> The good friend is far away   良朋悠邈
> I scratch my head and wait for long.   搔首延佇

Taken singly and in another kind of poem, no one would care to be
reminded that the phrases *liang p'eng* "good friend" and *sao shou*
"scratch the head" also occur in the *Shih ching*.[47] But in an archaizing
four-word poem like this one, every identifiable bit of *Shih ching*
vocabulary adds to the total effect, even when not as obviously
archaic as *yi-tsu*, for example, in line 4 of the same poem ("The
level roads are blocked" 平路伊阻).

> For long I yearned to live in Southtown—   昔欲居南村
> Not that a diviner told me to—   非爲卜其宅
> Where many simple-hearted people live   聞多素心人
> With whom I would rejoice to pass my days.   樂與數晨夕

This[48] needs no explanation. Yet if we refer line 2 ("Not because
I decided on the site through divination") to the proverb quoted
in *Tso chuan*, "It is not the site one divines for, but the neighbors,"[49]
it gains point and flavor.

The next example is harder to dispose of. When T'ao Ch'ien
wrote the line[50] "The dusty cup shames the empty wine cask,"
he was surely inspired by the *Shih ching* couplet,[51]

> That the bottle is empty   缾之罄矣
> The wine cask is ashamed of it.   維罍之恥

[46] "Hovering Clouds" 停雲, Ting 1.1a.
[47] *Shih ching* No. 164/3, 42/1.
[48] No. 1 of "On Moving House" 移居, Ting 2.15a.
[49] *Tso chuan* 左傳 20.16b (Chao 3) *SPTK* edition.
[50] "The Double Ninth, In Retirement," 九日閑居 Ting 2.4a.
[51] *Shih ching* 202/3.

The reader who is aware of the source can admire the skill with which the couplet has been transmuted into a perfect line, but the awareness is somehow distracting: there are no reverberations to intensify or complicate his appreciation of T'ao's poem. Here the poet is not drawing on the Classic as a source of strength, he is improving on it.

Also on the borderline between Types Four and Five is the use of a ready-made phrase or line solely as display. It is a compliment to the reader's erudition, which must be its own reward, for he gains nothing in understanding of the poem he is reading. T'ao Ch'ien wrote few purely formal social poems, but when he did, he was inclined to indulge in this sort of empty display. "At General Wang's Party for Departing Guests" begins[52]

The autumn days grow sharp and chill	秋日淒且厲
And all the plants are dry and sere.	百卉具已腓

Here a *Shih ching* couplet has been pressed into use[53] which says the same thing in identical words (T'ao has tucked in an extra word in each line to make it scan). We cannot suspect plagiarism, for he must have expected his readers to know the source. But once they recognized it, they could not make use of any part of their knowledge in interpreting T'ao's poem. For the *Shih ching* poem is a complaint about ill-treatment by someone who ends by saying

A gentleman has written this song	君子作歌
He did it to tell his grief.	維以告哀

It is I suppose not absolutely precluded that T'ao Ch'ien was thus deviously expressing his dislike of his host, but read this way the poem becomes merely impolite, not a better poem. I think this example can be assimilated to the Fifth Type, for the recognition of a source in no way affects one's reading of the poem, even though there is no doubt of the poet's having deliberately used the source. Earlier I quoted a couplet for the example of an allusion of the Third Type in the second line:

The hero makes the world his goal:
May I never recognize old age.

[52] Ting 2.18a, where the word 多 is a misprint for 秋.
[53] *Shih ching* 204/2.

The first line is clear enough, and becomes no clearer from the fact that it occurs verbatim in Ts'ao Chih's poem to his brother, Ts'ao Piao.[54] Now Ts'ao Chih's poety is not a text like the *Shih ching*, and there is no way of knowing whether T'ao Ch'ien expected the line to be recognized, or even whether he himself was aware that someone had used it before he did. But it is hard to believe that he could have cared whether or not it was familiar to his reader. The only way the information could be more useful than distracting is by preparing us to dissociate the line from the next one.

An instructive example is the couplet[55]

Little by little the autumn has come to an end,	靡靡秋巳夕
Chill, chill the wind and dew combine.	凄凄風露交

Ting Fu-pao cites one *Shih ching* line,[56] "Wind and rain are chill, chill," and Ku Chih another,[57] "The autumn day is chill, chill." Either one contains three terms which occur in T'ao Ch'ien's couplet, but neither is necessary as a source or even likely as his inspiration.

Lexical borrowings are not unlike the preceding category, of which they might seem to be a special case. On the other hand, they also have one thing in common with the second variety: they leave the sense of the line obscure until they are explained. However, they need not be explained by transferring their original context to the line in which they occur. All that is needed is a definition of "what they mean." They differ from ordinary elements of the vocabulary by owing their meaning to one specific use, usually in a well-known text. For example, the following lines contain an expression not immediately intelligible from its components:[58]

Sympathetic friends who know my tastes	故人賞我趣
Bring a wine jug when they come to visit.	挈壺相與至
Sitting on the ground beneath the pine tree	班荊坐松下
We keep on filling cups until we are drunk.	數斟巳復醉

---

[54] 贈白馬王彪, *Ts'ao Tzu-chien chi* 5.8b (*SPTK* edition).
[55] "The Ninth of the Ninth Month, 409," Ting 3.9b.
[56] *Shih ching* 90/1.
[57] *Ibid.*, 204/2 (Ku Chih 3.6b).
[58] No. 14 of "Drinking Wine," Ting 3.17b.

Taken at their face value, the words of line 3 mean "Spreading thornwood, we sit beneath the pine tree." The term *pan ching* "to lay out thornwood" occurs in a *Tso chuan* passage[59] quoted by Ting Fu-pao about a chance meeting between Wu Chü and Sheng Tzu; they "*pan ching* and ate together, talking about taking up service (with Ch'u) again." Tu Yü's commentary explains *pan ching* as "to spread thornwood and sit on the ground." As an allusion, *pan ching* means "to meet a friend by chance." In the present context it means no more than "to sit on the ground," and the *Tso chuan* passage has no relevance except as the first occurrence of what has become a common piece of vocabulary. Note that the word *ching* "thorny bush" is made no clearer by referring to the original, or to the commentary. Surely no one ever went out of his way to sit on thorns, and to the writer of the passage the word either meant something else ("mat" would make good sense) or he was using *pan* to mean not "spread" but "push aside."

The next two examples are to be found in the dictionary; each gets its meaning by a kind of ellipsis, and to that extent depends on the original context. But it is possible to understand each quite independently of that context, if you know its special meaning simply as a lexical item. T'ao Ch'ien's lines[60] can be translated,

My first joy will be to wait on my parents   一欣侍溫淸
My next pleasure to see my brothers.   再喜見友于

The word *yu yü* "friends with" means "brothers" only by virtue of its occurrence in the *Shu ching*,[61] "You are filial and friends with your brothers." The ellipsis had become an established word-play by T'ao Ch'ien's time, but even so its use in this poem verges on the affected and can be excused only as a parallel to *wen ch'ing* "warm and fresh" in the preceding line. This expression comes from the *Li chi*,[62] "What constitutes ritual behavior for a son is, in winter, to warm [his parents] and in summer to refresh [them], at night to make them secure and in the morning to pay his respects."

---

[59] *Tso chuan* 37.7a (Hsiang 26).

[60] "In the Fifth Month of the Year 400, Held up at Kuei-lin," Ting 3.2b.

[61] *Shang shu* 尙書 11.4a–b (*SPTK* edition): 惟孝友于兄弟. This is a *ku-wen* text, but the line is quoted from the *Shu* in *Lun yü* 2/21.

[62] *Li chi* 1/10.

The seventh category is the real non-allusion. It belongs in the list for two reasons: it looks like an allusion, and it will be cited by a commentator as though he thought it was one. The reason I am so confident it is not an allusion is that it makes nonsense of an otherwise intelligible line to refer it to the passage quoted. There could be doubtful cases which might belong either here or in the fifth category, but in all of them you could be sure no reference was intended by the poet.

The following example[63] surely admits of no argument:

With loosened belt relax in joy,	緩帶盡歡娛
Get up late and go early to sleep.	起晚眠常早

You loosen your belt to be comfortable (or take your pants off, but this is excluded in decent poetry). Your belt also grows loose when you lose weight, as you might do from worry or longing. It is the first which is the sole point of T'ao Ch'ien's line, and to be reminded here of the second meaning is a gratuitous irrelevance which can only mislead. Yet Ting Fu-pao quotes the couplet from the first of the Nineteen Old Poems[64]

You left and every day go farther from me,	相去日已遠
My garment's belt grows every day more slack.	衣帶日已緩

No doubt Ting Fu-pao did not misread the line or think of his quotation as an allusion to be read into T'ao's poem; he probably only wanted to show that he remembered another line with the words *huan* and *tai* in it, in addition to the more relevant Ts'ao Chih couplet which Ku Chih had cited:[65]

In their happiness they drink more than three cups	樂飲過三爵
And loosening their belts empty the dishes of dainties.	緩帶傾庶羞

Now this parallel does not constitute real allusion either, but belongs to my Fifth Type, where the identity is probably accidental but in any case was not intended to be noticed by the reader. It is not of the Sixth Type, for the two words together do not have any special meaning that is not directly apparent.

[63] No. 4 of the "Untitled Poems," Ting 4.5b.
[64] *Wen hsüan* 29.1b.
[65] "The Cither Song" 箜篌引, *Ts'ao Tzu-chien chi* 曹子建集 6.1a.

The next example comes from a poem I have already discussed, "Drinking Alone in the Rainy Season." The line "Can Heaven have departed from here" was puzzling, because it needed something beyond the overt statement to make sense in context, and this prompts one to look for an allusion. It was found, not in a verbally identical passage, but in a statement in *Chuang tzu* which made clear the association with the preceding line. Ku Chih, however, was struck by a much more similar line from Yang Hsiung's *Canon of the Great Mystery*, and he quoted the whole passage:[66]

> Approach Mystery and Mystery will draw near. Keep away from Mystery and Mystery will keep its distance. It is like the sky all cerulean—east, south, west, north: wherever you look up, there it is; but if you look down you do not see it. *Can it be that Heaven rejects man?* It is man that has kept himself away."

Only one word (*jen* "man" for *tz'u* "here") differs from T'ao Ch'ien's in the sentence *t'ien ch'i ch'ü jen tsai*, but for all the verbal likeness, this passage is one hundred percent irrelevant. "Can Heaven have rejected this (=wine)?—No, Heaven has not." Such a reading has nothing to do with this poem.

This last category of allusion (the non-allusion) is clearly a trap for the unwary, but so must some of the more valid types of allusion appear to be, at least as I have presented them. There is often an element of play involved in the use of allusion: the writer at once showing off and giving his reader a chance to match wits with him. This is the allusion as ornament. Where it becomes an organic part of the poem, it cannot be so easily dismissed. Sometimes, like ambiguity, it enables the poet to say more than one thing at once. It can include an ironical comment on the overt statement. It is allusion of the third and fourth types that is most likely to be fruitful in this way. The second type is at best a convenient shorthand, a way of saying much with one or two words. The fifth type is capable of subtlety and nuance: its contribution to the poem is less obvious and hard to assess, but still appreciable. The limitations of the first type I have already mentioned, and the seventh type makes at best a negative contribution.

[66] *T'ai hsüan ching* 楊雄, 太玄經 7.12b (*SPTK* edition).

I have limited this essay to examples of allusion from the works of a single poet. A wider selection of materials might well lead to another and more manageable scheme of arrangement; it would be useful to test it against writings of another period.

Some Literary Qualities of the Lyric (*Tz'u*)

by James J. Y. Liu

The purpose of this essay is to examine some of the distinctive qualities of the *tz'u* as a literary genre, especially in comparison with the *shih*. I shall endeavor to show some of the potentialities and limitations of the *tz'u*, or, in other words, some of the things one can do in it and some of the things one cannot. For the sake of euphony, I shall use the word "lyric" for *tz'u* and refer to *tz'u* writers as "lyricists" or "lyric poets."

It may be well to point out that to treat the lyric as a literary genre is not to deny the fact that it was originally written to existing music and meant to be sung. The reasons why I have chosen not to discuss the musical aspects of the lyric (apart from my lack of competence in musicology) are two. First, the music used for the lyric in T'ang and Sung times has not survived, except for seventeen tunes composed by Chiang K'uei 姜夔 (*ca.* 1155–*ca.* 1235) for his own lyrics and written down in a notation which has not been deciphered to the satisfaction of all,[1] so that discussions on the music of the lyric are bound to be, for the most part, highly hypothetical. Second, many lyricists themselves regarded the lyric simply as a poetic genre. This already happened even when the music was available, as in the case of Su Shih

---

[1] But cf. Julan Chao Pian, *Sonq Dynasty Musical Sources and Their Interpretation,* Harvard-Yenching Institute Monograph Series 16, 1967. Previous attempts to decipher Chiang K'uei's notation include Hsia Ch'eng-t'ao 夏承燾 *T'ang Sung tz'u lun-ts'ung* 唐宋詞論叢 (Shanghai 1956) pp. 94–144; Yang Yin-liu 楊蔭瀏 and Yin Fa-lu 陰法魯, *Sung Chiang Pai-shih ch'uang-tso ko-ch'ü yen-chiu* 宋姜白石創作歌曲研究 (Peking 1957); Jao Tsung-yi 饒宗頤 and Chao Tsun-yüeh 趙尊嶽 *Tz'u-yüeh ts'ung-k'an* 詞樂叢刊 (Hong Kong 1958), pp. 3–72 79–94; Ch'iu Ch'iung-sun 丘瓊蓀, *Pai-shih Tao-jen ko-ch'ü t'ung-k'ao* 白石道人歌曲通考 (Peking, 1959).

(1037–1101), and when we come to Ming, Ch'ing, and twentieth-century lyricists, who had no idea what the original music sounded like but only "filled in" the words according to the standard metrical patterns, to them the lyric could not be anything more than a literary form.

In general, on the basis of their respective attitudes to their medium, all lyricists may be divided into four groups, regardless of their assignment to various "schools" in traditional literary history and criticism. The first group consists of those who used the lyric as a literary form for a limited range of themes and moods, and who, at the same time, paid sufficient attention to the auditory qualities of the words so that they would be suitable for singing. Most T'ang, Five Dynasties, and early Sung lyricists, with the notable exception of Li Yü (937–978) in his later phase, would seem to fall within this group—poets like Wen T'ing-yün (812?–870?), Wei Chuang (836–910), Feng Yen-ssu (903–960), Yen Shu (991–1055), and Ou-yang Hsiu (1007–1072). The second group consists of poets who took the lyric simply as another poetic form and expressed themselves freely in it, without much concern whether their works were singable. Their lyrics may be called "literati lyrics" *(wen-jen tz'u)*, if we may coin a phrase *à la* "literati painting" *(wen-jen hua)*. The most outstanding representatives of this group are Su Shih and Hsin Ch'i-chi (1140–1207). To the third group belong lyricists who regarded the lyric primarily as a song-form and were preoccupied with the musical effects of their words, so much so that they were sometimes ready to sacrifice the meaning for the sound.[2] Among these lyricists may be mentioned Chou Pang-yen (1056–1121) and Chang Yen (1248–*ca.* 1320). The fourth group comprises the numerous writers who, since Southern Sung times, have imitated the works of earlier lyricists, syllable for syllable and tone for tone, without knowing the musical reasons which originally prompted the use of particular syllables and tones. Since we are here concerned with the literary qualities of the lyric, more attention will be paid to the first two groups of lyric poets.

---

[2] The notorious story about Chang Yen's father Chang Shu who changed the word *shen* to *yu* and then to *ming* has been told repeatedly (e.g. in Hu Shih 胡適, *Tz'u-hsüan* 詞選, Preface p. 10), but the reasons for the changes have been variously explained. Cf. Hsia Ch'eng-t'ao, *ut supra*, pp. 84–5; Ts'ai Chen 蔡楨, *Tz'u-yüan shu-cheng* 詞源疏証 (Nanking, 1932), Preface by Lü Ch'eng 呂澂, p. 2, and *hsia*, pp. 9–10; Ts'ai Te-an 蔡德安 *Tz'u-hsüeh hsin-lun* 詞學新論 (Taipei, 1963), p. 31.

Being a poetic genre, the lyric naturally partakes of the basic nature of all poetry, which I conceive of as a double exploration of "worlds" and of language. Briefly, by a "world" is meant a fusion of external reality and inner experience, and by "exploration of worlds" is meant the poet's probing into the nature of reality as well as his own mind. As for "exploration of language," this refers to the poet's search for the right words to embody the poetic world in a complex verbal structure.[3] These two aspects of poetry are of course closely interrelated, and in the ensuing discussions no attempt will be made to draw a rigid line between the two. Nevertheless, it may be useful to concentrate on one at a time.

It would be difficult to demonstrate which poetic worlds explored by the lyric are unique to it. We may, however, recognize some worlds as typical of the lyric but rarely seen in poetry in the *shih* genre. Moreover, though similar worlds may be explored in both genres, the mode of exploration may be quite different. Finally, we may, with less difficulty, point out certain worlds known to the *shih* but practically absent in the lyric.

One of the most familiar worlds in lyric poetry is that dominated by romantic love. This world is, of course, not unknown in the *shih*, but there it is not as frequently encountered as in the lyric, nor is it often presented with such directness and frankness as in the latter. Li Shang-yin's love poems in the *shih* form, for instance, have a degree of complexity and obliquity seldom seen in love lyrics. This is not to say that all love poems in lyric meters are similar; on the contrary, the world of love is explored in various ways by the lyricists. Let us begin with a lyric in which love is treated in a light-hearted manner:

Chang Pi (10th century)　張泌
To the tune *Huan Hsi Sha*[4]　浣溪沙

In the evening I chase a perfumed carriage into the
　　Phoenix City;[5]　　　　　　　　　　　　　晚逐香車入鳳城
The east wind lifts the light embroidered curtain aslant;　東風斜揭繡簾輕
Slowly she turns back her lovely eyes with a smile.　　慢回嬌眼笑盈盈

[3] For fuller discussions cf. James J. Y. Liu *The Art of Chinese Poetry* (London and Chicago, 1962; paperback edition Chicago, 1966) pp. 91–100; "Towards a Chinese Theory of Poetry," in *Yearbook of Comparative and General Literature* (Bloomington, Indiana, 1966), pp. 159–165.

[4] Since the names of the tunes are for the most part irrelevant, they are left untranslated.

[5] The capital city.

No word has passed between us—what shall I do?　　消息未通何計是
Let me pretend to be drunk and follow her along!　　便須伴醉且隨行
Vaguely I here her say, "What nerve!"　　　　　　依稀聞道太狂生

(李一氓校, 花間集, 香港, 1961, 頁 72)

The poet makes no pretense that this is anything more than a casual
love affair, and adopts a deliberately frivolous and gay tone, which is
emphasized by the colloquialism at the end. (Cf. below, p. 147.) The
scene is presented from the lover's point of view, but not without a
sense of the dramatic: the poet is emotionally involved in the situation he presents, yet at the same time sufficiently detached to be
aware of the part he is playing. This self-awareness, it seems to me,
saves the lyric from sentimentality.

In contrast, we may turn to a lyric which reveals the world of love
in a serious light:

> Ku Hsiung (10th century) 顧敻
> To the tune *Su Chung-ch'ing* 訴衷情

In the endless night, having deserted me, where have
　　you gone?　　　　　　　　　　　　　　　　永夜抛人何處去
No news of your coming!　　　　　　　　　　　絕來音
　　My eyebrows knit—　　　　　　　　　　　眉斂
My perfumed chamber closed,　　　　　　　　香閣掩
The moon is about to set.　　　　　　　　　　月將沈
How can you bear not to seek me?　　　　　　怎忍不相尋
How lonely in my quilt!　　　　　　　　　　怨孤衾
Only if you bartered your heart for mine　　　換我心爲你心
Would you know how much I miss you!　　　始知相憶深

(同上, 頁 131)

Here, the sufferings of a woman in love, as imagined by the poet,
are expressed in a forthright manner. The somewhat disjointed
structure seems to suggest the woman's restless and incoherent
feelings; the shift of focus back and forth between external objects
and inner feelings further reveals the world of tormented passion.
The last two lines remind one of Sir Philip Sidney's famous poem,
"My true-love hath my heart and I have his,"[6] but whereas Sidney's
poem rests on a rhetorical conceit intellectually worked out, the

---

[6] *The Golden Treasury*, no. xxiv.

present poem is a passionate cry, moving in its simplicity and naiveté.[7]

In many lyrics love is shown frankly in its erotic aspect, such as in the following one by Liu Yung (1004?–1054?):

To the tune *Chü-hua Hsin*　柳永　菊花新

Before lowering the perfumed bed-curtain to express her love,	欲掩香幃論繾綣
She knits her eyebrows, grieving that the night is too short.	先斂雙蛾愁夜短
She urges the young gallant to go to bed	催促少年郎
First, so as to warm up the mandarin-duck quilt.[8]	先去睡鴛衾圖暖
A moment later she puts down her unfinished needlework,	須臾放了殘鍼線
And removes the silk skirt, to indulge in passion without end.	脫羅裳恣情無限
Let me keep the lamp before the curtain	留取帳前燈
That I may look at her lovely face from time to time!	時時待看伊嬌面

(唐圭璋編, 全宋詞, 北京, 1965, 頁 38)

There is a shift from the objective to the subjective. In the first stanza, the poet describes himself in the third person as "the young gallant" *(shao-nien lang),* but at the end of the second stanza he speaks in his own person. (Although in the original the first person pronoun is not used, the tone is unmistakably that of the first person, while the woman is referred to by the third person pronoun *yi.)* Consequently the amorous atmosphere is increasingly intensified and a world of erotic intimacy is revealed.

In other lyrics we enter a world in which love is mingled with nostalgia and regret. A typical example is this one by Ch'in Kuan (1049–1100):

To the tune *Man-t'ing Fang*　秦觀　滿庭芳

The mountains are rubbed with light clouds,	山抹微雲
The sky adheres to the withering grass—	天黏衰草
The sound of the painted horn ceases at the watch-tower.	畫角聲斷譙門

---

[7] Cf. Wang Kuo-wei 王國維, *Jen-chien tz'u-hua* 人間詞話 (with notes by Hsü T'iao-fu, Peking, 1955) p. 47.

[8] A brocade quilt with two holes for the necks.

Let me stop my travelling boat	暫停征棹
And share a farewell cup with you for a while!	聊共引離尊
How many bygones of Fairyland—	多少蓬萊舊事
To look back is futile:	空回首
Nothing but scattered mists remain.	烟靄紛紛
Beyond the setting sun:	斜陽外
A few dots of cold crows,	寒鴉數點
A river winding round a solitary village.	流水遶孤村
Soul-searing	銷魂
Is this moment when	當此際
The perfume bag is secretly untied,	香囊暗解
The silk girdle lightly parted.	羅帶輕分
All this has merely earned me the name	謾贏得青樓
Of a fickle lover in the Green Mansion!	薄倖名存
Once gone, when shall I see you again?	此去何時見也
In vain are our lapels and sleeves stained with tears.	襟袖上空染啼痕
Where the heart saddens,	傷情處
The tall city wall stops one's gaze;	高城望斷
The lights are up: it is already dusk.	燈火已黃昏

(毛晉編, 宋六十名家詞, 四部備要本, 淮海詞, 頁 9 左)

In this lyric, the poet's sorrow at parting from someone he loves, his nostalgia for past joys, and his regret over the irrevocable passing of time and the inevitability of separation, are all perfectly blended with the external environment to form a special world. He first sets the scene effectively by using unusual verbs: the mountains are "rubbed" *(mo)* with clouds and the sky "adheres" *(nien)* to the grass (lines 1–2); then he introduces the theme of parting (lines 4–5). Lines 6–8 recall romantic affairs of the past: P'eng-lai, which I have translated as "Fairyland," may be used as a poetic euphemism for a house of courtesans, and since the poet uses the more explicit expression "Green Mansion" *(ch'ing-lou)* in the next stanza, it seems safe to take P'eng-lai in the same way. It is further possible that the allusion here might refer to a girl whom Ch'in Kuan is said to have met when he was lodging in a house called P'eng-lai Ko.[9] The "mists" in line 8 seem to have a double function: they represent bygone events which now appear vague and distant, but at the same time they may also describe the actual scenery. Thus we are imperceptibly

---

[9] Cf. Hu Yün-yi 胡雲翼, *Sung tz'u hsüan* 宋詞選 (Peking, 1962) p. 97.

brought back to the present. The remaining lines of the first stanza, much admired for their evocative power, paint a vivid scene of desolation, which enhances the mood of sadness. The setting sun, as is often the case in Chinese poetry, is associated with decline; the "cold" *(han)* crows and the "solitary" *(ku)* village further add to the feeling of desolation and chilliness. (Some editions have "myriad dots of cold crows" instead of "a few dots of cold crows"; I prefer the latter reading, which is more in keeping with the prevailing atmosphere.)

The second stanza expresses parting sorrow in a more direct manner. The "perfume bag" being untied is probably a souvenir being given by one of the lovers to the other. The "silk girdle," as Hu Yün-yi pointed out,[10] is a symbol of love, since it was common for lovers to tie a love-knot *(t'ung-hsin chieh,* or "same-heart knot") with a girdle. Thus, line 4 means that the lovers are too lightly parted, just as the girdle is. Lines 5–6, derived from Tu Mu's well-known lines

Awaking from a ten year old Yang-chou dream,
I have earned the name of a fickle lover in the Green Mansion[11]

suggest regret as well as irony: the poet has had no success in his official career, and even in love he is not credited with sincerity and seriousness. Circumstances oblige him to leave against his will, but the girl thinks he is merely fickle. The last three lines add a final touch to the landscape and bring the mood of the poem to the verge of despair—night has fallen and people in their homes have lit up their lamps, but the poet has to depart, leaving behind all that he loves in the darkness which his gaze cannot penetrate.

Many lyricists explore a world more elusive than that of love, one inhabited by groundless melancholy and ennui:

Yen Shu　　　　　　　　晏殊
To the tune *T'a So Hsing*　踏莎行

Little path scattered with red,	小徑紅稀
Fragrant country covered with green.	芳郊綠遍
By the lofty tower the trees display their dark, dark color.	高台樹色陰陰見
Why does the spring wind allow the willow catkins	春風不解禁楊花
To pelt one's face, helter-skelter, as one walks along?	濛濛亂撲行人面

[10] *Ibid.*
[11] Tu Mu 杜牧, *Fan-ch'uan wen-chi, wai-chi* 樊川文集, 外集 *(Ssu-pu pei-yao* ed.) p. 8a.

Emerald leaves hide the orioles,   翠葉藏鶯
Vermilion curtains bar the swallows.   朱簾隔燕
The incense smoke quietly follows the gossamers to
    drift in the air.   爐香靜逐游絲轉
As one awakes from a sorrowful dream induced by wine, 一晌愁夢酒醒時
The slanting sun is still shining on the deep, deep
    hidden courtyard.   斜陽却照深深院
                (全宋詞, 頁 99)

We need not follow those commentators who take this lyric as a
political allegory, but only see how the world of groundless melancholy is embodied in its verbal structure. The first three lines not only
paint a highly colorful scene but also hint at the passing away of
spring, for only a few fallen red petals remain on the little path while
the countryside is covered with lush green grass and the trees have
grown thick foliage. As the speaker walks along, he is annoyed by the
floating willow catkins that keep striking gently against his face, like
persistent melancholic feelings that refuse to be brushed aside. He
thereupon indulges in the poetic fancy that it is the wind that is to
blame for failing to forbid the catkins to annoy people.

In the second stanza the scene gradually moves to the interior. We
first observe the leaves outside the window, then the curtains that
exclude the outside world, and finally the intimate atmosphere inside
the room. The contrast between "emerald" *(ts'ui)*[12] and "vermilion"
(chu) in the first two lines of this stanza echoes the similar contrast
between "red" *(hung)* and "green" *(lü)* in the opening lines of the
first stanza, while the incense smoke that follows the gossamers to
drift in the air parallels the floating willow catkins and again seems to
symbolize elusive feelings of listlessness and melancholy. At the same
time, the incense smoke also suggests the extreme stillness and privacy
of the room. The last two lines heighten the mood of melancholy by
hinting at the regrettable passing of time. The world of this lyric is
subtle and fragile. It embodies a highly refined consciousness and
reflects a cultured and leisured environment.

Some lyric poets of the Southern Sung and later periods explored
worlds even more exquisite and rarefied than that revealed in the
lyric just quoted. An example may be given from Chiang K'uei:

[12] I am aware that strictly speaking *ts'ui* is not "emerald" but "green jade," but a little
poetic license might not be out of place.

To the tune *Nien-nu Chiao* 姜夔　念奴嬌

Preface.　Formerly I sojourned at Wu-ling, where the office of the judicial intendent[13] of the Hupei Circuit was located. By the ancient city wall were wild waters, and tall trees that reached towards the sky. With two or three friends I daily rowed a boat thereabout, and drank when we approached the lotus flowers. The atmosphere was secluded and peaceful, unlike the human world. When the autumn water was almost dried up, the lotus leaves stood about eight or ten feet above the ground. Thereupon we sat in a row under them. When we looked up, we could not see the sun; and when a cool wind came slowly, the green clouds moved by themselves. Occasionally, from where the leaves were sparse, we could peep at the pleasure-seekers in their painted boats, which also provided us with some enjoyment. Travelling to and from Wu-hsing, several times I have been able to wander among the lotus flowers. Also I sailed over the West Lake one night and found the view wonderful beyond compare. I therefore wrote these lines to describe it.

（序）予客武陵，湖北憲治在焉。古城野水，喬木參天。予與二三友日蕩舟其間，薄荷花而飲。意象幽閒，不類人境。秋水且涸，荷葉出地尋丈。因列坐其下。上不見日，清風徐來，綠雲自動。間于疏處，窺見遊人畫船，亦一樂也。揭來吳興，數得相羊荷花中。又夜泛西湖，光景奇絕。故以此句寫之。

Stirring the red: a single boat. 鬧紅一舸
I remember when I came 記來時
I had mandarin ducks for my companions. 曾與鴛鴦爲侶
Over the thirty-six pools where no one comes, 三十六陂人未到
Water-pendants and wind-skirts are numberless. 水佩風裳無數
The emerald leaves blown cold, 翠葉吹涼
The jade-like faces wearing off wine, 玉容消酒
Then a sprinkling rain over the rushes and reeds. 更洒菰蒲雨
Charmingly swaying, 嫣然搖動
The cold fragrance flies up my lines of verse. 冷香飛上詩句

[13] The expression *hsien-chih* in the preface refers to the office of the *t'i-tien hsing-yü*, translated by E. A. Kracke, Jr. as "judicial intendent" (*Translations of Sung Civil Service Titles*, Paris, 1957, p. 40).

At sunset	日暮
The green canopies stand erect.	青蓋亭亭
Not having seen your lover,	情人不見
How can you bear to leave, treading the ripples?	爭忍凌波去
I only fear your dancing dress will easily fall in the cold,	只恐舞衣寒易落
And grieve to enter the west-wind-blown southern shore.	愁入西風南浦
Tall willows casting shades,	高柳垂陰
Old fish puffing at the waves,	老魚吹浪
Invite me to stay and dwell among the flowers.	留我花間住
How many spreading leaves?	田田多少
How frequent the return journey by the sand?	幾回沙際歸路
	(同上，頁 2177)

In spite of the preface, which contains some surprisingly irrelevant
information, the meaning of this lyric is far from clear. We need not
try to find allegorical meanings in it; on the other hand, to say that
this is nothing more than a description of lotus flowers would be as
naive as to say that Mallarmé's *L'Après-midi d'un faune* is nothing more
than a description of a faun. Let us examine the poem closely and see
what different levels of meaning it may yield. The first line, by using
the striking verb "stirring" *(nao)* and the metonymy "red" for "red
lotus flowers," and by following this with the simple phrase "one
boat" *(yi ko)*, produces an immediate impact and makes us see the
boat making its way amidst innumerable lotus flowers. The next two
lines recall the past, with a possible allusion to a love affair, since
mandarin ducks of course symbolize lovers. The rest of the first
stanza may apply to the present as well as the past. The poet is as
much concerned with describing the lotus flowers he now sees as with
recollecting all the other lotus flowers he has seen before. In line 5,
the "water-pendants" and "wind-skirts," as Hu Yün-yi has noticed,[14]
are derived from a poem by Li Ho, where they are used to describe
the famous courtesan Su Hsiao-hsiao. By using these images, Chiang
K'uei implicitly compares the lotus flowers to beautiful women, while
likening the water drops on them to white jade pendants and the
leaves to wind-blown skirts. Line 7, "The jade-like faces wearing off
wine" *(vǔ jung hsiao chiu)*, is highly ambiguous. It could mean that the

[14] Hu Yün-yi *ut supra*, p. 347.

jade-like beauty of the lotus makes one sober up from the effect of wine, as suggested by Lo Ch'i,[15] or that the color of the lotus is compared to a woman's fair complexion from which the flush caused by wine is fading, as suggested by Hu Yün-yi.[16] In line 9, the word translated here as "charmingly," *yen-jan*, could be used to describe a "charming smile," and this is how Hu Yün-yi took it,[17] but I do not think it quite fits with "swaying" *(yao-tung)*, unless we think of the personified flower as smiling charmingly and swaying gracefully at the same time. Anyway, this implied personification is transferred from the flower itself to its fragrance, which "flies up" the poet's lines of verse. This striking conceit brings together the concrete and the abstract, the physical world and the mental. Furthermore, line 10 can bear two meanings: first, the poet's lines of verse have captured the beauty of the lotus, and second, the verse itself has a kind of chastened beauty comparable to the cold fragrance of the flower.

In the second stanza, the poet first compares the lotus leaves to canopies; then the flower to a goddess, by using the phrase "treading the ripples" *(ling po)*, which alludes to Ts'ao Chih's famous *Goddess of the River Lo (Lo-shen fu)*. He imagines the flower-goddess as about to leave, walking gently above the ripples, and asks her how she can bear to do so, not having seen her lover. He then shows apprehension that the coming of cold weather may cause the flowers and leaves to fall. Here the image of the dancing dress echoes the "wind-skirts" in the first stanza. Line 6 in the second stanza, *ch'ou ju hsi-feng nan p'u*, is syntactically ambiguous, and the translation given above is only one of several possible interpretations. Lines 7–9 refer more explicitly to the poet himself and suggest his reluctance to leave the scene. Line 10 in the original does not contain the word "leaves" but refers to them by the phrase *t'ien-t'ien*, which is used in an anonymous song to describe the lotus leaves spreading on the water—a device of substitution which Hu Shih condemned.[18] The last line is again ambiguous. Literally it says, "How many times the return road by the sand?" It could mean, "How many times have I returned home by the sandy shore?" or, "How many times shall I return by the sandy shore?"

[15] Lo Ch'i 羅泌, *Chung-kuo li-tai tz'u-hsüan* 中國歷代詞選 (Hong Kong, 1962), p. 272.
[16] Hu Yün-yi, *ut supra,* p. 347
[17] *Ibid.*
[18] Hu Shih, *ut supra,* p. 306

I have tried to preserve this ambiguity to some extent in the translation without making the line utterly meaningless in English.

Now that we have considered the individual lines, what total meaning can we see in the poem? What kind of world emerges from its verbal structure? We might say that it is mainly a world of imagination and aesthetic sensibility, with some emotional elements, though attenuated. On the physical level, the poet describes the lotus flowers, both the ones now present and those he has seen before. On the imaginary level, the lotus is personified and deified, and certain emotions are attributed to it. This may be regarded as a means by which the poet transfers his own emotions to the flower so as to externalize them and make them objects of aesthetic contemplation. On the aesthetic level, the poet's sensitivity to the beauties of Nature and his enjoyment of quiet pleasures are brought out by images appealing to several senses, yet he is not merely interested in sensuous enjoyment as an end in itself but consciously transforms it into artistic creation, as borne out by the line, "The cold fragrance flies up my lines of verse."

To turn to a totally different world, we may examine two lyrics which embody heroic sentiments. The first one is by the patriotic poet Lu Yu (1125–1209):

    To the tune *Su Chung-ch'ing*   陸游　訴衷情
    Formerly I travelled ten thousand miles in search of   當年萬里覓封侯
        honor;   匹馬戍梁州
    Riding alone, I guarded the Liang-chou frontier   關河夢斷何處
    Where have my broken dreams of passes and rivers   塵暗舊貂裘
        gone?
    Dust has darkened my old sable coat.

    The Tartars have not been vanquished,   胡未滅
    My hair has turned grey,   鬢先秋
    My tears flow in vain.   淚空流
    Who would have thought in this life   此生誰料
    My heart should be with the T'ien Mountains,   心在天山
    My body grow old by the shore?   身老滄洲

                                                       (同上, 頁 1596)

In the first line, the phrase translated here as "in search of honor," *mi feng-hou* (literally, "in search of a marquisate"), is a conventional expression for seeking official honors by military deeds. In the second line, Liang-chou (in modern Shensi) not only represents the distant frontier, but also refers specifically to Lu Yu's military career in that part of the country in his middle age. The next line may be taken to mean, "Not only have my exploits among mountain passes and rivers gone like dreams, but even these dreams are broken and cannot be found." In line 4, the poet alludes to Su Ch'in who, according to tradition, wore out his sable coat while trying to persuade the King of Ch'in to adopt his policies, without success. By means of this allusion, Lu Yu shows his own frustrated ambition to help recover North China from the Tartars. This feeling of frustrated ambition is further emphasized in the second stanza, where the contrast between the remote T'ien Mountains and the shore of the lake where the poet is living in retirement sums up the tragedy of his life. (The expression *ts'ang-chou* or "by the shore" refers to the life of a recluse.)[19]

The second lyric embodying heroic sentiments is by Huang Shu (1131–1199):

To the tune *Chiang Shen Tzu* 黃銖 江神子

The autumn wind whistles and stirs, the setting sun is red;	秋風嫋嫋夕陽紅
The twilight mist thickens,	晚烟濃
The evening clouds multiply.	暮雲重
Ten thousand blue mountains—	萬疊青山
Beyond which a returning wild goose cries.	山外叫歸鴻
Alone I mount the tower three hundred feet high,	獨上高樓三百尺
Leaning on the jade rail,	憑玉楯
Gazing at the tiered skies.	睇層空
In the human world, days and months quickly pass by.	人間日月去匆匆
Over the green *wu-t'ung*	碧梧桐
The west wind again sighs.	又西風
Amidst wanderings north and south,	北去南來
How many heroes have been worn out?	銷盡幾英雄
Let me throw my jade goblet beyond the heavens!	擲下玉罍天外去
So many things	多少事
Must remain unsaid!	不言中

(同上，頁 1677)

---

[19] For some of these notes I am indebted to Hu Yün-yi *op. cit.*, p. 253.

Here, too, the poet expresses his frustrated heroic aspirations and his regret over the passing of time, and these sentiments are intermingled with the natural surroundings to form a poetic world. The sad atmosphere evoked by the autumn wind, the setting sun, the twilight mist, and the evening clouds, is in consonance with the poet's state of mind, while the cry of the wild goose echoes his own sighs. The tower on which he stands is as lofty as his aspirations, and the *wu-t'ung* trees seem to share his apprehension of decline. Toward the end of the poem, the poet abandons all hope, including the hope of expressing himself fully, with a gesture that reminds one of Byron's "Dash down yon cup of Samian wine!"

The examples given above represent only a few of the worlds explored and embodied by lyrics, but space does not allow me to give more. I must refrain, for instance, from attempting to illustrate the world of inconsolable grief and utter despair in the last lyrics of Li Yü, or those of stoic calm and of irrepressible *joie de vivre* in some of the lyrics of Su Shih. Now, what of the worlds not found in the lyric? First of all, the lyric does not appear to be used as a vehicle for the exploration of social and political realities. There are no lyrics comparable to Tu Fu's war poems or Po Chü-yi's "New *Yüeh-fu*" ballads. This is probably because the lyric by its nature is unsuited to extended narrative or satire. (Satirical lyrics do exist, but they are rather rare.) Secondly, we do not find lyrics that explore the world of the supernatural, as do many of the poems of Li Ho and Li Shang-yin. Thirdly, we miss the world of self-oblivious contemplation of Nature, which we find in the best poems of T'ao Ch'ien and Wang Wei. Of course, there are many lyrics which sing of the beauties of Nature, but it seems to me they never quite efface the poet's own personality so as to present Nature as an end in itself. The lyrics of Chu Tun-ju (*ca.* 1080-*ca.* 1175), for instance, may bear a superficial resemblance to the Nature poems of T'ao Ch'ien, but in fact they are so self-consciously other-worldly that they sound more like popular Taoist songs, using the stock symbols of the fisherman, the wine jug, plum blossom, and so on. In brief, the lyric remains primarily a personal kind of poetry, a vehicle for the exploration of private worlds of sentiment and sensibility, rather than a social, religious, didactic, or intellectual kind of poetry. Even in Su Shih's and Hsin Ch'i-chi's lyrics on historical or philosophical themes, it is the poet's consciousness at the moment, rather than external reality, that engages our attention. On a lower level, though there are lyrics written for social occasions and Court ceremonies, they tend to be hackneyed and uninspired, much inferior to poems of a similar nature in the *shih* form. On the whole, as an exploration of worlds, the lyric is more limited in range than the *shih*, though the former has extended the realm of poetry into previously unknown worlds, some of which are more stark and intimate than those revealed in *shih* poetry, while others are more elusive, subtle, and rarefied.

In its exploration of language, the lyric vastly enlarged the boundaries of Chinese poetry and made possible almost infinite varieties of subtle and complex verbal structure. This exploration may be considered in various aspects, such as diction, syntax, rhythm, imagery, and allusions. Here we can only focus our attention on each aspect briefly.

As far as diction is concerned, three different styles in lyrics are discernible—the colloquial, the elegant, and the bookish. Naturally, similar styles can be found in the *shih*, but in the lyric there is a tendency to go to extremes, especially in the case of the colloquial style. The three styles are not mutually exclusive. The same lyricists may use two or three different styles in different lyrics, or even mix them in the same lyrics. For example, Liu Yung, Ch'in Kuan, and Huang T'ing-chien (1045–1105) all wrote some highly refined lyrics as well as some extremely slangy ones, and Hsin Ch'i-chi employed all three types of diction in his lyrics. The style of a lyric depends on the kind of world it embodies, and vice versa. Thus, lyrics embodying the world of love often adopt the simple colloquial style; those exploring complex worlds of ennui or aesthetic sensibility naturally employ the elegant style and those embodying philosophic attitudes often use the bookish style. For example, Chang Pi's love lyric given above uses the colloquial expression *t'ai k'uang-sheng* (literally, "a bit too wild"), where, according to Hu Shih, the colloquial suffix *sheng* is like the modern *hsieh* and means "a bit."[20] A more radical example of colloquialism is the following lyric by Huang T'ing-chien, which is so slangy that the translation here is only tentative:

[20] Hu Shih, *ut supra*, p. 22.

To the tune *Kuei-t'ien Lo Yin*　黃庭堅　歸田樂引

Facing the view, I'm getting thinner and thinner.	對景還銷瘦
I've been teased and made a fool of by this man.	被箇人把人調戲
I too have a heart—	我也心兒有
He misses me and calls me;	憶我又喚我
When he sees me, he scolds me:	見我嗔我
Good Heavens! How can one put up with this?	天甚敎人怎生受
We were lucky to have been intimate;	看承幸廝勾
Now, before the wine cups, I knit my brows again.	又是樽前眉峰皺
This man wonders why—	是人驚怪
He misled me and made me give way to him.	寃我忔懰就
"Let go! Give up!" (I said to myself)	拚了又捨了
"Certainly this time it's all over!"	定是這回休了
But when we meet, it's just the same as before.	及至相逢又依舊

(同上, 頁407, 參看張相, 詩詞曲語辭滙釋, 北京, 1953, 頁394, 627)

In contrast to this colloquial style, the original language of the lyrics by Ch'in Kuan, Yen Shu, and Chiang K'uei given above is elegant and oblique. As for the bookish style, Hsin Ch'i-chi and his followers habitually use such prose particles as *yeh* 也, *yi* 矣, *erh* 耳, *tsai* 哉 etc., and quote phrases from works like the Confucian *Analects* and the *Chuang Tzu*. Since the quotations would require too much annotation, I shall not give any examples.

Just as in diction, so in syntax the lyric displays opposite tendencies. While some lyrics follow the syntax of colloquial speech or of classical prose, others are often syntactically even further removed from prose than are poems in the *shih* form. For instance, in the lyric by Huang T'ing-chien just quoted, we find such colloquial constructions as *pei ko jen pa jen t'iao-hsi* (line 2, literally, "By (such) a man one is teased and fooled") and *ting-shih che-hui hsiu-liao* (line 12, literally, "Certainly, this time it's all over"). Such lines are impossible in the *shih*. Examples of lines following the syntax of classical prose may be given from Hsin Ch'i-chi. In one lyric he writes, *pei, ju lai ch'ien* 杯汝來前 ("Cup, come you forward"); in another one, *lai, wu kao ju* 來吾告汝 ("Come, let me tell you"); in yet another one, *yi shou t'ui sung yueh ch'u* 以手推松曰去 ("With [my] hands [I] push the pine, saying, 'Go!'").[21] Lines like these are never found in Regulated

---

[21] *Ch'üan Sung tz'u* 全宋詞, pp. 1915, 1944.

Verse *(lü-shih)*, though in the Ancient Verse *(ku-shih)* of such poets
as Han Yu we may find similarly constructed lines, which read more
like prose than verse. As for lyrics employing a syntax far removed
from that of prose, several features are notable. First, we often
encounter lines which contain no verbs, such as *shui-ching lien li po-li
chen* 水晶簾裏頗黎枕 ("Inside the crystal curtain, a glass pillow"), and
shou li chin ying-wu, hsiung ch'ien hsiu feng-huang 手裏金鸚鵡, 胸前繡鳳
凰 ("In [her] hands a golden parrot, on [her] bosom embroidered
phoenixes"). These lines are taken from the lyrics of Wen T'ing-
yün,[22] who is particularly fond of using lines consisting of a series of
noun phrases which build up an elaborate picture and produce what
might be called a "pointillistic" effect. Second, the syntax of some
lyrics can be highly flexible and ambiguous. In Su Shih's famous
lyric "Recalling Antiquity at Red Cliff" *(Ch'ih-pi huai ku)* to the tune
Nien-nu chiao occur the lines, *to-ch'ing ying hsiao wo, tsao sheng hua fa*
多情應笑我, 早生華髮 *(Ch'üan Sung tz'u*, p. 282). Some commenta-
tors take *to-ch'ing* ("[one who is] affectionate or sentimental") as the
subject and think it refers to the poet's deceased wife,[23] so that the two
lines mean, "The affectionate one [i.e. my wife] should laugh at me
for growing grey hair so early." Others take *to-ch'ing ying hsiao wo* to
be an inversion of *ying hsiao wo to-ch'ing*, so that the lines mean,
"People should laugh at me [or, I should laugh at myself] for being
such a sentimentalist that I am turning grey so early."[24]

Personally I am in favor of the latter interpretation, but the
existence of the former shows the ambiguity of the syntax.

Of course, syntax is closely bound up with versification, and it is
the greater variety of metrical patterns which enables lyricists to use
certain syntactic constructions not possible in the *shih*. For example,
the meter *Ch'ai-t'ou Feng* requires that the last line of each of the two
stanzas should consist of three reduplicated monosyllables. Thus, in
a famous piece of Lu Yu, the first stanza ends with *ts'o, ts'o, ts'o*
錯錯錯 ("Wrong, wrong, wrong!") and the second with *mo, mo, mo* 莫莫
莫 ("Don't, don't, don't!").[25] In the meter *Yi Ch'in O*, in both stanzas
the second half of the second line is repeated to form the third line:

[22] *Hua-chien chi* 花間集. pp. 2, 13.
[23] Fang Tsu-shen 方祖燊 in *Ku-chin wen-hsüan* 古今文選 Vol. II (Taipei, 1957) p. 668.
[24] Hu Yün-yi, p. 76.
[25] *Ch'üan Sung tz'u*, p. 1585.

Attributed to Li Po 傳李白作 To the tune *Yi Ch'in O* 憶秦娥.

    The sound of the flute chokes.   蕭聲咽
    The Ch'in lady's dream breaks in the moonlight   秦娥夢斷秦樓目
      over the Ch'in mansion.
    The moonlight over the Ch'in mansion—   秦樓月
    Every year, the colour of the willows   年年柳色
    Induces parting sorrow at Pa-ling.   灞陵傷別

    On the Lo-yu Heights, the cool autumn season.   樂遊原上清秋節
    On the ancient road to Hsien-yang, news is cut off. 咸陽古道音塵絕
    News is cut off—   音塵絕
    The west wind, the fading sunshine,   西風殘照
    The mausolea and palaces of Han!   漢家陵闕

                     (萬樹, 詞律, 卷四, 頁 15, 右)

Another notable feature of the lyric affecting both syntax and versification is the fairly frequent occurrence of enjambment, as compared
with its relatively rare appearance in the *shih*. Examples can be
found in the lyrics by Liu Yung, Ch'in Kuan, Chiang K'uei, and Lu
Yu given above. Two more examples may be given from Hsin Ch'i-
chi:

    ying-hsiung wu mi   英雄無覓
    Sun Chung-mou ch'u   孫仲謀處
    (Nowhere to seek a hero
    [Like] Sun Chung-mou [Sun Ch'üan])[26]

and

    chin-lai shih chüeh ku-jen shu   近來始覺古入書
    hsin-cho ch'üan wu shih ch'u   信著全無是處
    (It is only recently that I began to feel that the books of the ancients,
    If you believe them, are no good at all.)[27]

Lines like these add to the variety and liveliness of the lyric as well as
its structural complexity. Some other syntactic features of the lyric
have been discussed by Wang Li[28] and will not be mentioned here.
    Since this short essay is obviously not the place to go into technical
details of versification, I shall content myself with a few general
observations. It is sometimes said that the lyric represents a liberation

---

[26] *Op cit.*, p. 1954.
[27] *Op cit.*, p. 1944.
[28] Wang Li 王力, *Han-yü shih-lü hsüeh* 漢語詩律學 (Shanghai, 1958), pp. 659–664.

from the restrictions of Regulated Verse. This may have been partially true when the lyric first evolved, but it is certainly not true of the
fully developed genre as a whole. Anyone who has attempted to
versify in both genres can bear witness to the relative ease (on the
purely technical level) of composing an eight-line poem with the
requisite tone-pattern and rhyme, as compared with the far more
exacting demands of lyric meters. Even a nodding acquaintance with
the intricate tone-patterns and rhyme schemes of the lyric will
convince one that this is anything but a "free" verse form. To take
just one example, whereas in the *shih* one need only distinguish between level *(p'ing)* and deflected *(tse)* tones, in the lyric one often has
to differentiate the three kinds of deflected tones *(shang, ch'ü* and
ju).[29] Some lyricists, such as the poetess Li Ch'ing-chao (1084–*ca.*
1151), paid attention to the qualities of consonants and vowels as
well as tones.[30] Indeed, both in her conscious exploitation of the
auditory effects of language and in her virtuoso performances, Li
Ch'ing-chao might well have been the envy of Edith Sitwell! In short,
the lyric has greatly enriched the auditory effects of Chinese poetry,
even when the actual music originally used is lost, and has created
more subtle and varied sound-patterns than the *shih.* Thus, although
lyric meters have strict and complicated rules, the genre as a whole
does afford the poet far more metrical patterns to choose from than
the *shih* does.

With regard to imagery, some lyricists (such as Wen T'ing-yün)
rely almost exclusively on imagery to reveal a poetic world through a
synthesis of the external and internal elements of life, while others
(notably Li Yü and Hsin Ch'i-chi) often dispense with imagery but
seek to achieve their poetic purposes largely by means of direct
expression, auditory effects, or allusions. On the whole, lyrics employing elegant diction involve frequent use of imagery, while those
in the colloquial and bookish styles use imagery but rarely or not at
all.

The use of imagery in the lyric does not differ radically from that
in the *shih,* though some types of imagery seem to be more common
in the former, or are at least considered more appropriate. For

---

[29] Cf. Wan Shu 萬樹, *Tz'u-lü* 詞律, *fa-fan* 發凡 (SPPY), pp. 7b–9a; Hsia Ch'eng-t'ao,
ut supra, pp. 521–89; Ts'ai Te-an, *ut supra,* pp. 80–86.

[30] Cf. *Li Ch'ing-chao chi* 李清照集 (Shanghai, 1962), pp. 9, 25, 31, 79.

example, in a lyric by Ch'in Kuan to the tune *Huan Hsi Sha* occurs
the well-known couplet

> *tzu-tsai fei-hua ch'ing ssu meng*   自在飛花輕似夢
> *wu-pien ssu yü hsi ju ch'ou*   無邊絲雨細如愁

(The freely flying flowers are as light as dreams; The endless threads
of rain, as fine as sorrow.)[31]

Here, the "tenor" and the "vehicle" of each compound image are
inverted: instead of comparing dreams to flowers and sorrow to rain,
the poet does the opposite. Such images, highly admired as they are
in a lyric, would be considered too "delicate and ingenious" (*hsien
ch'iao* 纖巧) if used in Regulated Verse, let alone Ancient Verse.[32]
Compound images of substitution (those which replace the tenor by
the vehicle) also seem to be more common in the lyric than in the
shih. In one lyric alone, the one by Chiang K'uei given above, we
find several examples: "wind-skirts," "jade [-like] faces," "green
canopies," "dancing dress," all of which are substitutes for "lotus
flowers" or "lotus leaves." The excessive use of this kind of imagery
led to the writing of so-called "lyrics describing objects" (*yung-wu
tz'u* 詠物詞), in which one is not supposed to mention by name the
object described but has to resort to ingenious substitutes. This
naturally turned a legitimate poetic device into a form of riddle. A
similar device which also appears frequently in the lyric is metonymy,
such as the use of "red" for "flowers" and "green" for "grass" in the
lyric by Yen Shu, or the use of "red" for "lotus" in that by Chiang
K'uei. These two devices—imagery of substitution and metonymy—
have produced numerous clichés beloved by many latter-day lyricists
but rightly condemned by such critics as Wang Kuo-wei.[33] On the
other hand, one need not reject all lyrics that use familiar imagery,
for though they may lack originality in conception they often possess
a kaleidoscopic kind of novelty—the constituent elements are the
same, but the resulting pattern is different each time.

In the preceding pages I have merely touched on a few aspects of
the lyric, and the generalizations I have made would obviously need

[31] *Ch'üan Sung tz'u*, p. 460.
[32] Cf. Miao Yüeh 繆鉞, *Shih tz'u san lun* 詩詞散論 (Hong Kong, 1962), p. 6.
[33] Wang Kuo-wei, *ut supra*, pp. 20–21.

modification when applied to individual lyrics or lyricists. It is my hope to undertake a more detailed study of the lyric, as exemplified by major lyricists of the Sung period, along the lines suggested in the present essay.

Wu Wen-ying's
Tz'u: A Modern View
by Chia-ying Yeh Chao

For sheer bulk, the *tz'u* of Wu Wen-ying 吳文英, amounting to nearly 350 songs, are, with the exception of Hsin Ch'i-chi's, unequalled in the Southern Sung period. (Even so prolific a songwriter as Chou Pang-yen left less than 200.) Wu Wen-ying was not only a prolific writer, he was hardly excelled in technical skill or intellectual subtlety. He has never enjoyed Hsin Ch'i-chi's popularity, however, and critical opinion has been divided about the value of his work. Ever since Southern Sung times, Wu Wen-ying's *tz'u* have been misunderstood or simply not read at all. The oldest and most often repeated criticism comes from his contemporary, Chang Yen, who said in his *Tz'u Origins:*[1] "Meng-ch'uang's *tz'u* are like a fabulous building that dazzles the eyes, but when taken apart, the pieces do not fit." Even contemporary historians of Chinese literature still quote this remark in passing unfavorable judgment on Wu Wen-ying. Hu Shih, for example, in his *Anthology of Tz'u*[2] stated: "In all four of Meng-ch'uang's collections of *tz'u* there is hardly a single poem that is not a heap of allusions and clichés. What Chang Yen says (he quotes it) is quite right." Hu Yün-yi, in his *Studies in Sung Tz'u,* also works up to an appeal to Chang Yen's authority:[3] "There is one major flaw in Meng-ch'uang's *tz'u:* he is too addicted to allusions, too eager for ornamentation. This is a common fault among Sung *tz'u* writers, but it is most extreme in Meng-ch'uang. In his deter-

---

[1] Chang Yen 張炎, *Tz'u yüan* 詞源 B. 4 (*Tz'u-hua ts'ung-pien* ed.).

[2] Hu Shih 胡適, *Tz'u hsüan* 詞選 (Commercial Press, 1928), pp. 342–343.

[3] Hu Yün-yi 胡雲翼, *Sung tz'u yen-chiu* (Chung-hua shu-chü, 1929), p. 178.

mination to find an allusion, he pays no attention to the rhythm of the whole poem. Granted he gets some very good effects and writes some skillful lines, still they are only isolated beauties. He is quite incapable of creating a literary work through which flows a single emotional current. This is why he was criticized by Chang Yen. . . . ''

If we are to accept judgments like these, we must not expect much from Wu Wen-ying. For his anthology Hu Shih chose only two of his short verses, and one of them he omitted in his revised edition.[4] Hu Yun-yi was even more rigorous in applying his critical canon, for there is not a single poem by Wu Wen-ying in his *Hundred T'ang and Sung Tz'u*.[5] A more striking demonstration of critical disapproval would be hard to find.

This unfavorable opinion has not been universal, and there have been critics who praised him just as immoderately. Chou Chi (Ch'ing dynasty) gives him the most space in his *Anthology of Four Sung Tz'u Writers* and says:[6] "No one can equal Meng-ch'uang for elevation of thought or wide-ranging implications." Ko Tsai, in his *Seven Tz'u Writers*,[7] comes even more strongly to his defense, and Wu Mei, the modern critic, quotes Ko Tsai and adds his own praise:[8] "In fact Meng-ch'uang's genius was extraordinary and his poetry is by no means obscure. His great strength was precisely in letting profound ideas appear in the most extravagant passages; and one should not confuse profundity with obscurity. Chang Yen's criticism, comparing him with a fabulous building, is based on a lack of understanding. If you look at a whole poem, you find many unexpected insights, and if you take it line by line you also find excellences. The statement that the pieces do not fit is inappropriate."

All this praise was no doubt based on careful reading and a refined appreciation, but unfortunately it is couched in wholly abstract terms. As generalities they are fine, but they are not of the slightest help to anyone who does not already understand Wu Wen-ying's poetry, and some who cannot see what is so wonderful about it are

[4] *Tz'u hsüan* (revised ed.), pp. 344–345.
[5] *T'ang-Sung tz'u yi-pai shou* (Chung-hua shu-chü, 1961).
[6] Chou Chi 周濟, *Sung ssu-chia tz'u hsüan* (Hsin-hua shu-tien ed.), Preface, p. 3.
[7] Ko Tsai 戈載, *Ch'i-chia tz'u hsüan,* quoted in *Sung tz'u san-pai shou* (Kuang-wen shu-chü ed.), p. 328.
[8] Wu Mei 吳梅, *Tz'u-hsüeh t'ung-lun* 詞學通論 (*Kuo-hsüeh hsiao ts'ung-shu* ed.), p. 97.

likely to be goaded by such remarks into flat contradiction.[9] It is clear that evaluations so divergent must be based on quite different readings of the poetry, and so the first task of a would-be critic is to try to reach an understanding of each poem, which he will then share with his readers. What are needed and what are deplorably lacking are commentaries and exegesis. Chu Hsiao-tsang, after twenty years of study, during which he made four collations of Wu Wen-ying's *tz'u,* wrote a "small commentary"[10] limited to identifying personal and place-names and tracing a few allusions. It is no help to a beginner who tries to read this poetry, any more than Ch'en Hsün's "Explaining (Meng-ch'uang's) *tz'u,*"[11] which is so terse and enigmatic that the explanations are as hard to understand as the poems themselves.

There is no question but that Wu Wen-ying's poetry offers unusual difficulties; however, those same difficulties are very much a part of the interest and value of his poetry. The reader finds trouble, at least at the beginning, in devices of style and imagery which in modern times have become common in all the arts, not just poetry, and which are responsible for the charge of obscurity that is still brought against modern art. This explains why Wu Wen-ying was generally not understood or appreciated by Chinese critics in the past: his technique was simply at odds with traditional practice. But coming to modern readers in classical garb, something they are inclined to identify with a shroud, Wu Wen-ying has failed to find an appreciative audience among them as well. So the modern reader is likely to view him with distaste from a safe distance and then turn away before he can discover what he is missing. It is precisely

[9] Hu Yün-yi, for example (*Sung tz'u yen-chiu,* p. 179), after quoting Chou Chi's effusion ("His best *tz'u* shine with the radiance of heaven and the colors of clouds") comments: "This would serve as an appreciation of Chiang K'uei, but not of Wu Wen-ying." He adds, "Chou Chi gave Meng-ch'uang the leading position among his four *tz'u* writers and praised his 'unusual ideas and great beauties that maintain the rich texture of the Northern Sung.' This is piling exaggeration on top of exaggeration. Meng-ch'uang's *tz'u* wholly lack 'unusual ideas' and are even more devoid of any 'great beauties'. How can anyone say he 'soars to the skies and hides in the depths'?"

Hsieh Li-jo 薛礪若 says of Wu Wen-ying: "His talent was not great and his style is neither free nor powerful. He cannot approach Hsin Ch'i-chi, nor even tail along after Chiang K'uei. When Wu Mei spoke of his genius being extraordinary, he got it exactly backwards" (*Sung tz'u t'ung-lun,* p. 281).

[10] Chu Hsiao-tsang 朱孝臧, *Meng-ch'uang tz'u hsiao chien* 夢窗詞小箋.

[11] Ch'en Hsün 陳洵, *Hai-hsiao shuo tz'u* 海綃說詞.

because Wu Wen-ying combines classical and modern beauties—
and difficulties—that he falls between the two stools of ancient and
modern.

The most significant way in which Wu Wen-ying's poetry resembles modern poetry is in his complete indifference to the kind of
logical connections traditionally used in Chinese poetry. This
indifference leads to the confusing or intermingling of different times
and places in a way that generates obscurity, and the obscurity is
compounded by his creation of unorthodox and eccentric verbal
imagery. I would like to discuss each of these points in turn.

In traditional Chinese poetry, the structure of a poem is based
essentially on a logical sequence, whether the poem is narrative or
lyrical or descriptive of scenery. Long narrative poems have a beginning, a middle, and an end in logical temporal and spatial
sequence, for example, Ts'ai Yen's "Lament," the anonymous ballad
"The Peacock Flies. . . , " Tu Fu's "Northern March," and Po
Chü-yi's "Song of Everlasting Sorrow," all of which tell a consecutive story. Lyric poetry is equally direct and uncomplicated; cause
and effect are presented in directly intelligible terms: "Thinking of
you makes me old," "An empty bed is hard to keep alone," "Tears
fall like rain," "The departed grow every day more distant," "When
your griefs are many, you know the night is long"—these typical lines
from the "Nineteen Old Poems"[12] are all straightforward, immediately intelligible, and essentially logical. As far as descriptive
poetry is concerned, the critical verdict has always been for straightforward simplicity, ever since Chung Hung's expressed preference for
lines uncontaminated by allusion.[13] Wang Kuo-wei[14] objects to Chou
Pang-yen's line "Cassia flowers flow over the tiles" because of the
euphemism "cassia flowers" for "moonlight," and he quotes as
unexceptionable examples of description T'ao Yüan-ming's lines:[15]

> The mountain air is lovely as the sun sets,
> And flocks of flying birds return together.

[12] *Wen hsüan* 文選 (Yi-wen yin-shu-kuan ed.), 29. 1b, 2a, 3b, 4b.

[13] Chung Hung 鐘嶸, Preface to *Shih p'in* 詩品 (K'ai-ming shu-tien, 1930), p.
6b–7a.

[14] Wang Kuo-wei 王國維, *Jen-chien tz'u-hua* 人間詞話 (K'ai-ming ed.), pp. 20, 29.

[15] Ting Fu-pao 丁福保, *T'ao Yüan-ming shih chien-chu* 陶淵玥詩箋注 (Yi-wen yin-shu-
kuan ed.), p. 110.

It seems clear that Chinese poetry, whether narrative, lyrical, or descriptive, is most appreciated when it is intelligible in purely logical terms. Here Wu Wen-ying's *tz'u* are completely at variance with traditional critical standards. So Hu Shih, after quoting his poem on the magnolia,[16] could comment,[17] "This is a heap of clichés and allusions strung together without a particle of poetic feeling or a poetic concept to hold them together. First he talks about a person and then about the flowers, now about 'barbarian stench' and the Wu Park, and then the next thing we know he is in Hsien-yang seeing off a visitor." And Liu Ta-chieh, who quotes Hu Shih's comment, goes on to remark that Wu Wen-ying's poems are riddles. As an example he cites the *tz'u* "Kao-yang Pavilion"[18] and says,[19] "On the surface this is extraordinarily pretty, a 'fabulous building that dazzles the eyes,' but when you read it carefully, you discover that there are six or seven discrete parts without the slightest connection with one another, as though each were an independent entity rather than a unified poem. It lacks the wholeness and unity that are necessary qualities of a work of literature. It is quite as Chang Yen said: his poetry fails by having only the form without any internal coherence."

Obviously Wu Wen-ying's practice of merging time and space and confusing the real and the imagined has led to serious misunderstanding on the part of his readers, since even professional critics fall into the trap. It is inevitable that such a poet should be passed over by less experienced readers, repulsed by the external difficulties of his style and encouraged in their prejudice by the disapproval of such critics. But if we can take a new look at his poetry, not seeking for explanations in narrowly logical terms but trying to see how the emotional associations work, then we may uncover its extraordinary richness and beauty. Of the *tz'u* ("The Magnolia") so ruthlessly criticized by Hu Shih, the Ch'ing critic, Yang T'ieh-fu, said:[20] "The

[16] *Meng-ch'uang tz'u chi* (Shih-chieh shu-chü reprint of the Chiang-ts'un yi-shu ed.), p. 1a:瑣窗寒（玉蘭）.

[17] *Op. cit.*, p. 342.

[18] *Meng-ch'uang tz'u chi*, p. 91b:高陽台（落梅）.

[19] Liu Ta-chieh 劉大杰, *Chung-kuo wen-hsüeh fa-chan shih* 中國文學發展史 (Chung-hua shu-chü ed.), p. 261.

[20] Yang T'ieh-fu 楊鐵夫, *Meng-ch'uang tz'u hsüan chien-shih* 箋釋, I, 1, 2.

magnolia of the title is a symbol for the poet's departed mistress. In the first stanza he treats the woman in the guise of flower; in the second stanza he speaks about the woman directly." And Wu Mei has extravagant praise for the Kao-yang Pavilion poem that Liu Ta-chieh found so distasteful.[21] So when approached with the right expectations, these two poems do yield a satisfactory sense.

It is doubtful, however, whether Yang T'ieh-fu's method would lead everyone to a good understanding of Wu Wen-ying's poetry, for he uses the critical vocabulary (*pi* 比, *hsing* 興) associated primarily with the traditional interpretation of the *Classic of Songs*, bringing with it expectations that Wu Wen-ying seldom fulfills—for instance, the ideas of political loyalty and personal political aspirations that were read into the poems of the *Classic*.

Hu Shih's criticism itself suggests what is wrong with his reading: he finds no connection between the parts, because he is looking for the wrong kind of connection. Yang T'ieh-fu could see that the leap between the flower of the first and second lines and the woman of the third was not between two discrete things, but that the two were somehow one. The connection is not logical but associational. The poet, seeing the flower, remembers when the woman he loved was present, for at that time the flower and woman were together and in his mind remain inseparable. From the flower and the woman to the "barbarian stench" and the Wu Park may seem a bigger jump, but he is merely suggesting that the flower grew in the south. "Seeing a guest off in Hsien-yang" is an allusion to a line in a poem by Li Ho,[22] "The wilting orchid sees off the guest on Hsien-yang road." The flower calls up the whole idea of grieved parting, and Hsien-yang need not imply the city in Shensi itself, only the thing associated with it; nor does the "Wu Park" have to be the royal park of King Fu-ch'a of Wu. There is no occasion for annoyance with Wu Wen-ying for jumping around the map. This is not an example of confusing real places and real times, for here they are used symbolically, by way of allusion.

What would Hu Shih have made of lines like these?[23]

---

[21] Wu Mei, *Tz'u-hsüeh t'ung-lun*, pp. 97–98.

[22] *Li Ho ko-shih pien* 李賀歌詩編 (*SPTK* ed.), 2.1a: 金銅仙人辭漢歌.

[23] *Meng-ch'uang tz'u chi*, p. 3a: 霜葉飛（重九）.

> The painted fan sobs the cold cicada,
> Weary of dreaming, not knowing Man or Su.

The real and present cold cicada is juxtaposed with the real but past painted fan in present time and space, and the verb "sobs," which belongs with the "cold cicada," is placed after the "painted fan," fusing past and present through a subjectively interpreted sound. In the second line, "weary of dreaming" is the feeling experienced during the cold cicada's singing (present time), while Hsiao-man (or Fan-su) alludes (by way of two of Po Chü-yi's mistresses) to the girl who held the painted fan long ago. The two lines bring together objects and people and times associated in the poet's imagination in ways not subject to logical analysis. It is precisely in this illogical synthesis that the painted fan of Hsiao-man or Fan-su of long ago becomes the weary dream of today and sobs in the intermittent cry of the cold cicada. (For another example of Wu Wen-ying's inverted use of verbs see the last line of the *tz'u* "Music Fills the Sky" analyzed below.)

This first characteristic of Wu Wen-ying's poetry, the technique of fusing past and present, here and elsewhere, is something new in Chinese literature, but it has many parallels in modern Western literature and art—one thinks of Resnais' movies *(Hiroshima Mon Amour)*, of Faulkner *(The Sound and the Fury)*, not to mention Rimbaud and T. S. Eliot; in fact, it has become extremely commonplace in the twentieth century. So what in the past has seemed a major weakness in Wu Wen-ying's poetic technique today makes him interesting and accessible to modern readers, who from another time and another world than his can appreciate what he wrote.

The other characteristic of Wu Wen-ying's poetry is his creation of a new poetic vocabulary. Here again he relies on his own personal vision, in defiance of traditional expectations and logic. For convenience I shall use the term "verbal imagery" for this technique. In traditional Chinese literature the most respectable source of poetic vocabulary was the allusion. An allusion can be to a well-known anecdote, and then it requires that the reader supply as much of the story as is appropriate to the context of the poem. For example, take Li Shang-yin's lines:[24] "Miss Chia spied through the curtain on

---

[24] *Li Yi-shan shih chi* 李義山詩集 (*SPTK* ed.), 5.6a: 無題，二.

Clerk Han's youth;/Consort Fu left a pillow for the Prince of Wei's talents." Here the allusions are (1) to the daughter of Chia Ch'ung, who spied on her father's secretary, Han Shou, and fell in love with him;[25] and (2) to the story of Ts'ao Chih's supposed love affair with the Empress Chen as recorded in Li Shan's commentary on the *fu* "Goddess of the Lo River."[26] Li Shang-yin used these allusions to suggest a situation where a woman in love has made advances to a man, and his poem continues: "Don't let your susceptible heart vie with flowers in bloom,/For one inch of love-longing, one inch of ash." In such cases the allusion is part of the direct communication of the poem. An allusion can also be no more than a faint echo, a phrase used in an earlier text which the poet, perhaps unwittingly, incorporates in his own poem. Knowledge of the "source" serves only to reassure the reader that he is in the hands of an educated writer, one who has read the right books. From the rise of the Chiang-hsi school of poetry at the beginning of Southern Sung times, it became a critical doctrine that poets should find the vocabulary of their imagery ready-made. Huang T'ing-chien said of Tu Fu, meaning it as high praise, that he never used an expression that did not have its source[27]—in other words, that Tu Fu invented no unfamiliar imagery. The Ch'ing commentator Ch'ou Chao-ao set about proving the statement in his Tu Fu commentary, and you will find him supplying a wealth of gratuitous and quite unhelpful information about the most unremarkable piece of imagery. For example:[28] "On the River the waves couple with the sky in leaping,/Above the Pass wind-clouds touch the earth in casting shade." Here there is no anecdote or hidden meaning, just the Long River as Tu Fu saw it before him at K'uei-chou, and it is unlikely that he was thinking of any of the texts that Ch'ou Chao-ao quotes: first a line from a poem by Yü Yen: "From the Three Mountains the waves are high." Then *Chuang tzu*: "The Way couples with the sky." A poem by Yü Hsin: "In autumn air wind-clouds are high." A letter from the Han Emperor Wu to the Prince of Huai-nan: "Verging with the sky and touching earth." All that this proves is that before Tu Fu wrote his

[25] *Shih-shuo hsin-yü* 世說新語 *(SPTK* ed.), 3B.47ab.
[26] *Wen hsüan*, 19.7b.
[27] *Yü-chang Huang hsien-sheng wen chi* 豫章黃先生文集 *(SPTK* ed.), 19.23b.
[28] *Tu Fu yin-te*, 杜甫引得 2.467/32A/3: 秋興, 一.

poem, the combinations 波浪, 兼 (於) 天, 風雲 and 接地 had all occurred in texts that Ch'ou Chao-ao (and quite probably Tu Fu also) had read. But it has long been an expectation of readers of Chinese poetry that poets should not be innovators in the matter of vocabulary and imagery, and when they use allusions, that the allusions should be to familiar texts. The result is a poetry that is easy to understand. Wu Wen-ying's poetry conspicuously fails to conform to these expectations, and it is indubitably hard to understand. He is fond of allusions, but he alludes to unfamiliar texts, or worse, to stories and events which he did not himself learn from a written source. And in his use of imagery, he is likely to come up with something bizarre that he invented himself.[29]

For example, the second line of the "Magnolia" poem (the one Hu Shih objected to) reads 氾人初見. The Mao Chin edition has 記 *chi* for 氾 *fan*, and Hu Shih adopted that reading, which at first glance does seem to be better: "Remembering when she first appeared." This is not the only variant of the word *fan*. Another text writes 汜 *ssu*, which also makes sense as "river bank." The correct choice depends on recognizing a rather obscure allusion behind the expression *fan jen*. The story is told by the T'ang writer, Shen Ya-chih, under the title "An Account of the Unhappy Person by the Hsiang River."[30]

This tale is both remarkable and charming, but no one has written it down.... In the Ch'ui-kung period (685–689) a *chin-shih* of the academy named Cheng set out in the early morning on Bronze Camel Street. By the light of the moon he crossed the bridge over the Lo River. Hearing someone crying bitterly under the bridge, he dismounted to see who it was and found a young woman, who covered her face with her sleeve. She said, "I am an orphan. My elder brother looked after me, but my

[29] Shen Yi-fu 沈義父, *Yüeh-fu chih mi* 樂府指迷 (*Tz'u-hua ts'ung-pien*, II, 1) makes this criticism of Wu Wen-ying: "His weakness is in using allusions and imagery too obscure for anyone to understand." Cheng Wen-cho 鄭文焯, *Meng-ch'uang tz'u chiao-yi*, B. 19 (appended to *Meng-ch'uang ssu kao* in *Ssu-ming ts'ung-shu*) also criticized him in similar terms. Hu Yün-yi (*op. cit.*, p. 55) quotes Shen Yi-fu with approval and adds, "There is hardly a single long *tz'u* of his which can be read."

[30] Shen Ya-chih 沈亞之, *Shen Hsia-hsien chi* 沈下賢集 (*SPTK* ed.), 2.14ab. The word *fan jen* on its first occurrence is written *ssu jen* in this edition. There are also variant forms in the *T'ang tai ts'ung-shu* and *Kuan-ku-t'ang hui-k'o* 觀古堂彙刻 versions of this story, but *fan jen* is the most common orthography.

sister-in-law was bad-tempered and treated me harshly. Today I was
going to drown myself and in my misery was just waiting here a
minute." "Would you care to come home with me?" the young man
asked. She replied, "Even as your slave or concubine, I would not
mind." So they lived together. He called her *fan jen,* "the woman
adrift." She could recite the "Nine Hymns" of Ch'u and the "Summons
to the Soul" and the "Nine Arguments." Moreover, she could
compose tunes in the Ch'u style and write the loveliest sad songs. No
one was her equal. After a few years the young man went off to
Ch'ang-an. On the eve of his departure she said, "I am a relative of
the dragon of the Hsiang River. He sent me away in exile and I went
with you. Now the years of my banishment are up and I cannot stay
with you any longer, so I wish to say farewell." And she clung to him
weeping. He was unable to detain her, and she left.

Some ten-odd years later his elder brother was Prefect of Yüeh-
chou. On the Third Month Festival they climbed the Yüeh-yang
Gate-tower and looked out over the Isle of O. As they were feasting
and drinking the young man sang sadly:

> Feelings unfathomed
> Like waves surging
> As I remember the happy time
> On the Three Hsiang.

Before the song was finished, a gaily-painted boat came floating toward them. It carried an ornamented tower over one hundred feet high,
on which someone was dancing. She looked very unhappy and in
appearance resembled the woman adrift. In a moment the waves
rose and crashed angrily, and it was not seen where the boat went.

Wu Wen-ying's *tz'u* about the magnolia is written in remembrance
of his departed mistress, and the allusion to the woman adrift *(fan
jen)* is an appropriate way of intensifying the feeling he wants to
communicate. The line "The Woman Adrift first appears" refers in
the first place to today's flower, and so reminds him of the first time
long ago when he saw the woman who resembled the flower. Moreover, the woman was like the Woman Adrift of the story in her
beauty, her susceptibility, and above all, in the fact that she is now

separated from him. Flower and person are fused in these four words, which carry an extraordinary weight of suggestion. The misprint in the Mao Chin text transforms a subtle and profound expression into a shallow and obvious one. For the "Woman Adrift" not only refers to the person, it also serves as a symbolical term for the flower, while "I remember her as she first appeared" can refer only to the woman. No wonder that Hu Shih found the poem abrupt in its transitions and was oblivious to its beauty.

For another example of a faulty reading which obscures an allusion on which the point of a line depends, see lines 7–8 of "Music Fills the Sky" that follows. Like the preceding, the allusion is one not easily accessible or likely to be known to most readers. Such passages have been neglected by the commentators, not because they are obvious but for the opposite reason, as is shown by the tendency of editors to emend. Aside from the fact that the emendation makes no sense in context, it destroys the whole point of the line. So faulty texts have compounded the difficulty of understanding and appreciating Wu Wen-ying's *tz'u*, but the fault lies primarily with editors and commentators, and it is hardly fair to blame the poet for things that he simply did not write.

Each reader, of course, brings his own standard of erudition to the poetry he reads. What to one reader is obscure, even willfully so, to another may be commonplace. The first example, from a story by Shen Ya-chih, is not so well known as the allusions in Li Shang-yin's lines, coming from such texts as the *Shih-shuo hsin-yü* or Li Shan's *Wen hsüan* commentary and familiar to every literate person. However, even Shen Ya-chih's story hardly counts as obscure, at least not to Wu Wen-ying's contemporaries. His works were printed in Northern Sung times,[31] and the *fan jen* allusion also occurs in a *tz'u* by Chou Mi[32] (1232–1309?): "After years the *fan jen* appears again" (here also the term *fan jen* is used of a flower). And the allusion in the *tz'u* discussed below is merely using a bit of local color, familiar to Wu Wen-ying as a native of the place and also no doubt to the friend for whom he wrote the *tz'u*. Certainly he was not trying to make his poetry unintelligible.

[31] The *SPTK* edition is a photo reprint of a Sung Yüan-yu (1086–1093) edition, so the story circulated in print before Wu Wen-ying's time.

[32] Chou Mi 周密, *Ts'ao-ch'uang tz'u* 草窗詞 (*Kuo-hsüeh chi-pen ts'ung-shu* ed.), p. 47.

One might also say a word in defense of the poet's right to the vocabulary which he finds adequate and appropriate to his purposes. What he has to communicate is hard enough to get on paper, without limiting himself to the lowest common denominator of his potential readers' knowledge and intelligence. He should not sacrifice the unique meaning-loaded allusion that fits his needs just because one or another reader will predictably fail to recognize it. One can imagine Milton's reaction to the limitations which our modern education would like to impose on his use of classical allusion. Wu Wen-ying's fondness for allusions is not in itself a positive virtue, but, granted that he uses them skillfully, his poetry cannot with justice be called a mere "heap of allusions and clichés."

The other obstacle to understanding Wu Wen-ying's poetry is his unusual poetic diction and imagery. Take the lines:[33] "If flying reds were to go to the bottom of the lake,/Gliding through green waves are all the sorrowful fish." The expression "sorrowful fish" is quite without precedent. In Chinese writing generally, swimming fish are taken as symbols for a life of freedom and contentment, from the *Classic of Songs*[34] "Eagles fly and fish leap" and Chuang Tzu's[35] "In the moat the fish rejoice" to T'ao Yüan-ming's[36] "Standing by the stream I am abashed at the free-swimming fish," and Tu Fu's[37] "In the fine drizzle the fish come out" or Su Tung-p'o's[38] "Up winding reaches fish leaped," and Chiang K'uei's[39] "Old fish blowing the waves"—in all these lines the fish is untrammeled and carefree. In the face of this well-established tradition, Wu Wen-ying invents the phrase "sorrowful fish," which most readers will take as arbitrary and incongruous.

We must read the term in the context of the whole poem, which is pervaded by a tone of profound melancholy, where "the east wind

---

[33] *Meng-ch'uang tz'u chi,* p. 91a: 高陽台（豐樂樓）.

[34] *Shih ching,* No. 239/3.

[35] *Chuang Tzu chi-chieh (ch'iu shui)* 莊子集解（秋水） (Shih-chieh shu-chü ed.), p. 108.

[36] *T'ao Yüan-ming shih chien-chu,* p. 87: 始作鎮軍參軍經曲阿.

[37] *Tu Fu yin-te,* 2.372/9A/6: 水檻遣興, 一.

[38] *Su Tung-p'o yüeh-fu chien* 蘇東坡樂府箋 (Commercial Press ed.), 1.52b: 永遇樂詞.

[39] *Pai-shih Tao-jen tz'u chien-p'ing* 姜夔, 白石道人詞箋平 (Commercial Press ed.), p. 84: 念奴嬌.

hastens the declining sun's departure" and "beside the lamp I lean
on my pillow; it is raining outside, the incense burns." And added to
the loneliness, sickness: "emaciated beside the stream." In such a
mood and in such a setting, it is easy to transfer one's own feelings
even to inanimate nature, and it becomes particularly effective when
the conventionally cheerful fish are also infected with the poet's
gloom. The pathetic fallacy is not uncommon in Chinese poetry. Li
Ho writes:[40] "If the sky has feelings, the sky is too old," and Li
Shang-yin:[41] "Catkins scatter and threads bind, until the sky too is
confused." Here the ordinary impersonal sky is as subject to aging
as the poet or is as confused as he. No wonder, with the flying red
petals falling into the water and sinking to the bottom, that the
living, active fish swimming in the lake could become aware of the
passing of spring, and we should be prepared to let them share the
poet's own feelings about the event.

Another example of unconventional verbal imagery is:[42] "On
Arrow Creek a sour wind impales the eyes,/Creamy water stains the
flowers' stench." The "sour wind" is not Wu Wen-ying's own
invention, having been used first by Li Ho[43] and borrowed from him
by Chou Pang-yen,[44] but it is still a long way from the conventional
epithets applied to the wind, such as "cold" 寒 or "warm" 暖, as it is
ordinarily perceived through the sense of touch. "Sour" is of course
primarily a taste, which goes with vinegar or green plums. But in
Chinese usage it is also applied to sensations, usually unpleasant,
experienced in other parts of the body than the mouth; a "sour
pain" is a standard term for a muscular ache. The "sour wind" is a
sharp wind which is perceived as unpleasant as it blows in the eyes,
making them smart and water.

The creation of expressions like "sour wind" is a product of a poet's
special sensitivity to the world and of his ability to find adequate
verbal equivalents for his experience. Not all poets are creative in
this way, and Wu Wen-ying's fondness for borrowing from Li Ho

---

[40] *Li Ho ko-shih pien* (Chung-hua shu-chü ed.), 2.1a: 金銅仙人 ...
[41] *Li Yi-shan shih-chi* (Chung-yung ed.), 4.1a: 燕台詩, 一.
[42] *Meng-ch'uang tz'u chi*, p. 99a; cf. below.
[43] *Li Ho ko-shih pien, loc. cit.*
[44] Chou Pang-yen 周邦彥, *P'ien-yü chi* 片玉集 (*SPPY* ed.), 6.3.

(already remarked by Cheng Wen-cho[45]) shows them to be kindred spirits. Wu Wen-ying also makes his own innovations in these two lines. The "flowers' stench" (花腥), for example. The usual words favored by poets for the odor of flowers are those meaning "sweet-smelling" 芬, 芳, 馨, 香, etc. The word "stench" is used for strong-smelling things like fish or meat. In the present context the word is extremely evocative and carries a considerable weight of suggestion. The poem is written on the site of the ancient palace of Wu. The poet imagines that the flowing stream still carries the slops of the palace ladies, their bath water, redolent of their creams and unguents. As a result, it is not unadulterated flower fragrances that one smells; they are contaminated with the traces of face cream and powder, which naturally bring to the nostrils a fragrance not purely of flowers.

But the word carries yet another suggestion. This site of the old Wu palace has often been the scene of revolution and battles, of pillage and desolation as well as of prosperity and opulence. The poet today finds in the odor of the flowers another odor, that of bloodshed and decay, and this too is carried by the "stench." In this one word is combined the poet's feelings about the bygone palace ladies and the vicissitudes of time, the transience of beauty and power alike. It may be an unusual and almost shocking combination (stench of flowers), but it is justified by the effect achieved. It certainly cannot be dismissed as arbitrary or as a deliberate attempt by the poet to annoy.

So much in the way of generalities; let us now see how the bits and pieces of Wu Wen-ying's "fabulous structure" fit together to make a whole. I have chosen two *tz'u* for exegesis: "Music Fills the Sky" and "Eight-Rhymed Kanchou Song." Each is presented first in a close translation, followed by the Chinese text and a line-by-line commentary.

To the Tune "Music Fills the Sky"   齊天樂

On Climbing to the Grave of Yü with Feng Shen-chü   與馮深居登禹陵
   Events of three thousand years beyond the last crow;   三千年事殘鴉外
   Wordless, weary, I lean against an autumn tree.   無言倦憑秋樹。
   The flowing water changes channels,   逝水移川

---

[45] Cheng Wen-cho, *op. cit.*, "Much of his vocabulary comes from Chang-chi's (i.e. Li Ho's) poems, with the result that his constructions are bizarre. Today readers seldom look for the source and mistakenly suspect him of being too obscure" (quoted by Lung Mu-hsün 龍沐勛 in his *T'ang-Sung ming-chia tz'u hsüan*, p. 269).

High hills turn to valleys—   高陵變谷
How can one tell it was Holy Yü?   那識當時神禹。
Dark clouds, strange rain,   幽雲怪雨。
Green cress wets the empty rafter   翠荇澄空梁
In the depth of night flown away.   夜深飛去。
Wild ducks rise in the blue sky,   雁起青天
A few lines of writing, perhaps where concealed   數行書似舊藏處。
  of old.

Long we sit, quiet, by the western window,   寂寥西窗坐久
Friends who seldom meet,   故人慳會遇
To talk and trim the lamp together.   同翦鐙語。
Accumulated moss on the fragmented stone,   積蘚殘碑
Shattered scepter, broken circlet: 零圭斷璧
Repeatedly rub away the world's dust.   重拂人間塵土，
Frost reds stop dancing,   霜紅罷舞。
But still the mountain color is ever green   漫山色青青
Misty morning, hazy evening.   霧朝煙暮，
Springtime boats, tied to the bank,   岸鎖春船
Picture flags resounding devotional drums.   畫旗喧賽鼓。

The subtitle of this *tz'u* states that it is for Feng Shen-chü (Feng Ch'ü-fei, *chin-shih* 1241), a friend of many years' standing to whom Wu Wen-ying dedicated another *tz'u*.[46] Feng Ch'ü-fei resigned his post in the Imperial Family School in 1256 to protest the emperor's appointment of Ting Ta-ch'üan 丁大全 as political counsellor of the left.[47] This *tz'u* is written in a mood of high seriousness which a man like Feng Ch'ü-fei might be expected to appreciate.

The title further mentions Yü's grave, which the two men visited together. Yü is of course King Yü, the founder of the Hsia dynasty and controller of the flood, a ruler who brought order to a land racked by natural calamity. He is supposed to have died on Kuei-chi Mountain (in what is now Shao-hsing hsien, Chekiang province), while on a tour of inspection of Yüeh, and to have been buried there.[48] His temple was restored early in the Northern Sung period[49]

---

[46] *Meng-ch'uang tz'u chi*, p. 77b: 燭影搖紅（餞馮深居）.

[47] Feng Ch'ü-fei 馮去非, biography in *Sung shih* 宋史 (T'ung-wen ed.), 425.9ab.

[48] According to *Yüeh chüeh shu* 越絕書 (*SPTK* ed.), 8.65ab.

[49] *Ta-Ming yi-t'ung chih* 大明一統志 (Wen-hai ed.) 45.3014. The restoration was in the Chien-te period (963–967).

and was no doubt still there when Wu and his friend visited it; in fact he seems to allude to it directly in the poem.

The poem takes the reign of King Yü as its point of departure, "three thousand years" being approximately the period elapsed since his time. Of course three thousand is at once the most general and the most tradition-loaded of all large numbers ("three" and "thousand").[50] Three thousand years ago puts Yü well back in the mists of antiquity; at the same time it invests the poem at the start with an air of seriousness and of purpose.

The line continues with the enigmatic words *ts'an ya wai* "beyond the last crow," presumably based on what the poet saw as he reached the top of the mountain. What the words suggest is more explicitly stated in a couplet of Tu Mu:[51] "The empty sky is pale, pale; the solitary bird has vanished,/Ten thousand years of antiquity evaporate like this." The "last crow" is like the "solitary bird," suggesting that it was the only one left, and now even it is gone (or about to go). The word "beyond" is used in a similar way in Ou-yang Hsiu's lines:[52] "Where the level moor ends, the spring hills lie;/The traveller is beyond even the spring hills." Reading all this into Wu Wen-ying's line, we get something like "the last traces of the one remaining crow vanish into the pale immensity of the sky, and the events of the past three thousand years are even more irretrievably gone." The seven words of this line blend time and space, past and present, to create an impression of infinite distance and utter solitude. But what specifically was the setting? The poet had climbed a hill to visit the grave of King Yü, and it was Yü who inspired his admiration and regret. Of all the sage rulers of Chinese tradition, it was Yü who worked most unremittingly for the salvation of mankind and whose achievements were the greatest. He inspired another Sung poet, Hsin Ch'i-chi, to write:[53]

> Enduring, an achievement for all time,
> Unflagging, the bitter labor in his own day.
> (Because of it) fishes plunged into the depths

[50] Cf. L. S. Yang, "Numbers and Units in Chinese Economic History," in *Harvard Journal of Asiatic Studies*, 12 (1949), 218.

[51] *Fan-ch'uan wen-chi* 樊川文集 (*SPTK* ed.), 2.7a.

[52] *Sung tz'u san-pai shou* (Kuang-wen shu-chü ed.), p. 35.

[53] *Chia-hsüan tz'u pien-nien chien-chu* 稼軒詞編年箋注 (Chung-hua shu-chü ed.), p. 532.

And mankind lived on the level land.
The red sun still sinks in the west
And white waves always flow east.
It is not Gold Mountain I am looking at,
I am thinking of Great Yü.

In King Yü's time the people were plagued by flood waters and
wild beasts, and it was Yu who restored order to the world—fishes
plunged into the depths, birds and beasts returned to their proper
places, and mankind lived on the level land. The conditions were
then right for mankind to enjoy peace and prosperity, it was an
enduring achievement for all time, and all that it cost was one man's
dedicated effort. Today, "The red sun still sinks in the west,/White
waves always flow east," just as they used to (thanks to Yü), but
present-day troubles—war and social upheavals—are a thousand
times worse than the flood waters and wild beasts of antiquity. And
who today has the strength and the will to play the role of Yü and
save mankind from its troubles? This is what made Hsin Ch'i-chi
think of Yü as he faced Gold Mountain and this is why Wu Wen-ying
reflects on three thousand years of the past as he watches the last
crow disappear.

But today there is no King Yü. The crow is gone, and in the
vastness of sky and land what can a man hold on to? "Wordless,
weary, I lean against an autumn tree." It was Confucius who said,
"I would prefer not to talk,"[54] and the lady Hsi who said, "What
more is there to say?"[55] when she felt that she had disgraced herself.
The reason why the poet is wordless is that he cannot bear to say
directly and cannot express completely what is troubling him. All
that he can do is lean against an autumn tree, overcome by his
feelings. Of course, he may also be tired from the climb, as Yang
T'ieh-fu suggests.[56] But he has carried with him on that climb the
weight of three thousand years of human suffering and is in sore need
of relief, of some secure resting place. And what does he find? An
autumn tree, bare of foliage. The emotional impact of the line is
achieved entirely by indirection.

[54] *Lun yü*, 17/17.
[55] *Tso chuan,* Chuang 14.
[56] *Op. cit.,* 1.14.

He continues:

> The flowing water changes channels,
> High hills turn to valleys—
> How can one tell it was Holy Yü?

There is an echo of the "events of three thousand years" of the first line: it is the changes and transformations of three thousand years which he now views as he leans, weary, against the autumn tree. How many times has the east-flowing river changed its channel, while hills have eroded away and become valleys? The work of Yü, accomplished at what expense of effort, a work so vast that he must be called a god, "holy," a work which was to be an "enduring achievement for all time,"—all has been altered beyond recognition; the channel he dug for the River, the hills he bored through, all are gone: "How can one tell it was Holy Yü?" It is not the disappearance of the physical traces of his effort that distresses the poet, it is the accompanying changes in the human condition which are implied, and the fact that things are getting worse.

The next three lines of the poem seem on first reading to have nothing much to do with his theme. In fact, it is this sort of thing that has given occasion for the criticism of Wu Wen-ying's poetry as "superficial," "confused," and "obscure."

> Dark clouds, strange rain,
> Green cress wets the empty rafter
> In the depth of night flown away.

These lines have also been taken as an example of his remarkable poetic skill, "Bizarre concepts, beautiful colors, ascending to the sky and plumbing the depths."[57] The key to this admittedly obscure passage is the word "rafter," which must belong to the temple of Yü built beside the grave, about which there is a legend recounted in the Ming Gazetteer:[58] "There is a *mei*-wood rafter in Yü's temple. When they were building the temple in Liang times, a sudden rainstorm

---

[57] Chou Chi, *Sung ssu chia tz'u hsüan*, p. 7.
[58] *Ta-Ming yi-t'ung chih*, 45.3012.

floated a beam to the site, and this was the *mei*-wood rafter."[59] It further quotes the Illustrated Record of Ssu-ming 四明圖經: "On top of Ta-mei Mountain there is the *mei*-tree. It supplied the rafter for Yü's temple in Kuei-chi. Chang Seng-yu painted a dragon on it, and nights when there was a rainstorm, it would fly into Mirror Lake and fight the dragon there. Afterward, people noticed that the rafter was dripping wet. At first they were frightened at the prodigy and chained the rafter to a pillar. Although the rafter there today is from another beam, it is still fastened with a chain in memory of the event."[60] It is not surprising that Wu Wen-ying, a Ssu-ming man himself, would have known the legend of the rafter "in the depth of night flown away," and it clearly explains these otherwise puzzling lines, all except the "green cress."

I had originally thought of the kind of painted scene one sees on rafters in palaces and temples and took the word *p'ing* to mean "duckweed," as one detail of the painting. But the orthography of the word *p'ing* is a variant form which occurs in the "Heavenly Questions" *(T'ien wen)*, where Wang Yi's commentary explains it as the "God of Rain" 雨師.[61] This gives a satisfactory reading, "Green Raingod moistens the empty rafter," if one takes the epithet "green" as a bit of poetic license, as Li Ho spoke of the "whiteness" of the autumn wind.[62] But the real solution turned up in a reprint of a Southern Sung edition of the *Kuei-chi Gazetteer,* where the entry on Yü's temple reads:[63] "Twelve miles southeast stands Yü's temple. . . . When repairing it in Liang times, they lacked one rafter. In a sudden rainstorm a log came to hand in a lake, which they used to make the rafter. This was the *mei*-wood rafter. Nights when there is a great rainstorm the rafter is apt to disappear, and when it comes back again there are water plants on it. People believed it to be supernatural and fastened it with a great iron chain, but it still disappears

---

[59] Although written with the word *mei* 梅 (plum tree), it is certainly not a beam fashioned of fruit tree wood. Yang T'ieh-fu (*op. cit.*, p. 14) identified it with *nan-mu* 楠木, a cedar-like wood.

[60] *Ta-Ming yi-t'ung chih,* 45.3016.

[61] *Ch'u tz'u (SPTK* ed.), 3.18a.

[62] *Li Ho ko-shih pien,* 2.4b.

[63] *Kuei-chi chih* 會稽志 (Ts'ai-chü-hsüan 采鞠軒 1808 reprint of a Sung Chia-t'ai [1201–1204] ed.). It has a preface by the poet Lu Yu 陸游 (1125–1210).

sometimes." This passage is similar to the one quoted in the *Ming Gazetteer,* omitting the part about the painting and the dragon fight. Together, they supply the necessary information for a correct reading of the line. For the poet, it was no doubt all part of a commonly known legend, and there was no question of one or more written sources to which he was alluding.

The next line is also about something directly observed: "Wild ducks rise in the blue sky." From this we know that it is daytime and that the "depth of night" in the preceding line is not part of the present time of the poem; in fact, this abrupt transition throws into relief the unreality of the mythological passage, and we can see that the language is in keeping with the subject.

The next line, "A few lines of writing, perhaps where concealed of old," is first of all the sort of "sky-writing" that migrating ducks perform, something which Wu Wen-ying mentions in another poem:[64] "Who wrote the poem on this landscape?/Wild ducks scribbling across the tower." It also is related to the subject of his poem. The *Ming Gazetteer* says:[65] "Stone Casket Mountain . . . is shaped like a casket. Tradition has it that when Yü completed his labors to control the flood, he stored his books there." Another legend of Stone Casket Mountain recorded in the *Ch'ing Gazetteer*[66] says that Yü found a golden tablet with jade writing there. In any case, the wild ducks are flying off across the sky looking like a couple of columns of writing. Where they are headed is Stone Casket Mountain where Yü's books were once hidden, and now all that is left are the bird hieroglyphs and no longer any sign of Holy Yü. It is another reminder of those three thousand years and the changes they have brought.

The entire first stanza is written from the point of view of the poet without reference to his companions. With the second stanza, Feng Ch'ü-fei is introduced: "Long we sit, quiet, by the western window, / Friends who seldom meet, / To talk and trim the lamp together."

[64] *Meng-ch'uang tz'u chi,* p. 91.
[65] *Ta-Ming yi-t'ung chih,* 45.2996.
[66] *Ta-Ch'ing yi-t'ung chih,* 179.8.

These lines incorporate an allusion to Li Shang-yin's poem:[67] "When will we trim the lamp together by the western window/And talk about the time it rained at night on Pa-shan?" In Li Shang-yin's poem the meeting is the longed-for happy situation which has yet to occur, but here, although Wu Wen-ying and his friend are together, they are quiet, even lonely. They have been sitting there a long time, not ready for bed, but like Tu Fu and his wife reunited after long separation:[68] "The night grows late, we light a lamp/Face to face, it is as in a dream." Or in another poem where Tu Fu celebrates a reunion with a friend he has not seen for twenty years:[69]

> Friends have trouble meeting
> Just like morning and evening stars.
> On this auspicious night
> We share the light of the lamp.
> The time of youth did not last long;
> Both of us have grey hair now.

The feelings conveyed by the lines "as in a dream," "like morning and evening stars," and "the time of youth did not last long"— these are reason enough for them to sit quietly. When Wu Wen-ying continues with "Friends who seldom meet,/To talk and trim the lamp together," he is expressing the same sentiment as Tu Fu's "friends have trouble meeting," and "the night grows late, we light a lamp."

Following this account of meeting after long separation come the incongruous lines: "Accumulated moss on the fragmented stone,/Shattered scepter, broken circlet:/Repeatedly rub away the world's dust." At first glance these seem to have absolutely nothing to do with the lines immediately preceding, a characteristic example of what is commonly regarded as Wu Wen-ying's obscurity. The first two lines give a feeling of shreds and fragments and evoke a host of historical memories. The initial problem is to establish what the lines refer to: the "thick moss on the fragmented stone" should be the stone over Yü's grave, the one used as an anchor in lowering the coffin (窆石). The *Ming Gazetteer* quotes an "old source" which refers to the anchor-stone at Yü's grave and says that it had an in-

[67] *Li Yi-shan shih chi*, 6.7a
[68] *Tu Fu yin-te*, 2.52/8A/11.
[69] *Ibid.*, 2.17/20/2.

scription in ancient *li* script that was no longer legible and that a shelter had been built over it.[70] (Another source says that there was no inscription.)[71] Tombstones are of course as subject to the vicissitudes of time as any other human monument, but they are especially favored by poets. Li Po writes:[72] "Don't you see/The old tombstone of Yang Hu, from Chin times,/Tortoise head broken off, overgrown with moss?" The four hundred years from Chin to T'ang is but a fraction of the three thousand years that separated Wu Wen-ying from King Yü, and one would expect to find the stone split and the fragments moss-covered. The language used is particularly effective: the moss is not said to be "thick," but *chi* ("accumulated"), suggesting the time elapsed, and the stone is not simply fragmented but *ts'an* ("in remnants"), again emphasizing the end result of a long-lasting process.

The poet lists other relics, a scepter *(kuei)* and a jade disk (*pi*, "circlet"), likewise fractured and in fragments. These too are associated with Yü's tomb. The *Ch'ing Gazetteer* mentions[73] "a crimson scepter like the sun and a green scepter like the moon" which the Spirit of Mt. Wan-wei presented to Yü, and the *Ming Gazetteer* has an entry,[74] "In the Shao-hsing period (1131–1163) of the Sung dynasty, suddenly one evening a radiance was seen shining forth from in front of the temple, and when they excavated at the place, they found an ancient scepter, a jade disk, girdle pendants, and bracelets, which were stored in the temple. However, the ones preserved there today are not genuine." It is quite probable that both scepter and disk were in the temple when Wu Wen-ying and his friend visited it. The idea that these relics, fragmentary and broken, are all that is left from King Yü's time, is particularly poignant. Of his great engineering feats no trace remains, and of his beneficent rule only the tradition. But here at least is something tangible, if pathetically little, and the poet rubs them with his hand, not just once, but again and again *(ch'ung)*, lingeringly, regretfully, as though with this gesture he would undo the neglect of the centuries. It is not just dust

[70] *Ta-Ming yi-t'ung chih*, 45. 3016.
[71] *Chin-shih ts'ui pien* 金石萃編 (Ching-hsün-t'ang ed.), 11.35.
[72] *Li T'ai-po shih* 李太白詩 (*SPTK* ed.), 7.1b.
[73] *Ta-Ch'ing yi-t'ung chih*, 179.8.
[74] *Ta-Ming yi-t'ung chih*, 45.3016.

that he removes, but "the world's dust." The qualifier *jen chien* seems puzzling—dust *is* of this world, after all. The term is unquestionably functional and needs to be scrutinized carefully if we are to see how the poem holds together, for it provides the necessary link between the discontinuities of space and time that we have already observed in it.

Remember that we were abruptly jerked from the two friends talking and trimming the lamp together to the broken stone covered with thick moss: a change in space and time, from home (or an inn) to the temple, from night to the preceding day. The easiest explanation is that the first stanza describes the day's excursion to the temple, the second the noctural conversation about what they had seen there. This is all right as far as it goes, but Wu Wen-ying characteristically does not separate things out that neatly: he moves without transition from friends talking by lamplight to the shattered scepter and broken circlet of Yü's temple, from night to day, from separation and reunion of individuals to the ancient and modern of history. And by not making a clear distinction between these things, he conveys the impression that they are all connected; the time and space dimensions merge. Of course the fragmented stone and shattered scepter were objects seen that day in the temple, and the feelings of regret attached to them were a subject of conversation that night. They recall the good days of their own youth that will not return, the events there is no repeating, and their feelings are perfectly symbolized by fragmented stone and shattered jade.

When the poet says that they "repeatedly rub away the world's dust," he is talking about their own lives as well as about these relics of a more remote past. And the dust that has accumulated on their broken lives, that has overlaid their youthful dreams and aspirations, their hopes and plans and enthusiasms, this is the inevitable product of living in the world, just as the dust of the ages collects on artifacts three thousand years old.

This intermingling of past and present, of the personal and the historical, is what gives the poem its meaning. The juxtaposition of relics from King Yü's time with old friends talking about their own past, at once gives intensity and depth to their own experiences and imbues history with human feeling.

The next three lines take another unpredictable leap: "Frost reds stop dancing,/But still the mountain color is ever green/Misty morning, hazy evening." Here we have a new setting, abruptly leaving the dusty relics of the past and picking up an earlier seasonal clue, the "autumn tree" of line 2. For the "frost reds" are certainly maple leaves turned by frost. But this brief passage of natural scenery has a more important contribution to make to the poem than just to remind us of the time of year. The juxtaposition of fallen red maple leaves that fall in a fluttering dance and the unchanging green of the hills establishes that relativity of passing time which Su Shih defined in his "First *Fu* on the Red Cliff":[75] If you look at it in terms of its changes, then the world cannot endure for the wink of an eye; but if you look at its unchanging aspect, both I and all things are unending." What Su Shih says abstractly, Wu Wen-ying expresses in concrete images. The idea of transience is invested with feeling when embodied in something beautiful, alive, dancing. When the leaves fall they stop their dance, and they lose their color. They have been turned red by the frost, and in this transfigured state they cannot long endure: a most dramatic example of change and of the impermanence of beauty. What does not change is the green of the conifers on the hills, whether there is mist in the morning or haze in the evening. The contrast is emphasized by the first word of the line, *man,* which is hard to translate. It suggests indifference, also something done in vain. It is as though the frost-reddened leaves have stopped dancing and after their fall the indifferent mountains go on being green to no particular purpose in the morning mist and evening haze. What is past is gone for good, but human generations go on indefinitely. For all that they suggest the never-ending flux of things, these lines deal with scenery that could have been observed at Yü's tomb, but it was not necessarily what was seen on the previous day, for this is also a general statement about the way of the world.

The final two lines seem at first to be not only arbitrary, but also flatly contradictory: "To the bank is tied a springtime boat,/ Picture flags resounding devotional drums." After the autumn tree and the red leaves, a springtime boat does not fit. Either Wu Wen-

---

[75] *Ching-chin Tung-p'o wen-chi shih lüeh* 經進東坡文集事略 (*SPTK* ed.), 1.3a.

ying is showing a fine indifference to consistency or he is trying for a definite effect. To look first for a precedent: Tu Fu, for example, wrote his eight "Autumn Thoughts" poems and adhered to the one season until the very last poem, where we come across the line, "The lovely ones gather the green in spring for remembrances."[76] Commentators have confidence in Tu Fu's competence, and so Weng Fang-kang says of this line, "Miraculous radiance flickers forth—it demands an intuitive response."[77] One can be equally enthusiastic about Wu Wen-ying's line. When in the first stanza he says, "Word-less, weary, I lean against an autumn tree," he is reporting an event occurring on the day of the excursion. With "Frost reds stop dancing" he is not limiting it to the one day but extending the period to include the changes of the autumn season. "But still the mountain color is ever green" goes further; it is valid for morning mist and evening haze, for winter as well as autumn, and will be still true next spring. And below this mountain, next spring and every spring, one can see boats tied to the bank and everywhere the painted flags and the drums of the festival. But what festival? The *Shao-hsing Gazetteer* says:[78] "The establishment of Yü's temple fell on the day they sacrificed in Wu-yu to Yü. They sacrificed to Yü in Kuei-chi in spring and autumn. . . . In the fourth year of Ch'ien-te (966), Wu and Yüeh were ordered to build Yü's temple in Kuei-chi with five households to look after it. The supervisor offered sacrifices in spring and autumn." The *Ch'ing Gazetteer* adds,[79] "Since Sung-Yuan times they have always sacrificed to Yü there."

Consequently, the painted flags and devotional drums have to do with the festivities connected with a sacrifice to Yü's spirit, festivities that involve public performances. The painted flags are on the many boats assembled for the occasion or carried by the guard. The "resounding" goes of course with the drums, but placed between the two parallel terms "painted flags" and "devotional drums," it has to serve for them both: the flags are summoning and the drums are beating to attract the audience.

[76] Yeh Chia-ying 葉嘉瑩, *Tu Fu Ch'iu hsing pa shou chi shuo* 杜甫秋興八首集說 (Chung-hua shu-chü, 1966), p. 434.

[77] *Tu Fu yin-te*, 2. 469/32H/5.

[78] *Shao-hsing fu chih* 紹興府志 (K'ang-hsi ed.), 22.2.

[79] *Ta-Ch'ing yi-t'ung chih*, 179.8.

But why springtime boat? According to the Sung *Kuei-chi Gazetteer,* the fifth day of the third month is traditionally Yü's birthday, when there are the most people at the temple. For this occasion rich and poor, nobles and commoners all come out from the city in gaily painted boats. There are feasting and drinking, songs and dances, and people save up all year long for the celebration. So the word "spring" in the poem is intended to remind us of this most important annual festival at Yü's temple. But it is more complicated than that. Practically the whole poem is autumnal: the one remaining crow, the autumn tree, the quiet, the frosty reds, and now in the last lines all at once is the word "spring," flags, drums and gaiety—quite the opposite of lonely, quiet autumn. It may seem that the poet is trying to cheer himself—and us. But if we look at the three lines just before, we are reminded that what is lovely in autumn passes and what is unchanging carries over through winter and spring and the next autumn. So we must expect the spring festival to pass as quickly as the autumn one did. The word "spring" is a device for extending the scope of the poem. It does not change the dominant mood of regret, nor does it confuse the time-frame of the poem. What the poet is lamenting is not his observations on a single day's excursion. We look in vain today for traces of Yü's work, and the steady deterioration of the world follows a course as unalterable as the succession of the seasons.

Eight-Rhymed Kanchou Song　八聲甘州

An Outing on Mt. Ling-yen with Colleagues
from the Grain Transport　陪庾幕諸公遊靈巖

An endless void, mist to the four distances.	渺空煙四遠
What year was it	是何年
The meteor fell from a clear sky?	青天墜長星
Illusory green crags and cloud trees.	幻蒼厓雲樹
Celebrated beauty's Golden Chamber,	名娃金屋
Failed Leader's palace walls.	殘霸宮城。
On Arrow Creek a sour wind impales the eyes,	箭徑酸風射眼
Creamy water stains the flower's stench.	膩水染花腥。
At times tripping paired-lovebirds echo:	時報雙鴛響
An autumn sound in corridor leaves.	廊葉秋聲。
In the palace the King of Wu is dead drunk,	宮裏吳王沈醉
Leaving the weary traveler of Five Lakes	倩五湖倦容

To angle alone, cold sober.
Ask the blue waves: they won't talk.
How can grey hairs cope with the mountain's
    green?
The water envelops the void;
From the balcony's height
I follow random crows and slanting sun dropping
    behind Fisherman's Isle.
Again and again I call for wine
And go to climb Lute Tower:
Autumn level with the clouds.

獨釣醒醒，
問蒼天無語

華髮奈山青。
水涵空
闌干高處

送亂鴉斜日落漁汀。
連呼酒
上琴臺去
秋與雲平。

From the subtitle we know that this *tz'u* was written by Wu Wen-ying while accompanying his colleagues in the Grain Transport Office[80] on an outing to Mt. Ling-yen. According to Hsia Cheng-t'ao's chronology,[81] Wu Wen-ying was in Soochow around the year 1232 as an official in the granary; he was over thirty at the time. He had been a long-time resident in the Wu region ("I spent ten years in Wu parks"[82]), and clearly was familiar with the historical sites and monuments, of which the most evocative are the ones relating to the ancient conflict between Wu and Yueh, culminating in Wu's downfall under King Fu-ch'a. The situation in the last years of the ancient kingdom of Wu had its modern parallels. Wu Wen-ying himself was born some seventy years after the fall of the Northern Sung and died only twenty years before the end of the Southern Sung. He lived at a time when there was a constant threat of foreign invasion and when the country was governed by unscrupulous politicians. In such times a sensitive poet need not have been a patriotic hero to be affected by what was going on or to be obsessed by a sense of impending catastrophe: "Relics of a thousand years' rise and fall—/Half the hill declining sun and lonely cloud./We pour

[80] The term *yü-mu* 庾幕 seems to be only an elegant variant of *ts'ang-mu* 倉幕. *Yü* is defined in *Shuo wen* as "storage of water-transport," and Tuan Yü-ts'ai 段玉裁 para-phrases: "Grain is brought by water and stored" *(Shuo wen chieh tzu ku lin* 說文解字詁林 4136a). There were two granaries in Soochow, the one in the south, west of Tzu-ch'eng Gate, and the one in the north beside Ch'ang-men Gate. The former was for regular tax grain, the latter for special requisitions. Cf. Chu Ch'ang-wen 朱長文 *Wu-chün t'u-ching hsü-chi* 吳郡圖經續記 *(Illustrated Account of Wu Prefecture, Continued) (Lin-lang mi-shih ts'ung-shu* 琳琅祕室叢書 ed.), A 13b.

[81] Hsia Cheng-t'ao 夏承燾, *Wu Meng-ch'uang chi-nien* 吳夢窗繫年 (reprinted in *Meng-ch'uang tz'u chi*), pp. 3-4.

[82] *Meng-ch'uang tz'u chi*, 80b.

another libation to the ghosts of Wu." These lines[83] were written on the occasion of another pleasure trip with his colleagues; but this *tz'u* especially, where the setting is Mt. Ling-yen, covered with relics of antiquity, is unusual among those written during his Soochow period in its awareness of the tragedy of past and present. But where this poem is most outstanding is in the stylistic nuances and the inspired unconventionality of its ideas.

It begins with a scene out of Genesis: "An endless void, mist to the four distances./What year was it/The meteor fell from a clear sky?" This is bizarre and unearthly enough. With only five words the first line takes us far outside the world of man into a realm of infinite space, chill and empty; it leaves us wondering where there is any place for human life in such a setting, with no beginning and no end and wholly without substance. The abrupt interrogative, "What year was it?" prepares for the introduction of something more substantial, a meteor fallen out of the clear blue sky, by which we are to understand Mt. Ling-yen. It was no doubt the physical appearance of the mountain which inspired this unusual image. It is described in the *Ch'ing Gazetteer*:[84] "From the top you can look down on both Mt. Chü-ch'ü and Mt. Tung-t'ing. Over vast billows of mist the view stretches a thousand *li*." And the *Wu-chün Gazetteer* says:[85] "The mountain is 360 fathoms high; it lies three *li* from human habitation." These quotations give an idea of the mountain's height and isolation, and looking at it, it could well occur to the poet that it was a great meteorite fallen from the sky. Conceived in these terms, the question follows, when did the meteor fall? It is a wonderfully skillful use of language to evoke the impression made by the physical aspect of the mountain without using a single word of direct description.

As he climbs the mountain and comes across the ruins of the old palace of Wu, the poet can only deplore the passage of time and react profoundly to the changes it has brought. When a heap of rubble is all that survives a thousand years, what are the values in this

---

[83] "Magnolia Flowers: On Tiger Hill in the Company of Colleagues from the Granary," *ibid.*

[84] *Ta-Ch'ing yi-t'ung chih* (Chia-ching revised ed.), XXVI, Soochow section 12a.

[85] *Wu chün chih* 吳郡志 (Sung ed. reproduced in Chang Shih-ming 張石銘, *Ying Sung-Yüan shan-pen hui-k'an* 影宋元善本彙刊), 15. 1b.

impermanent human world of vicissitudes? What is its meaning?
Where does it come from? Is it any more than a senseless, unfeeling
stone cast down from the sky by chance? The question, then, is one
loaded with feeling: "What was the year/The meteor fell from a
clear sky?"

In line 4, the word *huan* ("illusory") evokes all the faded flowers
and vanished beauties of the past. The earth itself is no more than a
random fallen star, and the things on the surface of this insensate
stone give the illusory appearance of rise and fall, of growth and
decay. In the beginning something came from nothing, and there
were green crags and mist-enshrouded trees; but these are only bits
of natural scenery. Later man and his ephemeral works appeared:
the "celebrated beauty," the Golden Chamber, and the palaces of
the Leader of the States, the Hegemon who dominated his time. But
before the word "Leader" Wu Wen-ying slips in the qualifying
adjective "failed," and Fu-ch'a's great work of political unification
all at once collapses. And with it the famous beauty and the Golden
Chamber and all the other glories of his reign revert to nothingness.
So all that came into existence from nothing is now nothing again: is
it not illusion, all the endless human endeavor—human affairs with
their ups and downs, played out on the surface of a fallen star?
And so the word "illusory" connects the meteor of the first three
lines with the famous beauty and Golden Chamber of the following
three. The earth is a falling stone, human life vanishes like a con-
juror's illusion, there is no constancy in the world's affairs, and there
is no end to suffering and uncertainty. Even the opening line of this
poem "An endless void, mist to the four distances" rouses an inex-
plicable feeling of sadness.

The Golden Chamber is at once an allusion to the room where the
Han Emperor Wu proposed to lodge the woman whose beauty so
appealed to him as a boy,[86] and a reminder of the Palace Where the
Beauty Was Lodged (Kuan wa kung) built for Hsi-shih.[87] One can

[86] The anecdote is found in *Han Wu ku-shih* 漢武故事 (*Ku-chin yi-shih* ed.), 2a.

[87] "The *Yüeh chüeh shu* says that the people of Wu built the Palace Where the Beauty Was
Lodged (Kuan wa kung) on Polished Stone Mountain (Yen shih shan). The palace must
have got its name from its connection with Hsi-shih. Traditionally there is supposed to
have been a Lute Tower on the mountain. Also a Resounding Steps Corridor, the floor
of which was made of catalpa wood. When Hsi-shih walked on it, it echoed to her steps,
and hence the name" (*Illustrated Account of Wu Prefecture, Continued*, B.21ab).

imagine the grandeur of the palace as it must have been in the time
of King Fu-ch'a and the revels and festivities that he enjoyed there
with his favorite. But the King of Wu had other concerns than
amusing himself with Hsi-shih; he yearned to become Hegemon,
Leader of the Feudal Lords. We read in the *Historical Records*:[88]
"In the second year of his rule, King Fu-ch'a of Wu . . . attacked
Yüeh and defeated it at Fu-chiao . . . . In the seventh year he went
north to attack Ch'i and defeated Ch'u at Ai-ling. In the ninth year
he attacked Lu on behalf of Tsou . . . . In the spring of the fourteenth
year the King of Wu assembled the feudal lords at Huang-ch'ih to
the north, intending to be Hegemon over the central states so as to
fulfill the house of Chou."

If King Fu-ch'a had the hegemony so nearly within his grasp, why
does Wu Wen-ying call him the "failed Leader"? In the first place,
among the famous Hegemons of the Spring and Autumn period,
Fu-ch'a is not in the same class with Duke Huan of Ch'i or Duke Wen
of Chin, or even with Duke Mu of Ch'in or King Chuang of Ch'u.
Second, he comes late, at the very end of the period. Third, it was
only shortly after the assembly at Huang-ch'ih that he was defeated
by King Kou-chien of Yüeh, with the result that he lost his life and
his state was destroyed. This sort of leader, for all that he achieved
the hegemony, surely deserves the epithet "failed." And yet the
ruins of the palace among green crags and cloud-shrouded trees
which belong to the time of Fu-ch'a's failed leadership are visible here
today on Mt. Ling-yen. When we read the words "palace walls" we
think of their splendor as they were during Fu-ch'a's lifetime; but
"failed Leader" reminds us of his premature defeat, of the rapid
changes in the fortunes of men and nations, and all is reduced to an
illusory shadow play on a fallen star. It is a common enough experience to feel depressed by reminders of decayed grandeur; here
Wu Wen-ying's unique achievement lies in putting this enduring
human uncertainty in a setting that transcends the human time
scale.

The poem continues: "On Arrow Creek a sour wind impales the
eyes,/Creamy water stains the flowers' stench." These lines provide
further details of the cheerless scene of relics of the past, relics which

[88] *Shih chi* (Po-na ed.), 31.6ab.

Wu Wen-ying presents in his most eccentric style to convey every nuance of feeling. Arrow Creek (Chien ching) is the same as the Plucking Fragrances Creek (Ts'ai-hsiang ching) mentioned in the *Wu Prefecture Gazetteer*:[89] "Plucking Fragrances Creek is a small brook on the side of Fragrant Hill. King Wu planted fragrant plants on Fragrant Hill and had his harem beauties pick them as they drifted down the brook in boats. Today, viewed from Mt. Ling-yen, the stream flows straight as an arrow, and so the popular name for it is Arrow Creek."[90]

The "creamy water" suggests Fragrant Water Brook (Hsiang-shui hsi), also mentioned in the *Wu Prefecture Gazetteer*:[91] "Fragrant Water Brook flows through the old Wu palace. It is popularly said that it is where Hsi-shih bathed; people called it the 'rouge and powder pool'. It was the place where the palace ladies of the King of Wu washed off their makeup. Even today the spring above smells fragrant."

So both Arrow Creek and the creamy water of Fragrant Water Brook are near the Palace Where the Beauty Was Lodged.

"On Arrow Creek a sour wind impales the eyes." "Sour wind," as Wu Wen-ying uses the expression here, is not just another example of what I have called his modernity, a sort of sharpening of perception through the choice of unusual word-combinations. He has borrowed the term from a line in a poem by Li Ho,[92] and his whole line is so close to Li Ho's that the allusion is unmistakable: "From the Eastern Pass a sour wind impales the eyeballs." As a result, in addition to the heightened effect of the association between "arrow" and the verb "impales," the context of Li Ho's poem is available to add to the intensity of feeling of Wu Wen-ying's as we are reminded of what Li Ho said in the preface to his poem: "In the eighth moon of 233, the Emperor Ming of the Wei ordered his palace officers to pull in a cart the statue of the Immortal who holds a dish for collecting dew, the one which the Han Emperor Wu had erected, wishing to have it set up in front of his own palace. The officials had broken off the dish and were about to move the statue when tears poured from its eyes."

---

[89] *Wu chün chih*, 8.9b.

[90] The word 涇 is defined by Tuan Yü-ts'ai's *Shuo wen* commentary (4824b) as "course" (通) and is interchanged with 徑 "direct route, path."

[91] *Wu chün chih*, 8.10a.

[92] Li Ho (Shih-chieh shu-chü ed. of Li Ho's *Works* 李賀詩註, Taipei, 1964), p. 66.

According to Yao Wen-hsieh,[93] the T'ang Emperor Hsien-tsung was preparing to excavate Dragon Head Pond and build two palaces when Li Ho wrote his poem, intending it as a timely reminder that extravagant undertakings of rulers did not long endure. In Li Ho's poem it was the sour pricking of the wind in the face that made the tears flow. But even more it was the grief for the fallen mighty, for the ancient ruler whose line was ended. Li Ho's poem "On the Gilded Bronze Immortal Taking Leave of the Han" was written as a warning to the ruling emperor, using the example of the Han as a reminder that the T'ang could not last forever, and when Wu Wen-ying had climbed Mt. Ling-yen with the autumn wind in his face, he used Li Ho's phrase "A sour wind impales the eyes" to convey the feeling of sadness inspired by the ruins of the ancient palace of Wu, now overgrown with weeds, as he reflected on the lesson history had for his own time when another dynasty was on its last legs.

Fragrant Water Brook, in the poet's imagination, still carries the powder and unguents of the harem ladies of the Wu palace of old, and so he calls the water *ni,* "creamy" or "oily." The word is doubly effective, for besides being appropriate to the creams and powder washed off into the water, it also recalls Tu Mu's "Rhymeprose on O-fang Palace,"[94] where a line about the palace women of Ch'in reads: "The current of the Wei rises and is oily *(ni)* : it is because they dumped here the water in which they washed off their makeup." This provides another reminder of the transience of glory, for Tu Mu follows his description of the grandeur of the O-fang Palace with the abrupt sequel: "Once put to the torch by the Ch'u leader, alas the scorched earth!" And the piece concludes with the lament: "If later men pity them and fail to take them as a warning, these later men too will be pitied by still later men." In borrowing from Tu Mu the combination "creamy water," Wu Wen-ying shows the same skill as in his use of Li Ho's "sour wind," for in both cases the allusion reinforces the unusual language.

In the next phrase "stains the flowers' stench," the word *hsing* (stench) is even more remarkable than "creamy" or "sour," if only because unprecedented; besides, the effect does not depend on the reader's familiarity with literary antecedents. I have already dis-

[93] Yao Wen-hsieh 姚文燮 (chin-shih 1659), *ibid.*, p. 226.
[94] *Works (SPTK* ed.), I. 1b–2b,

cussed the unconventional nature of this epithet applied to the palace ladies' wash water and its contradictory associations with carnage and bloodshed, and need not repeat it here. It is in these three adjectives, applied to the wind on Arrow Creek, the water of the brook, and the flowers growing beside it, that Wu Wen-ying's artistry in words is displayed. What we have takes us a long way from the conventional lament for the past inspired by a sightseeing visit to some famous ruin.

"At times tripping paired-lovebirds echo/An autumn sound on corridor leaves." This gets a bit more complicated. It still deals with something from a vanished past, but it begins to treat illusion as reality. The "echo" is the sound of Hsi-shih's footsteps. The word *sa* ("child's slipper," translated "tripping") is used by Ssu-ma Hsiang-ju[95] in its other reading *hsi* to mean "lightly, swiftly"— of flowing water. Wu Wen-ying manages to combine the two meanings in what is really a verbal use. It is of course standard practice in Chinese to use as a verb a word ordinarily a noun: *lü*, for example, which is the noun "shoe" and a verb "to wear on the foot" or "to go in shoes." But here the noun *hsi* (or *sa*), "slipper" is being used as a verb with the added adverbial meaning "lightly, swiftly," giving something like "to step swiftly and lightly," "to go tripping along." The ordinary word would be *lü* 履 or *tao* 蹈 "to step," both lacking the extra meaning of "swiftly, lightly." So *shih sa* means "from time to time to go past trippingly with swift, light steps."

The "paired-lovebirds" *(shuang yüan)* are Hsi-shih's slippered feet. The term occurs frequently in T'ang and Sung *tz'u* for the embroidered slippers worn by women, and Wu Wen-ying also uses it elsewhere.[96] The *Wu Prefecture Gazetteer*[97] mentions a "Corridor of Echoing Steps" as a part of the Palace Where the Beauty Was Lodged and explains the name by saying that the corridor was built over a sound chamber of catalpa wood, so that when Hsi-shih walked along it, her steps resounded. Today as the poet views the palace ruins, he seems to hear from time to time the sound of Hsi-shih's quick steps: "At times tripping paired-lovebirds echo," but since he

---

[95] *Han shu pu-chu* 漢書補注 (ed. of 1900), 27B. 11b-12a.

[96] "Wind in the Pines," *Meng-ch'uang tz'u chi*, 62b: "Sad that the paired lovebirds do not come,/On the dark steps a night's moss has grown."

[97] *Illustrated Account of Wu Prefecture, Continued*, 21b.

lived some 1700 years after Hsi-shih's time, the sound must be imaginary. What has created the illusion of footsteps? The autumn wind whirling the fallen leaves in the corridor, "an autumn sound in corridor leaves"—and with this line the illusion that we hear the footsteps of Hsi-shih fades, and we are left with the melancholy rustle of dry leaves in the wind, autumn's most characteristic sound.

All this first part of Wu Wen-ying's poem is written directly out of what he observed on Mt. Ling-yen, some of it true and some false, part genuine and part illusory, the present scene blended with events of a thousand years ago; the inexpressible melancholy, the poet's sensitivity, the miraculous language—all out of reach of those who conceive of beauty only in conventional terms.

The second part of the poem begins abruptly: "In the palace the King of Wu is dead drunk,/Leaving the weary traveler of Five Lakes/To angle alone, cold sober." Where the first part was primarily descriptive, for all that it confused the real and the illusory, this part mingles past and present while concentrating on the state of the world. Ch'en Hsün[98] has explained these lines as drawing a parallel between Fu-ch'a's loss of his kingdom and the decline of the Southern Sung dynasty. It is an excellent interpretation and I have based my own upon it, but it has two weaknesses: it pushes the historical parallels too far in detail to carry complete conviction and it is written in a style terse to the point of unintelligibility.[99]

The palace in the first line is the Palace Where the Beauty Was Lodged; its physical ruins are there before the poet's eyes, among the green crags and cloud-enveloped trees on Mt. Ling-yen. The Five Lakes of the next line are Lake T'ai, whose "misty isles and vast

[98] Ch'en Hsün, *op. cit.*, 3b–4a.

[99] "The first three lines simply connect the two scenes of mountain and lake with the drunkenness of King Wu and the soberness of Fan Li. The 'blue waves' continue the 'Five Lakes,' and the 'mountain's green' follows on 'in the palace.' This is the most painful thing in the whole poem. To develop it a bit: it regrets Fu-cha's being duped by the King of Yüeh. Fan Li recognized that he was a dangerous bird of prey, but Fu-ch'a did not, and so was drunk; Fan Li was sober. The treachery of the Juchen surpassed even that of Kou-chien, and the abduction of Emperor Hui was more shocking than Fu-ch'a's defeat. The emperor's death in Wu-kuo ch'eng was more tragic than the episode of Pei-yu-wei. And finally the grief of the Southern Sung survivor was a different thing from Fan Li's carefree flight; the excursions to Ken-yüeh and the visits to Fan-lou were more abandoned than the dissipations in the old palace of Wu. The Northern Sung was finished, and the peace and security of the Southern Sung were precarious. Who is the 'weary traveler of Five Lakes' today? The word *ch'ien*, 'leaving,' implies that everyone else is drunk too. One wonders what Wen-ying's colleagues from the Grain Transport found to answer to this poem?"

reaches" are mentioned in the *Soochow Gazetteer* as visible from its top. Then two human figures are thrust into the scene, the King of Wu and the "weary traveler"; the former is King Fu-ch'a, whose drunkenness is his infatuation with Hsi-shih and the diversions he enjoyed in her company, unaware of the danger from his powerful neighbor, Kou-chien. The "weary traveler" is Fan Li, of whom it was said, "When Kou-chien destroyed Wu, he advanced as far as the Five Lakes. Fan Li took his leave of the king, saying, 'May Your Majesty continue to strive. I shall not return to Yüeh,' and he left in a light boat across Five Lakes. No one knew where he ended up."[100] And in the *Shih chi* account of Kou-chien,[101] "In the end Fan Li went away. From Ch'i he sent back a letter to the Great Officer Chung: '. . . The character of the King of Yüeh is that of a long-necked bird of prey. You can share trouble and hardship with him but not prosperity.' "

When the poem says "to angle alone, cold sober," it implies that Fan Li was the only clear-sighted and sober man in his time. The single word "to angle" recalls his carefree life in a boat on Five Lakes, while "alone" emphasizes his loneliness and his difference from the others who were drunk while he was sober. In Wu Wen-ying's time was there anyone like Fan Li, by exception sober? If there was, he was born into a world where everyone else was drunk, and he could only be a weary traveler fishing alone on Five Lakes. The word "weary" conveys his weariness with the instability of the world and with the bitterness and tragedy of the human condition. The word *ch'ien* means "to cause" and gives the sense "The only thing for a man to do who is as clear-sighted as Fan Li is to harbor no ambition beyond fishing alone—the only choice of a sober man in the midst of the drunken crowd." Finally, although the drunken King of Wu in his palace and the sober fisherman on Five Lakes belonged to different states, rival kingdoms of over a thousand years ago, now in Wu Wen-ying's poem there is only the opposition of drunk and sober, and in this opposition lies the sadness of the endless changes from past to present, the alternation of prosperity and decay, of peace and war. It is not necessary to limit it, as Ch'en

[100] *Kuo yü* (*SPTK* ed.), 21.9.
[101] *Shih chi*, 11.37ab.

Hsün did, to the threat of Kou-chien, which Fan Li recognized but of which the King of Wu was unaware.

In these two sentences one is carried from the mountain and lake present before the eyes to the millennial rise and fall of empires. In the following two lines, the "blue waves" and the "mountain's green" bring us back to the present landscape. Today's weary traveler finds in the mist-enshrouded blue waves stretching away to the horizon no answer to the agonizing question that so preoccupies him. "The mountain's green" picks up "in the palace" of line 11 and refers to Mt. Ling-yen with the ruins of the Palace Where the Beauty Was Lodged; "white hair" refers back to the weary traveler, clearly a persona of the poet himself. The confrontation of white-haired poet and evergreen mountain, the one so full of feeling, the other wholly indifferent, the weary traveler with his burden of grief and worry, the mountain with experience of the ever-changing current of history—how little can man's feeble strength hope for!

Certainly Wu Wen-ying's *tz'u* carries an enormous weight of feeling beyond anything made explicit in the words, and Ch'en Hsün is quite right to bring in the Juchen invaders and the troubles of the Sung empire. The old kingdom of Wu was destroyed by Kou-chien, and the Northern Sung was defeated by the Juchen. King Fu-ch'a was unwilling to accept the disgrace of his defeat and committed suicide at Yung-tung, but the Sung Emperor Hui-tsung and his son were taken prisoner and carried off north to die miserably in the territory of the invaders, surely a more shameful end. Wu Wen-ying, who must have thought of himself as a survivor of the Northern Sung catastrophe, both sober and aware of the precarious situation of the Southern Sung in its last years, could feel his own helplessness in the presence of the Wu palace ruins and the misty waves of Five Lakes; all he could do was deplore the situation, unlike Fan Li, who was free to leave the concerns of the state and end his days in carefree wandering. But aside from that, Wu Wen-ying saw a historical analogy between the China of his day and the old state of Wu, between himself and Fan Li. However, this is only a unifying thread that runs through his poem; there are further layers of feeling that cannot be restricted to any simple historical parallel.

We have yet to consider the last six lines:

> The water envelopes the void;
> From the balcony's height
> I follow random crows and slanting sun dropping behind
>   Fisherman's Isle.
> Again and again I call for wine
> And go to climb Lute Tower:
> Autumn level with the clouds.

In this passage the poet tears himself free from his preoccupation with the sorrows of history and of the present. The setting takes the place of emotions, or rather, becomes their vehicle. In the first line we see the water stretching out to merge with the sky, an endless, vast expanse, as far as the eye can reach. This is probably the actual view from Mt. Ling-yen, on which there stands a lookout tower named Enveloping the Void (Han k'ung) at just this place. According to the *Ming Gazetteer*,[102] it was built in the third century. Kao Ch'i wrote a poem about the view, with the lines:[103]

> Rolling billows under an endless sky
> From the twisting railing of the high tower on this mountain peak.
> Take your stand right on top of floating clouds
> And let your sight go beyond the departing birds.

Wu Wen-ying's line contains a reference to the name of the tower, but it is primarily a description: wherever one looks the scene extends to blend into the horizon. It is an isolated vantage point looking out over a bottomless immensity. The high balcony railing on which the poet leans to look out seems to be in the midst of this void. What is there in the whole vast universe besides this stretch of emptiness which swallows up his body? Far off in the distance a few isolated crows disappearing with the westward setting sun—all gradually vanishing in the far-off misty waves beyond the fisherman's isle. The word *sung* ("follow" or "accompany as a parting guest") suggests that he stares a long time, lost in his reverie; the grief that he feels in his loneliness, helpless to hold back birds or sun, is implied but not made explicit. At this point there is nothing more to do or say, and he can only call for wine over and over again. The repeated call

---

[102] *Ta-Ming yi-t'ung chih,* Soochow section, 8.9b.

[103] *Kao T'ai-shih ta-ch'üan-chi* 高太史大全集 (*SPTK* ed.), 14.18a; lines also quoted in the *Ming Gazetteer.*

suggests the urgency of an intolerable distress. Where does he intend
to drink his wine? On Lute Tower. Li Shang-yin's poem "Setting
Sun Tower"[104] has a couplet: "The flowers are bright, the willow
is dark, and the whole sky is melancholy;/From the second wall I
climb yet another tower." And Hsin Ch'i-chi: "The sky is far and
hard to reach, so don't stare too long./The tower is high, and you
want to go down, but still you lean."[105] A man in the grip of hopeless
sorrow will always want to go to a place with a distant view for a
final struggle and effort, and always it will intensify his grief. This is
the effect of Wu Wen-ying's last line, where after calling for wine, he
climbs up Lute Tower.

And what more is there to be seen from the top of Lute Tower?
"Autumn level with the clouds." Filling the void between heaven
and earth, outside the human world is nothing but this autumn air.
Here on the tower one feels oneself at last to be upon a level with the
clouds. But in the whole vast sky there is no place where a man can
get a breath of air untainted with autumn sadness.

These last four words take us to even further reaches of space and
stretches of emptiness, where the famous beauty and the Golden
Chamber and the failed Leader and the palace of the King of Wu
and the weary traveler are enveloped and dissolved in the mists of
the four distances. We are carried back to the opening lines of the
poem, which is like the snake of Ch'ang-an with its tail in its mouth,
and all the intervening confusions of true and false, past and present,
empty and actual, the implications and the marvels of style, all are
beyond description. Wu Mei said that Wu Wen-ying's greatest
excellence lay in the depth of thought he was able to convey in the
most rarefied flights of fancy—and in this poem are combined both
the fancy and the profundity.

[104] Li Shang-yin (*SPPY* ed.), 1.15b.
[105] Hsin Ch'i-chi (*SPPY* ed.), 4.2b.

The Conventions and Craft of Yuan Drama

by James I. Crump

I

The great discoveries of the thirties and forties and the piecemeal publication of Yuan dynasty drama (*tsa-chü* 雜劇) seem to have ceased and the corpus of this genre, it is generally agreed, has been increased by sixty-two examples.[1] All these were gathered together and published (in a format reminiscent of *Yüan-ch'ü hsüan* [*YCH*] 元曲選) in 1959 under the title *YCH wai-pien* (*WP*) 外編 a work which promises to become just as standard for the last sixty-two *tsa-chü* as *YCH* is for the first one hundred. One can now make the general statement that the 2,783 pages of these two publications contain—with insignificant exceptions—the entire genre, if we limit it to Yuan and very early Ming productions as has been the habit of most scholars in the past. *Pei-ch'ü* 北曲, that is *tsa-chü* using northern music and the form developed in Yuan times, continued to be written well into the Ming dynasty but they should be kept distinct from Yuan drama as a genre, for the *tsa-chü* of Yuan times was a wildly flourishing commercial enterprise while Ming examples were mostly hothouse varieties which throve only at court. Since the publication of *Wai-pien* we can now refer to all Yuan dramas by their serial arrangement in these two books: 1 to 100 in *YCH* and 101 to 162 in *WP*.

[1] For the sake of convenience I am treating *WP* 117, *Hsi-hsiang chi* 西廂記 and *WP* 140, *Hsi yu chi* 西遊記 in the same fashion as the newly discovered dramas.

It now seems quite obvious that interest in Yuan *tsa-chü* is waxing and is beginning to be characterized by a sounder critical approach. New publications east and west have certainly more than doubled the information on the genre that was available a scant ten or fifteen years ago. Since there are a number of technical considerations and additions which can be made now with every expectation of appreciative attention, though they would have been greeted with little understanding or enthusiasm a decade ago, I propose to examine briefly the meager but increasingly important information we have on how the Yuan dramatist incorporated some of the musical demands of his genre into the poetry of individual songs. I shall go on to show some of the ways in which the stiff requirements of song-sets (*t'ao-shu* 套數) and other conventions became flexible in the hands of the men who brought the genre to perfection.

II

Musical Convention and its Reflection in the Poetry of Yuan Drama

Yuan dramatists were poetic playwrights but they did, after all, compose their poetry to music and so were obliged to handle not only dramatic but musical conventions. Just as we may expect some reflection of musical phrasing in the lyrics that John Gay[2] wrote for his *Beggar's Opera*, so we may feel reasonably hopeful that the lyrics (arias) of Yuan drama bear some relation to the rhythmic element, at least, of the conventional tunes to which they were composed. The convention requiring the use of the same melody many times in Yuan dramas was a very strong one and it seems reasonable to expect that there is some common rhythmic framework which informs all lyrics written to the tune *T'ien-hsia lo* 天下樂, let us say, in whichever drama it may be found.

Someone with a reasonable grasp of the mechanics of Yuan dramatic arias can hardly read through the opening verses (*Tien chiang-*

---

[2] I single him out because there is much similarity of form between that ballad opera of his and Yuan drama. Cf. H. W. Wells, *The Classical Drama of the Orient*, Asia Publishing House, New York, 1956, pp. 24–25. But cf. also p. 131. Wells is quite right in saying that the tone of Yuan drama (and other periods of Chinese drama) is quite different from the satirical treatment of demi-mondaine subjects preferred by the majority of ballad operas during the brief heyday of that form, but for an examination of the range of topics cf. E. M. Gagey's *Ballad Opera*, Columbia University Press, 1937 and 1965, esp. pp. 6–7 where he gives a definition of ballad opera.

ch'un 點絳唇) of the first ten dramas in *WP* without being thoroughly convinced that the music they were all written to required the words to be grouped 4, 4, 3 for the first three lines and that the last two lines should probably be 4, 5. Reading a random choice of ten other *Tien chiang-ch'un* from *YCH* would not shake this conviction. As he reads further in Yuan drama, however, a student of the genre will be dismayed to find that he can seldom, if ever, come across another set of arias with such unarguable regular forms (*cheng-ko* 正格).

The longest and by far the most impressive work devoted to assembling rhythmic skeletons of the music behind the arias *(ch'ü)* is Wang Yü-chang's 王玉章 *Yüan-tz'u chüeh-lü* 元詞觪律, in three volumes, printed in 1936. This publication is called *shang-pien* 上編, implying that there was more forthcoming. Unhappily, no more did come forth. The *shang-pien* treats all tunes used in four of seven common modes employed in *YCH*.[3] In his preface the author explains how he went about reconstructing the rhythmical outlines:

I used the words to *ch'ü* found in the *Kuang-cheng* 廣正 the *Ta-ch'eng* 大成, the *Cheng-yin* 正音 and the *Ch'in-ling chien p'u* 欽定簡譜 to test and verify *(YCH)*, but those works have their lapses. For example, the *Kuang-cheng p'u* says of the Hsien-lü 仙呂 mode's *Tuan-cheng hao* 端正好[1] that "the words within stanza and line are not fixed but may be added to or subtracted from," but since one cannot tell *which* lines can be added to or subtracted from, this leaves him no place to begin. A more extreme case is the *Ta-cheng's* statement under the Cheng-kung 正宮 mode's *Tuan-cheng hao*, "the first and last lines of the fourth, fifth, sixth and seventh stanzas *(ch'üeh* 関) are all slightly different from the regular form—they constitute an 'augmented form.'" The books did not separate *ch'en-tzu* 襯字 ('stuffing') from the base characters correctly and so created an imaginary 'augmented form' to delude the eye of the reader. The above are examples of shortcomings found in the old formula-books and this is why my present volume relies on the language of the songs (in *YCH*) themselves plus some supplementary collation to furnish a base line for those who would like to write words to *(ch'ü)* forms.

[3] Wang Yü-chang, *Yüan-tz'u chüeh-lü*: ch. 1, Huang-chung kung 黃鐘宮; ch. 2, Cheng kung 正宮; ch. 3, Ta-shih tiao 大石調; ch. 4, Hsien-lü kung 仙呂宮. This leaves untouched the often-used Nan-lü 南呂, Chung-lü 中呂, and Shuang-tiao 雙調 modes, as well as the less frequently seen Yüeh-tiao 越調 and Shang-tiao 商調 modes.

[4] See schema below.

Few of us nowadays write words to *ch'ü*, but it is of the greatest consequence to reader, translator, and critic alike to discover the range of rhythmic flexibility, the loci of repetitions and similar information on the prosody of Yuan *ch'ü*, and all interested scholars must be impressed with the ordered flexibility shown in the following excerpt from Dale Johnson's analysis of Wang Yü-chang's work.[5]

Tuan cheng hao

The *cheng-ke* in this melody is (33775) but slightly over half of the arias are found to have from four to twelve 3-character *chü* 句 inserted into the body of the tune located in all cases after *chü* 4. In each case, the number of added *chü* is an even one and can be ranged in groups of balanced couplets. A 5-character *chü* always closes the aria.

YCH 21	*YCH* 19,51, 67,69,72,84	*YCH* 28,49, 82,93	*YCH* 59	*YCH* 40
000 1	000 1	000 1	000 1	000 1
000 2	000 2	000 2	000 2	000 2
0000000 3	0000000 3	0000000 3	0000000 3	0000000 3
0000000 4	0000000 4	0000000 4	0000000 4	0000000 4
- - -	- - -	- - -	- - -	- - -
- - -	- - -	- - -	- - -	- - -
- - -	- - -	- - -	- - -	- - -
- - -	- - -	- - -	- - -	- - -
00000 5	- - -	- - -	- - -	- - -
	- - -	- - -	- - -	- - -
	00000 5	- - -	- - -	- - -
		- - -	- - -	- - -
		00000 5	- - -	- - -
			- - -	- - -
			00000 5	- - -
				- - -
				00000 5

The more one reads of Yuan drama the stronger grows a subjective conviction that something very much like what Wang is trying to

[5] This and the next schema are used with the kind permission of Professor Dale Johnson, and are taken from his unpublished Master's thesis (University of Michigan), "*Form in the Arias of Yüan Opera.*" Cf. also his articles "One Aspect of Form in the Arias of Yüan Opera," in *Two Studies in Chinese Literature*, Michigan Papers in Chinese Studies, no. 3, 1968, and "The prosody of Yuan Drama," in *Toung Pao*, 56, 1-3, 1970, 96-146.

describe is indeed an aspect of the loosely ordered complexity of arias in the genre, but the difficulties involved in demonstrating the underlying rhythmic framework which should inform all arias written to the same tune are enormous. Johnson gives an example:

> . . . the base characters, not the *ch'en-tzu*, are the real keys to an understanding of the rhythmic and tonal structure of this music. Guided by rhyme schemes which point out the phrase final characters, the phrases can be uncovered, and once the *ch'en-tzu* have been 'cleared away' the base words are left standing, revealing the framework of the melody . . . . The following are all diagrams [by Wang] of the same aria, *T'ien-hsia lo*, but they are taken from four different plays. Note the high irregularity of the *ch'en-tzu* (represented by 'x'):

YCH 1

```
x x x o o o o o o o  r
              o o  r
            o o o  r
x x x o o x o o o o o  r
      x x x o o o
      x x x o o o  r
    x x x o o o o o
```

YCH 13

```
x x x x x x x o o o o x o o o  r
                  x x x o o  r
        x x x x x x x o o o  r
x x x x x o o o x o o o o  r
              x x x o o o  r
            x x x x x o o o  r
x x x x x x x x x x o o o o o  r
```

YCH 28

```
x x x o o o o o o o  r
              o o
            o o o  r
x o o o o o o o  r
      x x x o o o
      x x x o o o  r
    x x x o o o o o  r
```

YCH 41

```
o o x o o x o o o  r
      x x x o o
          o o o  r
    x x x o o o o o o o  r
x x x x x x x o o o
x x x x x x x o o o  r
  x x x o o x o o o  r
```

To a slight extent I am using the above display as something of a straw man, for I know that Wang is seriously mistaken in several places, but looking at these examples it becomes amply clear that Wang—or anyone else—has his work cut out for him if Yuan playwrights could sprinkle *ch'en-tzu* as freely as this through their arias.[6] The student's immediate reaction to this display is to enquire how Wang spots *ch'en-tzu*. A hasty answer would be that there are

---

[6] As far as our present knowledge goes a composer *may* put *ch'en-tzu* almost anywhere, but in fact a rough estimate of the state of affairs will show that somewhere in the vicinity of 90 percent of all *ch'en-tzu* appear as the opening words of a line (*chü* 句). Perhaps the

old texts in which the "stuffing" characters are printed smaller than the base characters, but a quick check of these will soon dispel any notion that Wang agrees with them or that they are reliable.[7] Barring these aids, there are a large number of delightfully musical nonsense syllables (*t'e-leng-leng-t'eng* 忞楞楞嶐, *shu-la-la-sha* 疎剌剌沙, *mi-liu-mo-luan-ti* 迷留沒亂的, *yi-liu-wu-luan-ti* 壹留兀亂的), movable interjections which can even fall between two closely-bound words (*yeh-po* 也波, *yeh-po-ke* 哥),[8] and a number of other musico-linguistic phenomena which might logically be considered *ch'en-tzu*. Inspection of Wang's work shows that some parts of these utterances are sometimes designated *ch'en-tzu*, but at other times they are considered to be base characters. Last, but most helpful, are the high-frequency introductory phrases which are vastly more important to the rhythm of both the dialogue and arias of Yuan dramas than to the conveying of meaning (*chih chien na* 只見那, *ti to-shao* 抵多少, *wu-ti-pu* 兀的不, etc.). Most students of Chinese would be able to spot these quite consistently as *ch'en-tzu* and most of the time Wang will agree— though not always and not consistently. As an experiment I once worked through the first act of *Yü-hu ch'un* 玉壺春 (*YCH* 28) and with the help of the *Hsi Chi-tzu* edition worked out base forms for all its arias. Later I compared them with Wang. To my delight we were of one mind six out of ten times (with minor variations such as my 7,5 and Wang's 7,2,3). Checking against other attempts, in which I

---

reader could get some idea of the effect if the *T'ien hsia lo* in *YCH* 1 were translated with the *ch'en-tzu* in parenthesis—as far as English sensibly allows:

> (Even the)
> Lantern makes solid its essence to pierce the crimson gauze and reveal—
> My minister, look, I pray—
> (At this)
> Thin, this delicate shadow of hers: exquisite!
> A chance meeting and she remembers to call herself "lowly one,"
> In fullest respect she titles me "Imperial Presence."
> (Surely we have here)
> No ordinary daughter of the common folk!

If this does not seem to match the sequence of "x"'s and "o"'s in the selection by Johnson, it is simply because no one-for-one correspondence is possible.

[7] An interesting partial exception to this statement is the congruence between much of *YCH* 28, 1 in the (*Hsi Chi-tzu*) *Ku-chin tsa-chü* 息機子古今雜劇 edition and Wang's decisions on which characters are *ch'en-tzu* (cf. below).

[8] Actually when a unit is used symmetrically in an aria and each use of the aria demands its presence (as with *T'ao-t'ao ling* 刁刁令 using *yeh-po-ke* as part of its last line) it must be treated as a special *ch'en-tzu* form.

seldom duplicated Wang's decisions on what characters to call *ch'en-tzu*, I was impressed by the fact that the *ch'en-tzu* in *YCH* 28,1 are strikingly confined to the last mentioned high-frequency introductory phrases—more so than any other drama I had worked with. Such phrases then are obviously closely connected with what Yuan dramatists thought of as *ch'en-tzu*.

Taken in its entirety, Wang's work is a great contribution but not quite the one he meant it to be. He gives the impression that he works from the language of the arias and establishes by reasonable means what characters are *ch'en-tzu* and when he "clears them away" there stand the base forms. In actuality he begins with formulae derived from one or another of the *ch'ü-p'u* and labors to brand as "stuffing" enough characters to make the evidence fit the formulae. Besides a large number of highly tendentious decisions about what characters are or are not *ch'en-tzu*, Wang further lessens his claim to credibility by *ad hoc* uses. For example, his ch. 4, p. 85 yields *yi ko-ko* 一個個, *shuang-shuang* 雙雙 and *ts'eng-ts'eng* 層層, all counted as "stuffing," but in the same aria *yi pu-pu* 一步步 and *yi tuan-tuan* 一段段 are counted base words; ch. 4, p. 76a has *liang-ko* 兩個 as base, but on the same page *yi ko* 一個 is given three times as "stuffing", and on p. 85b *t'a liang-ko* 他兩個 is all judged to be "stuffing" rather than three base words.

It became a popular artistic pastime during the Ming and Ch'ing dynasties to write new words to the *t'ao-shu* of Yuan dramatic form and a large body of "formulae" grew up. The authors of these were seldom more conversant with actual Yuan dynasty performances than is Wang Yü-chang, but all of them were anxious to discover the "rules" underlying the *ch'ü* forms.[9] There was strong conviction that these rules were rigid and extended even to certain requirements for tonal successions. Since even the *rhymes* of Yuan

---

[9] The psychology generally is of this order: there were fixed rules for *ch'ü. Ch'ü*, especially in the North, allowed for "stuffing." If one does not sort the "stuffing" from the base characters he will tend to miss the "proper" scansion. The final quirk (and it can be seen spelled out on p. 24 of Wang Ching-ch'ang's 汪經昌 *Ch'ü-hsüeh li-shih* 曲學例釋, Chung-hua Press, Taipei, 1962) is that the playwrights were only indifferently skilled in following "proper" formulae so, presumably, *they* should be faulted and not the manufacturers of formula books. Why one should not accept the fact that the playwrights are the craftsmen and it is up to us to discover what we can of their craft has never been made clear by men who have interested themselves in this aspect of Yüan drama.

dramatic arias are not required to be in the same tone (this is a freedom almost unique in Chinese poetry) and since the pressure of musical considerations would badly distort or erase most tonal distinctions, I cannot conceive of a composer for the stage worrying over traditional tonal euphony. Furthermore, I have never seen evidence of the existence of mandatory tone sequences adduced by any scholar which was not eventually contradicted by another scholar or by the arias themselves.[10]

Despite the disabilities which attach themselves to the study of *ch'ü* prosody, I am convinced that there is merit in what Wang has done and that with a more sophisticated approach something can be achieved far less ambitious than Wang's goal, but far sounder and more convincing than his conclusions. I hope that if my paper achieves nothing else it will at least convince the reader that the craft of composers in this genre consisted so often in the skillful manipulation of conventions that any hope of isolating *in detail* the rhythmic skeletons of musical conventions in Yuan dramatic arias by means of a *single* simple device like clearing away *ch'en-tzu* is doomed to disappointment. There is every hope, on the other hand, of being able to make many very helpful metrical generalizations—for example, the hearteningly consistent 4,4,3 (4,5) of *Tien chiang-ch'un* —once our sights are realistically lowered and more sophisticated concepts are brought to bear.

III

That Yuan drama has a large number of formal characteristics is widely known and commented on. But one is tempted to ask if the sixty new examples found in this century have caused us to revise statements made mainly on the basis of Tsang Mou-hsün's 臧懋循 selection *(YCH)* of 1615–1616. Choosing one highly consistent feature, the use of music in a single mode for any one act, for example, will give a fair yardstick, and since all Yuan dramas use

---

[10] Disagreement even over the "proper" base form is often found and disagreement over which characters to designate as *ch'en-tzu* is routine; cf. Aoki Masaru 青木正兒, *Gennin zatsugeki shokusetsu* 元人雜劇序說 (Chinese translation by Sui Shu-sen 隋樹森, Shanghai, 1941, p. 25), Wang Ching-ch'ang, *op. cit.*, p. 198, and Wang Yü-chang, *op. cit.*, ch. 2, p. 56a *et passim*.

the Hsien-lü mode, something pertinent to the entire genre may be said if we treat that mode *in extenso.*

The Hsien-lü mode had an overall reservoir of about forty-two different melodies,[11] of which *YCH* uses twenty-eight (two tunes it uses only once—*Ssu chi hua* 四季花 and *Yü-hua ch'iu* 玉花秋): by adding all sixty-two plays of *WP,* about a 50-percent increase in opportunity to use the twenty-odd unused melodies in the mode, it appears that there are only two more unquestionably new titles (*Ch'uan ch'uang yüeh* 穿窗月 and *San fan hou-t'ing hua* 三犯後庭花, both from 140, IV, 1,[12] and one questionable one (*Tan yen-erh* 單雁兒 from 148, 1 and 154) which is in fact the same as the *Yen-erh* we already know from *YCH.* One must conclude on the basis of these figures for the most regular of all modes in Yuan drama that the genre's form is remarkably conservative if not restrictive in the tunes that might be used from the Hsien-lü mode. About one-half the total available are actually employed. It adds a bit more to the picture to know that in *chu-kung-tiao* 諸宮調, a precursor of Yuan drama, the most used Hsien-lü melodies are the same ones we know from *YCH: Tien chiang-ch'un, Liu yao ling* 六幺令, *Sheng hu-lu* 勝葫蘆 and *Shang hua shih* 賞花時.[13]

To state the case in this fashion is to make the Yuan dramatist appear almost inhumanly patient with strictures. It also gives a false picture. In fact, though the demands of the *t'ao-shu* (song-set) give Yuan drama much of its agreeable compact construction, the song-set itself is like a bookshelf: the framework is there but each user fills it with items to his own taste. For example, the song-set for almost all first acts of Yuan drama is in the Hsien-lü mode and the dramatist wrote his initial aria-poetry to the tune called *Tien chiang-ch'un*—but

[11] The number given by *Chung-yüan yin-yün* 中原音韻, cf. Vol. 1, pp. 224–229 of *Chung-kuo ku-tien hsi-ch'ü lun-chu chi-ch'eng* 中國古典戲曲論著集成, Peking, 1959. This ten-volume set consists of critical editions for most of the extant works on music and drama from T'ang times to Ch'ing, and is superior to any similar collection. Sixty-one is the total given by T'ao Tsung-yi 陶宗儀 (T.九成, fl. 1360), whose discussion of Yuan *ch'ü* (date unknown) is included in most editions of *YCH.*

[12] There are three other kinds of *Hou-t'ing hua* in the repertoire.

[13] As a general rule, however, *chu-kung-tiao* uses many more tune titles than Yuan *tsa-chü* because it employs southern as well as northern forms. This and other information on the *chu-kung-tiao* is reported by Mme. Milena Doleželová-Velingerová, whose un-published dissertation (Praha) "*Čínské Vypravěčské Skladby: Chu-kung-tiao*" (Chinese Story-tellers' Compositions: the *Chu-kung-tiao*) deals with all extant examples of that genre. Cf. also the same author's *Ballad of the Hidden Dragon:* Liu Chih-yüan chu-kung-tiao (in collaboration myself), Clarendon Press, Oxford, 1971.

he *could* have used *Pa-sheng Kan-chou* 八聲甘州, and in three cases did. After one of these he always wrote his poetry to melody "b"—except in one case. After "b" he used "c"—but he could insert "r" or "s"[14] at this point and did in three cases, or he could dispense with "c" or "d" entirely and did so in seven cases. Beyond this there is almost no general statement that can be made about the progression of a Hsien-lü song-set except to note that the dramatist would wind up the song-set (and the act) with one of five possible coda titles. Even greater freedom was provided the composer by the fact that he could write his poetry to one of the melodies within the song-set and if he were not satisfied with the scope it gave him he could repeat the melody. An extension of this freedom—which seems to have been used with great musical subtlety in some cases—is to repeat sequences of melodies such as "sqsq" or "qtqr," "qtqrq." Related to this, in the options given the composer, were the coda chains often used in the Cheng-kung and Chung-lü modes. They run *ssu-sha* 四煞, *san-sha* 三煞, *erh-sha* 二煞 etc., and mean "fourth from final," "third from final" and so on.[15] The composer could choose to start the series anywhere that seemed appropriate (there are series as long as *wu-sha* 五煞 through *sha-wei* 煞尾, "coda"), but he might also use simply the coda alone.

Though what has been said above about the flexibility of musical structure is hardly exhaustive it does indicate that since the composer-poet could manipulate this area of the genre's strictures through such a large number of permutations he was likely to find some combination satisfactory to him as a poet. Another convention of Yuan drama closely related to the formation of the *t'ao-shu* is the matter of limiting singing parts to a single role[16] within any given act. This restriction was less of a restraint to the composer as poet—though it did in theory deny him the opportunity to work with the poetic effects possible through the emotional strophe and antistrophe of two or more characters interacting[17]—than it was to the dramatist.

[14] I am using here the lettering system found in "Song Arrangements in Shianleu Acts of Yuan Tzarjiuh," by Hugh M. Stimson, *Tsing Hua Journal of Chinese Studies* (New Series) Vol. I, 1965, pp. 86–106.

[15] In one confusing case, YCH 51, *Ch'ing-shan lei* 青衫淚, it runs 1, 2, 3, 4 instead of 4, 3, 2, 1. I know of no explanation for this.

[16] The exceptions are WP 114, *Tung-ch'iang chi* 東牆記 and 141, *Sheng hsien meng* 昇仙夢.

[17] Cf. below for more on this.

No matter how well a personality may dominate an act there has to be a certain sameness to the use of a single singing voice and a single viewing angle throughout the dramatic unit. There can be no surprise, no shifting of the audience's attention, nor even the refreshing effect of an astringent olive eaten between mouthfuls of sweet wine. In this area (which is essentially a theatrical one) the sixty-odd newly found Yuan dramas do bring forward new material to our consideration. After all, Tsang's *YCH* was directed at a reading audience of quite distinguished taste and he says in his introduction:

> "Some say that during Yuan times officials were chosen by having them write poetry to (operatic) songs. . . . Since the dramas were thus composed under examination conditions and within a short time interval, this is the reason all the great men of the era, Ma Chih-yüan 馬致袁, Ch'iao Meng-fu 喬孟符 and the like, always ran out of power after the fourth act. Others say that the examiner simply furnished the topic and then specified what songs were to be used together with the rhyme required. The dialogue parts were written by actors at the time of performance which is why they are so crude and repetitious—. but all this I am not disposed to argue about."

Further on he says:

> "In general, the marvel of Yuan *ch'ü* (arias) is that they achieve their effect with no effort. The finest of them should be ranked with our best *yüeh-fu* 樂府 songs even though the cruder among them include colloquialisms."

There is no question that Tsang thought of Yuan drama as Yuan *songs* and half believed their composers to have been office holders. There is reason to fear he edited his text to fit the taste of his readers and his own preconceptions. There is reason to hope that the sixty dramas brought to light in this century are relatively less "edited" and better reflect the fact that *tsa-chü* were, after all, dramatic performances which had to withstand the exigencies of the stage and exploit its powers, command the attention of an audience and insure its return. It is my opinion that this is the reason the restriction of singing to a single role is disregarded more often in the dramas to be found in *WP* than it is in *YCH,* though intrusion into the *t'ao-shu* of song performances extraneous to it is by no means foreign to *YCH*. For example, *YCH* 15,4: here Ts'ui-luan, the heroine and singing role, finally achieves revenge upon her perfidious husband and his equally perfidious second wife, the *ch'a-tan* 搽旦, or villainess role. When the two have been taken into custody the following appears in the script:

Ts'UI-LUAN: (angrily): Lock her up at once!

CH'A-TAN: Don't yammer so! When my father was in office he especially liked to sing *Tsui T'ai-p'ing*.[18] I even got so I could do it. Dear lady, listen while I sing it for you.

(sings):   *Tsui T'ai-p'ing* 醉太平
I see you are as brilliant as Cho Wen-chün
I see you are as beautiful as Hsi-shih
Why should you have been so light of hand, quick of foot
To steal? Surely this was perjury by Ts'ui T'ung.

Ts'UI-LUAN: Attendants, lock her up!

CH'A-TAN: Aiya! Here am I, a bride still wearing her phoenix cap and sunset robe, about to be locked in a cangue! Wait a moment! (Pantomimes removing of phoenix cap.)

(sings):   I take off my phoenix cap
With its eight treasures picked out in thread of gold.

(Pantomimes taking off the sunset robe.)

I unfasten my sunset robe.
These I bequeath to lady Chang as her dower
I would be happy now simply to be her maid.

Ts'UI-LUAN: Attendants, they are locked up and in custody. Take them off to stand before my father!

(EXEUNT)

Though this song is in the same mode as the rest of the act it stands out quite clearly from the song-set, for its rhyme is *ih* (class 4, *yü-mo*) where the rest of the act uses the rhyme *ien* (class 10, *hsien-*

---

[18] Despite the fact that this song is dragged in here by the heels it is interesting to note that her father *did* sing a *Tsui t'ai-p'ing* intrusively in the second act of this drama. This indicated attention to detail on the part of either the author or the editor.

t'ien).[19] What dramatic or poetic purpose is served by this particular intrusion is not clear (though the simple desire for a second voice may have been its only reason) but I suggest that whatever else it may indicate we should bear in mind that the urge to fatten parts was probably no less strong among stage people then than now.

A second use for the song intrusion in *YCH* is simply to bring on the dancing girls (or the Yuan dynasty equivalent thereof) and an example may be seen in 63,1. There the songs a group of entertainers sing are in a mode other than the act proper and their rhymes are *ai* instead of the act's *ung*. They would stand away from the song-set in a stage performance and the *YCH* text takes pains to make them stand out for the reader by dropping their titles below the height occupied by those from the song-set proper. It should be noticed also that these songs may actually *displace* the songs ordinarily expected— the effect is "a g (intrusion) h" where one usually finds "a b c d g h". In other words, the intrusion seems to oust tunes "b c d" by its presence: there is no other example in the Hsien-lü mode where song "a" is followed immediately by "g". I introduce this rather technical consideration because it may indicate another of some importance to any description of Yuan drama—insertion of songs which interrupt the song-set may have been done either by the performers *or* the composer. The dropping of a normal "b c d" segment when an intrusion is included may indicate the composer himself compensating and balancing his music and poetry. Whatever the general case, this particular example is not merely an intrusion; it generates a reciprocal effect upon the rest of the song-set.

The third and most frequent fashion of employing song intrusions is the sung epilogue (or epode?). This intrusion is sometimes straight, but more often comic. The best example of the latter I know appears in *YCH* 95, 3, *Wang chiang t'ing* 望江亭. This piece is perhaps the only surviving Yuan drama with its tongue so firmly in its cheek, so a farcical song interlude fits particularly well. The song terminating act three of *YCH* 95 is out of mode (probably it was not even "northern music"), out of rhyme, but perfectly in keeping with the intrusive comic song. The lyrics are as disreputable as the comic-

---

[19] Cf. however *YCH* 48, 3 where the monk sings a rollicking "dry bones" type of intrusion in the right rhyme, proper mode, and the tune is in proper sequence. This can be labeled intrusive only because it is not sung by the lead.

villains who have just been completely gulled and left in a drunken stupor by a heroine who displays more than a trace of raffishness herself. She has relieved them of their badge of office and the appurtenances to it—all of which they discover as they recover from insensibility:

OFFICIAL (speaking): But what can we do about it?

(Ma-an'erh) 馬鞍兒

SERVANT (sings): Think-on-it, con-cen-trate; fall down and yell.

SERVANT 2 (sings): Think-til-you, char-your-pate; my what a smell!

OFFICIAL (sings): Sodden with liquor fumes and yet burning as well.

TOGETHER (sing): No one will ask us so we'll never tell
Burning our incense and chanting our spell
We'll make her hot meat start twitching like hell!

OFFICIAL (speaks): Why, these rascals can even sing a southern style trio!

(EXEUNT)[20]

Before leaving this carefree bit of vulgarity I should like to point out that it is one of the most successful pieces of "lyric" poetry—that is, poetry which reflects musical rhythms—in Yuan drama. It sings even in modern pronunciation:

[20] The Yangs (*Selected Plays of Kuan Han-ching*, Shanghai, 1958) translate this as follows:
SERVANT: I stamp my feet in dismay! (敖 should be 叫)
SERVANT: Here's a fine to-do!
OFFICIAL: I am burning with secret rage!
TOGETHER: But we dare not let anyone know.
Let us go offer incense,
And lay a curse on that woman!
There is a shaft of what I take to be purest wit a few lines before this which goes:
OFFICIAL: Do you mean to tell me you can write as well, madam?
TAN: Oh sir, I have need to know (須識) about downsweeps (撇),
upright sticks (竪), drops of water (點) and strokes (劃).
Since she is posing as a fisherwoman I find this rather clever. The Yangs translate it:
OFFICIAL: I suppose you can read and write?
TAN: A little.
If it were not that I knew the variorum for this play I could not credit the fact that we use the same text.

This amalgam of earthy verse, jingling rhythm and farcical plot could not fail to be a box-office success.

I have no wish to imply that these are the only ways *YCH* employs intrusive songs, but it is my impression that something more than a majority of examples is covered by these three categories. *WP* dramas, on the other hand, not only make greater use of intrusive songs but employ them in a wider variety of ways. In addition to examples which parallel *YCH*, there is one case in *WP* of an "occasional song" *(hsiao-ch'ü)* 小曲 which is so closely integrated with the dramatic mechanism of the performance that motivation for the rest of the play would be entirely lacking without it. In the first act of *Huang hua yü* 黃花峪 (156), Liu Ching-fu's wife is asked by her husband to sing a song.[21] This attracts the attention of the drama's blackguard, which leads to intervention by Yang Hsiung and the

---

[21] Stimson, analysing the components of Hsien-lü song sets, quite properly ignores this Nan-lü song and the Nan-lü in 118, 1. He should have continued by ignoring the *Ch'ing-chiang yin* 清江引 of 126, 1, the two Chung-lü songs and their reprises in 115, 1, and the out-of-mode intrusions in 63, 1. They all bear the same marks: wrong rhymes, and not sung by singing roles. As I once pointed out ("Elements of Yuan Opera", *Journal of Asian Studies*, xvii-i, 1958, pp. 417-434) a similar intrusion appears in 126, 6 where two *ching* roles sing a *Nan Ch'ing ke-erh* 南清歌兒 with *ai* rhymes, not *ao* as they are in the arias.

eventual capture of the villain by Lu Chih-shen. In this case the song appears before the *t'ao-shu* begins; it has an *ai* rhyme as opposed to the *ang* rhyme of the rest of the act, and it is sung to a "southern" tune.[22]

Duets sung by *ching* 淨 (comic-cum-villain) roles are far more frequent in *WP* than in *YCH*. It seems that the very act of using more than one voice to sing a single song was considered ludicrous, rustic (?), and "southern"[23] by capital audiences, so there is almost always a hint of the comic about the singers of duets; but the one appearing in 118, 1, where two *ching* hope to catch the embroidered ball and sing a duet of disappointed hopes when they do not, seems not to be used for comic contrast so much as for simple variety. The kind of intrusive song found a number of times in *WP* but not in *YCH* is embedded in comic sketches reminiscent of the Jigs and Drolls of Elizabethan and Commonwealth drama—one must substitute song for dance to make the analogy close, but once that is done the similarity between the two comic traditions is quite striking. As I have pointed out elsewhere[24] I am of the opinion that some (cf. *WP* 126, 2) of the more elaborate farce sketches (complete with songs) with which dramas in *WP* are larded are in fact remains of *yüan-pen* 院本 that composers or players of Yuan drama gladly incorporated into their pieces for the sake of comic seasoning and musical variety. There are other interludes, mildly comic in tone (which being solo performances in song and speech are not likely to have been *yüan-pen*) used elsewhere in *WP* dramas for what I take to be reasons of musical variety. The most curious of these is the opening section of *WP* 115, 1 (*Yi-ch'iao chin lü* 圯橋進履). This interlude opens the drama as it stands today, but we know the first section of the script is

[22] Cf. *Yüan-chü chen-yi* 元劇斟疑, Shanghai, 1960, pp. 149–150. Yen Tun-yi believes the piece to be a pastiche of the three great *Shui-hu* dramas, *Shuang hsien kung* 雙獻功, *Li K'uei fu ching* 李逵負荊 and the Ming piece *Chang yi su ts'ai* 仗義疎財; he points out that the intrusive song itself may be an indication of the drama's late date since this same song is found in the 22nd act of the Ming period *Yu-kuei chi* 幽閨記, where it is unquestionably more apposite. Cf. *Liu-shih chung ch'ü* 六十種曲, ii, 2, p. 57.

[23] Was this, perhaps, the Chinese equivalent of the "West Country Bumpkin" complete with dialect ("Ud zooks here's a yellow would make a man zwear") who figures so largely in Elizabethan Jigs? Cf. Baskervill, C. R., *The Elizabethan Jig* (Chicago, 1929), pp. 428–432, and the part of Wat in *The Cheaters Cheated*, pp. 475–488.

[24] Cf. my article, "Elements of Yuan Opera", cited above, note 21; cf. also Hu Chi 胡忌, *Sung-Chin tsa-chü k'ao* 宋金雜劇考, Shanghai, 1959, pp. 80 ff.

missing and cannot, consequently, see just how it was mitered into the text originally. The sketch opens with Ch'iao, a Taoist Immortal, reciting what may have been his entrance lines:

> . . . the dark of night became my screen. I'd pop behind a chimney flue and if the owner was not in, silent as a wrack of smoke I burst the wall or roof-tile through to steal his cloth or filch his cloak. And why, you ask, should this have been? Because my Teacher taught me to . . . .

Ch'iao continues by relating his lamentable (for a Taoist Immortal) taste for dog meat and women and then sings *Shang hsiao-lou* 上小樓 (often used for intrusive songs) using *ieh* rhyme:

Deep in the hills I live, far in the wilds;
No neighbor to the east nor hut to the west.
I love the bitter wild-almond, the tiny mountain peach.
I sup on plainest fare: the yellow leek, the bamboo sprout and wild tea
    leaf;
Where I live the smoke of hearths is seldom seen.
Even calls of birds are still.
Gone is the lantern's gleam, the fire's glow,
Only the tips of trees against a partial moon and dawn-spent stars
Keep me company.

This is followed by three reprises, the first of which contradicts the above song completely by relating Ch'iao's craving for red meat, robbery, and violence. The second tells of his fearlessness in the face of any wild beast and the third of his addiction to venery and wine. The picture is not of the ever popular "sturdy divine" such as we find with Lu Chih-shen, *Shui-hu's* 水滸 immortal monk, but of an inept Taoist adept; it becomes a portrait of a farcical, bumbling immortal[25] as soon as he has sung his fourth song, upon meeting Chang Liang whose way is being barred by a menacing "tiger." Ch'iao the immortal says: Chang Liang, do you wish me to save you?

---

[25] Since the first page or more of this play has been lost we do not have a designation for the type of role Ch'iao 喬 is playing, but from his actions it is only sensible to conclude he wore *ching* (comic) make-up. This assumption is further strengthened by knowledge that there is a clownish Taoist nun playing a *ching* role, also called simply Ch'iao, in *Tung-hsüan sheng hsien* 洞玄昇仙. Cf. *Ku-pen Yüan-Ming tsa-chü* 孤本元明雜劇, vol. 28, 3, p. 4b.

CHANG: I wish you knew how I wish you to save me!

CH'IAO: I have no arts to save you, Chang Liang;

(sings):   But I think you've no cause to lose your life for no cause.

CHANG: Master, take pity on me and save me, will you?

CH'IAO: That is no tiger, Chang Liang, that's a very large pussycat
I raised myself and he's called Good Brother. If I call Good
Brother once he lowers his head, sheaths his claws and lies
prone. If I call him thrice, at the first call he crouches
beside me, on the second I mount him, and on the third I
fly into space on his back.

CHANG: Does the Master really have such powers?

CH'IAO: You don't believe . . . ? I'll call him . . . . Good Brother!
   [Tiger bats Ch'iao.]
Good Brother!
   [Tiger again bats Ch'iao.]

CHANG: Master! He's really a wild one, don't tease him!

CH'IAO: It's nothing, I raised him myself, my own Good Brother.
   [Tiger knocks Ch'iao down.]

CHANG: Master! You are an immortal, how can a tiger knock you
down? [Tiger drags Ch'iao offstage.]

CH'IAO: It's nothing, nothing, I raised him myse-e-e-lf. . . .

Taoist immortals and adepts are often seen in paintings and, if the
implications of this farce sketch are followed, it would appear they
were seen on the stage also, with "tigers" and other wild beasts as
their familiars and steeds. This episode, in fact, contains all the
ingredients of a conventional Taoist interlude—reference to alchemy,
eroticism, the powers of wine, appeal of the wilderness, the "tiger"
familiar, and even the wild tea of the mountains.[26] It was my opinion
almost a decade ago that this sketch, complete with its intrusive
songs, was a burlesque of the conventional Taoist interlude done by a

[26] The best English rendering of such an interlude is in H. Shadick, *The Travels of
Lao-ts'an*, chaps. 8–10, where we have the whole Taoist interlude complex, beginning
with (p. 89) the "tiger" (the quotation marks are to keep the unwary reader from seeing
Bengals in the snows of Northeast China's mountains), which is obviously a supernatural one and is connected with the mountain villa and its Taoists by implication,
and continuing through the joys of "mountain vegetables" and alchemy (p. 95), the
obliquely erotic (pp. 100–101), and wild tea (p. 102).

somewhat uncertain hand. I have found no good reason to change my mind since then. The songs, I believe, are intended to give dramatic variety and set the tone of supernatural while the final dialogue and stage business make a farce and parody of the conventional Taoist Immortal's ability to ride "tigers".[27] The poet or player incorporated the sketch and provided his script with added freshness by simply sliding it in between two songs of his *t'ao-shu*.

IV

Lines of Dramatic Development Available With the Conventions

So much for the range of variations in those conventions of organization which are related to the song-sets. I suggest that the playwright who was closely involved with a theater dependent on its box-office utilized these insertions into the main musical framework (itself already a very flexible affair) to produce scripts with still wider dramatic appeal and variety.

It will be noticed, however, in the examples given that there is no instance of full utilization of intrusive songs for dramatic effect. That is, the songs are not done seriatim with those of the *t'ao-shu* to produce a kind of musical dialogue with two distinct voices. The Yuan dramatist finally does achieve this effect with his song-sets by means of a *ho-t'ao* 合套 script (alternate songs are in Northern and Southern music and sung alternately by male and female lead) in 141, *Sheng hsien meng* 昇仙夢, which is a very late Yuan or early Ming production, but long before that time he was able to manipulate the available conventions of his genre and reach a high level of dramatic tension while violating none of the structures which give Yuan drama its unique, tight-knit texture.

Recited verse was a part of dramatic performance as early as the *Liu Chih-yuan* 劉知遠 *chu-kung-tiao*[28] and remains a part in modern times. When we read in Yuan drama scripts that a certain character

---

[27] I have not yet found a stage exit done on the back of a tiger (though *YCH* 98, 3 has a Taoist riding the force of a tiger's mighty fart all the way back to his temple); but a similar exit made mounted on a crane may be seen in *WP* 123 at the end of the "wedge."

[28] Without doubt it was used in early *yüan-pen* as well.

shih-yün 詩云 "recites in *shih* form" or *tz'u-yün* 詞云 "recites in *tz'u* form" we have no really clear idea what the vocal effect was. However, since some type of stylized declamation or chant (or even singing) has always been associated with these poetic forms we assume that something quite different from conversational voice was used in oral performances on the Yuan stage. The learned playwright had so many verses from the brushes of former poets at his fingertips that he could often say much of what he wished by simply tacking them together. The danger here is that they become perfunctory pastiche and certainly much entrance and exit verse in Yuan drama, and still more in Ming drama, is simply that. But the great dramatist can remain entirely within the ambit of his medium and produce passages which though partially derivative are both superb theater art and wholly satisfactory poetry by the skillful use of conventions available to him. My thesis has been from the beginning that the Yuan dramatist could move as freely as he wished within shackles of his own devising. Recited verse was one of the broadest areas open to exploitation. I hope the passage given below from *YCH* 15, 4 (*Hsiao-hsiang yü* 瀟湘雨) will demonstrate that despite the restrictions the song-set and the single singing role place upon poetic dialogue, the playwright has managed wonderfully well with what song and verse are available to him. In the first act the singing role, Chang Ts'ui-luan, was separated from her father when their ferry sank in a storm. She has suffered several years of vicissitudes including an unconsummated marriage, and now both father and daughter (she as a prisoner in manacles and cangue who is not supposed to survive her trip to prison) have taken shelter in the same posthouse though neither knows the other is there.[29]

CHANG   [Ts'ui-luan's father]: Hsing-erh, I am so weary from this entire day in the saddle that I must sleep for a while. Allow no one to disturb me for if I'm awakened I'll give you a beating. Tell the others what I have said.

---

[29] For my translation of the last act of *Hsiao-hsiang yü* cf. H. W. Wells, ed., *Asian Drama: A Collection of Festival Papers*, University of South Dakota (mimeo), Vermillion, S.D., May, 1966, pp. 53–83, "Colloquium and Translation".

HSING-ERH: Yes sir. Keeper, I order you to allow no disturbance
                 for my master is going to rest and if he is wakened
                 he'll beat me and I'll take care of you.

KEEPER: That I know!

            ENTER prisoner's guard and heroine.

TS'UI-LUAN: Dear brother, my guard, all the rain in heaven is
                 falling on us.

GUARD: This much rain could just drown a man. I wouldn't
                 mind resting a while myself. . . . Shamen Island
                 prison certainly takes a bit of walking to reach.

TS'UI-LUAN: Brother, the rain gets worse.

            [*ian* rhyme] *Tuan-cheng hao*

(sings):   So heavy the rain! Wind gusts as from a fan!
                 High in the empty air they both have twined
                     together,
                 Neither heeds the traveller's woes, both buffet his
                     head and face.

            Kun hsiu-ch'iu 滾繡毬

            That day near the bank of the stream,
            The rise of the shore,
            What chance had we against that towering wind,
                that curling wave?
            On each side the sight struck chill to the heart.
            The wind blew as though piercing us with arrows,
            The rain fell as water pours from a cistern.
            This storm I watch now I know bodes ill,
            My destiny provokes punishments and summons
                calamity.
            The water drenching this Hsiao-hsiang scenery
            Is dark with lamp-black that wet clouds paint across
                the skies,
            And tears flow from my eyes.

CHIEH-TZU: Here, here, now! Don't fuss about it. We'll go to the
                 Lin-chiang posthouse and spend the night. (Pan-
                 tomimes calling at the door.) Keeper! Open up!

KEEPER: Here's another one! Let me open the door. You two have a nerve, with the great judge in here trying to rest! Now you stay outside and if you make a rumpus I'll break your legs for you. I'm closing the door.

CHIEH-TZU: What luck! A great judge staying here so we can't even make a sound. Oh well, I'll take off my jacket and try to wring it dry. (Pantomimes undressing.) Yah! I still have a biscuit in my sleeve pocket. Might as well eat that.

TS'UI-LUAN: Brother what are you eating?

CHIEH-TZU: A biscuit.

TS'UI-LUAN: Brother, could I have some?

CHIEH-TZU: Every time I'm eating something you're looking for something to eat. Oh well, take some.

TS'UI-LUAN: Brother, could you give me a little more?

CHIEH-TZU: But it's only one biscuit! I give you some and it's not enough. . . . eh-h-h, I suppose I should give you the whole thing!

TS'UI-LUAN (sings): *Pan-tu-shu* 伴讀書

I plead with my guard for food but
How impossible to explain to him the hunger in me.
He has taken this storm-swept journey by force and
  walked me
Till my sinews are slack, my strength is gone and
  shudders of dizziness
Sweep my body, which is all pain and ten parts
  weary.
I, I, I must drowse, must sleep.

Hsiao Ho-shang 笑和尙

I, I, I have pressed on through this night which has
  seemed a year.
I, I, I hide my anger against heaven for
I, I, I must be paying in full some chilling oath
Sworn in a former life. My, my, my eyes are wept dry
My, my, my throat is cracked with sobs.
Come, come, come brother—How will I swallow this
  biscuit you have given me?

(speaks):   Aiyo heaven! Here am I in this place but who knows where my father is?

CHANG: Oh, Ts'ui-luan, my child, I shall die of grief over you. This moment through closed lids I saw my daughter before me. Just as she was telling me what happened to her years ago, someone startled me awake.

[six-four   My evening years came long ago.
ao rhyme   'My dream is broken, my spirit spent.'
atonal]   Soul wretched and hostel silent.
    And the path in the sky has reached autumn;
    The landscape is mournful.
    Night is endless in this river town.
    The sound of the watcher's bell vexes me.
    It makes an old man chill with dread
    Or simmer with impatience.
    Crickets of the cold chirp,
    Geese from the border fort cry,
    The wind of metal soughs
    And the rain rustles.

    It is probably that heartless wind and rain which keep my eyes from closing. "Melancholy as all the waters of the Hsiang which roll on forever. Like the rains of autumn—each drop the sound of grief itself." I just finished telling that worthless Hsing-erh not to allow any disturbance, but he's been careless no doubt, and should be given a beating.

HSING-ERH: I gave the hostler his orders but he paid no attention. I'll give him a beating. (Pantomimes beating the keeper.) You good-for-nothing, I told you there would be no rumpus, but you've wakened my master and he's going to beat me, so I'll beat you.

KEEPER: Uncle, stop! Go get some sleep yourself. It was all the fault of that prisoner's guard. I'm opening the door to beat that no-good. (Pantomimes beating the guard.) You, guard, I told you there was to be no rumpus! You and your snuffling and crying have waked up his honor and I've been taking a beating from his escort. Now you get yours!

GUARD: But it was all the fault of this hardcase!
(recites in *tz'u*)
[*u* rhyme]   Oh, you are a fine Meng Chiang-nü carrying winter
                    clothes a thousand li.
                  A virtuous Madam Chao whose scarlet skirt was
                    caked with earth. [?]
                  Though you weep more than Empress Ngo-huang
                  Who would want *your* tears to dapple the bamboo?

TS'UI-LUAN: Let me speak, brother, I am not allowed anger.
(recites in *tz'u*):
[*u* rhyme][30]   The wrongs I've suffered, who will plead them for
                    me?
                  From this day forth, brother, I shall swallow both
                    bitterness and voice.
                  Never again shall I wail or weep my pain.
(speaks):   Papa, how I miss you.

CHANG: Oh, Ts'ui-luan, my child, how I ache for you. I was
                  telling you the things that happened to me after we
                  were parted at Huai Ferry—but someone woke me
                  from my dream.
(recites in *tz'u*): First because my heart was ill at ease,
[*u* rhyme]   Next because my mind was all uncertain,
                  As soon as my eyes closed father and child were met
                    again.
                  Even as I struggled to tell the doubts of those years
                    gone by,
                  Suddenly the startled dream fled.
                  From where came the cruel sound; what was it?
                  —the clink-clank of armored horsemen?
                  —the cold, stiff thump of wet garments against the
                    laundry block?
                  —the chittering of crickets in a deserted stairwell
                    sounding through my window?
                  —geese returning to southern eddies from beyond
                    the reach of heaven?
                  But now I stop my chant and listen closely.

[30] The less poetic "tz'u" (and I use this term because the Yuan dramatists do, not
because they bear any resemblance to Sung dynasty *tz'u*) I have rhymed in an attempt
to make them stand out from the loftier diction of the more serious verse. The persistent
u (*yü-mo* 魚莫) rhyme extends through the entire set of "*tz'u*" irrespective of which
character does the reciting.

It is nothing but the wild wind and rushing rain that summon me awake.

I face this grey prospect having lost all who were close to me.

What wonder then grief sours the heart still more?

My child, do you yet live the life I knew

Or have you come back to this mansion earth in another form?

Are you wealthy, honored?

Or captive, slaved?

A white haired father in the lonely hostel ponders, wonders,

Ah, heaven!

But his daughter in the bloom of her years is somewhere anguished!

(speaks):   I told you, Hsing-erh, there was to be no noise! Now you've wakened me. (Pantomimes striking Hsing-erh.)

HSING-ERH: Don't beat me, master, it was that damned hostel-keeper. (He pantomimes going out and seeing keeper.) You, keeper! I told you there would be no disturbance; what do you mean by waking my master?

(recites in *tz'u*): I gave you a thousand commands, ten thousand warnings.

[*u* rhyme]   But you have allowed loud weeping and mournings.
                 And since my master beat "aiyah!" from me
                 I shall thump an "Uncle!" from thee!

KEEPER: It's all the fault of that guard outside this door so I am opening it and I'll beat that good-for-nothing guard!

(recites in *tz'u*): What matter if the rain has soaked you through and through,

[*u* rhyme]   It gives you no call to weep "wu-hu"
                 And if his escort gives me mine
                 I will break your mother's spine!

GUARD: All he hears is a raised voice.

(recites in *tz'u*): And his door pops open in a rage at the noise.

[u rhyme]   Had you ever wandered you would always be kin
                 To the traveler. Instead, you begin
                 Without question to belabor someone
                 Cursed with a manacle-bearing cangue-wearing
                     worry-minded tear-soaked stinking female
                 Who woke that posthouse mounted gold-badged
                     Panjandrum who first lops off a man's head and
                     then asks him what he's done![31]
                 I've put up with hunger and suffered cold, because
                 I've no love for the rod and now I find it's just
                 as close to my skin as before. It would be a lot
                 better to butt the wind and brave the rain on the
                 highroad again to find someplace else to spend
                 the night.

Ts'UI-LUAN   In all meekness I beg you, brother,
(recites in *tz'u*): Please hear my deepest feelings.
[u rhyme]   Find it in you to take pity on me
                 And you will be as much to me as my blood parents.
                 Speak no more of further travel,
                 Of blistered feet, the ropes of rushing rain,
                 The arrow wind's wild thrumming.
                 You talked of finding peace in this posthouse,
                 How can you drive us forth again by angry talk?
                 You would seek some barnyard inn or village public
                     house
                 But in this cavernous darkness who could find the
                     place?
                 I would end my life in the jaws of wild beasts
                 Or the bellies of the river's fish.
                 In no time the temples' matin bells will ring.
                 Allow us, I beg you, to shelter here still,
                 Out of the night rain on the Hsiao-hsiang.

CHANG: Well, dawn has come. Hsing-erh, go to the main
                 door, find the person who has disturbed this whole
                 night and bring him before me!
                     (Hsing-erh brings the guard and Ts'ui-luan.)

Ts'UI-LUAN (recognizing her father): It's my papa!

---

[31] The last line of this verse is made to suffer a grotesque metrical elephantiasis to
heighten its comic aspect. I have tried to approximate it in English by putting an
impossible number of feet between "someone" and "done."

CHANG: Ts'ui-luan, my child! Oh, where have you been these
                    three years?! What are you doing wearing cangue
                    and manacles!

Notice that Ts'ui-luan's aria is the reason for her father's first
declamation and Ts'ui-luan's first *tz'u* introduces her father's first
tz'u. There is an excellent theatrical irony brought about by allowing
the audience to see pathetic possibilities inherent in the situation
which none of the actors can discern. Besides this the author's skilled
use of verse creates a dramatic and poetic dialog (each character's
verse observes a proper decorum and buskin is not confused with
sock) to which the audience would have given serious attention—if
only because it was poetry. Furthermore, they would in all likelihood
have understood it completely—which was certainly not always the
case when the dramatis personae sang. The final section of the song-
set is delayed until the mechanics of recognition and reunion have
been worked out in another verse form, the *tz'u,* then the poetry of
the song-set takes over for final sentiments and the conventionalized
emotions of the finale.

With the information on the prosody of the dramatic *ch'ü* now
becoming available (especially through Johnson's work), it is
growing clearer that much of the verse declaimed (as opposed to
sung) in *tsa-chü* is actually mimicking what was done with the song
lyrics. Often authors seem to be writing what amount to songs for
recitation. What I once rather timidly suggested[32] I can now state
with a great deal more confidence: Yuan playwrights utilized the
metrics of their songs to write their verse as well. In my opinion this
interlude of "*tz'u*" found in the fourth act of *YCH* 15 is actually a
kind of musicless song-set. Note the use of a single rhyme throughout,
long and short lines, shifting caesura, and verses which are devoted to
the dramatic situation instead of generalized emotions. The author
has skillfully used the prosody common to his arias and has produced
something not to become a regular phenomenon for another century:
a piece of drama in which there is poetic dialogue divided among
many voices and not just poetic declamation patched into the
dramatic mechanism.

[32] Cf. *Occasional Papers,* Center for Chinese Studies, University of Michigan, No. 1,
p. 56, n. 1.

It is obvious, I believe, that the arias in *YCH* and *WP* are also working in the direction of multiple-voice participation in the poetic (i.e. sung) parts of the drama. Note the very frequent insertion of lines by the listener—"tell me how did it go then?" "I don't know that story, tell it to me"—which not only give the singer an opportunity for new lyric statements and shifts of subject but show the efforts of the dramaturgist to breathe into solo song (a static, not dramatic vehicle) the life and movement of drama. The playwrights had, only a short time before, taken the declaimed (not acted) *chu-kung-tiao* (Medley) and transformed it by just such means as these into genuine poetic drama, creating in the process a unique, germinal, and appealing genre.

Some Concerns and Methods of the Ming *Ch'uan-ch'i* Drama

by Cyril Birch

In this paper I examine three of those long, involved plays which flourished in the Ming period and were known under the generic name of *ch'uan-ch'i* 傳奇. *Ch'ing-shan chi* 青衫記 is to a large extent a reworking of the Yuan *tsa-chü* 雜劇 *Ch'ing-shan lei* 青衫淚, and thus suggests points of comparison between distinct dramatic forms. *Ming feng chi* 鳴鳳記 is a rare instance, for its time, of a drama built around contemporary events, and illustrates the involvement of the dramatist in the political life of his day. *Mu-tan t'ing* 牡丹亭 is much the best-known of the three, and justifiably so, for it is one of the great masterpieces of the *ch'uan-chi* genre and may be used as a measure of the height of the drama's achievement in Ming times.

Many, or most, of the more technical aspects and conventions of *ch'uan-chi* are omitted from the following accounts. There are numerous treatments of the evolution of *ch'uan-ch'i*, the prosody of song-patterns, conventions of performance, and so on. I would not wish to deprecate the importance of such studies or to suggest that the plays can be at all adequately treated without reference to their performance aspects. From the printed text of the play alone, however, it may be possible to illustrate something of the dramatist's approach to his subject, his skill in presenting his story through the medium of the dramatic form, and his debt and close affinity to the great fiction writers of the Ming period whose works up to this time have been more widely known and more closely studied.

I. *Ch'ing-shan chi*

Each of Po Chü-yi's two most celebrated romantic ballads provided material for a whole succession of plays. The tragic fate of Yang Kuei-fei as sung in the *Ch'ang-hen ko* 長恨歌 was related again by Po Jen-fu 白仁甫 in the Yuan *tsa-chü Wu-t'ung yü* 梧桐雨, by T'u Lung 屠隆 (*chin-shih* of 1577) in the *ch'uan-ch'i Ts'ai-hao chi* 彩毫記 and by Hung Sheng 洪昇 (1645–1704) in *Ch'ang-sheng-tien* 長生殿, to mention only the best-known of the works which have survived. The ballad *P'i-pa hsing* 琵琶行, with its glamorous ingredients of moonlit river, exiled poet and aging courtesan, inspired plays hardly less popular. Kubo Tenzui[1] treats of five plays on the theme. Two of these are too minor to concern us at present. A third was a favorite piece of the Ch'ien-lung period, Chiang Shih-ch'üan's 蔣士銓 *Ssu hsien ch'iu* 四絃秋. This is a four-act *tsa-chü* which contains many fine songs: Chiang is credited in one marginal comment with recapturing the "authentic tone of the Yuan dramatists" 元人本色. The play remains extremely faithful to the original poem, and was in fact written, as Chiang tells us in his preface, to set the record straight about Po Chü-yi and his relationship with the *p'i-pa* player.

It was a Yuan dramatist, no less a figure than Ma Chih-yüan 馬致遠 himself, who first knocked the record sadly askew with his *tsa-chü Ch'ing-shan lei*.[2] Ma's invention of a love affair between Po Chü-yi and the subject of his ballad was accepted by the Ming dramatist Ku Ta-tien 顧大典 (*chin-shih* of 1568) as the basis for a *ch'uan-ch'i* in 30 scenes, *Ch'ing-shan chi*.[3] The appended synopses will make clear the essential similarity of action between these two plays. More detailed study reveals, however, a host of differences, and consideration of some of the major disparities—of the innovations, that is to say, which Ku Ta-tien saw fit to make in his treatment of the theme—may give us a lead-in to some of the concerns and contributions of the Ming dramatists.

---

[1] 久保天隨, "Biwako no gikyoku" 琵琶行の戲劇 in *Shina gikyoku kenkyu* 支那戲劇研究, Tokyo, 1928.

[2] *Yüan ch'ü hsüan* 元曲選; for six other surviving editions, cf. Fu Hsi-hua 傅惜華 *Yüan-tai tsa-chü ch'üan-mu* 元代雜劇全目, Peking, 1957, p. 69.

[3] *Liu-shih chung ch'ü* 六十種曲. This collection was compiled by Yüeh-shih tao-jen, 閱世道人 (? Mao Chin 毛晉, 1599–1659) and published late in the Ming period by the Chi-ku ko 汲古閣.

First of all, the ex-courtesan of Po Chü-yi's original ballad has to
be given a name if she is to appear on stage. Rather surprisingly, Ma
Chih-yüan chooses the name of an authentic person, P'ei Hsing-nu
裴興奴, who is recorded in a contemporary source.[4] She and Ts'ao
Kang (her tutor in the plays) are there named as outstanding musicians of the Chen-yüan period, whence the saying is quoted "Ts'ao
Kang excels with the right hand, Hsing-nu with the left." Ma Chih-
yüan is less concerned with authenticity when it comes to supplying
companions for Po on his visit to Hsing-nu's house in the gay
quarter. Chia Tao, though contemporary with Po Chu-yi, is not
known to have been acquainted with him, and Meng Hao-jan was
a man of an age half a century gone. In fact, this latter choice may
reflect no more than Ma's fondness for this poet as a romantic
recluse, for he wrote a play, unfortunately lost, with Meng Hao-
jan's name as title.

Then, the lovers must be separated if they are to enjoy reunion at
Chiangchou. Po's demotion, the historical reasons for which are
well-known, is attributed by the Yuan dramatist to his excessive
fondness for wine and verse-making. Thus the upright Po is reduced
to a romantic Bohemian of the Li Po kind. As for Hsing-nu, she of
course must be forced into marriage with the tea-merchant. This is
brought about by the old mother-procuress, who is a stock figure of
Yuan drama. Her stratagem is crude but effective: a spurious letter
convinces Hsing-nu of Po's death. After their eventual reunion, Po
with never a scruple falls in with Hsing-nu's bold suggestion of
elopement, and leaves the unfortunate tea-merchant to explain to
unsympathetic officers just what he has done with his wife.

These crudities of plot, historical inaccuracies, and aspersions on
the character of Po Chü-yi have offended numerous critics.[5] In
defense of Ma Chih-yüan two points seem worth making. First, the
morality of the play conflicts, it is true, with the conventional code.
But it carries a step forward the romantic or humanistic ethic to the
championship of which so much of the vernacular literature is
dedicated. We are asked to consider the beauty of Hsing-nu, the

[4] The *Yüeh-fu tsa-lu* 樂府雜錄 by Tuan An-chieh 段安節 of T'ang, in *T'ang-tai
ts'ung-shu* 唐代叢書, *chüan* 11. The name of P'ei Hsing-nu appears, naturally, in the
section on "*P'i-pa.*"

[5] Kubo, *op. cit.*, p. 390.

talent of Po and the affection between the two; to set these against the
greed and treachery of the old woman and the boorishness of the
tea-merchant; and to judge whether the outcome, including the sad
fate of the innocent husband, is not in fact a manifestation of "poetic"
justice.

Secondly, the very crudities of the fiction fully justify themselves if
they offer the possibilities of dramatic effectiveness, of excitement on
stage. The stratagem to persuade Hsing-nu of Po's death makes
possible the beautiful laments of the second act, when Hsing-nu
makes sacrifices and the dramatist stretches his license so far as to
introduce a whirlwind, understood by Hsing-nu as a manifestation of
Po's spirit. Another visual high point of the play must surely be the
passage in the third act in which Hsing-nu, completely taken in by
the false letter and then suddenly confronted with Po at Chiangchou,
naturally assumes him to be a ghost. Love and longing fight most
touchingly with fear as she begs him to keep his distance, throws
money into the river as an offering to secure reunion after her own
death, but finally accepts his living presence.

Otherwise, the quality of *Ch'ing-shan lei* is synonymous with the
quality of its songs. Since Yuan drama is not my present theme, I
limit myself in this connection to quotation of Hsing-nu's song at the
opening of Act III, with the comment that this hardly seems inferior,
in its economy and freshness, to Ma Chih-yüan's own oft-quoted
Ch'iu-ssu 秋思 poem: Hsing-nu sings *(Shuang-tiao hsin-shui-ling)*:

Setting sun, wide sky, darkling river's meander,	正夕陽天闊暮江迷
Hills of Ch'u, folds of green, rest on the clear air.	倚晴空楚山疊翠
Ice-jar cosmos, sky to earth,	冰壺天上下
Trees tall and short are cloud-brocaded.	雲錦樹高低
Will someone ask Wang Wei	誰倩王維
For a landscape to transcribe this sorrow?	寫愁入畫圖內

Cf. *Ch'iu-ssu*:

Dry vine, old tree, crows at dusk,	枯藤老樹昏鴉
Small bridge, stream running, cottages,	小橋流水人家
Ancient road, west wind, lean nag,	古道西風瘦馬
The sun westering	夕陽西下
And one with breaking heart at the sky's edge.	斷腸人在天涯

One's first impressions on turning to Ku Ta-tien's *Ch'ing-shan chi*
after the *tsa-chü Ch'ing-shan lei* are that the length is much greater and
the poetry much inferior. At a similar moment in the play, the
opening of scene 28 in this case, Hsing-nu sings to the *p'i-pa* which is
her sole companion. If it is fair to compare the *Hsin-shui-ling* which
Ku gives Hsing-nu at this point with the song we have just seen, the
comparison is certainly not a favorable one:

Singing strings, metal pick, body of sandalwood	鯤絃鐵撥紫檀槽
Have made a knell for oh, so many who were young.	斷送許多年少
Startle the roosting bird from his still forest	空林驚宿鳥
Make dance the dragon in his dim ravine—	幽壑舞潛蛟
But no strum, no twang	切切嘈嘈
Can all express of this sad song of pining.	寫不盡相思調

Although he is telling essentially the same story, Ku Ta-tien offers
us a somewhat more acceptable portrait of Po Chü-yi. His exile to
Chiang-chou, though not for the authentic historical reasons, is at
least in tune with these. Scene 14 presents Po as an outspoken
memorialist of the kind the Ming court sadly needed and the Ming
dramatists were happy to supply if only on the stage:

> Troops ill-chosen, barely trained,
> Supplied or not at random
> Paid or not at the plotters' whim—
> How can eunuchs wield an army?

Po's taking of Hsing-nu into his household, carried out in so
scandalous a fashion in the Yuan play, here is greatly softened. First
we should note that Hsing-nu resists the tea-merchant with much
more determination than in Ma Chih-yüan's play. Then before she
can go to Po Chü-yi the troublesome husband is got rid of, simply
but effectively by drowning while returning to his boat after a
drunken spree. When Liu Yü-hsi suggests that Hsing-nu ("who as a
'state-registered entertainer' should in any case never have been
taken to wife by a commoner") may now revert to Po, the latter is
moved to demur. Liu Yü-hsi's response is indicative that the
dramatist is still not entirely easy about the propriety of all this:

Po: As Hsing-nu has been the wife of this merchant, I fear that
      what you suggest is impossible.

Liu: Lo-t'ien, you have lived a life of blameless virtue and your
conduct as an official has been without flaw. Surely you may
be permitted a romantic peccadillo *(feng-liu tsui-kuo* 風流罪過)
such as this?

By preferring the *ch'uan-ch'i* form to the *tsa-chü*, Ku Ta-tien
deprives himself of that tight unity which follows from the restriction
of singing to a single role. No longer is Hsing-nu at the center of the
action, no longer are situations contrived (e.g. Po's reported death)
in order to work their dramatic effect on her and on the audience
through her reaction. On the other hand, *Ch'ing-shan chi* takes little
advantage of the new freedom to present the sort of cavalcade we see
in *Mu-tan t'ing* or *Ch'ang-sheng-tien.* There is but one brief martial
interlude (scene 12), but one "spectacular" (scene 6) in addition to
the finale. On the whole, the structure of the play offers little more
than a simple alternation between the adventures of Po and those
of Hsing-nu.

If, then, the story is much the same, the portrait of Po improved
only a little, the songs inferior and the dramatic tension weakened by
length and disunity, we may fairly ask what if anything this new
presentation contributes to dramatic literature. I suggest that the
answer must be couched as much in terms of fiction as in those of the
drama, and that we must bear in mind the great strides that the art
of fiction was making in the later part of the Ming dynasty.

It is a prime concern of fiction to explore life at the mundane,
everyday level. If we examine the initial establishment of Hsing-nu's
situation in *Ch'ing-shan chi* we shall find her presented at exactly this
level. Nothing could be closer to the daily round of life than the
mother's advice to her, to stop dreaming of a husband and accept
more cheerfully her lot as a courtesan:

"Ah, daughter, today you talk of finding a husband, tomorrow you'll
talk of finding a husband—what's so great about finding a husband?
Marry some man, and before you've got past his gate his first wife
will be letting you know who she is. She'll soon have your coiled hair
scratched down, and you'll have to kneel or kotow any time she says
kneel or kotow. Nor will she let her husband sleep with you, and
then won't you be the neglected one with cold sheets and lonely
pillow? And supposing the old man does plead and pray till he gets

a night with you, then that first wife will be so jealous and sour, she'll grumble and nag and have you out of bed before dawn. What's more, all day through you'll be getting scoldings from her. You'll have nothing to wear, nothing to eat, you won't be able to come or go, climb or stoop, and then you'll be sorry you didn't take your mother's advice, and it'll be too late. Now go hurry and do your makeup and entertain your visitors, or I've got a whip here and I'll beat you to a pulp with no mercy if you go on like this."

This is highly effective advice and a highly effective passage, but in its easy loquacity and love of detail it smacks of the *Chin P'ing Mei* brand of fiction rather than of the dialogue of the stage. This kind of impression is further strengthened by the intricacies of the plans to "ransom" Hsing-nu. Anticipating Trollope or Balzac, Ku Ta-tien provides (scene 23) detailed information on the state of Po's savings and the market value of the handmaids' jewelry as they attempt to raise the necessary one thousand taels.

Hsing-nu, losing her central importance, becomes merely one of a whole gallery of characters. Again it is a characteristic of fiction to create a world of people and to explore the resulting network of relationships. In contrast, we think more commonly of dramatic personages in terms of the clash of two or three or four characters: Othello and Iago, Lear and his daughters. Hsing-nu reacts now not only with mother, tea-merchant, and Po Chü-yi, but with the latter's two handmaids also, Fan-su and Hsiao-man, who occupy the stage in their own right in scenes 4, 8 and elsewhere. This relationship between these two and their lord's new inamorata is a particular delight of the play. Hsing-nu's plight elicits their warm sympathy, they try to help her in the only way they can by sacrificing their jewels, and when the way is finally clear for her to join them in a *ménage à quatre* they welcome her with a simple song (scene 29):

> Parting brought twin lines of tears,
> Voice and visage blocked, the road far and dim.
> Now, a chance encounter where clouds and river meet,
> The mandarin duck follows in flight the wild goose.
> On bud-like feet she enters the painted hall,
> Together again we rejoice in her company.

All this sweetness, however, is not allowed to turn into syrup. Ku endows the two handmaids with a tart sense of fun, and introduces a clown *(ch'ou)* to help them out. And so, after they have exchanged obeisances with Hsing-nu, this dialogue follows:

> Fan-su, Hsiao-man: My lord, it has always been said that a returned wanderer brings more happiness than a new bride. Since Madam P'ei comes to my lord now both as new bride *and* as returned wanderer, your joy is easy to guess. But autumn nights are long—let us prepare a jar of wine and sit for a while with Madam P'ei in the lamplight.
>
> Po: It's getting late, there's no need for this. Do it tomorrow instead.
>
> Fan-su: My lord seems rather impatient!
>
> Hsiao-man: Sister, do be a little more tolerant.
>
> Fan-su: Well, then, we'll be off to bed now. Ling-lung, bring some tea for Madam P'ei.
>
> Boy (Ling-lung, *ch'ou*): Madam P'ei gets a headache when she hears the word "tea." Now she has joined the Po family she'd better drink plain *(po)* 白 hot water. . . .
>
> Hsiao-man (turning to go): My lord, tomorrow there will be visitors coming to congratulate you, and you will be drinking. You'd better be up early.
>
> Boy: It's not wine you'll be drinking, it's vinegar, of jealousy.

This low-pitched, unhurrying exploration of character, which is the glory of the Ming novels, is as typical of the texture of *Ch'ing-shan chi* as is high poesy of the texture of Ma Chih-yüan's play and, even more so, of Chiang Shih-ch'üan's *Ssu hsien ch'iu*. Ku Ta-tien makes surprisingly little out of the obviously "poetic" elements of the original *P'i-pa hsing*. (Chiang Shih-ch'üan's *Ssu hsien ch'iu* is the first of the "lute-song" plays to deal exclusively with the circumstances leading up to the composition of the poem, the first, that is to say, fully to exploit the glamour which Po Chu-yi's original work suggests.) And yet, he never questions the aristocratic set of values which exalts the poet Po Chü-yi and demands his romantic victory over the bourgeois tea-merchant. It is the grand paradox of a work like this that a scholar-official, writing a play which reads like a novel, should expend so much energy in denigrating the bourgeois

values which would no doubt predominate among his potential
audience. It is perfectly in order for Po Chü-yi to go a-whoring: in
this way he meets Hsing-nu and the romance is under way. When
the poor tea-merchant follows suit he falls in the river and drowns.
Style is the saving grace, and the boorish merchant doesn't even
know how to dress (scene 22).

It remains to draw attention to a technical device which strengthens Ku Ta-tien's play as it strengthens other and later plays and
novels alike. This is the device of centering much of the action in a
concrete object, which develops thereby a symbolic force. The title
Ch'ing-shan chi is as significant as the novel title *Shih-t'ou chi* 石頭記,
which appears to have been preferred over *Hung-lou meng* 紅樓夢, for
important reasons, by the commentator Chih-yen-chai 脂硯齋.[6] My
synopsis (below) shows that the adventures of the blue shirt provide
action for half the scenes of Ku Ta-tien's play. The shirt, in and of
itself, is the badge of Po's private life, his domestic self divested of
rank and office. By the act of pawning it to buy wine he adumbrates
his readiness to sacrifice for Hsing-nu's love. She, by redeeming and
returning it to the handmaids, imbues it with the qualities of a token
of fidelity. Fan-su and Hsiao-man, restoring it to Po Chü-yi with
some teasing (scene 23), hear the declaration of his longing for Hsing-
nu as, in the words of the popular saw, "sight of the object reminds
him of the person":

> Suddenly startled that this old garment should still be whole,
> Sorrow sinks to my shoes as fond remembrance breaks.
> Sight of the lost hair-ornament brings grief
> And sighs over the time wasted on trivial pursuits.
> After so many buffetings of fate
> Now my heart's banner streams afar.
> (This is the blue shirt that I lost in the capital.)
> So distant—by what fate shall I come to you?
> Could I be borne by wind and cloud to the maiden's chamber?

At last, when in scene 28 the action of the original poem is played
out and Po hears Hsing-nu's lute-song, he asks her "Do you recognize
this blue shirt?" and she replies:

---

[6] Cf. Wu Shih-ch'ang, *On the Red Chamber Dream*, Oxford, 1961, p. 100.

Now that you recall how you pawned your blue shirt when the wine
  was dear
I am forced to clutch my lute to me to hide my red gown.

By this time, the blue shirt has become a powerful enough symbol
to set against the red bridal gown which announces Hsing-nu's
married state, and these two lines most forcefully epitomize Hsing-
nu's past sorrows and present shame.

The blue shirt may also be said to "contain" Po as a spirit-tablet
"contains" the departed one. Alternatively, it symbolizes his unique
personal characteristics, as in Chao Shu-li's 趙樹理 modern story *Ch'uan-
chia-pao* 傳家寶, "The Heirloom," the old sewing-box which supplies
the title supplies also the clue to the system of values of the protagonist.

Like the pearl-sewn shirt (*Ku-chin hsiao-shuo* 古今小說 1), the stone
amulet of Chia Pao-yu or the portrait of Li-niang in *Mu-tan t'ing*, the
blue shirt both generates action and illuminates pattern. We might
consider it also as a symbol in a different sense: a sign that a new
kind of literary architecture is replacing the simple structural unity of
the *tsa-chü*.[7]

II. *Ming feng chi*

I am suggesting, then, that naturalistic detail, interplay of
character, and a more complex sense of structure are at least three of
the new contributions of the *ch'uan-ch'i* form, and that all of these
seem to point to a kind of symbiosis of drama with novel. But my
example *Ch'ing-shan chi*, though of interest for comparative purposes,
is not after all a major work of art. The remainder of this paper will
be devoted to two plays very different in nature but each a masterpiece of Ming drama: *Ming feng chi* and *Mu-tan t'ing*.[8] Works of this

[7] I have taken over some of these considerations of the symbolic function of the blue
shirt from discussion of the play with Prof. Lucien Miller, and acknowledge here my
indebtedness to him.

[8] Wu Mei 吳梅 (1883–1939), *Chung-kuo hsi-ch'ü kai-lun* 中國戲曲概論, posthumously
published Hong Kong, 1964, in a section on Ming *ch'uan-ch'i* cites 43 titles in an exclusive list of fine plays. The list excludes *Ch'ing-shan chi*. On the other hand, the *Ch'ü-
p'in* 曲品 of Lü T'ien-ch'eng 呂天成 (p. 321) ranks *Ch'ing-shan chi* as *shang-chung* 上中,
"middle of the upper level," whilst *Ming feng chi* (p. 336) is only *chung-shang* 中上,
"top of the middle level." *Mu-tan t'ing* is *shang-shang* 上上, "top of the upper level"
or "crème de la crème"; Kao Ming's *P'i-pa chi* 高明, 琵琶記 no doubt partly on account
of its venerable age and pioneering nature, is ranked as a "godlike work" (*shen-p'in* 神品).

caliber may fairly be used to test out Wu Mei's bold thesis:[9]

> I maintain that *ch'uan-ch'i* is the most straightforwardly honest (眞率) literary medium of any period whether ancient or modern. Its authors expressed in the finest phrasing what weighed on their innermost hearts, without thought whether of preservation and transmission, or of examination success or salary increment.[10] They wrote as they listed and their works are masterpieces of all time.

Ming feng chi is ascribed by the *Liu-shih chung ch'ü*[11] to Wang Shih-chen 王世貞 (1529–92), the outstanding man of letters of his day. But *Ch'ü-hai tsung-mu t'i-yao*[12] (p. 238) describes its author rather as a protégé of Wang's, Wang himself being credited with the authorship of scene 16 only.[13] In the *t'i-yao* entry on *Feng ho ming* 鳳和鳴[14] the name of the author of *Ming feng chi* is given as Liang Ch'en-yü 梁辰魚. This is a more acceptable attribution. Liang was a troubadour who "disdained the first degree examination," a wanderer and drinker whom Wang Shih-chen and his eminent colleagues held in high regard. The musician Wei Liang-fu 魏良轉 was a fellow-townsman (of K'un-shan), and the birth of the *k'un-ch'ü* 昆曲 genre is traced to the initial collaboration of Liang and Wei on the play *Wan sha chi* 浣紗記. This is the only *ch'uan-ch'i* credited to Liang by the *Ch'ü-p'in*.[15] But this same work (p. 326) describes Liang's significant admiration for the *ch'uan-ch'i Chiao-shang chi* 椒觴記 by Ku Mou-chien 顧懋儉. This play is based on the life of Ch'en Yüan-liang 陳元亮, "as the author seemed to be moved by the story." We should note that Ch'en Yüan-liang played *vis-à-vis* the Sung traitor Chia Ssu-tao 賈似道 the same kind of role that Yang Chi-sheng 楊繼盛 played, in *Ming feng chi*, against Yen Sung 嚴嵩 (though Ch'en was only degraded, not executed, for his leadership

---

[9] In his preface to *Ch'ü-hai tsung-mu t'i-yao* 曲海總目提要, compiled by Huang Wen-yang 黃文暘, b. 1736. Reprint by People's Literature Press, Peking, 1959, first preface, p. 2.

[10] Wu Mei surely has in mind here the old legend that Yuan writers practised the composition of *tsa-chü* in preparation for the examinations of the day.

[11] Cf. above, note 3.

[12] Cf. above, note 9.

[13] By the Ch'ing critic Chiao Hsün 焦循 in his *Chü-shuo* 劇說, 3. Scene 16 is in fact a *tour-de-force*, the longest scene in the play, devoted to the execution of Yang Chi-sheng.

[14] An anonymous *ch'uan-ch'i* which treats of the events of the later parts of *Ming feng chi*.

[15] Cf. above, note 8. The entry on *Wan sha chi* is on p. 321.

of opposition). Although the *Ch'ü-p'in* itself (p. 336) attributes *Ming feng chi* to Wang Shih-chen, Fu Hsi-hua[16] is noncommittal. He points out that several Ming catalogues fail to specify the authorship; that the Ming critic Wang Chi-te 王驥德 in his *Ch'ü-lü* 曲律 discusses Wang Shih-chen's *ch'ü* but makes no mention of *Ming feng chi;* and that Wang Shih-chen wrote a biography of Yang Chi-sheng which differed in numerous details from the play.

Ming feng chi was the major work to emerge, or at least to survive, from the political turmoil brought about by the greed and corruption of Yen Sung and his son Shih-fan 世蕃, the "Greater and Lesser Chief Ministers." Victims of the Yen tyranny included the Chief Minister Hsia Yen 夏言; martyrs to the cause of driving it from the court included the censor Shen Lien 沈練, Yang Chi-sheng of the Board of War and many others. Yang Chi-sheng's outspoken memorial enumerating the "ten crimes and five treasons" of the Yen family is a celebrated document included *in toto* in *Ming wen tsai* 明文在.[17] Shen Lien and his son are the heroes of the *hua-pen* 話本 story *Shen Hsiao-hsia hsiang-hui Ch'u shih piao* 沈小霞相會出師表,[18] which incidentally, as may be inferred from the title, uses the *Ch'u shih piao* of Chu-ko Liang as a thematic symbol of the kind I have noted above in the case of the "blue shirt." Plays about the "resistance movement" against Yen Sung include *Chung-min chi* 忠愍記, *Fei-wan chi* 飛丸記, *Tan-hsin chao* 丹心照 (*t'i-yao* 1713), *Ch'u shih piao* (*t'i-yao* 1872), and *Chieh chung ch'an* 傑終禪 (*t'i-yao* 2027). To repeat, *Ming feng chi* represents only one of a considerable number of dramatic or fictional treatments of a matter which "weighed on the innermost hearts" of the men of Chia-ching. (*Ming feng chi* was, however, one of the more effective treatments. *Ch'ü-p'in*, p. 336, refers to it as "a very detailed record of all the events concerned, which prompts one with his own hand to plunge a knife into the traitor Yen Sung." This enthusiasm is somewhat qualified, though, by the rest of the comment: "The songs are clear and singable, but wearisome in their abundance.")[19]

[16] *Ming-tai ch'uan-ch'i ch'üan-mu* 明代傳奇全目, pp. 50–51.

[17] *Chüan* 30, Basic Sinological Series edition vol. I, pp. 241–49.

[18] *Ku-chin hsiao-shuo* 40.

[19] No doubt it was objection to what was considered excessive length which prompted the ranking of *Ming feng chi* below the level of *Ch'ing-shan chi*, cf. above, note 8.

Ming feng chi is conceived on a majestic scale. Its protagonists are the political giants of the Chia-ching period. Important contributions to the action are made by no less than seventeen high officials, all but three of whom have appeared on stage by scene 9. Although, in conformity with the conventions of the *ch'uan-ch'i* form, a single scene seldom involves more than two or three personages, the offstage presence of the remainder is always palpable: the kaleidoscope turns, but each new facet of the story is colored by all its neighbors. And like an evil stain, the power of Yen Sung suffuses every life. In the early action, this power reaches its zenith with the overthrow of the Chief Minister Hsia Yen, who has urged in vain the policy of resistance in full-dress debate with the traitor (scene 6). Yang Chi-sheng pits raw but rash courage against Yen Sung and his son, and suffers torture, exile, and at last execution. This execution (scene 16) marks the low tide of the loyalist fortunes. Against Yen Sung's subsequent excesses is set the rising anger of the major characters, Tsou Ying-lung 鄒應龍 and Lin Jun 林潤. These two opened the action in scene 2 (following the prologue), but have been seen hitherto only in a preparatory role. Their time is not yet come, and they face the setback of punitive appointments at the fringes of the empire while three newcomers carry forward the mission of Yang Chi-sheng in attacks, again abortive, on the Yen family (scene 27). At last Tsou Ying-lung gathers together all the threads spun by the vicious spider Yen Sung and topples him from the center of his web. The downfall of the house of Yen is complete when Lin Jun illuminates the domestic scene, the villainies perpetrated by Yen Shih-fan against his humble neighbors. For once at least, the grand finale with its joyous reunions and distribution of honors is a fully justified and truly inevitable resolution of the action. Inevitability has been indeed the keynote throughout the play, as retribution in the persons of the young heroes Tsou and Lin broods, gathers, and finally swoops down on the evil at the nation's heart.

This grand scale of action, with its eminent personages and its major national concerns, is matched by a sweeping geographical range of movement. A complete map of China would be crisscrossed by a plotting of the action, from the court in Peking to the defense of the northern frontier, to the pirate raids against Fukien, to Yunnan where Lin Jun is banished, to the wanderings of the martyrs' widows in Kwangsi or Chekiang. The dramatist is not merely using the license provided by the absence of stage-sets to dispose of his characters for a scene or two. He is underscoring the nationwide nature of the catastrophe of an evil dictatorship, he is mirroring very sharply a growing sense of nationhood.

Contrast and variation in the scale of action is appropriately accompanied by a flexibility of language. Yen Shih-fan's private plot against Yi Hung-ch'i (scene 31) is conducted by means of low-keyed naturalistic dialogue. In complete contrast, Hsia Yen and Yen Sung dispute defense policy (scene 6) in high-flown rhetoric with numerous historical precedents set like gems in passages of *ssu-liu-wen*. Some of the flowers of speech are unusually interesting, as when in scene 39 a girl abused by Yen Shih-fan lays plaint before Lin Jun. Her account of her seduction is couched very largely in *tz'u* and *ch'ü* titles used with punning effect, as ". . . when we got to the *Phoenix Chamber,* he waited till it was *Quiet All About,* then he dragged me under the *Gold-Broidered Curtain* and loosened my *Fragrant Gauze Girdle.* . . ." One is reminded of that late chapter of *Ching hua yüan* which clothes an allegory on avarice in the names of ancient coins, or of the *reductio ad absurdum* of this particular literary game, *Finnegans Wake,* where, on pages 583–584 for instance, Joyce puns on the names of a crowd of contemporary cricketers to describe a very different if no less energetic sport.

Much of the verse of *Ming feng chi* is more or less utilitarian, e.g. the *ch'ü* which gives the gist of Yang Chi-sheng's memorial in scene 15. Much is pastiche, as the old *tz'u* lines with which the two wives lament their husbands' absence in scene 26.[20] But there are times when the *ch'ü* rise nobly to the occasion, as when Yang Chi-sheng's widow in scene 16 embraces his corpse before the executioners and sings a *Shua-hai-erh:*

See clouds of sorrow as sad plaints fill the skies,
Alas for those who part in life or endure death's separation!
Soon, soon these poor remains will be beyond my sight,
The close bond joined in childhood this dawn has snapped,
The close bond joined in childhood this dawn has snapped!

[20] After her opening song, Tsou's wife recites Li Yü's 李煜 *Lang-t'ao sha* 浪淘沙 "*Lien-wai yü ch'an-ch'an*" 簾外雨潺潺 with only two lines revised.

The ape's cry rends the bowels, wailing the moon from silent hills
Yet cannot pluck out the sword that stabs my heart.
(My lord)
A thousand-league courser, swift as "Flying Gold,"
Changed now into a cuckoo weeping blood.

Even so, plain dialogue can sometimes be more effective than
songs which sink beneath their weight of allusions. In scene 5, the
sycophant Chao Wen-hua tries to warn Yang Chi-sheng against his
outspokenness:

Chao: In times like these a man should study the cricket. If it
         keeps its mouth shut and its tongue well-hidden it can live
         in peace and be everywhere secure. If it still insists on
         opening its mouth it is asking for death.

Yang: What man can avoid death? The cricket singing on an
         ancient bough at least dies clean and undefiled. The fly
         trapped in a muddy pit may well keep its mouth shut, but
         its death is a degradation.

We have to expect a certain proportion of stock ingredients, of set
pieces without which no play on themes from official life would be
complete. Not surprisingly, these passages in the main are given to
Tsou Ying-lung and Lin Jun, the young and rising stars who signal
the fall of the house of Yen. The vows of brotherhood (scene 2), the
partings as the examinations loom (scene 22), the laments of the
abandoned wives (scene 26) and the final reunions, all these are
stock elements which could almost be interchanged with corresponding scenes in the great precursor *P'i-pa chi* or in many another play.

In contrast with these elements and in resumption of a theme I
have already touched on are certain features which would be
equally or even more at home in a work of fiction and which suggest
again the closet drama. Character-riddles are a case in point.
Riddle-predictions, oracularly issued in scene 8, are resolved in
scenes 36 and 41. As in the prime example of this device, the riddle-
poems of ch. 5 of *Hung-lou meng*, the riddles are formulated around
the dissection of graphs, e.g. "high mountain" *kao shan* 高山 for the
personal name of Yen Sung. The "case-histories" of scene 23, the
stories of the victims of Yen Shih-fan's greed, are just that: prose
fictions, narrated each by a personage who has appeared on stage for

this purpose only. Lastly, the sub-plot which features Yi Hung-ch'i (scenes 31–32) has the earmarks (the "clever stratagem" *hao chi* 好計, the providential savior) of a *hua-pen* which has been incorporated into the action.

These sequences, one feels, must surely be equally effective whether performed on stage or read in the silence of the studio. Scenes which depend for full effect on stage performance are very few, but they still occur. Scene 33 must have been a great favorite as a comic interlude. The two sycophants Yen Mao-ch'ing and Chao Wen-hua decide, each independently of the other, to purchase longevity pills from a hermit in the Western Hills for presentation to Yen Sung. Each man, chancing on the other en route, attempts in vain to conceal his true intention and destination, to throw the other off the scent and to be alone in winning the hermit's favor. These futile efforts surely present a diverting spectacle as the two dodge about the stage spying on each other and at every new point of the journey bumping into each other again.

The despicable Chao Wen-hua, though his role is *ch'ou*, is much more than a mere buffoon. It is his function to reveal the depths of evil of his master Yen Sung. Yen dominates the play, of course; but the national suffering that results from his dictatorship is more vividly brought to the stage by indirect comment than it ever could be by Yen's own actions or admissions. Scene 21 is central to the play in more senses than the merely numerical. In this scene Chao Wen-hua, as Yen's appointee, parades before us as a Commander-in-Chief who would be fully at home in a Gilbert and Sullivan opera. Persuaded by his troops to sacrifice to the Dragon-King of the Eastern Ocean, he agrees only when assured that he may keep for himself the sacrificial vessels afterwards. The monk brought in to conduct the ceremony calls twice on eighty thousand bodhisattvas, then the third time on only forty thousand. Questioned on the discrepancy, he explains that half the number was fictitious for ration-drawing purposes, and he has cancelled them out of fear of an investigation. After the ceremony Chao proposes to retain the monk and his five hundred disciples, to furnish "captured enemy heads" in case of his own failure otherwise to provide these. Finally, the troops are instructed not to molest the enemy until the latter have had time to complete their accumulation of plunder.

Thus the criminal follies of Yen's subordinates illustrate the master's misrule. And although the circumstances are a comic invention, they are unhappily authentic. The murder of civilians to provide "captured enemy heads" is one of the specific crimes laid at Yen Sung's door in Yang Chi-sheng's actual memorial, referred to above. The monstrous character of Yen Sung is no fiction. In the play it is brought out by means both indirect and direct. One of the subtlest of the means used is the contrast between the reactions of others to the virtuous and the villainous respectively. In scene 11, the noble widow of the martyred Hsia Yen receives aid from Yang Chi-sheng even though the latter is himself in exile. The contrast is provided by scene 37, when Yen Sung has been ousted and banished in his turn back to his native place. Everyone he meets, from the high eunuch who is an old friend down to the humble guard at the posting-station, treats him with icy indifference. Heaven itself, it seems, takes a hand when Yen Sung's boat gets stuck in a frozen river. This chill retribution, so richly deserved and so effectively contrasted with the warmth of sympathy prevailing among the erstwhile dictator's victims, is thus presented with strong visual as well as dramatic impact. The art of mime was surely no less highly developed in Ming times than now, and we may easily imagine the fruitless straining and heaving of the boatmen as under curse and threat they struggle to free abstract boat from imaginary ice.

Ming feng chi, with its material from contemporary political life,[21] is a prime example of dramatic treatment of "what weighed on the innermost hearts" of the men of Ming times. *P'i-pa chi* is by and large devoted to the resolution of conflicting relationships, when the claims of family clash with those of loyalty to the prince. The issue persists, and is faced in *Ming feng chi* by the three memorialists of scene 27. Wu Shih-lai has his mother's blessing on his memorial, even though the ensuing disgrace will deprive her of his support, for she proclaims that "the person of one who enters office belongs henceforth not to his parents but to the court." The dilemma of Chang Chung is even more movingly presented and suggests that the natural love of wife and children was gaining ground over the ritually prescribed devotion to parents, even though the demands of honor remained

---

[21] Wang Shih-chen, the patron of the play, conducted his own celebrated feud with Yen Sung, as witness his biography in *Ming-shih* 明史, 287.

after all paramount. Unlike Wu, Chang Chung feels unable to reveal to his wife his intention to attack Yen Sung, in that he lacks confidence in his own ability to withstand the pleas his wife would be sure to make. He therefore deceives her, telling her that the coffin he has had prepared is for a needy stranger, and sends her to their home out of harm's way. In the *tiao-ch'ang* 弔塲 he reveals true nobility of purpose: "If by ridding the world of these traitors I can bring security to every husband and his wife and to every mother and her son, then there need be no speaking of the distress brought to my own family." More touching still is his concern that the sacrifice should be of himself alone and without peril to others. In order to forestall demonstrations after his death and the inevitable punishment of sympathizers, he orders that his coffin be made ready outside the torture-chamber and sealed immediately his corpse enters it.

III. *Mu-tan t'ing*

The genesis of this, the third and greatest of the five plays of T'ang Hsien-tsu 湯顯祖 (1550–1617), lies neither in an earlier play nor in contemporary events. It is to be found in a little group of disparate works of fiction to which T'ang makes explicit reference in his preface to his own play:

> There is a resemblance between the story which is told of Prefect Tu and the stories from the Tsin period of the children of Prefect Li Chung-wen of Wu-tu and Prefect Feng Hsiao-chiang of Kuangchou; I have somewhat altered and elaborated on these. Prefect Tu's flogging of the scholar Liu likewise resembles that of the scholar T'an by the Prince of Sui-yang in Han times.

The "stories from the Tsin period" are from a work entitled *Fa-yüan chu-lin* 法苑珠林;[22] the daughter of the Prefect Li Chung-wen 李仲文 dies at the age of eighteen *sui*. Her ghost appears in a dream to the son of her father's successor in office. The young man "marries" her, but her father, angered by a report that his dead daughter's shoe has come into the young man's possession, insists

---

[22] The stories are reprinted in *Ch'ü-hai tsung-mu t'i-yao*, *chüan* 6, entry on *Huan-hun chi* 還魂記 (the alternative title of *Mu-tan t'ing*).

that the grave be reopened. This is premature, and the story ends
with the ghost's lament that she cannot now succeed in returning to
life.

The son of Prefect Feng Hsiao-chiang 馮孝將 likewise dreams of a
visit from the ghost of a girl of eighteen or nineteen *sui*, who seeks his
aid in securing her return to life so that she may be his wife. In this
case the attempt succeeds.

The story of the scholar T'an is from *Lieh yi chuan* 列異傳, and tells
how T'an takes to wife a girl who proves in fact to be a corpse
midway on the road back to life. Her father, the Prince of Sui-yang,
recognizes a pearl-embroidered gown as the property of his deceased
daughter, accuses T'an of robbing her tomb and flogs a confession
out of him. All ends happily with the opening of the tomb and the
girl's restoration to life and formal marriage to T'an.

T'ang Hsien-tsu's more comprehensive source, however, is the
first piece he mentions, the "story which is told of the Prefect Tu."
This is the *hua-pen* story *Tu Li-niang mu-se huan-hun* 杜麗娘慕色還魂,
justly characterized by C. T. Hsia as "this drab tale. . . . probably
little known even during the late Ming period."[23] The *hua-pen*
supplies the playwright with a basic set of events, including, of
course, those indicated by the title, i.e. the pining and death of Tu
Li-niang and her miraculous resurrection (through the intervention
of her lover Liu Meng-mei). T'ang incorporates snippets of the actual
text of the *hua-pen* into his play, as for example in Li-niang's lament
uttered shortly before the dream-appearance of Liu Meng-mei in
scene 10, *Ching-meng* 驚夢, or the dialogue between Liu and the
ghostly Li-niang in scene 28, *Yu-kou* 幽媾.

But T'ang Hsien-tsu does a great deal more than borrow a somewhat grotesque skeleton from the storytellers, flesh it out with
stage personages, and drape it with dramatic verse. Out of his own
rich store of invention he creates a masterpiece which sustains its
narrative appeal despite the inordinate length of fifty-five scenes, and

---

[23] C. T. Hsia, "Time and the Human Condition in the Plays of T'ang Hsien-tsu,"
in Wm. Theodore de Bary, ed., *Self and Society in Ming Thought*, Columbia, 1970, p. 273.
The story is contained in the late-Ming collection *Ch'ung-k'e tseng-pu Yen-chü pi-chi*
重刻增補燕居筆記. Professor Hsia most kindly supplied me with a duplicate of the
photographic copy of the story which he had been able to obtain from the Naikaku
Bunko in Tokyo. The only other set of the *Yen-chü pi-chi* is held by the library of National
Peking University.

which illuminates a profound philosophical truth despite the fantastic trappings of dreams, ghosts, demons, and exhumations. Not surprisingly, the *hua-pen* story virtually disappeared from view, whereas T'ang's play created a stir in its own day and won an enduring popularity. A note by T'ang's contemporary Shen Te-fu 沈德符 describes it as "passing from house to house, read aloud by one family after another, threatening to put the *Western Chamber* itself out of business."[24] T'ang Hsien-tsu himself, in retirement from office, participated in producing and directing his own plays. Performances continued through the Ch'ing dynasty, and Hsü Shuo-fang[25] estimated that about a quarter of the scenes were still in the repertoire towards the close of the dynasty. In the twentieth century, Mei Lan-fang had a particular fondness for *Ching-meng*, and the poet Hsü Chih-mo records in his diary an amateur performance of this scene in which he played opposite Lu Hsiao-man.

Many of the elements that have contributed to the play's perennial appeal are totally absent from the *hua-pen*. There is mention in the original tale of a tutor for Li-niang, but no hint of the richly comic Tutor Ch'en who introduces himself in scene 7, *Kuei-shu* 閨塾, with the lines

> Droning verses, re-revising
>   lines composed last spring
> pondering, my belly filled,
>   the taste of the noontime tea;
> ants climb up the table leg
>   to skirt the ink-slab pool
> bees invade the window-screen
>   to raid the blooms in the vase.

This celebrated scene consists essentially of attempts by the uninhibited maid Ch'un-hsiang to brush aside, from the path of the slowly awakening Li-niang, the old tutor's efforts to block out the spontaneity of spring. Although Ch'un-hsiang is punished for her pains, we may gauge her success by the fact that Tutor Ch'en, at the point of his exit, joins the girls in a chorus:

[24] *Ku ch'ü tsa-yen* 顧曲雜言, quoted Hsü Shuo-fang 徐朔方, preface to the 1963 edition of *Mu-tan t'ing* by People's Literature Press.
[25] *Loc. cit.*, note 23.

What a waste of
   this new green gauze on the sunlit window!

Tutor Ch'en is in fact already half won-over to Li-niang's cause, and subsequently develops in the most interesting way to become her champion against the rigidity of her father Tu Pao.

   The rebel Li Ch'üan is T'ang's innovation, and a vehicle for topical reference. Critics have singled out the close parallel between Tu Pao's stratagem for the suppression of Li Ch'üan's rebellion and the method used in actuality by the general Cheng Lo 鄭洛 in 1570. In that year, under the premiership of Chang Chü-cheng 張居正 (with whom T'ang Hsien-tsu early came into conflict), Cheng Lo "pacified" the Mongols under An-ta 俺答 by enfeoffing the Mongol princess San-niang-tzu 三娘子. In T'ang's play, Tu Pao correspondingly buys off the rebel Li Ch'üan by enfeoffing the latter's wife. Thus Liu Meng-mei to Tu Pao, in the final scene of the play:

How can you claim you pacified Li Ch'üan, when all you did was give his wife a pacifier![26]

By the time T'ang wrote his play the peace that Cheng Lo had purchased had long been broken, and indeed T'ang's friend Wan Kuo-ch'in 萬國欽 had been punished for advocating more active resistance when the Mongols raided Kansu again in 1590.

   T'ang introduces a wealth of plot elaborations to support an overall structure which, in essence (see appended synopsis), requires the dispersal of his cast of personages followed by their gradual reassembly. All the incidents concerning Li Ch'üan's rebellion, the separation of Prefect Tu from his wife and the false report of her death, even the beating of Liu Meng-mei taken over from the *Lieh yi chuan* anecdote, all these are in one way or another related to this basic structural pattern.

   Seldom in all of this involved narrative is the vein of comedy left untapped for very long. Tutor Ch'en, as already indicated, is a powerful comic creation. So is the Taoist Nun Shih, who with her attendant novices provides scenes of uproarious and sometimes outrageous bawdy (scene 17, *Tao-hsi* 道覡, consists mostly of one

---

[26] Li Ch'üan's personal name means "whole," and the original has "How can you claim you pacified Li Whole when all you did was pacify Li Half (Li Pan 李半)?"

hundred and sixteen puns, frequently salacious, on phrases from the
Ch'ien-tzu-wen 千字文, the "thousand character primer"). Both
Tutor Ch'en and Nun Shih are used from time to time to achieve the
kind of shock-restorative effect familiar to us from Shakespeare's use
of the drunken porter in *Macbeth*. Thus Scene 20, *Nao-shang* 鬧殤,
offers us Li-niang's death and her parents' prolonged keening. But
no sooner has Li-niang passed from the stage than Nun Shih enters,
to tease Li-niang's grieving maid with broad hints of an easy time of
it now that her mistress is gone; and no sooner does Prefect Tu speak
of provisions for his dead daughter's shrine than Tutor Ch'en
seizes the opportunity for a characteristic pun:

> Tu Pao: There are some thirty acres of grace and favor lands lying
> fallow, whose yield will supply the costs of the shrine.
>
> Tutor Ch'en: Aha, these grace and favor lands will grease and
> flavor my diet!

Such a detail as this provides a clue to the function of all the
large inventiveness of incident and humor that invests the play. By
furnishing a setting of such earthy solidity T'ang Hsien-tsu lends
credence to the preposterous progress of dream love, ghostly courtship, and revivification of the bride. It is easy for us to accept the
social and psychological truth of the play's most celebrated scenes,
Ching-meng and *Hsün-meng* 尋夢 and the others, whose sublime
poetry carries the poignancy of Li-niang's longing for love and fears
for the transience of youth:

> By winding walks I left my dream
> and lost him, fading.
> Now jade-like charms grow chill in chamber's depth
> where soul must languish
> while as the mist the petal
> or the moon the cloud
> a flicker of untold love
> touches the morning. . . .
> My toilet made at last, I sit alone
> listless as the incense-smoke I watch,
> no peace of mind
> until the choking weeds that breed distress are rooted out,
> and the shoots of joy can grow.

> Whom to please if I mask my sorrow with smiles?
> —My vision quivers in a blur of tears.[27]

But it is equally essential that we accept the poetic or spiritual truth of Li-niang's resurrection, which is the material demonstration of the power of love. And we are helped in this at every stage by the cumulative detail, the warm and almost novelistic realism of the macabre scenes of Hades, of love beyond the grave, and of the literal exhumation of Li-niang's uncorrupted body.

What, then, is this message of the power of love? It is most succinctly stated in the author's preface:

> Has the world ever seen a woman's love to rival that of Tu Li-niang? Dreaming of a lover she fell sick; once sick she became more deeply attached; and finally, after painting her own portrait as a legacy to the world, she died. Dead for three years, still she was able to live again when in the dark underworld her quest for the object of her dream was fulfilled. To be as Li-niang is truly to have known love.
>
> Love is of source unknown, yet it grows ever deeper. The living may die of it, by its power the dead live again. Love is not love at its fullest if one who lives is unwilling to die for it, or if it cannot restore to life one who has so died. And must the love which comes in dream necessarily be unreal? For there is no lack of dream-lovers in this world. Only for those whose love must be fulfilled on the pillow, and for whom affection deepens only as old age draws on, is it entirely a corporeal matter. . . .
>
> Ah me! The affairs of mortal men find no ultimate solution in this mortal world. I claim no omniscience, but constantly strive to use reason as a guide to my understanding. And though I speak of things reason must deny, how can one be sure that these are necessarily to be found in love? (第云理之所必無, 安知情之所必有邪?)

If I have correctly understood that concluding rhetorical question, perhaps the answer to "how can one be sure?" might be suggested. By accepting not the literal truth (of course), but the essential poetic or symbolic truth of the events of T'ang's play, one would indeed have "found in love" things that "reason must deny."

The conflict is between *ch'ing* (feelings, love, or even passion) and *li*. I have translated *li* as "reason," but it is generally to be understood, I think, in this context, as "the principles governing the

---

[27] From scene 14, *Hsieh-chen* 寫眞.

propriety of human conduct," and more particularly as the narrowly rational which inhibits the spontaneity of human affection: in application to the world of women, it is the restrictive code which denies them initiative in love. T'ang's preface is to be read against the background of the melancholy statistic[28] that the *Ming shih* contains at least four times as many biographies of "Chaste Wives and Virtuous Daughters" as any earlier standard history.

C. T. Hsia begins his penetrating article on T'ang Hsien-tsu's plays[29] with an account of the playwright's debt to the philosopher Lo Ju-fang 羅汝芳, who saw "as the animating principle of the universe the phenomenon of life itself, or the endless process of birth and growth. This ceaseless vitality he regards as something intrinsically good, and he would equate the term *sheng* 生 (life, vitality) with the term *jen* 仁 (humanity, love)." The triumph of Tu Li-niang is in complete accord with this position, and in fairly marked contrast, on the other hand, with the sterner ethos of the *Ming feng chi*. The author of the latter play, as we have seen, was bothered by conflicts between familial loyalties and duty to the state, and established the overriding *li* of public over personal interest. Tu Li-niang is a very different figure from the wives of Yang Chi-sheng or Chang Chung. She rejects the *li* which denies her personal fulfillment (at least until such time as the perfect match may have been contracted for her by her parents) and dares to assert her own desires in a "licentious dream." And it is the great daring of T'ang Hsien-tsu not only to present the dream on stage, but to make it come true.

The theatrical craftsmanship which expresses this philosophical position through the medium of a *ch'uan-ch'i* play is consistently successful. Comparison of my synopsis of action with the chart of the play's structure (both appended) will demonstrate the dramatist's skill in varying pace and mood without ever failing to move his story forward.[30] Set pieces of types common to Ming drama, such

[28] Cited by Hsü Shuo-fang, *loc. cit.*

[29] Cf. above, note 23.

[30] The chart is based on Chang Ching's 張敬 analysis of *Mu-tan t'ing* in *Ming-Ch'ing ch'uan-ch'i tao-lun* 明清傳奇導論, Taipei, 1961, pp. 113–116. The chart illustrates the distribution of scenes of the following varieties: transitional (short to average length, little singing, narrative in function); martial; comic; major (important developments of plot or mood, often including fine songs); and grand scenes (considerable length, important action, numerous singers, often a locale—e.g. the Imperial court—which would involve especially lavish costumes and groupings of extras).

as scene 8, *Ch'üan nung* 勸農, or scene 41, *Tan-shih* 耽試, are interspersed with scenes of swift action; "grand scenes" offering a display
of pageantry are spaced throughout the play; contrast is used to
maximum effect, as when the delicate beauty of the lovers' reunion
in scene 28, *Yu-kou*, is immediately saved from excess of saccharine by
the low farce of the following scene *P'ang-yi* 旁疑, in which Nun
Shih suspects her young novice of a clandestine visit to Liu Meng-
mei.

   But the real triumph of *Mu-tan t'ing* is the perfect embodiment of
the philosophical dispute (of *ch'ing* over *li*) in the conflict of wills
between Tu Li-niang and her father Tu Pao. The conflict is apparent
from the earliest scenes: on his first appearance in the play Tu Pao
admits that no arrangement has yet been made for Li-niang's
betrothal though she is at the marriageable age, and very shortly
he is reprimanding his wife for permitting the girl to spend her time
in idle pursuits. When Li-niang has dreamed her dream of love and
died her death of longing, Tu Pao is naturally full of grief. But whereas in the original *hua-pen* story the news of his daughter's rebirth is
immediately accepted by Tu Pao, in the play his dedication to
reason stands as a powerful block to his spontaneous affection, and
keeps him obdurate in refusal to acknowledge either daughter or
son-in-law until the very last scene of grand reunion. His recognition
of his daughter is made the ultimate test of love's supremacy over
cold reason. By scene 48 all obstacles but one have been removed:
Liu Meng-mei has married Li-niang and has succeeded in the
examinations, the rebellion of Li Ch'üan has been put down, and
mother and daughter have been reunited. Yet still the father holds
out against the joyful truth.

   Tu Pao is not at all an unsympathetic figure. Despite the equation
with Cheng Lo (see above) and the fine irony that elevation to the
premiership is actually his reward for a mean and demeaning stratagem against the rebels, he is in no way put forward as a corrupt,
grasping or traitorous official of the stock melodramatic sort. In
scene 8, *Ch'üan nung*, a highly stylized dramatization of rituals which
go back to the earliest centuries of Chinese agriculture, he is portrayed as a benevolent and beloved steward, naively remote from the
actual soil the peasants till but nonetheless a source of blessing to his
community. The key to what "weighed on the innermost heart" of

T'ang Hsien-tsu lies precisely in the contrast between Tu Pao's just benevolence in public life and the harsh tyranny he wields over his daughter in private. It is precisely that a man capable of stooping to the bribery of a miserable rebel should express himself with such righteous indignation when his wife permits their daughter a daytime nap. Tu Pao is a moderately honest and kindly man, yet *something* renders him all but incapable of accepting the news of his only child's return from the dead. That "something" is *li*.

This pathos of Tu Pao's position is brought out again and again, and as early as scene 16, *Chieh-ping* 詰病, when the maid reveals Li-niang's dream to the girl's mother. Tu Pao laughs off his daughter's desperate sickness as "a slight fever," scoffs at his wife's requests for the intercession of Taoist wizards but recommends that Tutor Ch'en read her pulse. Tu Pao is particularly scornful of the suggestion of lovesickness: "According to the ancients a man should take a wife at thirty, a girl marry at twenty . . . such a little innocent, what can a child like that know of 'love'?" And this, of course, comes when the atmosphere of the stage is heavy with the impending death of Li-niang.

By exposing Tang Hsien-tsu's preoccupation with the tyranny of time, in all of his plays, C. T. Hsia offers us new insights into the situation of Tu Li-niang and makes clear the distinction between her status and that of a potential tragic heroine. She is supremely courageous, supremely committed to love only when she is released from time, in dream or in death; after her resurrection she returns to the world of convention. But the overall and ultimate mode of *Mu-tan t'ing* is not tragic but magnificently comic. It is of prime importance to Li-niang's role that she continue her struggle, after her assumption of mortal, decorous wifely status, to attain the supreme goal, the blessing of her father. Love fulfilled sustains her every whit as strongly as did love withheld or love in the shades, until the great climactic moment of confrontation with her father in the final scene. Overcome with emotion, Li-niang faints away: and it is precisely at this moment that the force of her emotion overcomes the rational incredulity of her father.

In a famous T'ang story, the power of love wrings an involuntary cry from the lips of a mother and prevents the attainment of Taoist abstraction. In *Mu-tan t'ing*, the power of love wrings from the lips of Tu Pao the admission and acceptance of his daughter's return to life, and ends the long tyranny of the coldly rational over the spontaneous affection of the heart. Here, to conclude, is the central passage of this all-important final scene of the play:

Emperor:
Hear the Imperial decree: having given careful attention to the deposition of Tu Li-niang, we are no longer inclined to question the fact of her rebirth. Now let our eunuchs escort her past the Audience Gate, and let father and child, husband and wife acknowledge each other and all return home to resume their proper relationships.
(Shouts of "Long live his Imperial Majesty"; procession).

Madam Chen (wife of Tu Pao):
Felicitations, my lord, on your high advancement.

Tu Pao:
How could I even have hoped to find you safe and sound, my dear!

Li-niang (weeps):
Oh my father!

Tu Pao (refuses to look at her):
Here in broad daylight—keep your distance, demon, keep your distance. Tutor Ch'en, I'm beginning to entertain suspicions about Liu Meng-mei, that he is a ghost also.

Ch'en (laughs):
Then he must be the Demon Kick-the-Dipper!

Madam Chen:
Now that we find our son-in-law to be the new Prize Candidate, our daughter's return to life is doubly joyful! Come sir, salute your mother-in-law.

Liu Meng-mei (bows):
I was remiss in welcoming you, mother-in-law, on your arrival here, I humbly ask your pardon.

Li-niang:
Congratulations, sir, my best congratulations.

Liu:
Who told you my news?

Li-niang:
I heard it from Tutor Ch'en.

Liu:

But I have been the victim of your father's rage.

Ch'en:

Young sir, salute your father-in-law.

Liu:

As my father-in-law I salute you, Yama, authentic King of the Ten Levels of Hell!

Ch'en:

Ah, young sir, let me try to ease matters between you: now that

>   man and wife have ridden round
>   the transsubstantial wheel
>   and our Lord the Prince smiles on
>   the course you have set
>   do not fear His Excellency the Minister will disclaim
>   his dowry obligations.
>   Let us now see mother and daughter
>   father and son-in-law
>   signed, sealed and delivered.

Liu:

Guards, here I am, a criminal.

Ch'en (laughs):

You're joking with these men—

>   what a sense of humor!
>   We hail your seizure of the cassia-bough from heaven,
>   yet close-matched to this feat
>   was the snatching of a sweet flower from caverns of earth!

Li-niang (sighs):

Tutor Ch'en, if you had not brought about that stroll of mine in the rear garden, how would I ever have set eyes on this captor of the cassia-bough?

Tu Pao:

Devil-talk! There has been no matching-up of family rank and status—what is this nonsense about "setting eyes" on Liu Meng-mei?

Li-niang (laughs):

It's the sight of his

>   black silk scholar's cap
>   and court robes draped about him

> gives a spark, spark
> sparkle to my eye.

Ah my parents, there are people who build high towers decked out with colored silks, yet even in broad daylight can't succeed in attracting a son-in-law of official rank. And here I your daughter from ghostly caverns of my dreams have made the conquest of no less than the Prize Candidate—what's this talk now of "family rank and status"? It must be that as a

> descendant of Tu Fu
> you are grown so used to browbeating your daughter
> you fail to recognize the eminence
> of a scion of Liu Tsung-yuan!

Father, Please acknowledge me as your daughter.

Tu Pao:
Leave this Liu Meng-mei, and I will acknowledge you when you return to my house.

Li-niang:
> You would have me return to my girlhood home,
> quit my husband's house.
> I'd be an azalea blooming still for you
> but that would not stop the cuckoo's crimson tears.[31]

(she weeps):
Ai-yo, here before
> the father I knew in life
> the mother who gave me birth
> my dizzy soul loses its hold on sense.

(she faints away).

Tu Pao (startled):
Li-niang, my daughter!

---

[31] Cf. above, the song of Yang Chi-sheng's widow from *Ming feng chi*, and also E. H. Schafer, "Li Te-yü and the Azalea," in *Etudes Asiatiques*, XVIII-XIX, 1965, pp. 105-114: "The ninth century poet Yung T'ao, on hearing the song of the hawk-cuckoo, wrote about its blood staining the boughs of the azalea, and the tenth century poet Ch'eng Yen-hsiung borrowed the image:
> Doubtless it is the blood from within its mouth
> Dripping to form the flowers on the branch."

Appendix: Synopses

I: *Ch'ing-shan lei*

Act I: Po Chü-yi and two friends, Chia Tao and Meng Hao-jan, visit the house of P'ei Hsing-nu, a courtesan who longs to quit her occupation and marry but is prevented from doing so by a greedy mother-procuress. Hsing-nu treats her guests very lightly, but as the evening progresses becomes attracted to Po and asks that he visit her alone on the next occasion. Wedge: The Emperor demotes Po, who must now take leave of Hsing-nu after their six months' liaison and go off to exile in Chiangchou.

Act II: Hsing-nu has made a vow no longer to entertain patrons but patiently to await Po's return. The mother however schemes to marry her to Liu Yi-lang, a wealthy tea-merchant. She sends Hsing-nu a false letter announcing the death of Po. Hsing-nu is heart-broken and consents to marry Liu.

Act III: Po Chü-yi entertains his old friend Yüan Chen on the latter's boat. Hsing-nu plays her *p'i-pa* on a nearby boat, while her husband is away drinking. Po suspects that the player is Hsing-nu and summons her. She can be convinced only with difficulty that Po is a living man rather than a ghost. After hearing Hsing-nu's story Po composes his *P'i-pa hsing*. Hsing-nu puts her drunken husband to bed, then returns to run away with Po to the capital. On the following morning Liu wakes to find his wife gone, reports this to the local officers but is arrested on suspicion of her murder.

Act IV: Yüan Chen memorializes the Emperor to the effect that Po Chü-yi has been unjustly banished and that Hsing-nu has been wronged by her mother and the tea-merchant. The Emperor recalls Po and summons Hsing-nu to tell her story. Moved by this, the Emperor confirms the marriage and orders the punishment of the old woman and the tea-merchant.

II: *Ch'ing-shan chi*

Scene 1: No dialogue. Arias celebrate friendship, outline action.

Scene 2 : Po Chü-yi and Yüan Chen lament corruption of times, but decide to attend examinations in capital.

3 : P'ei Hsing-nu laments courtesan's life; her mother scolds her, paints black picture of concubine's life (which is Hsing-nu's dream).

4 : Po's two handmaids, Fan-su and Hsiao-man give farewell party for him.

5 : Very short, no dialogue: Po and Yüan sing hardships of road.

6 : Spectacular, many extras: Po and Yüan awarded *chin-shih* in examination before Emperor, given appointments in capital.

7 : Long: led by Liu Yu-hsi, Po and Yüan visit Hsing-nu, who plays lute for them. Po pawns his blue shirt to buy wine. Hsing-nu, drunk, asks him to stay; equally drunk, he agrees.

8 : Po's handmaids lament his absence, then welcome news of his success.

9 : Chü K'o-jung announces his rebellion and plans march on Ch'ang-an.

10 : Po and Yuan feast Liu on his departure as Governor to Chiangchou.

11 : Eunuch made Generalissimo to suppress rebellion.

12 : Short battle scene: Chu defeats eunuch's army.

13 : Hsing-nu redeems blue shirt, daydreams of marriage with Po. She and mother flee rebel disorders in capital.

14 : Po memorializes on military situation, is demoted to Marshal of Chiangchou.

15 : Hsing-nu and mother find shelter in countryside.

16 : Po visits Hsing-nu's house, learns she has fled.

17 : Very long: tea-merchant Liu Yi-lang visits Hsing-nu, who rebuffs him. Mother promises Liu that increased intimacy will result as Po's absence lengthens.

18 : Very short: Po arrives at Chiangchou.

Scene 19: Long: Hsing-nu returns blue shirt to Po's handmaids. They promise to tell Po of the mother's plan to wed Hsing-nu to tea-merchant.

20: Po sends his man for the handmaids to console his exile.

21: Long: invitation (scene 20) arrives as handmaids are entertaining Hsing-nu and mother. Mother prohibits Hsing-nu from accompanying them to Chiangchou, but they promise that, if she will wait, they will raise her "ransom."

22: Tea-merchant Liu, comically resplendent as suitor, succeeds in purchasing Hsing-nu from mother. Hsing-nu has no choice, but vows death before dishonor.

23: Handmaids rejoin Po, return blue shirt and tell him of tea-merchant's pursuit of Hsing-nu. They offer their jewels to ransom her. Po still lacks sufficient money, but decides to send a messenger immediately with what he has plus blue shirt "as evidence."

24: Messenger offers mother 300 taels, but is informed that Hsing-nu has left as wife of tea-merchant.

25: Po drinking with handmaids in celebration of autumn, receives messenger's reply.

26: Yüan Chen arrives on tour of inspection, Po and Liu greet him, exchange poems and plan a shipboard party for the evening.

27: Hsing-nu resists tea-merchant, who accepts servant's advice to console himself with wineshop girls until wife's resistance weakens.

28: Long: Hsing-nu's lute-playing at Chiangchou overheard by Po and friends, who invite her aboard their boat. News comes that tea-merchant, drunk, has fallen into river and drowned. Po's friends agree that he may now with propriety marry Hsing-nu.

29: Hsing-nu enters Po's home. After some comic (mock-jealous) exchanges with his handmaids, she and Po extol their reunion.

Scene 30: Grand *t'uan-yüan*. Po receives congratulations of Yüan and Liu. Three wives sing ditty of connubial bliss. Imperial messenger announces Po's recall to capital as Secretary of Board of Rites and Han-lin Academician.

III: *Ming feng chi*

Scene   1: Prologue briefly narrates the action.

    2: Tsou Ying-lung and Lin Jun exchange vows of brotherhood and visit tutor Kuo Hsi-yen.

    3: Grand Tutor Hsia Yen reveals his desire to recover Ho-t'ao and fear of treachery from Yen Sung.

    4: Chao Wen-hua fawns on Yen Sung.

    5: Yang Chi-sheng is refused admission to Yen Sung's mansion when he attempts to warn Yen that he has memorialized against him.

    6: Hsia Yen and Yen Sung dispute border policy.

    7: Yen Sung bribes eunuchs to accuse Hsia Yen of treason.

    8: Tsou and Lin obtain predictions from temple in Fukien.

    9: Honest but timid high officers bewail execution of Hsia Yen.

    10: Hsia Yen's widow and concubine leave for exile.

    11: Yang Chi-sheng, himself in exile, aids Hsia's widow.

    12: Wife of Tsou Ying-lung aids Hsia's concubine.

    13: Yen Shih-fan feasts henchmen.

    14: Yang Chi-sheng writes new memorial against Yen Sung.

    15: Yang submits memorial.

    16: Yang is executed, widow stabs herself.

    17: Ryukyu chieftain sends raiding parties against China coast.

    18: Lin Jun flees invading pirates, takes refuge with Tsou Ying-lung in Hangchow.

    19: Tsou Ying-lung sends Hsia Yen's posthumous son to Kuo Hsi-yen for safety.

Scene 20: Yen Sung appoints Chao Wen-hua to pacify pirates.

21: Chao proceeds against pirates.

22: Tsou Ying-lung and Lin Jun leave for *chin-shih* examinations.

23: Tsou and Lin, now *chin-shih*, visit tomb of Hsia Yen, then learn of misdeeds of Yen Sung and his son Shih-fan.

24: Yen Shih-fan has Tsou and Lin sent to perilous border appointments.

25: Tsou and Lin leave for northern border and Yunnan respectively.

26: Wives of Tsou and Lin lament husbands' absence.

27: Tung Yu-hai, Chang Chung, and Wu Shih-lai memorialize against Yen family.

28: Wu Shih-lai's mother encourages him to submit memorial at risk of death.

29: Chang Chung prepares his own coffin and sends his wife home.

30: Officer of guard, ordered by Yen Sung to murder the three memorialists, sends them to exile instead.

31: Yen Shih-fan plots murder of wealthy young neighbor Yi Hung-ch'i, but fails.

32: Yi escapes to take refuge with Kuo Hsi-yen.

33: Yen Mao-ch'ing and Chao Wen-hua, Yen Sung's henchmen, visit Western Hills to purchase immortality pills for presentation to Yen Sung.

34: Tsou Ying-lung on return from border learns of Yens' latest villainies.

35: Wives of Tsou and Lin visited by Kuo Hsi-yen.

36: Kuo Hsi-yen is executed, but Tsou Ying-lung memorializes against Yens and wins Imperial decision to investigate.

37: Yen Sung and Yen Shih-fan, disgraced, are mocked on their journey home.

38: Lin Jun, on the way to new appointment near Yen Sung's home, meets Hsia Yen's widow.

Scene 39: Lin Jun collects evidence of Yen Shih-fan's crimes against his neighbors.

40: Yen family makes restitution to its victims. Shih-fan executed, Lin Jun presents his head before spirits of victims.

41: Tsou Ying-lung and Lin Jun reunited, Imperial edict restores honors to living and dead.

IV: *Mu-tan t'ing*

Scene   1: Prologue, events briefly narrated.

2: Liu Meng-mei declares his ambition.

3: Tu Pao hires a tutor for his daughter Li-niang.

4: Tutor Ch'en receives Tu Pao's invitation.

5: Ch'en enters Tu's family.

6: Liu Meng-mei seeks a patron.

7: Tutor Ch'en teaches Li-niang from the *Book of Songs*.

8: Tu Pao "speeds the plow" in his district.

9: Maid Ch'un-hsiang tells of Li-niang's awakening to the spring.

10: Li-niang dreams of love with Liu Meng-mei.

11: Li-niang's mother is concerned for her daughter's health.

12: Li-niang recalls her dream.

13: Liu leaves for the capital.

14: Li-niang paints her own portrait.

15: Barbarians plan attacks.

16: Ch'un-hsiang tells Li-niang's parents of her walk in the garden.

17: Nun is brought to cure Li-niang.

18: Tutor Ch'en and nun try to cure Li-niang.

19: Rebel Li Ch'üan plans action.

20: Li-niang dies, Tu Pao appointed to pacify rebellion

21: Liu Meng-mei receives assistance from patron.

Scene 22: Liu falls sick, Tutor Ch'en takes him in.

23: Ruler of Hades permits Li-niang to fulfill her predestined love.

24: Liu Meng-mei finds Li-niang's portrait in the garden.

25: Ch'un-hsiang and Madam Tu offer incense to Li-niang's spirit.

26: Liu falls in love with the portrait.

27: Nuns witness visit of Li-niang's ghost to Liu.

28: Meeting of Li-niang and Liu.

29: Old nun suspects young nun of visiting Liu.

30: Nuns try to catch Li-niang with Liu.

31: Tu Pao arrives at new post.

32: Li-niang reveals her identity to Liu.

33: Liu plans to reopen Li-niang's grave.

34: Nun gets recipe for reviving Li-niang.

35: Grave opened, Li-niang revives.

36: Nuns disperse in guilty fear.

37: Tutor Ch'en finds the empty grave.

38: Rebel Li Ch'üan plans attack on Tu Pao.

39: Liu Meng-mei and Li-niang reach Hangchow.

40: Liu's servant receives news of Liu.

41: Liu succeeds in examinations.

42: Tu Pao proceeds against rebels.

43: Tu arrives in Huai-an.

44: Li-niang asks Liu to visit her parents.

45: Tutor Ch'en is given false news of Tu's wife's death by rebels.

46: Ch'en reports to Tu Pao.

47: Tu Pao "pacifies" Li Ch'üan.

48: Mother and daughter reunited.

49: Liu waits to visit Tu Pao.

50: Tu Pao refuses to see Liu.

Mu-tan t'ing: Chart of Structure

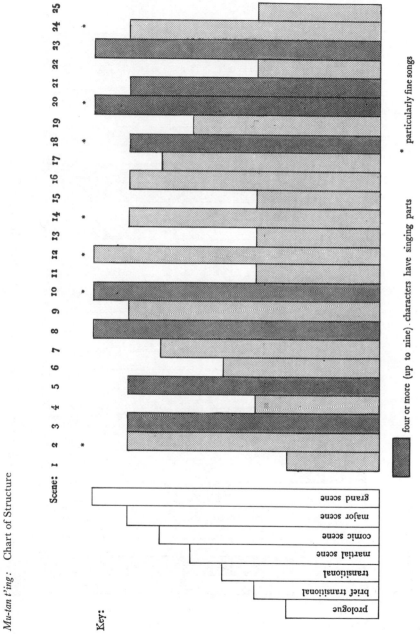

Scene: 1 2 3 4 5 6 7 8 9 10 11 12 13 14 15 16 17 18 19 20 21 22 23 24 25

Key:

grand scene
major scene
comic scene
martial scene
transitional
brief transitional
prologue

four or more (up to nine) characters have singing parts

* particularly fine songs

Chart of Structure (continued)

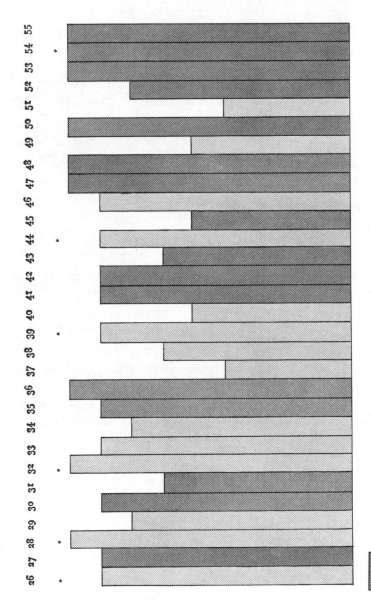

four or more (up to nine) characters have singing parts

* particularly fine songs

Urban Centers: the Cradle of Popular Fiction

by Jaroslav Průšek

There are not many cases in the history of the opposite ends of Eurasia when the lines of development in a certain domain of human activity so closely approached each other in East and West as they did in the literature arising in the cities of Europe and China, around A.D. 1300. Creations of a type of literature represented in Europe by the belletristic *oeuvre* of Giovanni Boccaccio and the *Canterbury Tales* of Geoffrey Chaucer also appear in the Chinese urban milieu, and a comparison of these literary products of a similar social environment would throw much light on their analogies and differences and would contribute notably in helping us to build up a picture of the environment which begot them. In China, this literature flourished much earlier—at the latest under the Southern Sung (1126–1279); but otherwise it has many traits in common with the corresponding European literature and mainly grows out of the same soil. Only the Chinese soil is richer and more finely prepared: Hangchow, the capital of the Southern Sung, not far from the mouth of the Yangtze River, was a city of a million inhabitants[1] with a complex economical and cultural life, and having as its hinterland an immense empire with a population of about 60 million inhabitants.[2] In all these respects, China was far ahead of contemporary Europe and bears some resemblance rather to Europe in the era of early capitalism.

[1] J. Gernet, *La vie Quotidienne en Chine à la veille de l'invasion Mongole 1250–1276.* Paris, 1959, p. 27.

[2] *Ibid.*, p. 69.

The greater influence of urban elements in the whole life of the country, especially after the forced shift of the capital to the wealthy seaboard after 1126 (when the northern part of the Empire was lost along with the capital, Pien-liang) manifests itself in literature as a certain tendency toward popularization, as an endeavor to appeal to a wider circle of readers; this is the main feature differentiating the literature of the Sung from the preceding T'ang literature. These tendencies, already apparent in the literature of the Northern Sung, mature under the Southern Sung and effect the shift of the gravitational center to quite new literary genres. Intimations of this trend appear in the time of the Northern Sung, for instance, in the tradi-ditional literature cultivated by the literati in the crystal-clear style of the essay, less burdened with quotations and striving to render a direct experience. The then fashionable lyric (*tz'u* 詞) abandons the great themes of T'ang poetry and tries to record the intimacy of transient moments and feelings. Certain poets such as Liu Yung 柳永 compose their poems already with an eye to mass consumption, collaborate with professional singers and so come closer to the professional folk authors. The colloquial language also found its way with increasing frequency into the lyric; indeed, it also began to infiltrate philosophy, records of the sayings of various philosophers appearing in the colloquial language (*yü-lu* 語錄).

The main manifestation of this democratization of culture was the rise of a whole stratum of folk artists, strictly specialized, who catered to the spiritual entertainment of the very varied groups of town population, from court circles to the lowest social levels. They comprised, in addition to men and women singers of songs of various kinds, specialists in certain types of ballads, such as ballads to the accompaniment of the drum (*ku-tz u-tz'u* 鼓子詞); long narrative compositions, in which the narrative sections in prose create only the framework for complexly arranged suites of lyrical songs, alternating according to a complicated set of rules—the ballads, *chu-kung-tiao* 諸宮調, from which later developed the Chinese *singspiele;* rudiment-ary forms of stage art, such as puppet and shadow plays, pan-tomimes, ballet performances, comic numbers, and so on. The European *joculatores*,[3] who remain a more or less undifferentiated

---

[3] Cf. V. Cerny, *Staročeská lyrika milostná* "The Old Czech Love Lyric," Praha, 1948, ch. *Gens jucunda joculatorum*, pp. 105-128. Also V. Cerny, *Staročesky mastičkár* "The Old Czech Quacksalver," Praha, 1948.

mass, can in no way bear comparison with the wide range of popular town artists, and especially not in respect to specialization and variety. This, too, is proof of the more richly developed character of the Chinese towns as compared with those of Europe.

Among these artists pride of place belonged, both as regards the fruits of their creative activities and the exceptional influence they exercised on the whole further development of Chinese literature, to the storytellers, usually called *shuo-hua-ti* 說話的, narrators of works of fiction. The interest these artists aroused at that time is already apparent from the fact that we find a comprehensive record of their activities in five descriptions of the then principal towns,[4] and that a whole book is dedicated to them by Lo Yeh, from the end of the Sung era.[5] It is evident that storytelling occupied the place in the cultural life of the town-dwellers which the theater was to gain later.

The Beginnings of the Professional Storytellers under the T'ang

Storytelling, as the professional art of spoken narration, arose under the T'ang, but achieved its full blossoming under the Sung, when it first acquired its mature form. It seems that the main impulse for the development of storytelling (*shuo-ch'ang wen-hsüeh* 說唱文學, "narration recited and sung") under the T'ang was the preaching of the propagators of Buddhism, which became the favorite entertainment of the broad masses. Soon the actual theme of the preacher, the interpretation of some sacred writing, provides only the core round which new elements accumulate: the narrator tells other stories as well, at first from the life of Buddha and of other Buddhist saints, but later no doubt stories of other origin. In translations of sūtras a mixed style was already employed, prose sections alternating with verse; in preaching, the verse sections were often sung, usually to the accompaniment of some musical instrument, and so arose the above-mentioned *shuo-ch'ang wen-hsüeh*, the basic form of Chinese popular literature. The language of these expositions of Buddhist Scriptures

---

[4] Description of Pien-liang (Kai-feng), in *Tung-ching Meng-hua-lu* 東京夢華錄, by Meng Yüan-lao 孟元老; description of Hangchow in *Tu-ch'eng chi sheng* 都城紀勝, by Nai-te weng 耐得翁; and then also in *Hsi-hu lao-jen fan-sheng-lu* 西湖老人繁勝錄; *Meng liang lu* 夢梁錄, by Wu Tzu-mu 吳自牧 and *Wu-lin chiu-shih* 武林舊事, by Chou Mi 周密. All taken over into *Tung-ching Meng-hua-lu, wai szu chung* 外四種.

[5] Lo Yeh 羅燁 *Tsui-weng t'an-lu* 醉翁談錄.

which were probably also committed to writing for the use of those who could not attend the sermons, and then for the general reader, was still a kind of compromise between the classical written language and the purely colloquial language; it tends toward one or the other sphere according to the genre and to the level of the writer. Often these productions are referred to as *pien-wen* 變文, according to the predominating genre, in the sense of texts *(wen)* relating strange incidents *(pien)* from the life of Buddhist saints, eventually also of heroes of secular character, regularly written in proso-metrical style. But the popular literature of this time, as it has come down to us in the Tun-huang caves in Western China, from the period around A.D. 1000, is both as regards subject matter and form much too varied to be comprehended under the term *pien-wen*. In that body of works we find in rudimentary form all the kinds of popular literature, from pure prose to compositions in mixed style and on to epic ballads and lyrical songs.

Despite the fact that in the domain of religious narration there arose as early as T'ang times some of the greatest creations of Chinese epic literature, such as for instance *Wei-mo-chieh chiang-ching pien wen* 維摩詰講經變文, "Exposition of the Vimalakirti Sūtra,"[6] comprising over 30 *chüan*,[7] and despite the fact that this production greatly influenced the further development of Chinese literature, it is still relegated to its periphery. Its character is still mainly religious and does not consciously set itself a literary aim, it has only a secondary relation to reality—through the medium of some traditional text or material—and, in some instances, actually only repeats and elaborates folklore motifs.[8] On the other hand, we cannot regard even this production as being of folklore character. Its creator is often an adequately educated professional: a Buddhist monk or a zealous believer, and probably already under the T'ang there appeared also the lay professional storyteller, differing in his whole habitus from the

[6] Wang Chung-min 王重民 and others, *Tun-huang pien-wen chi* 敦煌變文集 vol. 2, p. 517 *et seq.*

[7] Cheng Chen-to 鄭振鐸, *Chung-kuo su wen-hsüeh shih* 中國俗文學史, Peking, Tso-chia ch'u-pan-she, 1954, p. 205.

[8] For example the narrative *K'ung-tzu Hsiang T'o hsiang-wen shu* 孔子項託相問書, cf. *Tun-huang pien-wen chi*, vol. 1, p. 231. Compare A. Waley, *Ballads and Stories from Tun-huang*, London, 1960, p. 91. Probably also the story about Meng Chiang-nü (Waley, p. 145), then the ballad of Tung Yung (Waley, p. 155) and others.

folk singer or reciter, who has still not broken away from the collective from which he sprang.[9] The subject matter of the greater part of these productions is not material circulating in a folk community, but consists of themes taken over from literature, especially religious but also secular. This literature also differs from traditional folklore literature in its forms, some of which are of very complicated structure. There are for example intricate mosaics of prose and verse, as in *pien-wen*, various poetical forms (among them the long ballad composed in seven-syllable verses, which then remained for ages the basic form in popular epic), various metrical patterns not far removed from poetry and, finally, forms of ancient character taken over from orthodox writings, such as *fu*.

This literature, however, has often a two-sided character: it is presented to an audience orally, like folklore, but its main source is normal written literature and it in turn has a tendency to be fixed in writing; it thus forms a kind of bridge between literature and folklore; also the terms used for storytelling, such as *shuo-shu* 說書, "to interpret books," *yen-yi* 演義, "to explain the sense," and others, indicate that one of the primary functions of this activity was to expound works of recognized literature to the masses, and storytelling always remained true to this function, even though in later times it often interpreted works which themselves were the product of the storyteller's art.

The storyteller's production of the T'ang era, such as was preserved in the Tun-huang caves, decisively influenced Chinese literature in its further course. It obviously stimulated interest in the epic and it is not unlikely that the flourishing of the T'ang stories of the literati was promoted by the appearance of this popular literature. A feature of this early literature was an interest in contemporary

[9] Of the existence of professional storytellers there can be no doubt, see J. Průšek, "Researches into the Beginnings of the Chinese Popular Novel," pt. 1, *Archiv Orientální* 11 (1939), p. 108. I think, too, that the reference is to the recital of a professional storyteller in the comment which Yüan Chen made on his own poem, sent to Po Chü-yi (Yüan Chen, *Ch'ang-ch'ing chi* 元稹, 長慶集. *Szu-pu pei-yao*, ch. 10, p. 4a), where he mentions the recital of the tale, *Li Wa chuan* 李娃傳. This note circulates in two versions, but in opposition to Ch'eng Yi-chung 程毅中, *Sung Yüan hua-pen* 宋元話本, Peking, Chung-hua shu-chü, 1964, p. 5, note 2, it is my opinion that in either case it is a matter of a recital by a professional storyteller and not of a recital by the author of the recited tale, Po Hsing-chien 白行簡 himself. A point that would speak against the tale being told by Po Hsing-chien is the time at which the recital took place and its duration (4 a.m.-10 a.m.).

history, not without a certain political slant,[10] and sharply edged social criticism,[11] so that this literature became the voice of the masses also in the ideological sense.

The Sung Storytellers

The Sung storytellers are distinguished by two basic traits: their specialization, which in itself speaks for the professionalism and maturity of their art, and, on the other hand, their popular character. For even when they gained the favor and patronage of the highest classes with their art, they remained first and foremost folk artists, never crossing the dividing line between the people and the ruling class of literati, and therein lies the basic difference between their productions and those of the officially recognized literati. Proof of their folk character is to be found in the nicknames under which a number of them went, especially the tellers of short shories, *hsiao-shuo*: "Wine," "Gruel," "Jujube," "Old Clothes," and so on.[12]

Nevertheless they too paid court to traditional learning, as Lo Yeh stresses in his description of them: "These storytellers, though they belong to a negligible sphere of learning, do try to pick up as much as possible and do not belong to the category of average persons with merely superficial knowledge; for them it is a rule that they must be widely read and be thoroughly acquainted with their subject matter."[13]

Their popular character is to be inferred from the places where they perform; in addition to various temples, tea-rooms, and so on, especially entertainment parks (*wa-tzu* 瓦子) with narrow streets

[10] In the Tun-huang caves a fragment has been preserved of the story of Viceroy Chang Yi-ch'ao 張義潮, who about 857 inflicted a crushing defeat upon the Tibetans who had undertaken a raid upon Chinese territory. The relation was probably written at a time not too remote from the events described and extols the commander who forced the barbarians to retreat. See *Tun-huang pien-wen chi*, vol. 1, p. 114 *et seq.* A similar tendency is apparent in another fragment from Tun-huang, telling of a nephew of the afore-mentioned commander, Chang Huai-shen 張准深 by name, who defeated the Uighurs. This relation was written down most probably in the years 874–879. Cf. *Tun-huang pien-wen chi*, vol. 1, p. 121 *et seq.*

[11] The note of social criticism is sounded especially in *Yen-tzu fu* 燕子賦, *Tun-huang pien-wen chi*, vol. 1, p. 249 *et seq.* Cf. A. Waley, *Ballads*, p. 11, "The Swallow and the Sparrow."

[12] "Researches, Continuation," *Archiv Orientální* 23 (1955), pp. 649–650.

[13] Lo Yeh, p. 3.

bordered by rows of little shops, reminiscent of bazaars in pre-Revolutionary Chinese towns. There, sometimes also in permanent booths, *kou-lan* 勾欄,[14] the storytellers practiced their art, trying with their voice, sometimes accompanied by instruments,[15] to compete for an audience with their much noisier rivals, tumblers and jugglers, wrestlers, singers of both sexes, or the cries of vendors offering their wares. We must attribute an occasional harsh and penetrating note in their productions to the necessity of making themselves heard above the din of brazen competitors.

The storytellers were organized in guilds, as were all working people in the cities at that time; in the sources,[16] mention is made of a "Society of Good Debaters" *Hsiung-pien-she* 雄辯社, and of the fact that the storytellers were divided into "schools" *chia* 家; it is probable that all their work had a strongly guild character. The storytelling profession was evidently in many cases hereditary,[17] and so highly specialized groups grew up with their own stock of themes, their own methods of artistic composition, certain clichés and techniques. All this was of great importance in the history of Chinese literature. For the first time there appeared in China a literary professional, for whom literature was not a diversion or hobby (as it was among the gentry, who wrote for their own amusement or for literary fame), but a source of livelihood requiring a perfect mastery of the craft.

Descriptions of storytellers speak, as a rule, of four schools, and it seems that this division actually corresponds to the basic groups of storytellers, as regards both subject matter and form: tellers of shorter secular tales, *hsiao-shuo;* narrators of histories, usually long workings-up of various chronicles; expounders of Buddhist scriptures, probably also long texts; and narrators of religious stories of Buddhist

[14] Cf. *Hsi-hu lao-jen fan-sheng-lu* in *Tung-ching Meng-hua-lu*, p. 123: "In the Northern Bazaar . . . two booths were always reserved for the telling of histories"; two storytellers recited throughout their lives exclusively in the Northern Bazaar.

[15] The narrators of short stories were also called *yin-tzu-erh* 銀字兒, which is the name of a musical instrument, see "Researches," pt. 1, p. 123 and note 2.

[16] *Wu-lin chiu-shih*, ch. 3.

[17] Cf. J. Prǔšek, "The Narrators of Buddhist Scriptures", Archiv Orientální 10 (1938), p. 377; "Researches, Continuation", p. 648; *Ch'ing-lou-chi* 青樓集 *Ts'ung-shu chi-ch'eng*, Shanghai, Commercial Press, 1939, p. 6, par. *Shih Hsiao-t'ung* 時小童, speaks of a mother and daughter who were professional storytellers.

character.[18] We could characterize these groups, too, from the point of view of their relation to reality; this relation is weakest in the expounders of Buddhist scriptures, into which only very occasionally do echoes of life penetrate, as was also the case with *pien-wen*. At this time *pien-wen* were being transformed into *pao-chüan* 寶卷, "precious rolls," which have remained up to modern times the favorite reading of Chinese women.[19] Otherwise there is little of substance that we can say about the reciter of Buddhist sūtras.

Religious Narratives and Historical Tales

A very popular theme in Buddhist religious narration is that of the pious patron affording hospitality to monks; another is the theme of meditation and spiritual enlightenment.[20] The most important product of this group of storytellers and one of the oldest survivals of storytellers' literature is the first version of the relation about the monk Hsüan-tsang, who at the time of the T'ang Emperor T'ai Tsung, 627–649, set out to cross Central Asia to India in order to bring back with him the sūtras (*Ta T'ang San-tsang ch'ü ching shih hua* 大唐三藏取經詩話 or *tz'u hua* 詞話, "Relation interspersed with poems about the Monk San Tsang, or Hsüan-tsang, in the time of the Great T'ang Dynasty, and of how he set out in quest of the Sūtras"). The text still dates perhaps from the time of the Northern Sung and is as yet only a brief and fairly primitive storyteller's manual, containing 17 episodes. Already in this version, a miraculous monkey appears as the monk's guide, but he does not yet bear the name Sun Wu-k'ung, "Sun that has grasped emptiness"; the other two guides figuring in later versions are not yet created. Fantastic episodes telling for the most part of meetings and skirmishes with a variety of demons and set almost exclusively in quite imaginary milieus are very close to the fantastic ghost stories which at that time were one of the most popular parts of the storyteller's repertoire. In addition to this attempt at a synthetic working up of Hsüan-tsang's adventures, there existed single stories or episodes which were later incorporated in the famous work compiled by Wu Ch'eng-en 吳承恩, the present-

---

[18] Cf. "Researches," pt. 1, p. 125 et seq.

[19] "The Narrators of Buddhist Scriptures," pp. 378–379.

[20] I discuss the examples preserved in "The Narrators of Buddhist Scriptures."

day *Hsi yu chi* 西遊記, "Journey to the West".[21] A version fairly close to the present-day text already existed in the time of the Mongols.

Other religious narratives were strongly influenced by secular tales; into them criminal, erotic, and other motifs find their way.[22]

Much more closely related to reality are the historical tales, which we may divide into two groups according to whether they treat of recent events or are historical tales in the usual meaning of the word.

We pointed out above that among the finds in the Tun-huang caves were narrations about contemporary events with strong political, eventually patriotic, coloring. The Sung storytellers carried on this tradition and undoubtedly a number of their relations were imbued with a strong patriotism. Good examples are the tales of a certain Wang Liu tai-fu 王六大夫, who in the period Hsien-shun (1265–1274) narrated "Stories of the Restoration (of the lost parts of the Empire)" and the "Biographies of the Famous Generals of the Revival Period during the reigns of the Emperors Kao Tsung (1127–1162) and Hsiao Tsung (1163–1189).[23] This is evident from the words of Lo Yeh, who says of these historical narrations: "When they tell about the traitors to their country, full of falseness and cunning, then even the most stupid begin to curse, when they speak of loyal and devoted servants of the State, how they suffered wrong and were suffocated by hatred, even those with hearts and bowels of iron break out in weeping."[24] The political passions of the Sung era are reflected, for instance, in the tale of the hatred of the people for the reformer Wang An-shih, entitled *Ao Hsiang-kung* 拗相公.[25] The policy of Wang An-shih was taken over by the Appeasement Party and so probably became the target for attack of the storytellers, all of whom were supporters of the War Party. Especially passionate is the note of hate for the Appeasement Party in *Hsüan-ho yi-shih*

---

[21] Among the *hua-pen* which Lo Yeh includes in his list in the introductory chapter of *Tsui-weng t'an-lu* there appear two or three relations which passed over into the later *Hsi yu chi.*

[22] Cf. "The Narrators of Buddhist Scriptures."

[23] Cf. "Researches," pt. 1, p. 124.

[24] Lo Yeh, p. 5.

[25] *Ching-pen t'ung-su hsiao-shuo* 京本通俗小說 in *Sung jen hua-pen pa chung* 宋人話本八種, Shanghai, Ya-tung t'u-shu-kuan, 1928 (cited then under *Ching-pen*), p. 105.

宣和遺事, which is a collection of various relations and anecdotes compiled perhaps for the use of a storyteller.[26] This work was compiled shortly after the fall of the Sung dynasty in 1279. Echoes of political strife are to be heard in other tales also.

Even purely historical narratives, however, not only entertained with colorful descriptions of various events, battles, and struggles, but aimed at the same time to communicate to the people a very definite moral and philosophical conception of history, which we might call popularized Confucianism. In these narratives it is a law of historical destiny that after a period of flowering and unifying of the Empire there follows its decline and fall, ending in chaotic struggle. Out of that struggle can rise victorious only he who has the welfare of the people at heart, who aims at becoming a good ruler, and who, full of modesty and humility, cares for a good administration, gives the country peace and calm, and protects it from the attacks of enemies.

Narrators of history take as their principal heroes those figures who embody such a conception as this of a ruler's obligations, as for example Wen-wang, the founder of the power of the Chou, or Liu Pei, the founder of the small empire Han in Szechuan, in the time of the Three Kingdoms (221–263).

Undoubtedly, these old Confucian principles acquired a new significance in the political struggles of the Sung and still more after the subjugation of the country by the Mongols. We can suppose, too, that a certain political coloring attached to the popular relation of how shamefully rulers behaved to their servants and of how cruel were the consequences. For, as we know, lively recollections were preserved among storytellers up to the end of the Sung of General Yüeh Fei, who was shamefully executed in 1141, on pressure by the Appeasement Party, and of other commanders who vainly strove to regain the lost territories in the north. Proof that the storytellers had real political influence on the masses is a report from the year 1357 that one of the Hangchow storytellers organized a fairly

[26] *Hsüan-ho yi-shih* (new edition Shanghai, Commercial Press, 1934). The opinion cited of this book is expressed by Ch'eng Yi-chung (see note 9, above). For the dating of *Hsüan-ho yi-shih* cf. J. Průšek, "Popular Novels in the Collection of Ch'ien Tseng," *Archiv Orientální* 10 (1938), pp. 282–285.

extensive plot against the Mongols,[27] and there is no doubt that it was especially this political background that stimulated an interest in history.

Already under the Sung the whole of Chinese history was worked up into a series of historical narrations. The sources make specific mention of a history of the Three Kingdoms, of Han, Chin, Sung, Ch'i, Liang, T'ang, and of a General History by Szu-ma Kuang.[28] Under the Northern Sung are listed as individual specializations the relations about the Three Kingdoms and the Five Dynasties,[29] and it is no wonder, therefore, that the texts of both these narrations have come down to us from the beginning of the Yuan era.

In all, six texts of historical narrations have come down to us: (1) "Relation of the Expedition of King Wu against Shang";[30] (2) "The Annals of Seven States, Continuation; Yüeh Yi hatches Plots against the State of Ch'i";[31] (3) "Ch'in swallows Six States; Biography of the First Emperor of Ch'in";[32] (4) "History of the First Han Dynasty, Continuation, the Empress Lü has Han Hsin executed";[33] (5) "History of the Three Kingdoms",[34] and (6) "Relation of the Five Dynasties".[35]

These chronicles are usually classed along with novels (*hsiao-shuo*) which, however, is not in accord with their true character. Already the fact that among these historical narrations appears Szu-ma Kuang's "General History" points to these relations being designed more for instruction than merely for entertainment. And

[27] T'ao Tsung-yi 陶宗儀, *Cho keng lu* 輟耕錄, Shanghai, Fu ying shu-chü, 1885, ch. 27, p. 18b, "Hu Chung-pin Organizes the Masses" 胡仲彬取衆. It is interesting that the sister of this storyteller was also initiated into the storyteller's art.

[28] Cf. *Meng liang lu*, ch. 20. Compare "Researches," pt. 1, p. 124 and Lo Yeh, p. 4.

[29] "Researches," pt. 1, p. 115.

[30] *Wu wang fa Chou p'ing-hua* 武王伐紂平話.

[31] *Ch'i kuo ch'un-ch'iu p'ing-hua, hou chi, Yo Yi t'u Ch'i* 七國春秋平話, 後集, 樂毅圖齊.

[32] *Ch'in ping liu kuo p'ing-hua; Ch'in Shih-huang chuan* 秦併六國平話. 秦始皇傳.

[33] *Ch'ien Han-shu p'ing-hua, hsü-chi, Lü hou chan Han Hsin* 前漢書平話 續集. 呂后斬韓信.

[34] *San-kuo chih p'ing-hua* 三國志平話; the five chronicles mentioned were printed in the years 1321–1323, in a uniformly illustrated edition by the Yü family of Chien-an in Fukien. Of all five there are photo-facsimiles, and the first four were published in the collection *Ch'üan hsiang p'ing-hua* 全相平話, undated; the fifth chronicle was published in 1929 by Commercial Press, Shanghai. All five were published in modern format by Ku-tien wen-hsüeh ch'u-pan-she, Shanghai. Our citations are from these modern editions.

[35] *Wu tai p'ing-hua* 五代平話, published in 1911 by Tung K'ang; citations are from the modern edition of 1925 by Commercial Press.

then the texts which have come down to us preserve, despite all the
imaginary and fantastic detail, the ground-plan of chronicles, that
is, their basic structure is prescribed by the history of a certain
period, or at least of a given time-span. It would, therefore, be more
correct to speak of them as chronicles, not unlike our own chronicles
of the Late Middle Ages and the Renaissance, where the endeavor to
provide entertaining reading mingled with the aim to instruct. The
ratio of the two elements varies from one narrative to the next,
evidently according to the wealth of the historical materials which
the author had at his disposal and according to his preferences.

All the titles of these popular works contain the designation
p'ing-hua. This term was used already under the Sung not only for
narrations of history, but for narration in general.[36] Obviously this
designation is connected with the terms *p'ing-shih* 評釋, "to criticize a
poem and explain its meaning," *p'ing shu* 評書, "to expound," and
p'ing-shuo 評說, "to explain a tale"; it is thus not very far from the
later commonly used term *yen-yi* 演義, "to expound the sense." It
indicates that the storyteller's aim was not only to narrate an entertaining story, but also to assess historical personalities and their
deeds, as was implied from the first in the Confucian conception of
history. From the formal point of view, the term *p'ing-hua* is used for
a narration of some length, in which the poetical inserts are only
recited and not sung. Herein lies an important difference from the
storyteller's *hsiao-shuo*, short tales called *tz'u-hua* 詞話, narrations
interpersed with poems which were sung. In general, it may be said
that in *tz'u-hua* the poetical, and especially the lyrical, components
were of much greater importance, as we shall see below, for they
became the basic structural material in the creation of lyrico-epic
forms, these being probably also in respect of composition much more
precise than were *p'ing-hua*, where the predominance of prose gave
the storyteller greater freedom in the handling of his narrative. In
p'ing-hua, the verse-sections, of which there are usually fewer than in
tz'u-hua, are mostly in the form of *shih* and serve, as a rule, to give a
résumé of a situation or to express moral judgments and the like.

---

[36] In the tale, *K'an p'i-hsüeh tan cheng Erh-lang-shen* 勘皮靴單證二郎神, in *Hsing-shih
heng-yen* 醒世恆言 new ed., Peking, Jen-min wen-hsüeh ch'u-pan-she, 1957 (cited below
under *Heng-yen*), ch. 13, p. 243, is a description of a storyteller reciting his tale in the
palace of a high official. A storyteller who recites love stories is spoken of as *Shuo-p'ing-
hua-ti hsien-sheng* 說評話的先生.

Very frequently they are introduced with the phrase "we have a poem, which is proof of this" 有詩爲證; thus their function is not to strengthen the emotional element, as in *tz'u-hua*, but rather the intellectual element, by instructing and explaining. The poems are mostly introduced as the productions of persons figuring in the narration. In keeping with the historical character of the narrative is the occasional use in poems of various archaic forms.

The language of *p'ing-hua* contains far fewer colloquial elements than the storytellers' short tales—usually called *hua-pen*—and approaches a simplified form of the classical language *wen-yen*.

Historical narration of the Sung era created the firm structure of historical novels or, as we said above, of popular chronicles or "histories," which continued to be composed up to the war with Japan and were popular reading among the general public. The maturity of the creative principles of this genre can best be assessed by the fact that in the following Mongol period Lo Kuan-chung could make them the basis for one of the greatest works in Chinese imaginative literature.

Short Stories, Characters, and Environment

a) The upper classes

If we were able to discern certain new traits in the genre of historical narration, which assume almost revolutionary character, as for instance their sharp political slant—the reflection of the political views of ordinary folk, which has few parallels in older Chinese literature—we are certainly entitled to speak of the positively revolutionary turning-point marked by the productions of the fourth group of storytellers, the narrators of *hsiao-shuo*, translatable in this context as "short stories." That this category of storytellers' works was even at that time considered to be something original and different from the output of the other schools is clear from the way in which the sources stress again and again that the other storytellers were afraid of the narrators of *hsiao-shuo*, for they, with their short compositions, were dangerous competitors.[37]

---

[27] This fact is stressed by both *Tu-ch'eng chi-sheng* and *Meng-liang-lu*, cf. "Researches," pt. 1, pp. 123–124.

The innovatory character of this category is best realized if we compare its products with the mature tale of the T'ang literati. This we are in a position to do, because the T'ang story is also a shorter form (though not a short story in the modern sense, because it usually consists of series of episodes) and thematically the two genres roughly conform. Indeed, as we shall show, the storytellers' short stories frequently made use of subject matter of T'ang tales. Nevertheless, there is an essential difference amounting to a revolutionary dividing-line between the two forms.

This is especially apparent in the democratization of the content. The T'ang tale of the literati, written in the old classical language, was a purely aristocratic type of production. The heroes of these tales are, without exception, members of the highest classes: young literati, dignitaries, warriors, aristocratic maidens, or the courtesan friends of the literati. Ordinary folk rarely appeared in these tales, and then only in the role of servants or other subordinates. In the folk stories the authors' field of vision widens out till it encompasses the whole of contemporary society, and most importantly there is a change in the social accent and scale of values. It is as if the authors had climbed down the rungs of the social ladder to observe the society and social phenomena of their time and apply to them the yardstick in use at those lower levels.

This change of standpoint comes out clearly in those cases where the folk author choses the hero of his tale from among the ruling class, as did the authors of the T'ang stories, for example, a member of the literati or of the military profession. As presented by folk authors, such a figure acquires new features, is brought into conformity with folk taste and ideals and is located in a purely folk context, his character thereby undergoing substantial modification.

And even where the folk author takes over the traditional image of an historical personage and does not reshape it in accordance with his own predilections or ideas, he at least furnishes it with details which bring the figure closer to the folk environment. This is well illustrated in the tale, "How poor Ma Chou found his opportunity with the help of a vendor of dumplings," *Ch'iung Ma Chou tsao chi mai tui ao* 窮馬周遭際賣䭔媼,[38] of which the hero is Ma Chou, the

---

[38] *Ku-chin hsiao-shuo* 古今小說, Peking, Jen-min wen-hsüeh ch'u-pan-she, 1958 (henceforth shortened to *Ku-chin*), ch. 5.

famous minister of the second emperor of the T'ang dynasty, T'ai Tsung, 627–649. The story is based on the biography of this eccentric scholar, which is contained alike in the Old and in the New History of the T'ang, and keeps in general fairly closely to it, except that it underlines the nonconformist, eccentric behavior of the hero. But it adds to his life story an important episode not present in the official history: Ma Chou, after long groping, finds his way to position and office thanks to a woman who sold dumplings and who was recommended to him by his uncle-innkeeper. By means of this episode, the figure of the famous dignitary is drawn into the orbit of simple folk and, indeed, identified with them, for the minister rewards his protectress of humble origins by taking her to wife and, at least through this bond, becomes a man of the people.

Other tales show a significant transformation of the whole character of the historical personality, who becomes the hero of a new tale molded to the pattern of taste of a popular public. Such a complete transformation of character and of historical fact is exemplified in the tale, "How the first emperor of the Sung dynasty, Chao K'uang-yin, accompanied for a thousand miles the girl Ching-niang," *Chao T'ai Tsu ch'ien li sung Ching-niang* 趙太祖千里送京娘.[39] The founder of the dynasty is here described in his wanderings through China, meeting with various adventures, not seldom of doubtful character, engaging in skirmishes, and performing wonders of daring and courage. Evidently the tale was part of a whole cycle telling of these adventures. It is thus clear that the emperor's portrait was brought closer to quite a different social type, one much more popular among both audience and storytellers, namely, the type of a folk hero, or even a folk bandit.

In several tales, these elements are so emphasized that future emperors and generals are described at the beginning of their career as hooligans and thieves. The storyteller who already in the introductory episode informs his listeners that the hero is predestined to rise to the highest honors crystallizes his tale in a paradox, as for example in the tale of the meeting of the future emperor Kuo Wei 郭威 (951–959) with his general Shih Hung-chao, *Shih Hung-chao*

---

[39] *Ching-shih t'ung-yen* 警世通言, Peking, Jen-min wen-hsüeh ch'u-pan-she (cited hereafter under *T'ung-yen*), ch. 21.

lung-hu chûn-ch'en hui 史弘肇龍虎君臣會.[40]   On the one hand, he constantly speaks of his heroes as persons destined to rise to the highest dignities; on the other, he describes them as loafers and social outcasts. It is a positively heretical rejection of the Confucian theory that Heaven appoints to the office of government persons embodying the principle of Good. Whereas in contemporary European literature, in Boccaccio and Chaucer, folk types appear in the comic roles, here on the contrary the main actors in what is often rough burlesque are the future emperor and his general.

We can also observe in certain tales that the storyteller regards the representatives of high society with the unimpressed, even impudent eye of a gamin, who knows no respect for persons and who enjoys sharpening his tongue on the faults and weaknesses of the mighty. Such a mocking attitude is apparent in the story about the god Erh-lang, whose crime a leather shoe brings home to him, *K'an p'i hsüeh tan cheng Erh-lang shen*.[41]

Naturally it could be objected that the story is about the Emperor Hui Tsung, at whose door was laid the blame for the catastrophe which brought about the downfall of the Northern Sung, and that here we have one of those perverted emperors whose deeds were always depicted in the blackest of colors. If we consider, however, that this tale (according to the list drawn up by Lo Yeh) was already on the repertoire of storytellers under the Southern Sung, we are amazed at the daring with which a storyteller speaks of a not-so-remote ancestor of the ruling family and of the highest holders of office, and certainly we should scarcely find a parallel to match it in contemporary European literature.

Undoubtedly we could speak here of a certain democratic quality in the atmosphere of these tales, where the fact is recognized of existing differences in respect of power and wealth, but it is not by any means taken for granted that those to whom fate has been kinder are in any way essentially different from those who form the dregs of society. Moreover, mere chance may in a moment reverse their fate. Quite alien to this climate are European mediaeval conceptions of the Lord's Anointed, of the Divine Right of kings, of once a nobleman always a nobleman, and so on.

[40] *Ku-chin*, ch. 15.
[41] *Heng-yen*, ch. 13.

Figures from higher circles are seen by the storyteller as from a distance, nor are they usually drawn in such detail as those from social levels nearer to him. Like dangerous forces they lie in wait in the background and any meeting with them ends, as a rule, disastrously.

b) The lower classes

The strength and revolutionary significance of the storytellers and their art lies, however, not in their portraiture of members of the upper classes, but in the perfect characterization of ordinary people. Whereas the aristocratic authors of the T'ang tales chose as the heroes of their stories, as we pointed out above, only members of their own class, the storyteller takes a quite insignificant figure from the people about him, often directly from the street, and makes him the hero of his piece. In their works the Chinese people for the first time ascend the literary stage, with all their good and bad qualities, with their whole mode of life and thought, and practically overrun it, something which is not repeated in Chinese literature till the literary revolution of 1919. The great majority of the heroes of these tales belong to the lower strata of the city population, artisans (such as carvers of jade), umbrella-makers, shop assistants, small trades-men and shopkeepers, private teachers, clerks, monks, and even coolies, thieves, loafers, and social outcasts. As for women, instead of high-born maidens and glamorous courtesans, there appear in the tales of the storyteller the humble wives of lowly folk, daughters of bourgeois families, cast-off concubines, despised servants and slaves, sometimes far from attractive harlots.

The preponderance of themes taken from city life and this focusing of attention on the lower and often the lowest strata of the city population is without analogy in the European literature of that time, Boccaccio and Chaucer not excluded.

Still more striking is the author's attitude to the small folk from the streets and alleys of Chinese cities. In European mediaeval authors, the small artisan or tradesman has a place in literature only as a figure of fun. In Chinese tales, there is not a trace of an attitude of ridicule toward characters of low or humble life. Not even when the author of the tale, "Judge Pao Lung-t'u Avenges an Injustice Through Three Manifestations," (*San hsien shen Pao Lung-t'u tuan-*

yüan 三現身包龍圖斷寃,[42] which according to Lo Yeh was also in the repertoire of the Sung storytellers) describes a quite naturalistic scene, where a little servant has her ears boxed at night by her mistress for swooning at the sight of an apparition instead of preparing the soup ordered for refreshment, is there a trace of irony or humor in the description. Even a little drudge is taken altogether seriously, as is also the cardplayer and drunkard to whom the mistress marries her, the couple then becoming the principal figures in the exposure of a crime. And not even where the author describes what from the point of view of his society is the most revolting of crimes, namely, the murder of a father for gain, does he fail to describe the misery of those involved and adds, moreover, that the sons were slow-witted and ignorant of law and order.[43]

Storytellers are thoroughly familiar with their milieu, know their characters inside out, look around them without sentimentality and without illusion, and so describe their world and its inhabitants with remarkable truthfulness. We are thus fully entitled to speak of realistic tendencies and realistic elements in their works.

Let us take, for instance, the tale entitled "The Honest Clerk Chang," *Chih-ch'eng Chang chu-kuan* 志誠張主管.[44] With what virtuosity does the storyteller describe the chief character, the humble shop-assistant! In following the story we experience as at first hand the narrow circumstances of the "little man," overflowing with respect for his employer, who feeds and clothes him. We feel the eternal fear he has of the highly placed and especially of State offices and institutions. He only needs to catch sight of an official notice or be shouted at by somebody and he at once takes to his heels. With similar art does the author sketch in the figure of his mother— a woman embittered by a hard life, loving her son but at the same time rather egoistically shielding him as the only prop of her old age. She looks at everything with mistrust and suspicion. For the first time in Chinese literature the author of this tale gives a true-to-life picture of the hard, monotonous life of a little man, in which the only

---

[42] *T'ung-yen*, ch. 13.

[43] In the tale *Shen Hsiao-kuan yi niao hai ch'i ming* 沈小官一鳥害七命, *Ku-chin*, ch. 26, p. 395.

[44] *Ching-pen*, p. 83.

excitements are the New Year Illuminations and the occasional thrill of a crime.

The artistic mastery of the storytellers reaches a high-point in the portrayal of the principal figures in the tale "The Goddess of Mercy," *Nien-yü Kuan-yin* 碾玉觀音:[45] a carver of jade working in the prince's palace and a female slave, an embroiderer in the same household. When the slave wants to take advantage of the confusion following an outbreak of fire in the palace and presses the carver to flee with her, the artisan hesitates, not that he would not have a wife and his own home, but out of fear for the consequences. The girl, on the other hand, evidently hardened by the harsh life of a slave, is not to be deflected from her purpose. When the carver hesitates she uses a threat to force him to flee. But as soon as the man agrees, the woman at once subordinates herself to him, for he, the husband, makes the decisions, as was the custom in the patriarchal family. Rarely in the world literature of the time would we find such a realistic description of the relations between two young people— not lovers, but actually a betrothed couple, which is a characteristic detail. In the tale, there is practically no mention of love, the girl only recalls on what occasion she was betrothed to the carver.

Far ahead of its time is the objectivity with which the author of the tale manipulates the clash of forces which leads to the ultimate tragedy. If we compare this tale with the pattern on which it was perhaps based,[46] our first impression is that the author aimed to underline the emotional element, the cruelty of the prince who, directly or indirectly, destroyed four lives (he himself cut off the girl's head, her parents drowned themselves for shame and the girl's spirit brought about the carver's death). We may even see in the working up of the materials a clearly social and possibly also anti-feudal tendency. This is all negated, however, by the fact that the prince of the story—whose identity is only indicated by his title, which was nevertheless a quite sufficient clue for the audience—is not just another prince, but the famous hero, Han Shih-chung 韓世忠, one of the chiefs of the War Party and the principal supporter of General Yüeh Fei, a victim of Court intrigue, whose deeds as

---

[45] *Ching-pen*, p. 1.

[46] Perhaps the original version of this tale is reproduced in the book *Yi-wen tsung-lu* 異聞總錄, *Ts'ung-shu chi-ch'eng, ch'u-pien*, Shanghai, 1937, p. 12.

we saw above were celebrated by the narrators of political history. When General Yüeh Fei was executed, the prince withdrew into retirement and sought distraction in ramblings beside the Western Lake, which provides the storyteller with the introductory motif: the prince catches sight of the girl embroidress on one of these spring excursions. This identification of the prince's personality and the storyteller's assessment of his character alter the whole emotional atmosphere of the tale: what we have before us is not a sentimental story of a poor girl, or of an unfortunate couple destroyed by a cruel prince, but a situation created by the natural and logical workings of a feudal society. Every attempt at free decision or action on the part of unfree people must end in catastrophe. The prince acts as every feudal lord would act in his place, and the storyteller does not introduce into the picture any kind of moral evaluation. Perhaps he only heightens the horror of the culminating scene by having the fugitive couple brought before a terrifying commander for whom it is a delight to cut off a human head. With similar objectivity the storyteller draws in certain negative traits in the runaway pair.

The Composition of the Tales

Corresponding to the realistic conception of the characters is the essentially realistic build-up of the scenes. Here, however, we observe considerable differences between the individual tales in the methods of realization. We may distinguish two extreme types: a descriptive-realistic type and what we might call a lyrico-epic type. In the former—an instructive example is the tale, "the devoted son, Jen Kuei, thanks to his fiery temper, becomes a god," *Jen Hsiao tzu lieh hsing wei shen* 任孝子烈性爲神,[47] the author at the beginning presents his hero and furnishes the necessary information about the scene of the action, the origins of the hero, and his employment. Then, with a fine feeling for characteristic detail, he gives a full account of all the happenings up to the definitive winding up of the plot. The narrative unfolds, as a rule, along a single time-stave, which may also have a parallel part, the action proceeding only along one line, the other being brought meanwhile to a halt. Although the author characterizes his figures mainly by their actions and speeches,

[47] *Ku-chin*, ch. 38.

as has always been the way throughout the whole history of Chinese fiction, he selects the details of the narration so aptly and appropriately that he conjures up a certain emotional atmosphere or the state of mind and feeling of the person described, with the sure mastery of a great artist; as an example, we may cite the dialogue between the embroidress and the carver of jade, and we could list without difficulty any number of such perfectly observed scenes.

These precise drawings of little figures, detailed descriptions of their clothes and dwellings, the careful reproduction of their movements, gestures, and actions, and, finally, the accurate record of their conversations and monologues, all have their parallel in the equally detailed and exhaustive descriptions of the capital cities in which the storytellers practiced their profession. The authors of these descriptions of Kaifeng and Hangchow record with a similar passion for every tiny fact and insignificant detail the panorama of those cities, and it is probable that these works point to the source from which this particular approach to reality springs.

The above-mentioned literary descriptions of the towns indicate by their very titles the emotional springs from which they arose: the earliest of them is called "Dream of the Splendour of the Eastern Capital" (Kaifeng), another bears the title "Dream of Past Glory," and a third "List of the Sights of the Capital." In all these instances, the authors indicate by the titles that the main impulse which moved them to these descriptions was their love for their native town and the varied life of its busy streets.

If such accurate description recalls the tradition of Chinese historiography in its scrupulous respect for truth or rather authenticity, in general conception as well as in every detail we may observe yet another conception, which has links rather with the tradition of Chinese poetry. From thence comes the subtle economy in the build-up of the picture, the power to evoke atmosphere by the skillful juxtaposing of several selected shots from reality. With how small a number of short shots does the storyteller manage to tell the tragic story of the runaway couple in the tale of "The Goddess of Mercy" to which we have repeatedly referred! The introduction is as effective as that of any of the poems of Tu Fu. The prince returns from a spring outing and catches sight of an old man and a girl beside a bridge. Without our learning the reason, the prince orders his adjutant to bring the girl to the palace the next day. Only later do we find out that the girl was wearing a nicely embroidered sash and that they were seeking an embroidress at the palace. Thus the girl is presented and no more is said about her. In a similarly brief scene, the carver of jade is introduced and then follows the brilliantly rendered scene of the fire and the flight of the engaged couple. In no more than six or seven short "takes" the whole story is pictured. If in the previous category of tales a comparison springs to mind with the detailed, carefully drawn pictures by painters and writers of the cities which were a product of the Sung era, and in general with the realistic, finely wrought drawings of that time, this almost impressionistic manner reminds us of the contemporary pictures in Chinese ink, where a certain figure is only lightly sketched in, along with a few isolated scenic shots, the rest being enshrouded in mist and left to the viewer's imagination. No more does the author wish to recount the story in detail, but gives only the sharp, essential contours of the key-points of the tale; it is obvious that his main aim is not description or narration but evocation. His method is more that of the lyric than of the epic, insofar as we associate our idea of epic with the elaborate and fluent description of events or episodes, such as is employed in the above-mentioned tale of "The Devoted Son Jen Kuei."

Proof that the author of the tale "The Goddess of Mercy" consciously aimed at creating an artistic form essentially different from the realistic tales with their wealth of descriptive detail is the sparseness of the prose sections and the abundance of lyrical songs which, like luxuriating foliage, hide from view the simple trunk and few branches of the plot. The stress is clearly on the lyrical element and so arises—perhaps in conscious opposition to the over-pedestrian character of the descriptive-realistic tale—a new lyrico-epic form, which is perhaps the most original contribution of the Sung storytellers.

Verse in these tales is used for descriptions of the outward appearance of the character and his personal traits and for descriptions of various happenings: it is clear that these poetical descriptions served not only to introduce a certain colorfulness into the tale and heighten its aesthetic quality, but had the further function of detailed prose description for which the narrative technique was not yet adequate.

The poetical descriptions, however, not only characterize a certain person or happening, but still more generalize these features, giving them a universal and often typical quality.

We are thus confronted with two contrasting traits in our tales. On the one hand the authors of realistic–descriptive tales strive to give them the topical and specific quality of actual happenings. As we noted above, the time and place are precisely described, as are also the particulars identifying the heroes. But opposed to this specific reality, opposed to a world accurately taped and ticketed is set another world, universal and timeless. It seems as if the accurately described and precisely characterized actor did after all represent an eternal type, play a universal role.

This impression of two-planed structure, of the juxtaposition of two worlds—one that is epic, individual and mutable, and another that is lyrical, eternal and immutable, or at least repetitive—is particularly strong in the lyrico-epic type of story. For instance, in "The Goddess of Mercy" this impression is directly suggested in the lyrical introduction, a suite of poems on Spring, which describes the season's various phases, ending with a sad poem lamenting the emptiness of Nature when spring departs. The placing of such a lyrical composition, with introduction, culmination and melancholy close at the beginning of a tale similarly composed, suggests a lyrical parallel to, or indeed a kind of metaphor of, the epic content: human fates are like flowers in spring and it is one of the laws of man's lot, after a short time of flowering, to wither and decay.

And even though the poetical elements are not everywhere handled with such consummate art and do not always form so important a part of the structure, nevertheless they give these tales a quite specific character which has won for them a special place in the history of Chinese fiction. It is, for example, above all the lyrical description (interwoven with poems) of the colourful New Year festivities at home in the south, in Hangchow, contrasted with which is the sad picture of captives in the north, in Peking, at that time in the hands of the Jurjets, which makes of the story "How Yang Szu-wen met an old acquaintance in Peking"[48] a great work of

---

[48] *Yang Szu-wen Yen-shan feng ku-jen* 楊思溫燕山逢故人, *Ku-chin*, ch. 24. This tale was in the repertoire of the Sung storytellers, for it appears under the title, *Hui ku hsia* 灰骨匣 "The Casket of Ashes," in Lo Yeh's list.

art, in spite of the creaking banality of the story of retaliation for marital unfaithfulness in the second half. Without its lyrical component, the Sung *hua-pen* would often be nothing more than a naive story, and it is this artistic composition based on contrasting elements which we must make the focal point of all our critical considerations, and especially of our thoughts as to who the authors were of such skillfully composed works.

The Authors of Hua-pen

Before turning to the question of the authorship of these tales we must draw attention to one important fact. Not all the tales which we can assign with a fair degree of probability to the Sung period show such perfect artistic mastery as those we have so far mentioned. Especially the materials in the oldest collection of *hua-pen, Ch'ing-p'ing-shan-t'ang hua-pen* 清平山堂話本,[49] compiled by Hung Pien 洪楩, contain only a few artistically truly valuable works. I think that a fair idea of the artistic level of the repertoire of the Sung storytellers is to be gained from an investigation of the list of narrations drawn up by Lo Yeh. Of the 108 listed narrations of the category *hsiao-shuo*, about 17 have been preserved in their original form, 3 have been more or less altered and in one case the situation is not clear.[50] Of this number, 10 or 11 are tales of the first rank— several of them have been cited above—but the rest are a pretty mixed bag. If we presume that the better rather than the inferior tales are likely to have been preserved, we must suppose that the greater part of the tales circulating among the storytellers were second-rate productions, of no great artistic standing, and that the collection *Ch'ing-p'ing* probably reflects the average of this output.

If we base our consideration on the information supplied by Lo Yeh and an analysis of the tales listed by him, we see that a considerable part of the *hua-pen* were only very little worked-up versions of T'ang tales taken over from collections such as *T'ai-p'ing kuang-chi* 太平廣記. Examples are the tale *Li Ya-hsien* or "The Story of a Blue

[49] New edition Shanghai, Ku-tien wen-hsüeh Ch'u-pan-she, 1957. Hereafter cited as *Ch'ing-p'ing*.

[50] A detailed analysis of Lo Yeh's catalogue was published in the Collection Dissertationes, Prague, 1968.

Bridge," *Lan-ch'iao chi* 藍橋記, the texts of which have been preserved by Lo Yeh.[51] The two tales are only slightly altered repro-
ductions of the original texts, the former of the tale *Li Wa chuan*,
which as we saw above, a storyteller had already recited under the
T'ang,[52] and the latter of a tale by P'ei Hang 裴航.[53] The text of the
second tale is also preserved in a version showing very little diver-
gence from it in the collection, *Ch'ing-p'ing*.[54] Evidently the storyteller himself or assisted by a scholar had adapted the original text of
the T'ang tale. More complicated sections of the original tale are
rewritten and the difficult turns of phrase of the classical language
are replaced by expressions in more general use. Appended to the
text in *Ch'ing-p'ing* is a short introduction in verse and an epilogue.
I think that here we have the most rudimentary form of the storyteller's manual—a simple reproduction of the borrowed text, which
the storyteller probably then elaborated in the course of its narration.
For the following considerations about the authorship of the storytellers' texts it is noteworthy that even this unworked-up manual has
come down to us in two versions, and because it is mentioned also in
the catalogue, *Pao-wen-t'ang*,[55] we come to the conclusion that it was
probably also circulated in print, for only thus can we explain the
fact that so many copies have been preserved. Evidently there was a
wide demand for such texts and so they were printed and published.
Naturally we also come across cases in which the original version of
the T'ang tale was worked up into a very artistic and comprehensive
epic, as for example the tale about the head of the eight immortals,
Chang Lao, which is catalogued by Lo Yeh[56] and is preserved in
Ku-chin, ch. 33.

   We pointed out above that one of the main functions of storytellers was to interpret literary works to an illiterate public and they
seem to have remained true to this mission even when they created

---

[51] Lo Yeh, p. 113 and p. 88.

[52] Cf. note 9.

[53] *Tai-p'ing kuang-chi* (henceforward cited as *T'ai-p'ing*). Peking, Jen-min wen-hsüeh
ch'u-pan-she, 1959, ch. 50, vol. 1, p. 313.

[54] *Ch'ing-p'ing*, p. 49.

[55] *Ch'ao shih Pao-wen-t'ang shu-mu* 晁氏寶文堂書目, by Ch'ao Li 晁瑮 Shanghai,
Ku-tien wen-hsüeh ch'u-pan-she, 1957.

[56] Lo Yeh, p. 4, under the title *Chung sou shen chi* 種叟神記. Based on the tale *Chang lao*
張老, *T'ai-p'ing*, ch. 16, vol. p. 113.

original artistic forms often more perfect than were their patterns. Even then they mostly take over their theme from some traditional text, and Lo Yeh has recorded for us the names of books on which the storytellers drew very often for their subject matter:besides *T'ai-p'ing kuang chi*, there was Hung Mai's *Yi-chien-chih* 洪邁，夷堅志，*Lǔ-ch'uang hsin-hua* 綠窗新話, also a book comprising various stories written in *wen-yen*, and then several books today no longer extant.

If we go through the texts contained in the *Ch'ing-p'ing* collection we find there folklore themes, sometimes very ancient,[57] the rather naive belletrization of local legends,[58] the not very interesting working-up of various historical tales,[59] somewhat unskilled stories about popular poets,[60] love stories in the classical language taken over from the traditional repertoire,[61] moralizing tales,[62] along with several lively and interesting stories of adventure[63] and of crime,[64] of which we shall speak below.

Clearly, then, the *hua-pen* comprise very heterogeneous materials and considerable differences in the literary level, and we must take this into account in seeking an answer to the question of who were the authors of these texts. There is some evidence already of that duality of character which accompanied Chinese popular literature up to the literary revolution. On the one hand, in it arise the greatest works of Chinese literature, such as the most famous Chinese novels and plays, and on the other hand it is altogether peripheral literature,

[57] For instance, the narration about Tung Yung, *Tung Yung yü hsien chuan*, 董永遇仙傳 *Ch'ing-p'ing*, p. 235. A ballad with the same subject matter had already been found in the Tun-huang Caves, see *Tun-huang pien-wen chi*, vol. 1, p. 109.

[58] "How in Cha-ch'uan, Hsiao Ch'en demoted the King-Overlord (Hsiang Yü)," *Cha-ch'uan Hsiao Ch'en pien pa-wang* 霅川蕭琛貶霸王, *Ch'ing-p'ing*, p. 313.

[59] An example is the narration about General Li Kuang, the valiant fighter against Hsiung-nu, *Han Li Kuang shih hao Fei-chiang-chün* 漢李廣世號飛將軍, *Ch'ing-p'ing*, p. 298.

[60] For example "Liu Ch'i-ch'ing amuses himself with poems and wine at the Chiang-lou," *Liu Ch'i-ch'ing shih chiu wan Chiang-lou chi* 柳耆卿詩酒翫江樓記, *Ch'ing-p'ing*, p. 1.

[61] For example the love story of Szu-ma Hsiang-ju and Cho Wen-chün, *Feng-yüeh Jui-hsien-t'ing* 風月瑞仙亭, *Ch'ing-p'ing*, p. 38.

[62] For instance, the tale *Yin-chih chi shan* 陰隲積善, "By Secret Good Deeds He Gained a Blessing," *Ch'ing-p'ing*, p. 115.

[63] "Narration about the hero Yang Wen, called The Tiger Barring the Way," *Yang Wen Lan-lu-hu chuan* 楊溫攔路虎傳, *Ch'ing-p'ing*, p. 169.

[64] For example "On the monk who by means of a letter hatched a plot," *Chien-t'ieh ho-shang* 簡貼和尚, *Ch'ing-p'ing*, p. 6.

near to our books for popular reading, *Volksbücher*, and *boulevard* or bookstall literature.

It is noteworthy that under the T'ang the composition of tales in the classical language is the fashion among the literati, thanks to which we have a number of outstanding tales which are among the finest treasures of mediaeval Chinese and, indeed, world fiction. This tradition does not continue, however, under the Sung and the tale in *wen-yen* does not develop further. In the following Mongol period the attention of the literati is entirely focused on the drama. Thus the question arises as to whether a part of the energies of the literati which they devoted in the T'ang era to the classical tale and, in the time of the Mongols, to the drama, was not dedicated under the Sung to the *hua-pen*. It is necessary to bear in mind the very striking fact that in every description of the capital cities of the Sung era mention is made of the storytellers, whereas in similar descriptions of the Ming period we hear only of blind storytellers; evidently in the Ming period storytelling was no longer an art worthy of admiration, but became a popular entertainment catered to by professional purveyors, of good standard, but not an art in the earlier sense. I think that we can explain this qualitative change only by presuming that in later times the creative activity of authorship—the composition of storytellers' texts—became separate from the reproductive activity of the storytellers—their oral presentation.[65]

I believe we may seek at least some of the authors of *hua-pen* in the same milieu that produced the authors of stage plays in the following epoch. I have in mind the milieu of the *shu-hui* 書會. *Shu-hui* were societies of literati interested in popular literature within which various kinds of popular works grew up, especially plays, but also the ballads *chu-kung-tiao*, various songs and possibly also the texts of *hua-pen*. In *Lu kuei pu*,[66] "List of Spirits," a list of the names of such popular authors, the core of which was probably a list of the members of a certain *shu-hui*, there appears by the name of the dramatist Lu

---

[65] This is excellently expressed by Mr. Ch'en of Hai-ning in the epilogue to *San kuo chih p'ing-hua* (cf. note 34, above): "The present-day reciters of books . . . always take as their basis tales composed by people of an earlier time and only elaborate and develop them in the telling. In former times, however, each of the storytellers exercised his invention and on occasion created new works . . . ."

[66] Chung Szu-ch'eng 鍾嗣成 in *Lu kuei pu, wai szu chung* 錄鬼簿, 外四種, Shanghai, Ku-tien wen-hsüeh ch'u-pan-she, 1957, p. 17.

Hsien-chih 陸顯之 the note: "he has (that is, he composed) the tale about the good fellow, Chao Cheng" (有好兒趙正話). We have good reason to believe that the tale composed by this dramatist is identical with a tale preserved in *Ku-chin,* ch. 36, under the title "Sung Szu-kung causes the miser Chang great trouble," *Sung Szu-kung ta nao Chin-hun Chang* 宋四公大鬧禁魂張.[67] This indicates that we must probably look for other authors, especially those of mature tales, in the milieu of the *shu-hui* where unusually favorable conditions prevailed for this kind of production.[68] It was an environment of warmly congenial comradeship, where every artistic effort was keenly appraised. An interest in the life and work of kindred spirits was also the main impulse leading to the drawing up of these lists, which were intended to provide a permanent record of friends working in a domain of common interest. Mainly, however, the *shu-hui* milieu gave authors the necessary preliminary training without which we cannot imagine the rise of notable works of popular literature. Persons well versed in literature and loving its freer forms mingled here with professionals[69] and themselves acquired professional training,[70] which was an essential preparation for the composition of all kinds of works, and especially of *hua-pen.*

We could thus place to the account of such literary amateurs especially the above-mentioned lyrical tales, for skill in the composition of poems was the principal attribute of the cultured man. The

[67] In the first part of the tale the principal hero is Sung Szu-kung, but in the second part it is Chao Cheng, who outwits his teacher. Moreover, in the poems celebrating Lu Hsien-chih mention is made of one of the famous deeds of Chao Cheng, which occurs also in the tale of how he dug down to Prince Ch'ien's treasury and there appropriated to himself immense wealth. The character of the story, too, corresponds perfectly to the description of the literary work of Lu Hsien-chih, as it is described in the festive poem.

[68] Further support for our view is that Lo Kuan-chung 羅貫中, the author of the *San-kuo chih yen-yi,* appears in the Supplement to *Lu kuei pu,* p. 102.

[69] It is probable that one professional of this kind, at least for some time, was the dramatist Kuan Han-ch'ing 關漢卿 and that another was the author of the ballad *Hsi-hsiang-chi chu-kung tiao* 西廂記諸宮調, Tung Chieh-yüan 董解元, who topped the list of authors in *Lu kuei pu* p. 6. Support for this view would be the fact that only his family name, with the designation, *chieh-yüan,* has come down to us; this is how, in our sources, artists in the bazaars and especially storytellers are designated. The main core of members of the *shu-hui* were, however, amateurs, those "dukes, nobles, and high officials" enumerated in the introduction to *Lu kuei pu,* p. 7.

[70] At the beginning of the play *Chang Hsieh chuang-yüan* 張協狀元, preserved in the *Yung Lo ta tien hsi-wen san-chung* 永樂大典戲文三種, Ku-chin hsiao p'in shu chi yin-hsing hui, 1931, the members of the *shu-hui* are introduced who wish to measure their skill against that of professional actors in the performance of this play.

later Ming tales, motivated above all by moralizing tendencies, no longer possess lyrical character. In this lyrical quality, the *hua-pen* are close to the Yuan *tsa-chü*, and therein we may see support for our view that they are the product of the same environment.

It is possible that there existed a quite specific impulse leading to the fixation in writing of storytellers' texts in a form not very different from that in which they have come down to us. The well-known authority on popular literature, Feng Meng-lung, at the beginning of the seventeenth century, expressed the view that such tales were written for the Emperor Kao Tsung, who was very fond of such narrations.[71] Actually we know from the sources that there existed at the Court a professional *shu-hui*[72]—in our view an authors' organization—which perhaps prepared various popular texts for the use of the Court. As all sources stress that the storytellers' tales were short, we can suppose that for their performances at court they prepared texts not unlike the extant *hua-pen*. Insofar as they wished to include in their repertoire lyrico-epic works of the kind we spoke of above, they could not employ the technique of present-day storytellers, that is, freely elaborating their theme, in the course of recital. They must have been obliged to keep to carefully prepared outlines not permitting of much variation, if the whole composition was not to collapse. Here perhaps is the impulse which led to the creation and commitment to writing of carefully prepared texts, which came to be regarded as patterns for authors working in this domain. The hope of success and of reward at court may well have stimulated also amateur authors organized in *shu-hui*. The sources also mention that tales were actually composed at the Court.[73]

---

[71] Preface to *Ku-chin*. We have no proof that the preface was written by Feng Meng-lung himself, but it is very likely.

[72] *Wu-lin chiu-shih*, ch. 6.

[73] The compilation of a narration intended directly for the Emperor Kao Tsung and drawing for its subject matter on the recent hostilities against the Jurjets is mentioned in *San ch'ao pei-meng hui-pien* 三朝北盟會編 *Yüeh-tung chi* 1878, ch. 149, *Yen-hsing hsia chih* 炎興下帙, 49, p. 11a: "When Shao Ch'ing was pardoned he was appointed General Commissary for the Marine, in the State Council, *shu-mi yüan*. Prior to that, when Tu Ch'ung was defending Chien-k'ang (south of present-day Chiang-ning hsien, in Kiang-su), a certain *ping-yi lang*, Chao Hsiang by name, defended the water gate there. The Jurjets conveyed themselves across the Yangtze and Shao Ch'ing began to assemble bands of volunteers (against the Jurjets); Chao Hsiang was taken captive by Shao Ch'ing. Not till Shao Ch'ing was pardoned did Chao Hsiang manage to escape and return home. He became the protégé of the Imperial eunuch, Kang. Kang was an excellent (reciter of)

In investigating the probable authorship of our tales we keep coming up against the two-fold character typical of all aspects of the storytellers' activities which we called to attention above in our analysis of the artistic quality of their creations. Authors show an intermingling of brilliant amateur writers from among the educated class, as probably was Lu Hsien-chih, with professionals of folk origin who had little formal education. Similarly, the activities of storytellers have their setting in various strata of the social hierarchy. Some of them spent their whole lives in the bazaars and in various places of entertainment in the capital, and proof of their belonging to the common folk is to be found in their thoroughly vulgar nicknames, cited above. Others were able, through their art, to gain patrons among the highest levels of society of the capital. In the list of popular artists in *Wu-lin chih-shih*,[74] five of the reciters of *hsiao-shuo* have the further designation, *yŭ-ch'ien* 御前, "before the Emperor," probably indicating that they were called upon to recite before the Emperor, and beside the names of two storytellers stands Te-shou kung 德壽宮, the name of the palace where the Emperor Kao Tsung, known as a lover of popular tales, resided after his abdication. The storytellers of no other group are thus designated; this undoubtedly testifies to the great popularity of the short tales, *hsiao-shuo,* also in the highest circles, and so it is not surprising that the works of highest artistic quality are to be found in this category. This also supports our hypothesis of the motives which led to the written fixation of texts of this category.

---

hsiao-shuo, and the Emperor was fond of listening to him. Kang thought to procure some new materials, in order to compose a tale. And so he bade Hsiang describe to him in detail the whole course of events from the time Shao Ch'ing got together his bands, the loyalty and falseness of his supporters and the strength and weakness of his subalterns. All this he described very clearly, and on the basis of his relation the eunuch compiled his story and recited it when he waited upon the Emperor. The Emperor was pleased with it and so he learned in this way that Shao Ch'ing was a valuable man and rejoiced at the undoubted virtue and loyalty of his faithful and righteous subjects." Here we have another proof of how these narrations were linked up with contemporary events, and then we are given an accurate description of the creative process of which such a narrative was the outcome: the collection of interesting materials, the compilation of the story—evidently in writing—and its recital to an audience. It is clear that in cases such as this there was no improvisation, but the whole performance was carefully prepared. From this, too, it is evident that texts thus prepared were suitable for publication for a wider circle of readers.

[74] Pp. 454–456.

The Storytellers' Specialization: Tales of Love

There can be no doubt that this extremely diverse public for which the storytellers worked forced upon them sharply demarcated specialization, which in any case follows from the specific character of the storyteller's vocation, for the individual storyteller can master only a limited number of themes and acquire only a limited stock of expressive means, literary procedures, flourishes, and professional clichés. This tendency toward specialization was further strengthened by the inherited nature of the vocation and by the strict division of work everywhere in the guild organization. Our sources speak of four schools or categories *(chia* 家*)*, but at once add that each has its "(inherited) specialization," *men-t'ing* 門庭. And then both sources and preserved texts show that within the framework of the individual schools a still narrower and more concentrated specialization prevailed. Above we briefly described the various kinds of religious and historical narratives; naturally, in the case of the *hsiao-shuo,* as the most numerous group, this specialization was still more detailed.

Records of the storytellers' activities contained in individual descriptions of the Sung cities repeatedly combine in a single group tales of love (*yen-fen* 煙粉*,* more exactly tales about women),[75] about beings endowed with supernatural powers and bogies (*ling-kuai* 靈怪), and finally, romantic tales (*ch'uan-ch'i* 傳奇). Lo Yeh, on the other hand, separates these groups, but if we study the examples which he cites we see that a broad contamination of subject matter takes place, that we could speak of the individual "specialization" or *men-t'ing* (Lo Yeh also uses this term), rather as of certain types of narration, in which this or that type of theme predominates, which however does not mean that the storyteller could not freely incorporate other motifs, if he felt the need for them. In many cases, we shall be at a loss to decide whether to assign the tale to this or that category. And so the linking up of the above-cited three specializations has its justification; we could characterize this broader group as narrations ranging between pure love stories on the one hand and pure bogey tales on the other, with various combinations of the

[75] Ch'eng Yi-chung, *op. cit.* 79, note 2, explains that *yen* means "to blacken eyebrows" and *fen* "powder, face make-up." These terms indicate that the reference is to women, especially those whose business was the seduction of men.

two types of motif in between, but also with the eventual addition of motifs of another kind.

We shall leave for later our discussion of the pure ghost stories and confine ourselves here to an especially striking trait in this group, namely, the constant commingling of ghost and love motifs, so that the linking of the three specializations is based on good grounds. Very frequently the woman figuring in our tales as a mistress or wife is a vampire or other monster and the man's relations with her end in tragedy, insofar as he is not saved by some monk versed in the casting out or destruction of devils.

The reasons for this phenomenon are not hard to discover. In most of the tales, where the principal characters are two young people, the erotic element is little developed. The young woman usually becomes the man's wife without any great ado, and the motif of wooing, which is usually the main part of European stories, is reduced to a secondary episode, so that the backbone of the story is shifted elsewhere. In consequence, the storyteller was obliged to look round for other motifs to add interest to his narration—that is, either for crime or ghost motifs. Actually he thereby expressed the living experience of his environment, where extramarital love was usually a dark and destructive passion spelling disaster. The ghost motif is only a metaphorical parallel to the real-life situation with which the story-teller was familiar. Besides, we must admit that the supernatural motif often enables the storyteller to describe with greater authenticity the living milieu and the character of the persons involved than in some European tales of the corresponding category, where artificially constructed "natural" obstacles to the course of true love often deform the living context and disposition of the heroes much more radically.

Tales of Crime and of Adventure

The other large domain of motifs which enabled the storytellers to construct exciting stories was that of crime and adventure. Again the other sources combine specializations in these themes in a single group, whereas Lo Yeh divides them into several classes: crime stories 公案, themes relating to fencing with the long sword 朴刀, and stories about fights with cudgels 捍棒; the tales that have come down to us show that in this category a truly high degree of specialization took place, perhaps higher than in any other category. Though a certain start had previously been made in the creation of tales of adventure in the T'ang *ch'uan-ch'i* we can nevertheless say that this category is the most original product of the Sung storytellers. Here their close ties with the common folk come out most markedly, and here consequently the most intensive use is made of the elements of realism and naturalism. It is only natural that in narrations about crimes—*kung-an* means a lawsuit or criminal case—we make contact with the most brutal aspects of human relations and often with the most degraded strata of society. The longing for sensation, for themes which would excite and hold the interest of the audience, leads the authors to seek for ever more drastic and terror-inspiring subjects, so that we could draw up a whole scale of themes, from a simple lawsuit between relatives about property in what is probably the oldest tale of this type,[76] to the thirteen murders for the sake of a copper in a late Ming imitation.[77] A favorite theme is a demonstration of how a trifling cause—a joke,[78] excessive love for a bird,[79] and so on, can have the most terrible consequences. The motives for crimes are more often erotic or trivial rather than greed for money, for the authors do not, as we noted above, unjustly brutalize even their negative heroes from the lowest classes. The plot culminates, of course, in the exposing of the crime and in the punishment of those who committed it, in which connection two directly opposite solutions are presented: in certain tales, the main role in bringing the crime to light falls to a judge of genius who, thanks to his perspicacity, sees through the web of lies and falsity. As early as the Sung era the figure was created of the celebrated judge, Pao "Dragon Plan," who then became the hero of crime thrillers for centuries to come.[80] Judge Pao was an historical personage, in real life the high official Pao Cheng 包拯, as were the majority of the persons mentioned in the tales, which is also interesting proof of the close ties these tales

[76] *Ho-t'ung wen tzu* 合同文字, "The Contract," *Ch'ing-p'ing,* p. 33.

[77] *Yi-wen ch'ien hsiao-hsi tsao ch'i yüan* 一文錢小隙造奇冤, "A small quarrel over a single copper coin causes extraordinary evil," *Heng-yen,* ch. 34.

[78] In the tale, *Ts'o chan Ts'ui Ning* 錯斬崔寧, "How Ts'ui Ning was executed by mistake", *Ching-pen,* p. 131.

[79] Cf. note 43, above.

[80] Cf. notes 42 and 76, above.

had with reality. But not all judges were of this kidney and crime
stories tell of errors of justice, when brutal judges forced confessions
from their victims by torture and condemned innocent persons to
death.[81] Here sharp criticism is voiced of brutal legal methods to
which the novels of the Chinese reformers of the beginning of the
twentieth century were to return.

Special attention is devoted in a number of tales to the exposing of
a crime, often after considerable complications and often (and this
is typical for the atmosphere of these narrations) with the help of
supernatural powers.[82] But at least in one case, in the repeatedly
cited tale about the false god Erh-lang, the storyteller jettisons all
these chance and supernatural elements and writes a pure detective
story, anticipating all the methods of the classical European story of
crime, not excepting the inductive method of investigation, and even
introducing into the tale two detectives, a stupid inspector, who is
completely bamboozled, and a smart ordinary policeman who, with
the help of precise methods of investigation, lays a cunning criminal
by the heels.

Observable within the framework of the story of crime, in a
number of instances, is a change in the moral assessment of the hero
and, along with it, a change in the whole conception of the tale. The
criminal is no longer described as a person morally to be condemned,
but on the contrary the author admires his daring and resource,
laughs at his pranks that cause great trouble to detested usurers,
misers, and men of wealth, and finally comes to see in him a real
hero, an outlaw who takes from the rich and gives to the poor, an
embodiment of folk shrewdness and cunning. This upside-down
conception of a criminal is a feature of the tale described above as
probably the work of the dramatist, Lu Hsien-chih, telling about a
band of thieves led by Sung Szu-kung, Chao Cheng, and others.[83]
Here the author with evident enjoyment describes the forays of this
band and leaves to the end the remark that Judge Pao finally
succeeded in restoring order in the capital. This new moral assessment, however, brings the *kung-an* tales nearer to the tales of adventure, the tales of outlaws and folk heroes, the chief contents of which

[81] Cf. note 78, above.
[82] This is the case in "Three Manifestations," cf. note 42, above.
[83] Cf. note 67, above.

are duels and fights with staves and the long sword. These bandits, too, regularly begin their career with some offense against the existing order and thereby become outlaws, fleeing to the swamps and mountains where they form bands and carry on hostilities against the power of the State. They engender such respect that in the end they are pardoned, enter the Emperor's service and win glory and position. An important part of the tales of adventure was just this attainment of glory and the making of a fortune.[84] It is evident that the authors of the descriptions of the Sung capitals had good reason for linking tales of adventure with the *kung-an* tales.

All these tales had a tendency to grow into cycles; it was always easier to think out ever new adventurous episodes for a hero whose type was already popular with audiences than to create new characters and invent for them new and original features.

Naturally, from our standpoint, the most important work of the storytellers in this specialization was the cycle of tales about the bandits from Liang-shan-po. The account of narrations about the heroes of Liang-shan-po, as preserved in *Hsüan-ho yi-shih*,[85] still corresponds precisely to these tales in Sung descriptions, for it is clear that the tale ended with the pardoning of Sung Chiang and his being sent against Fang La, an undertaking in which he so distinguished himself that he was appointed Imperial Commissioner, *chieh tu shih*.[86] It was Shih Nai-an who first gave this narration quite a new meaning and reshaped it into a grandiose tragedy and a great warning: when bandits are shown mercy and enter the Imperial service, they perish one after another. Only those survive who prefer to escape and live their lives in the dark places of society. Besides attempts at working up whole cycles such as we possess in *Hsüan-ho yi-shih*, Lo Yeh records four tales about various heroes of the *Shui-hu*.[87] The fact that these four tales are distributed among all three specializations into which Lo Yeh divides tales of adventure offers proof on the one hand that we can really group all these themes under the single higher category of tales of adventure, and on the

---

[84] "Researches," pt. I, p. 123.

[85] *Hsüan-ho yi-shih*, cf. note 26, above, *yüan chi*, p. 36 *et seq.*

[86] *Idem, hsia chi*, p. 5.

[87] They comprise these narrations: *Shih-t'ou Sun Li* 石頭孫立, *Ch'ing-mien shou* 青面獸, *Hua ho-shang* 花和尚 and *Wu hsing-che* 武行者.

other that these tales existed independently and were not yet incorporated into a synthetically worked-up whole.

Fighting, duelling, and heroic deeds are the eternal themes, in
endless variations, which fill the pages of these tales. We can presume
that these themes of the tales of adventure were closely akin to the
tales of "iron knights," which means "things like soldiers, horses and
the tumult of battles," mention of which is also made in the descriptions of the cities.[88] Because in *Wu-lin chiu-shih* there appears one
storyteller beside whose name is the note, "the mail-clad guard," it is
not impossible that the description cited relates to the narrations of
veterans who themselves took part in such battles.[89] This would
explain the difference in quality between these tales and the historical
narrations, which are also crowded with descriptions of battles and
skirmishes, so that they too become an endless mummery of fights
and affrays.

It is worth our while to give some thought to the reasons for the
popularity of these heroic subjects in Chinese popular literature and
to the types of character which figure in them. We spoke of them
above in connection with the historical narrations. The predominant
type is a bold, fearless brawler, never daunted and without any
qualms, who rushes intrepidly to the aid of those who are being
wronged, but who also, without any great scruples, assaults and kills.
The impression it makes on us is as if Chinese society, representing
through its literati a type of man completely bound by the prescrip-
tions of morality, ethics, and custom, a man fully socialized, should
create in these figures an ideal in all respects the complete opposite,
a free and uncurbed individual, who must however be prepared to
pay the price for his freedom from all restraint. We must ask ourselves whether the storytellers did not here purposely propagate a
certain human ideal existing in the subconscious of the common
people and providing a contrast to that typified in the ruling gentry.
It is of interest that in several crime stories, too, the author extols a
man of the people who does not shrink from even multiple murders to
avenge a wrong that has been done him. In the storyteller's rendering
such a man, precisely because of his uncurbed natural disposition,

---

[88] Cf. "Researches", pt. 1, p. 123.
[89] Cf. "Researches, Continuation," p. 638.

becomes a god after his death.[90] If we recall the eternal revolts of the people, on a scale and with a frequency which is without parallel elsewhere, which punctuate the whole of Chinese history, and always at the head of which stood such untameable characters, we can easily grasp the special social and directly class-determined significance of this ideal. It is a canonized resistance of the people; according to the storytellers, a man should at no price submit to humiliation, better to lose his life, but never must he fail to defend himself and avenge a wrong.

From the literary point of view, these tales enriched Chinese literature with portraits of sturdy, indomitable characters, as if hewn out of stone, and yet completely authentic and full of the flush and vigour of life, whose like we shall scarcely find anywhere else in mediaeval literature. These narrations also discovered for Chinese fiction the Chinese countryside, for whereas most other tales had a town or some indeterminate milieu as their background, for the bandits the storyteller had to go to the country and so learned to create those monumental backcloths of Chinese mountains and rivers which are the setting of the novel, *Shui-hu chuan*, and provide the realistic analogy to lyrical Chinese landscape painting.

Ghost Stories and Tales of Fantasy

We have already noted in the preceding pages that alongside of fighting motifs, it was especially motifs of mythological origin that overran narrative fiction. The fondness for these motifs is apparent, too, from the fact that Lo Yeh reserves to this category three specializations: the above-mentioned stories about beings endowed with supernatural powers and ghost stories, which merge with love stories; tales about gods and immortals 神仙; and finally tales about the magical arts or sorcery 妖術. Clearly the mythological view of the world is still alive among people, the creations of mythology exist in people's minds side by side with real things, not yet having been relegated to the domain of the unreal. And so the storyteller can make free use of them without embarrassment, mythological motifs providing equally valuable and important materials in the con-

---

[90] Cf. Note 47, above, the tale of Jen Kuei.

struction of the plot as real motifs. It is certain, too, that the interest in supernatural motifs founded in this basic mental situation was in certain cases stimulated by specific literary impulses. We have repeatedly pointed out the strong influence exercised by T'ang tales of the literati on the production of the storytellers, who again and again drew upon the T'ang *ch'uan-ch'i* for their subject matter. And in the T'ang tale, in keeping with its markedly romantic mood, an important place was occupied by stories of supernatural beings, fairies, and immortals. Thus about five of the nine tales which Lo Yeh cites as examples of tales about divinities and immortals were clearly based on T'ang tales; it would seem that we come across all these themes in *T'ai-p'ing kuang-chi*.[91] On the other hand, so far as I know, real "horror" stories about vampires and various monsters sucking the blood and strength of human beings and demanding bloody sacrifices occur only rarely in T'ang tales; here the storyteller obviously drew in the main upon folk fantasy and developed its horror elements. By combining and reassembling these folk elements he then succeeded in creating perfectly bloodcurdling tales, in which horror is piled upon horror.

In a number of tales, three monsters appear. They might include a woman who died an unnatural death, or a being endowed with supernatural powers, in the shape of a snake, a hare, or a hen. The demon assumes the form of a lovely woman and entices a handsome young man into her house, whereupon her assistants want to tear out his heart and devour it. Always at the last moment the youth is saved by a Taoist monk, less commonly a Buddhist monk, who catches the demon or kills it.[92]

We said above that in these tales of terror the storytellers drew for inspiration upon folk superstitions and fantasy. It would however be a mistake to suppose that the storyteller took all these ghosts and demons as seriously as did his superstitious contemporaries. In several cases the author actually underlines the fantastic and im-

[91] Those comprise the narrations *Chung sou shen chi*, see note 60; *Chu yeh chou* 竹葉舟, *T'ai-p'ing*, ch. 74, vol. 1, p. 462, *Ch'en Chi-ch'ing* 陳季卿; *Huang-liang meng* 黃梁夢, *T'ai-p'ing*, ch. 82, vol. 1, p. 526, *Lü weng* 呂翁: *Fen ho-erh* 粉合兒, *T'ai-p'ing*, ch. 274, vol. 3, p. 2157, *Mai fen erh* 買粉兒; *Hsü Yen* 許岩, perhaps *T'ai-p'ing*, ch. 47, vol. 1, p. 294, *Hsü Hsi-yen* 許棲巖.

[92] *Hsi-hu san t'a chi* 西湖三塔記, *Ch'ing-p'ing*, p. 22, *Lo-yang san kuai chi* 洛陽三怪記, *Ch'ing-p'ing*, p. 67, and others.

probable character of his tale; for instance, in the tale "How the Stars of Good Fortune, Wealth and Longevity descended to this Earth,"[93] there are so many of these miraculous leaps and turns that we cannot help suspecting that we have here not an attempt to work upon people's superstitious fears and terrors, but an intentional phantasmagoria, an essay in the grotesque. In these "horror" stories a humorous note makes itself heard and the final effect is not of a terrifying procession of demonic spirits, but simply of a grotesque whirl of masks.[94]

We must not forget that the storyteller, bound by political considerations and by the sensitive reactions of his audience, had little opportunity to indulge in free flights of fancy. The postulate of truthfulness and seriousness, strong in the classical literature, operated equally restrictively in popular fiction as a set of psychological checks or curbs. The storyteller sitting in the circle of his listeners could not poke fun at the various weaknesses of his fellow creatures as could his European colleague, protected from the criticism of the targets of his wit by his noble patrons. I should say that the strict realism with which a story from real life is rendered needed to be offset by a domain where fantasy could come into its own, to satisfy the longing for the grotesque and the absurd. It seems to me that the mythological elements and tales were the same kind of reaction to the extreme realism of one part of the storytellers' production, as dadaism, surrealism, poetism, and other anti-realist trends were a reaction against the prolific realism dominating European literature more or less up to the First World War. Out of these anti-realistic, grotesque, and fantastic tendencies then sprang a work that completes the complex of great novels stemming from storytellers' activities: alongside the romantic chronicle (San kuo chih), the novel of adventure (Shui-hu chuan), the realistic–naturalistic description of manners (Chin P'ing Mei), the creation of pure fantasy takes its place in the novel Hsi yu chi.

[93] Fu lu shou san hsing tu shih 福祿壽三星度世, T'ung-yen, ch. 38.

[94] We have reliable proof that the tale "The Ghosts' Lair," Hsi-shan yi-k'u kuei 西山一窟鬼, Ching-pen, p. 51, was not interpreted as a horror tale, but rather as a tale of humorous character. There existed in Hangchow, at the end of the Sung era, a tearoom kept by mother Wang and called "The Ghosts' Lair," evidently after this tale. See "Researches, Continuation," p. 652. If the tale evoked feelings of horror, its name would surely not be used for the name of a tearoom.

Just as crime stories intrude into religious stories, so conversely do ghost or horror stories find their way into crime stories.

The mingling of elements of the most varied provenance and character is then the basic compositional principle in storytellers' relations and to this we must attribute a considerable part of their high artistic level and interest. Quite fantastic is the ability of the authors to mingle with a bold and absolutely sure hand mythological with realistic elements, lyric with epic, and description and dialogue. The predilection for sharp contrasts, probably stimulated by the need to amaze, attract, or surpass competition, led the storyteller to compose works which, in their clear-cut contours and high relief, are unparalleled in earlier ages and only rarely matched in later literature.

The Early Chinese Short Story: A Critical Theory in Outline

by *Patrick Hanan*

The Chinese vernacular short story has almost always been dealt with from the point of view of the literary historian. Besides bibliographical and textual matters, the noteworthy scholarly works on the subject have most often been concerned with genetic questions, especially the relationship of the short story to oral literature, or else with questions of social context and social reference.[1] In particular, no one has attempted to describe it as a genre, that is to say, to anatomize the body of Chinese narrative fiction and to show what distinguishes the short story from its other parts.

Yet basic questions are implied here. Are the vernacular short story and the classical tale distinct as genres, or merely by virtue of the language they use? Does the short story differ significantly, at all stages of the history of Chinese literature, from the category of works to which we apply the catchall word "novel"? If it does differ significantly, are the boundaries always drawn in the right places? In other words, are there short "novels" hidden among the short stories, or perhaps some long "stories" among the novels? Is the

---

[1] Exceptions in European languages include the following: J. Prušek, *Die Literatur des Befreiten China und ihre Volkstraditionen*, trans. Pavel Eisner and Wilhelm Gampert (Prague, 1955), esp. pp. 469–535; J. L. Bishop, *The Colloquial Short Story in China, A Study of the San-yen Collections* (Harvard 1956), esp. pp. 29–46; C. Birch, "Some Formal Characteristics of the *Hua-pen* Story," *Bulletin of the School of Oriental and African Studies* 17.2 (1955), 346–364; C. T. Hsia, "To What Fyn Lyve I Thus? Society and Self in the Chinese Short Story," *Kenyon Review* 24.3 (1962), 519–541. Also J. Prušek, "The Creative Methods of Chinese Medieval Storytellers," in *Charisteria Orientalia*, pp. 253–273. Birch's article is the only one of these works which is directly concerned with genre characteristics. Its aims and approach are, in general, different from those of this essay.

short story one genre, or more? Many of these questions cannot be answered with the methods of analysis that we have at hand. The tools of dissection, let alone the names of the classes, are hopelessly clumsy; the terms we use are the terms of convenience rather than the terms of scholarship. A new analysis needs to be made.

In any such classification, objective analysis of the existing works must take precedence over historical explanation. To take as an example the most common kind of historical explanation, the tracing of a class of literature to its origins, we cannot say that a distinct historical origin proves in itself that one class is distinct from other classes. The two kinds of approach—objective analysis and historical explanation—can be reduced to two questions: In what significant ways do the two kinds differ on their own evidence? Why do the two kinds differ? The first question refers to the method of objective analysis and the second to that of historical explanation. In genre classification, the second method is clearly subordinate. If the two kinds under review do not differ significantly—in terms, let us specify, of both formal and non-formal characteristics—they cannot be considered distinct.[2] If they do differ significantly, it is usually possible to find an accompanying historical explanation to corroborate the distinction. ("Explanation" does not mean direct causation; the question of historical causation in literature is infinitely complex.) This, essentially, is the part played by historical explanation.

The fact that historical explanation is subordinate does not mean that historical *development,* the development of genres in time, can be ignored. The relationships among the genres of narrative fiction are not immutable. As each succeeding member of a class or genre may change the constitution of that genre, so each genre may change with respect to other genres. It is not apparent, for example, that the short story in the time of the *Chin P'ing Mei* bears the same relation-

[2] The conception of genre which is accepted in this essay is essentially that discussed in René Wellek and Austin Warren's *Theory of Literature* (New York, 1962): "Genre should be conceived, we think, as a grouping of literary works based, theoretically, upon both outer form (specific meter or structure) and also upon inner form (attitude, tone, purpose—more crudely, subject and audience)" (p. 231). "Formal" in our definition refers to Wellek and Warren's "outer form"; "non-formal" refers to their "inner form." To their definition, there is also added the specific requirement that a genre be not merely based upon inner and outer form, but that it be distinguishable from any other genre by both formal and non-formal criteria.

ship to that novel as it does to the *Shui-hu chuan*. The conception of a genre is thus a useful critical tool for a limited period of literary history.

There are two main objections to any analysis of the various kinds of Chinese narrative fiction. Both objections concern the division of Chinese literature into certain large entities called "literatures" and ask whether it is valid to distinguish kinds of fiction within one "literature" from other kinds within another "literature."

There is great value in thinking of Chinese literature as plural. Thus, according to the medium of communication, there might at a given time be as many as three concurrent literatures, an oral literature addressed to a listening audience, a recognized literature addressed to a highly lettered reading public, and a vernacular literature addressed to a broader reading public. The criteria which distinguish one literature from another are a distinct medium of communication, a distinct authorship, and, to some degree at least, a distinct public.[3]

"Literature falls into two great parts not so much because there are two kinds of culture, but because there are two kinds of *form: the one part of literature is oral, and the other written.*" What Milman Parry calls "form" is approximately what Northrop Frye calls "genre."[4] It is obvious that oral literature must be considered as oral literature, and that in an analysis of the genres of fiction it cannot be considered alongside written literature. The problem arises in considering the early texts of the vernacular literature. There is no doubt that the stuff-material of many of these works existed once in oral literature. There is also no doubt that the written versions endeavor to suggest

[3] The idea of different concurrent "literatures" is treated in very general terms, as it applies to China, in Patrick Hanan, "The Development of Fiction and Drama," *The Legacy of China*, R. Dawson, ed. (Oxford, 1964), pp. 116–120. The theory on which the idea is based derives from H. M. and N. K. Chadwick, *The Growth of Literature*, Vol. III (Cambridge, 1940).

[4] Milman Parry, "Whole Formulaic Verses in Greek and Southslavic Heroic Song," *Transactions and Proceedings of the American Philological Association*, LXIV (1933), p. 180, quoted and discussed in Robert Scholes and Robert Kellogg, *The Nature of Narrative* (New York, 1966), p. 18; Northrop Frye, *Anatomy of Criticism: Four Essays* (Princeton, 1957), pp. 247–248. Frye's "genres" are distinguished by their respective "radicals of presentation." He discerns two radicals of presentation in a written work told by a narrator. For our purpose, such a work, e.g., some of Conrad, Sherwood Anderson, etc. is written narrative. The fact that it is "assimilated" to oral literature by the presence of a narrator merely distinguishes it from other kinds of written narrative.

an oral performance. In thinking of them as stories written *ab initio,*
are we vitiating any comparison we may make? Are we not perhaps
doing as stupid a thing as comparing a play with a piece of narrative?
For various reasons, I think not.

First, while we cannot doubt the connection of many stories with
oral literature, the statement that any considerable number of them
represent a story-teller's *script* is unproven.[5] It is one of a number of
widely accepted notions about fiction for which the bases of belief
have not been investigated. On the other hand, there are stories
which say explicitly that they have been derived from oral literature,
in the sense that they have been compiled from stuff-material which
had existed orally.[6] This is a very different matter, and such stories
can legitimately be considered as written literature.

Secondly, no one has yet succeeded in showing, on the basis of
observable features, that stories which are supposed to be directly
related to a story-teller's script differ significantly from the rest. Thus,
even supposing there are among our early extant stories some which
reproduce the texts of the story-tellers, they are still not distinguishable from stories compiled or composed as written pieces for a
reading public. There is really no bar to our considering all of the
stories together as examples of written literature.

The other objection concerns the validity of any comparison
between the classical tale, the *ch'uan-ch'i,* which is supposed to
belong to the recognized literature, and the vernacular story. But
even if they do belong to two different literatures, I doubt whether
comparison is invalidated. The great difference is between oral and
written literature, rather than between different written literatures.
The fact that the classical tale and the vernacular story belong to
separate literatures would be part of the historical explanation which
would corroborate a distinction based on objective analysis. But in
fact, the conception of different, concurrent literatures, while

---

[5] The story that is generally thought to represent oral literature most directly is the
Wen-ching yüan-yang hui (No. 24 in the list at the end of this essay). It has often been claimed
that this story is a *ku-tzu-tz'u* 鼓子詞 of the Sung dynasty. Whether it is a *ku-tzu-tz'u* is
uncertain, but the presence of Ming place names in the text means that it is unlikely to be
Sung. What casts doubt on the claim that it directly represents a piece of oral literature is
the fact that the prologue story is *textually* related to a T'ang dynasty classical tale. If we
are to suppose that this prologue story has been added to it in its written form, what other
changes may not have been made? It can scarcely be considered as a text for recitation.

[6] Cf. e.g., *Ku-chin hsiao-shuo* 15 (i.e., B in the list) and *Ching-shih t'ung-yen* 13.

generally valid and useful, is certainly not valid for the tale and the story during the whole of their history. Feng Meng-lung 馮夢龍 at the close of the Ming dynasty published both vernacular stories and classical tales, in the *San yen* 三言 and the *Ch'ing shih* 情史 especially;[7] a number of the latter are apparently versions of the former. The criteria of a literature should include both distinct authorship and, in some degree, a distinct reading public. Here we have neither; clearly the distinction between the two literatures has broken down.

1.   *Vernacular Fiction and the Classical Tale*

The primary distinction is not between the classical tale and the vernacular short story, but between the classical tale on the one side and the whole of vernacular fiction on the other. The distinction is more fundamental than that between one genre and another; it proves, in fact, to concern narrative method as such. The choice of a particular language, classical or vernacular, is merely one of the elements within the total narrative method.

Comparison is more than merely a formal necessity. It helps to distinguish, as little else can, the peculiar features of the narrative method of vernacular fiction. Nonetheless, any brief comparison must be at the highest level of generalization. It cannot help but seem like a travesty of scholarly procedure.

One method which will serve our present, modest purpose is to compare the stories and tales which treat the same stuff-material. There are dozens of such pairs of stories, most notably in the work of Feng Meng-lung, but also elsewhere.[8] Though little attention has

---

[7] No one article treats the correspondences between vernacular story and classical tale in the work of Feng Meng-lung. The best work on the "sources and influences" of the *Ku-chin hsiao-shuo* stories is still that of Wu Hsiao-ling 吳曉鈴 in *Han-hiue* 漢學 2 (Peking, 1947), 444–455. Sun K'ai-ti 孫楷第 did much the same for the *Chin-ku ch'i-kuan* stories in his introduction to the Ya-tung edition of 1933. The remainder of the stories in the *Ching-shih t'ung-yen* and the *Hsing-shih heng-yen* are treated by Chao Ching-shen 趙景深 in two articles contained in his *Hsiao-shuo hsi-ch'ü hsin-k'ao* 小說戲曲新考 (Shanghai, 1939), pp. 1–29. There are other works that treat single stories at greater length.

[8] Cf. note 7 above. I am excluding from consideration those versions in classical Chinese which are extremely brief, merely a précis as compared with the vernacular work. References to pairs will be found in the works cited above, and also in modern annotated editions of the *San yen*. Note the *Hsing-meng p'ien-yen* 醒夢駢言, a Ch'ing short story collection which contains twelve vernacular versions of *Liao-chai chih-yi* stories. Note also that Průšek, "Creative Methods," treats a pair of stories in great detail.

been paid to them except as sources, they are of great significance to
the critic. So truly does each member of the pair conform to its type
that it is generally not possible to tell from inspection which is
based on which. Thus a comparison of some of these pairs should give
a good idea of the essential differences between the two narrative
methods. Although there is not space here to compare them in
detail—something on the lines of the careful, critical studies of
Auerbach's *Mimesis* is really required—the following points are
derived from such a comparison.

The obvious, basic difference is the means of presentation.
Whereas the tale uses a variety of means, but most commonly the
device of the self-effacing omniscient narrator, the vernacular fiction
is narrated by an author who assumes the persona of the public
story-teller addressing his audience. If we use the word "rhetoric"
as Wayne Booth uses it in his *Rhetoric of Fiction*,[9] to denote the
mediating activities of the author, his intervention, open or secretive,
in the story, then the rhetoric of the tale is either implicit or deliberately unobtrusive. By contrast, the rhetoric of vernacular fiction is
explicit and even obtrusive. One of the functions of the introductory
remarks or prologue is just this—to make the rhetoric explicit, to give
a deliberate "distancing effect."[10] The scattered poems, the occasional pretended altercations with the audience, the frequent
summaries, all serve a similar purpose. It seems as if the rhetoric of
the vernacular fiction deliberately calls attention to itself.

I believe that it is possible to discern three modes of narrative in
the vernacular fiction, all of which may be used, side by side, at
frequent intervals, in the same work. Furthermore, transition from
mode to mode is always clearly marked, and deliberately so; it
strikes the reader like an abrupt change of gear. At a highly abstract
level, ignoring the clearly marked transition, I daresay it would be
possible to make a similar claim of any kind of fiction in any literature. But whereas in other cases such an analysis would be merely
tendentious, the explicit nature of the authorial rhetoric, as well as
certain corresponding formal features, makes it both natural and

[9] Chicago, 1961.
[10] *Op. cit.,* p. 155.

necessary in Chinese fiction. Let us name these the modes of *commentary*, *description*, and *presentation*.[11]

The mode of commentary is explicit in that it is clearly marked by what scholars sometimes call "story-teller phrases." It includes the introductory remarks or prologue, explanation given during the course of the narrative, comments both in verse and prose, the summaries. In each case, transition to the mode of commentary is marked. Explanation, for example, is either cast into the form of an altercation with some mystified questioner in the imaginary audience, or introduced by some such word as *yüan-lai* 原來. The occasional verses have a double function. The verse often has a proverbial, gnomic force and adds to the effect of conventional public wisdom that the mode of commentary generally contrives to give. More important, it is further set off, and the mode of commentary made more explicit, by the fact that it differs prosodically from its context.[12]

The mode of description has its own distinct markers and, generally speaking, its own distinct prosodic form. The description is usually cast into the form of a passage of parallel prose, full of stereotyped, classical language and rather overblown imagery. Its markers are the terms *tan chien* 但見, *chih chien* 只見, and the like.

The mode of presentation is not always marked, although terms like *ch'ieh shuo* 且說 and *ch'üeh shuo* 却說, for example after an explanation or a poem, often serve as markers. It consists of dialogue and narrated action, and makes up the greater part of the work. In terms of an old-fashioned kind of criticism, this mode may be described as *showing* rather than *telling*.[13] Of course, it is an illusion to imagine that one can ever escape into pure dramatic fiction; as Booth

[11] Note that both the mode of commentary and the mode of description serve generalizing functions, as distinct from the mode of presentation. The mode of commentary is partly commentary but it also summarizes. The two functions are interwoven, and it would be an artificial distinction to speak of separate modes of commentary and summary. The mode of description is formulaic, in the sense that oral literature is formulaic. Hence its emphasis on the general rather than on the particular. Note also that the mode of description is only one way of describing. The function of description is also performed, generally in a less striking manner, within the mode of presentation.

[12] Several important functions of the mode of commentary are here passed over. These consist of the "management" of the plot, particularly its pace and direction, as well as the controlling of the reader's response. The vernacular literature leaves less room for the reader's imagination and much less room for different kinds of response. Another aspect not dealt with is that of traditional elements in the language.

[13] *Rhetoric of Fiction*, pp. 3–19.

says, the author's viewpoint is always present for anyone who knows how to look for it.[14] But this illusion is precisely what many novelists strive for. In some measure, the vernacular fiction achieves it by declaring the author's mediation so openly and honestly in the mode of commentary that the reader tends to overlook what is smuggled in inside the mode of presentation.

The obvious difference between the two narrative methods is, of course, that of language. This is one of the elements of the narrative method, and choice of narrative method implies, at the same time a choice of language. It is thus no accident that use of the classical language is generally found together with implicit rhetoric and that the vernacular is found together with explicit rhetoric.

The difference between the effects of classical and vernacular narrative prose may be summed up, very roughly, in terms of two pairs of opposites: the vernacular tends to be referential and denotative, whereas the classical tends to be elegant and evocative; and the vernacular tends to be exhaustive, whereas the classical tends to be concentrated and elliptical. Vague though these characterizations are, they will have to serve here as signposts pointing toward a general distinction. The vernacular narrative prose tends to be exhaustive and denotative, therefore expressions like the "relative weight" of a word or phrase, or "what is left unsaid," have little meaning. Yet such considerations are vital in reading the classical tale; the art of reading a tale seems often to consist in recognizing "what is left unsaid" or in perceiving some key word or phrase. (Part of the reason that English translations of the tale often fall flat is that translators have not succeeded in rendering these qualities.) Though the vernacular narrative prose does change—one finds in the Ch'ing dynasty novels a greater tendency to use the vernacular evocatively— the denotative-exhaustive use is still paramount, and may be regarded as the staple kind in vernacular fiction.

The contrast between exhaustive and concentrated is, however, much more than a matter of prose style. It points to a fundamental difference in the two narrative methods toward the depiction of reality. Exhaustiveness implies an interest in particularity, and the vernacular aims at particularity, while the classical does not. By this

[14] *Op. cit.*, p. 20.

is meant particularity of person, of time, of place, of time and place in the larger sense, i.e., distinct historical background. The vernacular is full of "testifying detail."[15] Characters are always named, whereas in the classical fiction sometimes only the surname is given, sometimes not even that. The character is described, often in great detail, and he is placed, geographically, temporally and sociologically. More important, his speech is, so far as possible, individualized, a thing barely feasible in classical Chinese.

The vernacular fiction shows great concern for spatial and temporal setting. Elaborate calendars of events can be extracted from long works like the *Shui-hu chuan* and the *Chin P'ing Mei;* with their constant reckoning of time, they can even become wearisome. The contrast with classical fiction is quite clear. In many pieces of vernacular narrative, there is an implied claim to cover all elapsed time, sometimes on an hour-by-hour scale, unless it is otherwise stated. When time has to be skipped it will often be signaled by some such term as *pu t'i* 不題; otherwise the illusion is given that all time has been accounted for. It is an exaggeration, but not an outrageous one, to say that the vernacular fiction tries to give the impression that it is presenting a totality of experience within an accepted frame of reference. When the experience is to be cut short, or summarized, we are told so. This confirms the statement above about the separation of the modes in vernacular fiction, that the obtrusiveness of the mode of commentary generally allows the mode of presentation to claim to provide a complete and objective *showing*.

The qualities we have pointed to in vernacular fiction, with the exception of its explicit authorial rhetoric, have a certain consistency among themselves. It is possible to characterize the narrative method succinctly. To a considerable degree, it is the method which Ian Watt has called "formal realism."[16]

Formal realism is formal "because the term realism does not refer to any special doctrine or purpose, but only to a set of narrative procedures which are so commonly found together in the novel (of Defoe, Fielding, etc.) and so rarely in other genres, that they may be

---

[15] Ian Watt, *Rise of the Novel* (Berkeley, 1957), p. 34, quotes Hazlitt on Richardson's novels: "It is like reading evidence in a court of justice." The introductory markers to the mode of description often ask: "What did he look like?" or "How was he dressed?"

[16] *Rise of the Novel,* pp. 9–34.

regarded as typical of the form itself." That is to say, it refers to a set of narrative procedures which make up the "lowest common denominator" of the narrative method characteristic of the novel. These narrative procedures consist principally of the use of non-traditional plots, of particularity as to person, place and time, of the provision of a distinct historical background, and of the use of descriptive and denotative language. In most of these respects, Chinese vernacular fiction has been observed to employ the narrative procedures of formal realism. In each respect, with the single exception of the use of non-traditional plots, in which it seems to me that no distinction can be drawn, the classical fiction either lacks the quality described, or possesses it to a smaller degree.[17]

There is a compelling reason for adopting this kind of notion. We have begun by considering the vernacular and classical fiction as distinct in form. If our analysis has been successful, we might expect to find that they are also, in a broad majority of cases, distinct in function. That is the other side of the ideal equation in genre study, distinct form implying distinct function. Had we begun by considering some such thing as the "imitation of reality," conceived as a function of literature, we might have concluded that our sample had, to some degree, the same pattern of form. That is the side of the equation from which Auerbach's *Mimesis* proceeds; we cannot utilize his conclusions, however valuable they may be. On the other hand, we can agree with Watt that "there are important differences in the degree to which different literary forms imitate reality; and the formal realism of the novel allows a more immediate imitation of individual experience set in its temporal and spatial setting than do other literary forms" (p. 32). Applying this to Chinese fiction, we must acknowledge that, in general and allowing for innumerable exceptions, vernacular fiction, fiction that uses the method of formal realism, does imitate reality to a significantly greater degree than classical fiction.

The force of this characterization of narrative method can best be seen in an actual comparison. "Formal realism" is a term which purports to sum up certain narrative procedures in the novels of

---

[17] This is not the place to speculate as to why formal realism, if it is formal realism, should have been developed in China in this period. One factor may have been the close relationship of the Chinese historiographical tradition to Chinese fiction.

Defoe, Richardson, and Fielding, the consistent use of which distinguishes that kind of novel from earlier fiction. If our analysis of the narrative method is correct, we may expect to find a radical difference between the Chinese vernacular fiction and the genre to which it is sometimes likened, that of the Italian and Spanish *novella*.

There are certain obvious parallels. If we take the *Decameron* as our example, we will note the presence of a narrator, the existence of a prologue or introductory remarks, and the similarity of a number of plots. But these parallels are trivial compared to the difference in narrative method. The Italian stories show little attempt at particularity, of time, or place, or person. Often their characters are not named, especially the humbler characters. Time is seldom particularized, and there is no claim to account for time on a day-by-day scale. The only historical background worthy of the name is that of the frame story itself. There are compressions of the narrative, even at high points of the story, which would be inconceivable in the Chinese.[18] Dialogue in the *Decameron* is used less for the purpose of individualizing the speakers than for advocacy, for making set debating speeches. The language of the narrative is elegant and literary.[19] All this is far removed from the exhaustive narration, the attempt to put each event in its physical and temporal setting, of Chi ıese vernacular fiction.

2. *"Short Story" and "Novel" Before 1550*

If we think of a genre as a class of literary works distinguished from other classes by a set of formal and non-formal characteristics,[20]

---

[18] Take the story of Isabetta, the *Isabella* of Keats. Even in this story, which stands apart from the other Decameron stories because of its grimness and its suspense, there is little attempt to locate the story and little real attempt to build up to the moment of revelation.

[19] Cf. Maurice Valency's introduction to *The Palace of Pleasure*, Harry Levtow and Maurice Valency, eds. (New York: Capricorn Books, 1960), p. 8: "The stories of the *Decameron* are set in a richly cadenced prose, copious and balanced, and the speech of the Florentine merchants is made to swell majestically through the resonant periods of ancient Rome."

[20] Of course, a genre is not just a convenient concept for the systematizing critic, it is also something real to the writer; when he is writing in relation to a literary tradition, he is almost inevitably concerned with genre, whether he realizes it or not. This is what gives the concept of genre value for the critic.

we are forced to take account of the development of genres in time. Since each class is defined in terms of its differences from other classes, any mutation of one genre may require that other genres also be redefined. To provide a historical point of reference, therefore, we should first consider the vernacular fiction in its earliest period.

Anyone who deals with early fiction runs straight into the most difficult scholarly problem in this field—the problem of dating. This is not the dating of editions, nor the dating of pieces of oral literature which use the same stuff-material, but the dating of the earliest written version of the story. The problem is especially acute in the case of the shorter pieces, the so-called short stories. Apart from one story which survives in a 1498 edition, there are no other editions earlier than those of the 29 stories published by the Ch'ing-p'ing-shan-t'ang 清平山堂 about 1550.[21] Yet scholars have claimed to

[21] This is an approximate date. For a summary of the evidence relating to the collections, cf. André Lévy, "Etudes sur Trois Recueils Anciens de Contes Chinois," *Toung Pao* 52 (1963), 97–106. It is generally accepted that the stories once circulated under the title of *Liu-shih-chia hsiao-shuo* 六十家小說 *(Stories by Sixty Authors)*. It has not hitherto been pointed out that there is a title *Yüan-jen* 元人 *liu-shih-chia hsiao-shuo (Stories by Sixty Authors of the Yüan Dynasty)* among the works listed at the head of the *Hsü Chin P'ing Mei*. It is contained in the first edition, of which the author's preface is dated 1660, and in certain subsequent editions.

Lévy points out (pp. 103–106) that some of the surviving parts of the collections may not be from the original edition, in view of obvious differences of lineation, quality of paper, etc. He examines a story with a large lacuna and compares it with two other versions. One of these clearly derives from the kind of edition that had the lacuna; the other is the original *kind* of edition—the lacuna is filled in with the equivalent of exactly two double pages of text. There are many possible explanations, but perhaps the most likely is that the Ch'ing-p'ing edition we have in this case is printed from the original blocks, of which two were missing by the time the edition was made. However, Mr. Lévy also suggests that, because of disparities within the same part of the collection, we may have to reckon with the possibility that some later editor has rearranged the stories. Here he is on dangerous ground. Apart from the question of why any editor should rearrange the stories while retaining the old format, there is positive evidence that the division we now have existed at a very early stage. Of the twenty-nine stories that survive in whole or part, twenty-four are mentioned in the *Pao-wen-t'ang shu-mu* 寶文堂書目 (Lévy is incorrect in asserting, p. 105, that only one of the two stories discovered by A Ying 阿英 is mentioned.) The five that are not listed in the catalogue comprise one entire section of the book *Yü-ch'uang chi* 雨窗集, first part. This must mean that by the time of the compilation of the catalogue, this sectional grouping already meant something.

It seems reasonable to accept provisionally the view that the *Ching-pen t'ung-su hsiao-shuo* 京本通俗小說 is based on the *San yen* collections. If so, it is of no interest to us in this article. Evidence for the view is found in Nagasawa Kikuya 長澤規矩也, *Shoshigaku ronkō* 書誌學論考 (Tokyo, 1937), pp. 147–153. Yoshikawa Kojirō 吉川幸次郎 *Chūgoku sambunron* 中國散文論 (Tokyo, 1949, p. 192), states that he has compared the text of one story in both versions and has come to that conclusion. More recently, Ma

place scores of stories at points as far back as the twelfth century. And there is a widely accepted view, consistent in general if not in detail which allocates certain stories to the Sung, certain to the Yuan, certain to the early Ming, and so forth.[22]

Let us look briefly at the argument used to support the dating. They are of two kinds, bibliographical and textual, i.e. based on features of the stories themselves. The bibliographical evidence is extremely meager. An early work, possibly of the Yuan dynasty, the *Tsui-weng t'an-lu* 醉翁談錄[23] lists scores of stories, some of which clearly make use of the same stuff-material as extant stories. But although the work has often been used to date stories,[24] its use is questionable. It refers explicitly to oral literature, not written literature, and all that it tells us is that the stuff-material of such-and-such a story was current in oral literature in Yuan times or earlier. Unless one subscribes to the unlikely proposition that every oral story had its own prompt-book and that all the extant stories are directly based on those prompt-books, one cannot use the *Tsui-weng t'an-lu* as evidence for the date of the first written version. The sole early reference which is clearly to something written is contained in the *Lu-kuei pu* 錄鬼簿.[25] It is to the story of Chao Cheng 趙正, one of the heroes of the extant story, *Sung Ssu-kung ta nao "Chin-hun" Chang* 宋四公大鬧禁魂張,[26] and it is quite possible that the latter represents

---

Yau-woon 馬幼垣 and Ma Tai-loi 馬泰來 in *"Ching-pen t'ung-su hsiao-shuo ko-p'ien ti nien-tai chi ch'i chen-wei wen-t'i"* 京本通俗小說各篇的年代及其眞僞問題. *Ch'ing-hua hsüeh-pao*, New Series, 5.1 (July, 1965), 14-29 give a good deal of evidence, without, however, having seen either statement. A comprehensive study of textual variants is needed.

[22] Cf. e.g., Cheng Chen-to 鄭振鐸, *"Ming-Ch'ing erh-tai ti p'ing-hua chi"* 明清二代的平話集, *Chung-kuo wen-hsüeh yen-chiu* 中國文學研究 (Peking, 1957), I, 360-474. This is the most comprehensive attempt at dating. There is a great deal of scholarly literature on the subject, including, for example, the article by Ma Yau-woon and Ma Tai-loi mentioned in note 21 above. A revision and elaboration of Cheng's methods, which are not consistently applied in his article, are to be found in Yen Tun-yi's 嚴敦易 appendix to his edition of the *Ku-chin hsiao-shu* (Peking, 1955). Cheng's article was first published in the *Hsiao-shuo yüeh-pao* 小說月報 22.7-8 (1931).

[23] This is the work by Lo Yeh 羅燁. There is a Sung work of exactly the same title by Chin Ying-chih 金盈之.

[24] Cf. e.g., T'an Cheng-pi 譚正璧 *Hua-pen yü ku-chü* 話本與古劇 (Shanghai, 1956), pp. 2-12.

[25] Cf. *Chung-kuo ku-tien hsi-ch'ü lun-chu chi-ch'eng* 中國古典戲曲論著集成 (Peking, 1959), II, p. 116.

[26] *Ku-chin hsiao-shuo* 36.

the story referred to. Since the author's name is given, we may take it
to be a Yuan story. Apart from the *Lu-kuei pu*, there is no reference to
a written version of a story until the compilation of catalogue *Pao-
wen-t'ang shu-mu* 寶文堂書目 in the mid-sixteenth century.[27] This
catalogue lists twenty-four of the twenty-nine Ch'ing-p'ing-shan-
t'ang pieces, plus more than twenty titles of pieces that have survived
in later collections.[28] Thus from the bibliographical evidence, all one
is entitled to say is that there were somewhat above fifty pieces
existing in written versions by about 1550. Apart from the Chao
Cheng story, which could conceivably represent a written version of
the Yuan dynasty, and one other piece, the *Ch'ien-t'ang meng* 錢塘夢,
which survives in a 1498 edition,[29] the stories cannot be dated more
precisely than this.

However, the scholar's main recourse has been to internal
evidence, evidence drawn from the text of the short story. Unfortunately, it has been used so unsystematically, and with so many
unspoken and unfounded assumptions, that the results are of little
value. It is safe to say that there is not a single piece of positive
evidence among all the criteria used by Cheng Chen-to and later
scholars which will date a story reliably to either the Sung or the

[27] See note 21 above. Both stories discovered by A Ying are listed in the Pao-wen-t'ang
catalogue.

[28] On the question of the identification of *Pao-wen-t'ang shu-mu* titles as references to
stories that are extant, cf. T'an Cheng-pi, *Hua-pen yü ku-chü*, pp. 38–54. He lists a total of
53 titles which, he considers, refer to extant stories. Twenty-four of these are to Ch'ing-
p'ing-shan-t'ang stories. Not all of the remaining twenty-nine identifications can be
accepted, however. No. 1 survives, if it survives at all, only as an integral part of a longer
work; it cannot be said to exist as a story in its own right any longer. No. 6, if we accept the
view that the *Ching-pen t'ung-su hsiao-shuo* derives from the *San yen*, cannot be the *San yen*
story Mr. T'an identifies it as. Nos. 45 and 46 survive only in post-*San yen* collections. Both
are well-known stories from early *ch'uan-ch'i* literature; we cannot suppose with any
confidence that they are the works referred to in the catalogue. One of the stories discovered by A Ying, the *Fei-ts'ui hsüan* 翡翠軒, is not in Mr. T'an's list, although it is
referred to explicitly in the catalogue. He has alternative identifications for No. 52, the
San meng seng chi 三夢僧記; Wu Hsiao-ling's suggestion, in the review of *Ku-chin hsiao-
shuo* already referred to, is to be preferred to either. There are thus twenty-five fairly
reliable references to *San yen* and other stories, and twenty-four to Ch'ing-p'ing-shan-
t'ang stories, a total of forty-nine. Five Ch'ing-p'ing stories are not listed in the catalogue,
nor is the *Ch'ien-t'ang meng*. This makes a total of fifty-five early stories. Note that we cannot
always be certain that our extant version is the one referred to in the catalogue. For
linguistic reasons which it would be inappropriate to give here, story No. 32 is almost
certainly a late story.

[29] It is prefaced to the 1498 edition of the *Hsi-hsiang chi* 西廂記, a photographic reproduction of which is contained in *Ku-pen hsi-ch'ü ts'ung-k'an*, First Series.

Yuan dynasty.[30] And negative evidence, of course, provides only a *terminus post quem*, not a *terminus ante quem*. For example, the discovery of a distinctively Yuan place-name in a story will not prove that the story is Yuan, only that it is unlikely to be Sung. This essay is not the place to pursue the point; the writer is preparing a separate article on the subject. All one can say is that the reliable knowledge we have at present is restricted to the evidence of the editions and the bibliographies.

We are compelled therefore to choose 1550 as the terminal date of the early period. Before this time, there existed the fifty-odd pieces we have mentioned and the other pieces, most of them longer, the so-called novels. However, some of the shorter pieces are not vernacular fiction within the definition we have given in Section 1. Even in the most tolerant view, a story which is written throughout in classical Chinese, which has no mode of description and no mode of commentary except for a *hua shuo* 話說 at the beginning and a four-line poem at the end, does not belong to the vernacular fiction. When these pieces have been discarded,[31] the number of shorter pieces drops to forty-two, almost all of which are easily accessible. The so-called novels we should consider are those that exist in editions from before 1550 or are mentioned in the *Pao-wen-t'ang shu-mu*. The sole exceptions are the historical narratives of Hsiung Ta-mu 熊大木.[32] Popularized history is not necessary fiction, and the works of Hsiung Ta-mu do not share the features of the vernacular literature.

In grouping these pieces into genres, length is not, in itself, a primary criterion.[33] Nor is the fact that some of the pieces are divided

---

[30] Cf. the works by Cheng Chen-to, Yen Tun-yi, and Ma Yau-woon already referred to.

[31] Ten stories included in the Ch'ing-p'ing collections are excluded for these reasons. They are the ten stories not listed at the end of this essay. In each case, the grounds for exclusion are clear. At least one of the ten has a close textual relationship with a T'ang *ch'uan-ch'i* story. Another, the *Fei-ts'ui hsüan*, is not accessible: I am relying on A Ying's description of it as a classical tale (*Hsiao-shuo hsien-hua* 小說閒話, rev. ed., Shanghai, 1958, p. 24). Three stories outside the Ch'ing-p'ing collections are also excluded. They are *Ku-chin hsiao-shuo* 25, a classical tale in form; the Tu Li-niang chi 杜麗娘記 and the *Kuo Han yü hsien* 郭翰遇仙, contained in later editions of the *Yen-chü pi-chi* 燕居筆記 both of which are classical tales. Excluding these thirteen, we have a total of forty-two.

[32] Cf. Sun K'ai-ti, *Chung-kuo t'ung-su hsiao shuo shu-mu* 中國通俗小說書目 (rev. ed. Shanghai, 1957), pp. 28, 42, etc. The *Liang Kung chiu chien* 梁公九諫 should also be excluded on similar grounds.

[33] E.g., the sections of the *Hsüan-ho yi-shih* 宣和遺事 that concern the *Shui-hu* legend are shorter than most "short stories."

into chapters. For even those pieces which are not in chapters are sometimes divided into sections, each of which ends on a note of suspense, with a couplet or so speculating on what will happen next. The difference between this kind of informal subdivision and the formal subdivision of the chapter is too technical a matter to base a classification upon.

I suggest that the most significant formal criterion is none of these things, but instead a matter of the organizing principle on which the works are built. If we use the word "plot" to mean the sequential structure of events in the work, we can distinguish two fundamentally different kinds of plot. At one extreme, we have the plot which, no matter how intricate it may be, is all of one piece; nothing substantial can be subtracted from it without destroying it as a plot. At the other extreme, we have the plot which is a framework for a series of loosely linked segments, some of which could be removed without doing irreparable damage to the whole; potentially, these segments are minor plots in their own right. Let us call these polar types the *unitary plot* and the *system of linked plots*. As an example of the former, we may take the *Chien-t'ieh ho-shang* 簡貼和尚 story.[34] There is the initial trick, hidden from the readers, its temporary success, its discovery, the reunion of husband and wife, the punishment of the villain. This is clearly a unitary plot; each part contributes significantly to the whole. As an example of the latter, the system of linked plots, we could take the Wu Sung chapters of the *Shui-hu chuan*. Each of Wu Sung's adventures consists of an almost perfect unitary plot in itself, and some of them could, with a little bridging of the gap, be removed from the text without great loss. But although the Wu Sung chapters form a system of linked plots, they are themselves linked to other systems, for example the chapters that deal with Sung Chiang. There is a master-link between the two systems, in this case the recurring motif of the chance confrontation that ends in firm friendship. Therefore, in the *Shui-hu chuan* and in certain other works, there is a level of organization above the kind we have been speaking of, a superstructure—in this work the assembling of the heroes, the birth and death of the rebellion—which controls the various systems of linked plots.

[34] See no. 22 in the list at the end of this essay.

If we consider the early vernacular literature in the light of these distinctions, we shall have no difficulty in recognizing that the works commonly thought of as "novels" are to be classified as systems of linked plots, either at the simple level of the Wu Sung chapters or at the complex level of the *Shui-hu chuan*. On the other hand, the "short stories" can by no means all be thought of as having unitary plots.

There are as many as seven of the "short stories" which can reasonably be classed as systems of linked plots on the simple level, rather than as unitary plots. They are: the Chao Cheng story (A in the list at the end of this article), the sole story which can be considered with some reason to be as early as Yuan; the stories of Shih Hung-chao (B), Yang Wen (C), Cheng Hsin (D); the story of the *shan-t'ing-erh* (E); the stories of Chang Ku-lao (F) and Tung Yung (G). Let us examine some of these stories.

The Chao Cheng story, quite incidentally, bears a certain general resemblance to a well-known type of international folk-tale, the Master Thief.[35] The story begins with a number of tests in which the pupil outwits his mentor in crime, and continues with a series of daring burglaries. There is a half-hearted attempt to structure the story upon the theme of the stinginess of one of the victims, but the story does not have a unitary plot. The focus of narration, which in Chinese vernacular fiction almost always follows one of the characters, makes here the kind of switch, after a chance encounter for example, that we are accustomed to in the *Shui-hu chuan*. As a result there is more than one main figure in the story. There are loose ends left untied. Where the unitary plot is, in essence, the engendering of a crisis and its solution, this is a series of loosely linked adventures, with a somewhat random beginning and no proper end. At the close of the story we are even told that the thieves continued on in this manner for many years until they were finally swept away by the new broom of Judge Pao. The story is, in fact, a system of plots linked by the characters of Chao Cheng and his accomplices. It is on the simple level, i.e., on the level of the Wu Sung chapters; the theme of stinginess is used only to give it some semblance of unity.

The Shih Hung-chao story is a typical *fa-chi pien-t'ai* 發跡變泰 story.[36] In the special meaning this phrase has in the fiction of the

---

[35] Cf. Stith Thompson, *The Folktale* (New York, 1951), pp. 174–175.

[36] This expression is completely misunderstood by T'an Cheng-pi, *op. cit.*, p. 3.

early period, it refers to the rise of an upstart hero, and since the Five Dynasties seem to have been the great age for upstart heroes, most *fa-chi pien-t'ai* stories draw subject matter from that period. In this story, we have the characteristic features of the type—the unruly, even criminal boyhood, the magical signs of future greatness, the first army command, military and political success. Usually, the upstart is sought out by a wife who intuitively discerns his greatness; this happens to Kuo Wei, whose adventures are intertwined with Shih's. The subject matter and conventions of this story are closely akin to those of the *Wu-tai-shih p'ing-hua* 五代史平話, which is itself, formally speaking, a series of linked plot systems; it has, however, little real attempt at a superstructure.[37] In form, the Shih Hung-chao story is a very diffuse system of linked plots, of which the links are the two comrades Shih and Kuo.

Similar judgments apply, in some degree, to the five other stories.[38] The Yang Wen story is a series of plots around the career of the hero. Significantly, he is described as related to the Yang family of the Five Dynasties and the Northern Sung, of whom an oral cycle was current by the Yuan dynasty at the latest.[39] The Cheng Hsin story is a *fa-chi pien-t'ai* story with a strong supernatural element; it is clearly a system of linked plots. The Chang Ku-lao story is about a divine being; the plot is loosely linked, and the focus of narration moves abruptly from one person (the father), who is never heard of again, to another (the son), who has scarcely been mentioned before. No single crisis is engendered, and no crisis is solved. The Tung Yung story, though less loosely linked, is similar; nevertheless, it is on the edge of this group of stories. Another borderline story is the *shan-t'ing-erh* (E). The focus moves from the thieving servant to the merchant's daughter, and the servant is heard of no more. Another character, the knight-errant, appears out of nowhere. One might argue that the story has a unitary plot in that the merchant's dismissal of the dis-

---

[37] At various points, the work regards the Five Dynasties as a period of utter chaos from which the gods (and the first Sung emperor) delivered China, but this is merely a *pro forma* superstructure.

[38] A significant correlation with these results is supplied by oral literature. Five of the seven stories have counterparts in oral literature listed in the *Tsui-weng t'an-lu*. Only six of the remaining thirty-five short pieces of vernacular fiction have such counterparts. And fully five of these six belong to a distinct kind of story—the virtuoso.

[39] Cf. the references to oral literature at the beginning of the *Tsui-weng t'an-lu*.

honest servant leads directly to the kidnapping of the daughter, and that she is rescued only by the self-sacrifice of the knight-errant. But the arrangement of the plot scarcely supports this; loose ends are left, and the segments of the plot are very loosely linked.

There are no precise ways of describing the abstraction we call plot. In striving after definitions that will work in actual classification, one is inevitably driven to the use of metaphor, and mixed metaphor at that. The movement of the unitary plot "comes full circle," and so forth. It leaves no loose ends. It consists of the posing of a single kind of problem, the engendering of a single kind of crisis, and the solution of that problem or crisis. The linked-plot system, despite the fact that its segments are often potential unitary plots, is linear, not circular, in nature. It sometimes branches off from one character to another so that one hardly knows who is to be regarded as the main character of the work. Typically, it does leave loose ends. In the majority of cases, the line of the plot is biographical, and the sanction for the linked plots is nothing more than that they show the same person in action.

The broad distinction between "linked" and "unitary" is a distinction of form. The non-formal distinction which, allied with this, will set the two classes apart as genres is already implicit in what has been said so far. The seven works we have mentioned, like the longer "novels," are distinguished from the stories with unitary plots by the kind of hero they possess. Yang Wen is a warrior-hero in the spirit of his ancestors. Kuo Wei, Shih Hung-chao and Cheng Hsin are warrior-heroes or adventurers aided by the supernatural. Chao Cheng and his accomplices are, if we accept the comparison with the *Shui-hu chuan*, to be regarded as heroes. Although they are thieves, they are given precisely the same degree of approbation as some of the thieves and outlaws of the *Shui-hu*. The daring robberies, depending very often on the imaginative use of drugs, are features in both works. To be sure of the general point, one need only look at the *jou man-t'ou* 肉饅頭 incident in the Chao Cheng story; it is identical with the incident that occurs twice in the *Shui-hu chuan*,[40] and it has the same significance. The knight-errant of the *shan-t'ing-erh* story is a warrior-hero, even if the other characters in the same story are not.

---

[40] Chapters 17 (reported) and 27 of the 120-chapter editions.

Finally, the main characters of the Chang Ku-lao and Tung Yung stories either are from the beginning, or end up as, supernatural creatures.

In attempting to distinguish the *Chin P'ing Mei* from the novels that went before it, i.e., the linked works of this essay, I have had recourse to the notion of the lifesize character as contrasted with the larger-than-life character.[41] The characters of the *Chin P'ing Mei* were, on the whole, lifesize, as were many of the minor characters of the earlier novels; the main characters of those novels, on the other hand, were larger than life. This set of terms may be applied, in the same manner, to the characters of the linked work and the unitary work, respectively. However, the distinction between lifesize and larger than life is a fairly crude one, and deserves to be refined. There is a distinct advantage in substituting for it Northrop Frye's formulation of the scale of what he calls "modes" in narrative forms.[42] Much abridged, it consists of the following:

> Fictions, therefore, may be classified, not morally, but by the hero's power of action, which may be greater than ours, less, or roughly the same. Thus:
>
> 1. If superior in *kind* to other men and to the environment of other men, the hero is a divine being, and the story about him will be a *myth* in the common sense of a story about god. . . .
> 2. If superior in *degree* to other men and to his environment, the hero is a typical hero of *romance*, whose actions are marvellous but who is himself identified as a human being. . . .
> 3. If superior in degree to other men but not to his environment, the hero is a leader. He has authority, passions and powers of expression far greater than ours, but what he does is subject both to social criticism and to the order of nature. This is the hero of the *high mimetic* mode, of most epic and tragedy. . . .
> 4. If superior neither to other men nor to his environment, the hero is one of us: we respond to a sense of his common humanity, and

[41] "A Landmark of the Chinese Novel," *University of Toronto Quarterly* 30.3 (April, 1961), 325–335.

[42] *Anatomy of Criticism*, pp. 33–34. Frye goes on to make the observation (p. 50) that the more complex works of literature combine their modes, so that a character can be seen at various levels according to the viewpoint taken. Although this notion can be applied very successfully to certain works, in particular the *Chin P'ing Mei*, it is an elaboration for which there is no space in a short essay like this.

demand from the poet the same canons of probability that we find in our own experience. This gives us the hero of the *low mimetic* mode, of most comedy and realistic fiction. . . .

5. If inferior in power and intelligence to ourselves, so that we have the sense of looking down on a scene of bondage, frustration and absurdity, the hero belongs to the *ironic* mode. . . .

The advantages of this formulation are, first, that it provides a scale; indeed, the idea of a scale is more important than the particular gradations marked on that scale. Secondly, by defining his modes in terms of the powers of action of the hero instead of some other quality, Frye has enabled us to apply his idea to particular cases with less ambiguity.

On a scale of this kind, we can see at once that the linked works stand higher than the unitary works considered as a group. In my view, the linked works also stand higher than almost any one of the unitary works considered on its own. One result of this is that the heroes of the unitary stories can never be viewed in a tragic light; their heroes are almost always on the low mimetic or ironic scale.

The "demon" stories (17, 18, 19), which indubitably have unitary plots, may at first sight seem to be an exception. These are the stories in which a young man is first seduced and then threatened by a group of animal-spirits masquerading in human form. Of course, these stories are full of supernatural beings, but the whole point of them is that the hero is all too humanly powerless; he is as ineffectual as the reader himself would be, trapped in a like situation. The stories are designed to make the reader's flesh creep. Despite appearances, they are to be classed as low mimetic.

Our distinction between linked and unitary fiction has been based on what we can observe by reading the fiction itself, that is to say, by objective analysis. We have not made inferences based on the manner in which the works came to be written. But it is, of course, easy enough to see how the formal and the non-formal characteristics of the linked fiction came to be associated. It was the great hero, the man larger than life, who was too large a figure for any one of his adventures to exhaust. He was more than the connecting principle in a system of linked plots, he was the reason for the system in the first place. Character and plot stand in a basically different relation to each other in the linked fiction. The character is the primary thing, and the plots are the hero in action—the only way in which the hero can be revealed.

3.   *Kinds of Short Story Before 1550*

Among the stories with unitary plots—let us call them simply short stories from this point on—there are further distinctions to be made. Although they have not the scope of the distinctions made so far, they are comparable in character to the distinctions between genres. It scarcely matters whether the classes that result from the analysis are called genres or sub-genres.

In not all of the stories is the plot, as such, of the same importance. At the one extreme we have the story for which the plot is the main concern, for which the chain of cause and effect—whether true cause and effect or coincidence in the guise of cause and effect does not matter—is almost an obsession. Such stories seem to exist solely for the completion of the train of events which has been set in motion. At the other extreme, there is the story which indubitably has a unitary plot but in which the chain of cause and effect is not stressed, and in which the main interest lies in *some other thing*. Specifically, this other thing is either the virtuosity of the poet-hero, or the thematic value, as distinct from the plot value or narrative value, of the story.

There are twelve stories, numbered 1–11, 35 on the attached list of early stories, which may be classed as *virtuoso* pieces.[43] (Another name might be stories of preciosity.) In each of them the hero is a poet, in most cases an actual poet and not a fictional one. A large part of the function of many of these stories is to provide a context for the poems that the hero composes at will. The plot, such as it is, is that context and little more. The high points in the story do not really concern the plot, but rather the poet-hero's own existence, his reactions, es-

---

[43] There is a significant correlation with oral literature, as we have mentioned in note 38 above. Of the twelve "virtuoso" pieces, five have counterparts in the oral stories listed in the *Tsui-weng t'an-lu*. Only one of the remaining twenty-three stories has such a counterpart, and even that one is only a probable identification (Story 23). This means that, in terms of the extant works, the *Tsui-weng* list is related mainly to linked fiction and the virtuoso stories.

pecially his response in verse to the situation in which he is placed by the plot.

This kind of subject matter is not peculiar to the vernacular short story. It is much more common in the classical tale, and indeed some of these stories do have counterparts in Sung dynasty classical fiction.[44] The virtuoso stories tend to have fewer of the characteristics of formal realism, for example the complete physical and temporal setting, than do the other short stories. In language also, they are closer to classical fiction. This is not the place in which to try to work out a scale which would run from classical to vernacular, but as a simple rule of thumb, the distinction between the words which generally introduce direct speech will do. Narrative prose which is more vernacular uses *tao* 道; narrative prose which is more classical uses *yüeh* 曰. Of the twelve stories in the virtuoso group, eight make consistent, or at least frequent, use of *yüeh*,[45] while all but a couple of the twenty-three stories outside this group use *tao*. In keeping with their use of a more classical language, the virtuoso stories also emphasize the typical virtues of elegant concentration in prose.

If the function of the plot is the main formal characteristic of this group, its main non-formal characteristic is the kind of hero it has. The heroes are people of some importance, they are literati, and the "social affinities" of this class of fiction are with the literati, but only in the sense, let me hasten to explain, that the style of life and the supposed values of the literati are portrayed in it.[46] As fictional

[44] E.g., story No. 6 has a counterpart in the *Tsui-wang t'an-lu, jen* 王 *chüan* I, and story No. 9 has a counterpart in the *Ch'ing-so kao-yi* 青瑣高議 of Liu Fu 劉斧 (*pieh-chi* 別集 *chüan* 4). Much more important is the general affinity between the stories contained in these two works, as well as in the *Lü-ch'uang hsin-hua* 綠窗新話 and the virtuoso story. No study exists, to my knowledge, of the virtuoso classical tale in Sung, Yüan, and Ming times, important though it was. Such a study might well throw interesting light on the virtuoso story in the vernacular literature, and perhaps in the oral literature as well. Note that not all of these twelve are devoid of plot. Nos. 9 and 35, for example, contain a good deal of incident; both have potentially interesting plots. The interest, however, is not developed.

[45] The eight are: Nos. I, 2, 4, 6, 7, 9–11. No. 35 is uncertain. I do not have the text at hand and am depending on notes made some time ago, among which this point is not mentioned.

[46] The phrase is borrowed from Frye (p. 306), "the social affinities of the romance, with its grave idealizing of heroism and purity, are with the aristocracy." It is used here to mean something much less definite than the sociological group or groups from which author and audience come. It refers here to the style and life and the values of the literati, not necessarily as they were in actuality but as they were in the popular mind. "Social affinities," then, denotes a kind of subject supposedly characteristic of a social class together with a certain kind of tone or attitude toward that subject.

characters, the heroes stand somewhat higher on the mimetic scale than do the heroes of the other short stories. They have some ideal characteristics, and they have notable powers of expression.

There are two anomalous stories which share one or two of the features of the virtuoso story and may perhaps be mentioned here. They are the well-known story of Li Ts'ui-lien 李翠蓮 (12), and the *Ch'eng fo chi* 成佛記 (13). The most important part of the Li Ts'ui-lien story consists of her rhymed and patterned diatribes, while one important part of the other story consists of the girl's verse riddles, as she matches wits—and fists—with the local priests. The plot in each case is rudimentary, consisting mainly of a series of simple contexts which the girl turns into comic situations. Both stories, but particularly of course the latter, have religious significance.

The other kind of story which relegates the plot to a subordinate position is the *thematic* story, the story that concentrates on thematic rather than narrative values. The purpose of this kind of story is to demonstrate a moral example, to drive home a lesson. If such stories were reduced to the status of anecdotes, they would not lose all of their force, and this is perhaps why they make less use of the procedures of formal realism than some other groups of stories. Three stories may be considered to belong to this class (14, 15, 16), although it should be noted that the criteria for it are by no means as clear as for the virtuoso group. Story No. 14 contains a positive example of filial piety, and No. 15 an example of personal honesty. There is little attempt to create a temporal and physical setting, and the small springs of tension that normally make up a plot are noticeably missing. It may seem surprising to find the *Ho-t'ung wen-tzu* 合同文字 story classed as an exemplary tale, but the fact is that it excludes most of the details which might have contributed to the tension and which, in the Yuan play that uses the same stuff-material, give a rather different effect.[47] The third story, No. 16, is found as the

---

[47] Whereas in the play, the boy's aunt snatches away the contract, the sole evidence of his identity and his sole claim to a share in the estate, in the story she does not. The judge's verdict is, therefore, perfectly obvious. Because of this and other examples of greater interest in plot, it has usually been supposed that the play is based on the story. In fact, I believe it can be shown that the opposite is true, that the story derives fairly obviously from a play, not necessarily the extant one. Although it is not textually parallel to the play, the story breaks into sections just where the play breaks into acts. The dialogue is very close in substance, though not textually. Up to this point, one has no evidence as to which is based on which. But if one looks at the counterpart in the story to the beginning

prologue story attached to the linked narrative about Chao Cheng (A). It has not, I think, been pointed out that it also exists independently.[48] It is the only one of the three stories which provides a negative example. It can be taken at its face value as an exemplary tale which carries the grim warning that sudden and spectacular wealth is bound to bring ruin to the recipient. The last word is the executioner's, as he says to the hero: "Since you knew your wealth would destroy you, why didn't you give it away to others?" The edifying death of the hero's concubine only adds to the exemplary tone. In this story, as in the other two, the characters are fairly high on the mimetic scale.

4.   The Plot-Centered Story Before 1550

The short stories we have still to consider are those to which the value of the plot is central. There are eighteen such stories which are known to have been written before 1550. They are alike in that they all have unitary plots and in that their heroes are all on the low mimetic or ironic level.

The principal factor which divides these stories is that of the narrator's point of view. In the one kind, the point of view is that of "selective omniscience," to use the terrible expression that is in vogue.[49] While laying bare part of the situation, the narrator purports not to know the truth of the other part; in a typical case, he does not reveal that some trick or imposture in the story is in fact a

---

of Act III, one finds an unmistakable dramatic technique. The boy has set off home. Suddenly, the story switches to the uncle who, one day fifteen years later, chances to ruminate on the subject. In doing so, he tells us that he has married again. Then the story switches to his wife, who one day just happens to think of the relatives and to wonder what would happen if they returned. Then, of course, the boy knocks on the door. This is just what happens in the play at this point, except that we do not see the uncle; there is no need, for in the play he has taken a new wife before the action begins. Another possible indication of dependence on a play is the striking number of instances of the word *yün* 云 introducing direct speech. For example, in the part of the story that corresponds to Act III, it occurs ten times out of fifteen, excluding direct questions only. It is, of course, one of the common ways of introducing direct speech in the written texts of the drama.

[48] It is also found in various editions of the *Yen-chü pi-chi*. The *Pao-weng-t'ang shu-mu* entry has been connected with the *Yen-chü pi-chi* story, but it has not, to the best of my knowledge, been noticed that this story is the prologue to *Ku-chin hsiao-shuo 36*.

[49] Cf. e.g., Norman Friedman, "Point of View in Fiction: The Development of a Critical Concept," *PMLA*, 70.5 (December 1955), 1160–1184.

trick or an imposture. The climax of such stories is the moment of revelation. The other procedure is that of cards-on-the-table omniscience; the narrator knows everything that is germane to the plot and tells everything. However, he also goes further than this. Not only does he know everything, he positively glories in his knowledge and is tempted to predict what will follow. In the one case, the narrator betrays only partial knowledge and his narrative method stresses revelation. In the other, the narrator has full knowledge and his narrative method stresses prediction.[50]

The "revelation" procedure is found in two types of stories, the demon stories and one of the categories of crime stories. To some degree, it is also found in the two ghost stories. There are three demon stories, 17, 18, and 19, all of which are of the same general pattern, and two of which are so alike they may be said to have come from the same matrix. These two have identical features of plot, the young man who meets a beautiful girl, makes love to her, finds that she and her "mother" and her companions are in fact demons in human form, overhears someone being killed, is threatened with death, escapes and so forth. The reader is not told the true identity of the girl until the young man realizes it himself. These three stories clearly belong to a recognizable type, and they even have some of the same stock furniture.

Revelation does not play the same central part in the two ghost stories, 20 and 21, which hardly form a clearly recognizable type. The stories do, however, resemble each other to some degree. In each case, the ghost of the dead wife appears without its being realized that she is a ghost. And in each case, the story ends with the wife's ghost claiming the life of a husband who has been disloyal.[51]

The two crime stories that make use of revelation procedure are numbers 22 and 23. Both are remarkably ingenious works. The second story qualifies as one of the few real detective stories before the Ch'ing. The reason it qualifies, of course, is precisely that the

---

[50] The two procedures can be found together. For example, in the *Shui-hu chuan,* the chapter endings often function as prediction, while some of the stories, notably the theft of the birthday gifts, are narrated with the aid of the revelation procedure.

[51] Note that in story 20, the husband has given false evidence against his wife in order to save his own neck. This point is not clearly made at the end of the story when his own life is claimed.

Western notion of the detective story implies both selective omniscience in the author or narrator as well as revelation as an indispensable part of the plot. In the first story, we are not told that the
sending of the message is a trick by which to compromise an honest
woman; there is a certain amount of room for surmise, but, strictly
speaking, our knowledge is limited to that of the enraged husband.
The second story is also concerned with seduction. Again there is
ambiguity, but we are not told the identity of the woman's nocturnal
visitor. We are left to wonder whether he may be the supernatural
creature he claims to be. Both stories deal with examples of brilliant
trickery, and as if in recognition of his brilliance, neither criminal
appears in a particularly hideous light. We shall see the point of this
judgment in considering the next type of short story.

The omniscient "prediction" procedure is found in all of the
remaining eleven stories, numbers 24 through 34. The first ten of
these form a distinct group.[52] Typically, they consist of the working
out, before the reader's gaze, of the disastrous effects of some initial
act of folly or crime.[53] The narrator frequently intervenes after some
seemingly innocuous action and predicts, in general terms, the
consequences that will follow it. Many of the stories are studded with
half-a-dozen or more such predictions.[54] The reader feels, not the
mystification that the "revelation" stories induce, but a sense of
foreboding joined with an intense curiosity as to the precise form of
the outcome. The use of prediction appears also as an overriding
concern on the part of an omniscient author for the chain of cause
and effect. Although the causes given are sometimes no more than
coincidences, the effect is that of a tightly reasoned plot.

[52] The story that does not fall into this group is No. 34. It adopts the prediction procedure, but in other respects it is quite distinct from the other stories. It is a demon story in
subject, but not in type. There is a supernatural helper whom the reader knows about
from the beginning. This might seem to ally it to some of the linked stories, but it has, on
the whole, a unitary plot. The only part which might make us think it was a linked story is
the hero's suppression of a local bandit, an episode which has nothing to do with the rest of
the story.

The other stories are sometimes loosely called *kung-an* stories by other scholars, but this is
a misnomer. In some of them there is no trial at all, and in others it is of no significance.

[53] One of the stories, No 31, is set within the framework of supernatural causation. This
is probably not to be taken too seriously, for at the end it is reduced to a matter of opinion,
"when people of a later time discussed this affair," etc. Apart from the beginning, the story
is a perfect example of the type.

[54] Examples are: No. 25 with four, No. 26 with eleven, No. 27 with six.

This is the most numerous type of plot-centered story. It is remarkable also as the type of story for which it is hardest to find a parallel in classical fiction.[55] None of the stories has a complacent ending. One story ends with the hero's shriek of despair as he throws himself into the river. Almost all of the stories contain murders, and some contain several murders. One of the mildest is the *Chieh-chih-erh chi* 戒指兒記 No. 27, a story which is on the borderline of this group; all it can boast is the death of the love-stricken hero in the midst of his love-making. So used are we to thinking of the late-Ming story as typical of Chinese vernacular fiction that it is hard for us to realize that this stark kind of fiction is in fact the most significant kind of short story of the early period.

Stark it certainly is. Some of the stories read like the *Newgate Calendar*. Almost all of their characters are on the ironic level, not even on the low mimetic. The villains are the prisoners of their passions, locked within their lust or greed or bottomless frivolity. Story 24 in particular, and so some extent stories 29 and 31, are *intended* to be studies of ungoverned lust, perhaps nymphomania, whatever they may seem to the modern reader. Seductive and faithless woman as an agent of a man's ruin appears in most of these stories, but not all. Greed is the motivating force of story 28, physical love of 27, and frivolity, ostensibly at least, in the case of No. 33. Even the relatively blameless characters are shown in a harsh, intolerant light. The victims, whom we might expect to find pathetic, are often seen pejoratively. The victim of story 28, for example, might seem to deserve some sympathy. Certainly in a play which used the same stuff-material we would see a wholly innocent person. But Master Shen is shown to us as a spoiled son, a spendthrift, who wastes his time on frivolous pursuits. The first victim of story 33 is a completely ineffectual man, capable of playing a stupid

---

[55] These ten stories differ significantly from the other kinds in various ways. They are not closely related to classical fiction, as the virtuoso stories are. They are not closely related to early oral literature as the linked fiction and the virtuoso stories are. None of these ten has a counterpart listed in the *Tsui-weng t'an-lu*, as against five of the twelve virtuoso stories. In fact, if one considers stories that have possible sources, i.e. oral or written parallels before 1550, these stories differ markedly from the others. All seven of the linked stories mentioned have such sources. As many as nine of the twelve virtuoso stories have possible sources. Only two of these ten have possible sources; both of those are in the drama, and the claim is made below that those two stories are to be distinguished from the rest.

and cruel trick on his concubine. The hero of story 25 is a man who, heedless of all warnings, marries a prostitute who has no love for him. And the hero and chief victim of 26 first installs a concubine in his own household without his wife's consent, and then deserts both wife and concubine to dally with a courtesan in the capital.

It might be said that these stories give the anti-heroic view of life. But that would not be correct. What they show us is a purposive selection of events and people to support a pejorative view of life. Even the characters who cannot be described as stupid, brutal, venal or avaricious, are often belittled, as we have said, by some subtle means. It is impossible to see any of them in a pathetic, let alone tragic or noble, light. There is no one of the stature of Wu Sung to take on the role of avenger. Such avengers as there are are usually cuckolds or fools, whose bumbling act of vengeance is robbed of any ennobling quality. The hero of story 29, for example, the nearest approach to the figure of the righteous avenger, is both cuckold and fool. Following his wife to her house, he is trapped in the lavatory —significant detail!—and soundly beaten on the pretext that he is thought to be a burglar. Even then he does not realize the truth; he has to hear other people joking about the episode before he will take action. All the time he is exhorting himself to be a "real man" (*hao-han* 好漢). Despite his martyrdom at the end of the story, so redolent of the penultimate scene from a play, he is a poor creature, whose powers of action and intelligence are severely circumscribed.

Nevertheless, this story and No. 25, the hero of which is delivered from the consequences of his folly by an astute judge, do stand higher on the mimetic scale. Both men are diabolically schemed against, and this fact seems to outweigh that of their own stupidity. It amounts to historical explanation to say so, but it may well be significant that these stories are the only ones of the ten to have counterparts in the early drama.[56]

Two stories, Nos. 27 and 30, are on the edge of this group. Both stories are clearly of the same general type as the other eight, which may be characterized as "folly and consequences," but the main characters of both are on the low mimetic level rather than the ironic.

---

[56] None of the plays survive. For whatever is known of them, cf. the article by Wu Hsiao-ling, p. 454 and the *Ch'ing-p'ing shan-t'ang hua-pen* (T'an Cheng-pi, ed.), pp. 211–212.

It is probably no coincidence that both stories concern love affairs. Even so, in the two surviving texts of No. 27, one published by the Ch'ing-p'ing-shan-t'ang about 1550, the other in the *San yen* of the 1620's, we can notice a tendency to soften the starkness of the story. All six of the dire predictions of the earlier version have been cut out, together with some of the physical detail of the hero's death from sexual exhaustion. Instead, it is explicitly described as a "romantic story" (*feng-liu-ti shih* 風流的事) and a "lovely tale" (*chia-hua* 佳話).[57] Even the least pejorative of the "folly and consequences" stories was too harsh for the taste of the *San yen* editor. We shall return to the changes made in this story, as well as those made in No. 26, in the next section. But from these few details one can gain some hint of the differences between this kind of fiction and the typical late-Ming story.

5. *Some Historical Perspectives*

Genre classification tends to give an impression of greater uniformity than is justified. In fact, of course, there is a wide range of differences within the classes we have described, and it takes a systematic analysis to see that the members of each class can be grouped together.

Having made this reservation, we must still be surprised at the degree of uniformity that exists among these thirty-five stories, the only stories that we can confidently assign to the period before 1550.[58] There are kinds of story not found among them which, for many readers, are the Chinese short story in essence. There are no

---

[57] The rewritten version of story No. 1 even describes itself as a *feng-liu chia-hua*, cf. below.

[58] It is worth noting that, even if we had rashly accepted the references in the *Tsui-weng t'an-lu* as references to written literature, we should not have had to sacrifice very much of this uniformity. Sun (pp. 3–16) identifies thirteen stories in all from the *T'an-lu*, two for certain and eleven with some reservation. We have included seven of these already, the two certain ones and five of the possible ones, because written versions of them did exist before 1550. They are: D,11, 2, 7, 9, 35, C. The six remaining stories are: *Ku-chin hsiao-shuo 5; Ching-shih t'ung-yen* 10, 13, and 30; *Ch'u-k'e P'ai-an ching-ch'i* 初刻拍案驚奇 28 (prologue); story No. 6 (prologue). Of these six, KC5, TY 10, and both prologues are clearly to be classified as virtuoso stories; TY 13 is a "revelation" crime story; TY 30 begins like a demon story, ends like a fairy story. If these were added to existing numbers, we should have: 16 virtuoso; 4 demon (one of which is admittedly borderline); 3 crime revelation. There would be no increase in the "prediction" stories at all. Note that not all of Sun's identifications are acceptable even as to stuff-material.

love stories, for example, if we except a couple of virtuoso stories; there is not a single story that tells of love between a well-matched couple who triumph over difficulties. Again, with the exception of a virtuoso story or two, there is not a single story of a good-hearted singing-girl; singing-girls are invariably held to be the cause of some feckless man's ruin. Nor, again with the exception of one of the virtuoso stories, is there a story of a young man succeeding in the examinations and launching his career. For that matter, there is no story of a young man up for examinations and let loose in the great city.[59] There is not a single story of economic success; there is no patient artisan or tradesman who makes good and is able to rise in society. Nor—this *has* been remarked before—is there a single pornographic story.[60] Finally, there is no historical story, in the sense of a story in which events, characters and background— historical or intended to seem so—have a thematic value of their own.

Is one justified in assuming that because such types and subjects do not exist among the thirty-five, they did not exist at all in the short story of the early period? This is not an easy question to answer. On the one hand, the number of stories is probably large enough to support certain kinds of generalization. However, it will have been noticed that our two main criteria for the early stories were inclusion in the Ch'ing-p'ing-shan-t'ang collections or mention in the Pao-wen-t'ang catalogue. Our conclusions, therefore, were dependent on only two sets of circumstances, the editing of the former and the compilation of the latter. Furthermore, it can, I believe, be demonstrated that there is a correlation between the collections and the catalogue;[61] if so, this would reduce the two sets of circumstances to one. Thus a very small number of personal judgments may be responsible for our knowledge of the early short story. While this fact does not necessarily invalidate our conclusions, it cannot help but condition them.

[59] Except for No. 35, a virtuoso story.

[60] Cf. Cheng Chen-to, "Ming-Ch'ing," p. 376.

[61] Only five of the twenty-nine stories of the Ch'ing-p'ing collections are not listed in the Pao-weng-t'ang catalogue (cf. note 21 above). These five belong to one section and comprise the whole of that section. In addition, the arrangement in the *Pao-weng-t'ang shu-mu* of entries that refer to Ch'ing-p'ing stories is far from being a random one. Two or more such entries are listed next to each other on three occasions.

From the evidence provided by the thirty-five stories, then, we can deduce that the short story has a history of a clear-cut kind that has not been suspected before. Obviously, the dichotomy between *hua-pen* and *imitation hua-pen* that so dominates the histories of literature will not do; the latter is a term so vague it can mean almost anything, while the former rests on an assumption that cannot be proved. But, equally clearly, the theory of the static genre as outlined by Cheng Chen-to among others,[62] the theory that holds that the short story changed, if at all, only to become more bookish and more moralizing, simply does not fit the facts. Even in its early period, the short story consists of a number of genres or sub-genres. As we shall see, its history is full of change, whether it be interaction among its own genres, producing mutation or synthesis, or with those of the novel, linked or otherwise. The types and the subjects common among the later stories which we noted above are merely the roughest indication of the nature of these changes.

There is no point in trying to generalize in a few pages about the whole subsequent history of the short story. Unless the study is done with at least the degree of system and detail that was shown in Sections 3 and 4 above, it is not worth doing at all. Such a study must await a different occasion. All we can do here is to test our criteria against some of the seemingly new developments in vernacular fiction of the sixteenth and early seventeenth centuries, particularly in the novel *Chin P'ing Mei* and in the identifiably late stories among the *San yen* collections. We shall omit the *Lung-t'u kung-an* 龍圖公案 stories because of their specialized nature,[63] interesting though some of them are as specimens of fiction on the ironic level.

If we had set the terminal date of the early period at 1600 instead of 1550, and so included the *Chin P'ing Mei*, our analysis would have appeared very different. The main differences between linked and unitary fiction were found to be, on the formal level, a difference in plot, and on the non-formal level, a difference in mimetic scale. It would have been easy enough to distinguish the *Chin P'ing Mei*

[62] Cheng Chen-to, p. 364. This is not to deny that there is a lack of obvious technical experimentation, although there is more than is generally realized. However, there are no autobiographical tales, etc. In this obvious sense, the form of the classical tale was much freer.

[63] The *Hai Jui kung-an* 海瑞公案 stories are also omitted. Most of the crime-case stories that so flourished around the year 1600 are not vernacular fiction, however.

from the linked novel—its plot is not linked and its characters are low mimetic at best—but it would have required an extra step to distinguish it from the short story. The plot of the *Chin P'ing Mei* is unquestionably unitary. It is a remarkable plot in that it resolves for the first time in the Chinese novel the perpetual tension between the parts and the whole. In governmental terms, the relation between the superstructure and the parts of the Chinese novel may be anything from the centralized dictatorship of the *Hsing-shih yin-yüan chuan*, a novel with a short-story plot, to the near-anarchy of the *Ju-lin wai-shih*. But the plot of the *Chin P'ing Mei* is, nonetheless, radically different from the unitary plots of the short stories. Reverting, as one inevitably does, to metaphor to describe its plot, one tends to describe it not in terms of line or contour or even sequence, but of the close texture of daily life. The creeping pace of time passing is its great feature. And it is this closeness of texture, so perfectly suited to the novel's preoccupation with showing interpersonal relations comparatively and competitively,[64] that distinguishes it, on both formal and non-formal grounds, from the short story.

The main characters of the *Chin P'ing Mei* are, as we said, low mimetic at best.[65] But even this is a point of great significance for the later short story. In taking a couple of linked plots from the *Shui-hu chuan* and expanding one of them to nearly the full length of the novel, the author of the *Chin P'ing Mei* has changed the characters irrevocably. The larger-than-life character, Wu Sung, is expelled, literally and figuratively. The remaining characters, which in the *Shui-hu chuan* are on the ironic level, are raised to the level of the low mimetic. Sometimes there is a degree of ambiguity in the author's attitude, but in general there can be no doubt of the truth of this statement. From the moment that P'an Chin-lien sings her first dramatic soliloquy,[66] she ceases to be an ironic figure. The same may be said of Li P'ing-erh, whose death is attended with genuine pathos. Yet she is an adulteress and bears the main responsibility for her

[64] Cf. Hanan, "A Landmark of the Chinese Novel."

[65] To a novel like the *Chin P'ing Mei*, these notions should be applied in a more complex fashion (cf. note 42 above).

[66] In chapter 8.

husband's death. We can imagine how the early story would have dealt with her.

This is the most pervasive general difference between the stories of the two periods. Where the characters of the early plot-centered stories are presented pejoratively, the characters of the later stories are often sympathetic human beings within reach of pathos and even tragedy. It is nothing less than a general rise in mimetic level. The textual changes made in the *San yen* versions of stories 26 and 27 provide good evidence of this. The changes made in No. 27, slight though they are, are designed to reinterpret the story as a "romantic tale." In No. 26, an extra section has been added at the end, punishing the blackmailer and—much more important—softening the harsh judgment passed on the hero.[67] This latter story also makes an interesting contrast to a late story, *K'uang T'ai-shou tuan ssu-hai-erh* 況太守斷死孩兒; though the second story cannot be shown to have been influenced by the former, it has enough of the same elements of plot to arouse that suspicion.[68] The heroine is now on the low mimetic level, and her death is felt to be tragic.[69] It is scarcely

[67] Lévy, "Etudes," pp. 137–147, has reproduced materials from the modern edition by T'an Cheng-pi to show how much the *San yen* versions differ from the Ch'ing-p'ing versions. However, there is much more to the changes than can be shown by the mere counting of characters. As we have seen, the *San yen* version of No. 27 is nothing less than an attempt to reinterpret a "folly and consequences" story as a "romantic tale." The paragraph added to No. 26 is important mainly in that it partially exonerates the foolish hero. There is a comment right after this episode that gets to the heart of the matter. "When people told this story, they all held that, although Ch'iao Chün was a lecherous person, he had never actually harmed anybody. . . ." The important thing is to show in what direction the changes lead. This study still needs to be done for the stories as a whole. When it is done, we may be able to judge the *kind* of changes that have perhaps been made in other stories as well, stories of which no earlier version is extant.

[68] For a stimulating study of the later story, cf. C. T. Hsia, "To What Fyn. . . ." The similarities may be roughly listed as follows:

    a. a slight similarity in names: Ch'iu Yüan-chi/Ch'iao Yen-chieh; Yü-hsiu/Hsiu-ku.

    b. The villain (*p'o-lo-hu*) is described in much the same manner.

    c. In each case, a young servant is the seducer.

    d. He seduces maid or daughter as well.

    e. The villain has the body or the secret of the body's identity.

    f. The body is thrown into the river.

Note how in the later story, the emphasis is largely on the indictment of the blackmailer. This is the case only in the altered version of the other story.

[69] In the early story, there are two women, the wife and the concubine. The heroine of the second story combines some of the features of both women, although it is not suggested that she is derived from them in any significant sense. The point is that in the early story such a character did not exist.

necessary to elaborate this general argument. Characteristic figures like Tu Shih-niang 杜十娘,[70] whose death has the elements of tragedy in it, or the courtesan in the story of the oilseller,[71] or the women in the *Chen-chu shan* 珍珠衫 story,[72] or Yü-t'ang-ch'un 玉堂春,[73] are, in terms of the mimetic scale, new creations, quite inconceivable among the early stories.

In some later stories one fancies there is an effect on the plot, though no doubt it is misleading to think of abstractions like plot and character as entirely separate entities. Even in a story like that of Yü-t'ang-ch'un, one feels that the sympathies aroused by the main characters are beginning to dictate the course of the plot. These sympathies dictate that "everything comes out all right in the end," a fact which seems to disqualify some of these stories as the most serious kind of literature. This is the tendency which Edwin Muir, in a different context, describes thus: "The plot, in short, is in accordance with our wishes, not with our knowledge. . . . It is a fantasy of desire rather than a picture of life."[74] It seems as if this change accompanies the raising of the mimetic level, as if the characters escape from the iron laws of the "folly and consequences" story to fly to a kind of story without laws at all, except those dictated by the sympathies they themselves induce. During the course of this flight, we have some of the best of the short stories, that of Tu Shih-niang and the *Chen-chu shan*, for example. At its close we have, in some cases at least, the contrived situations and the ideal, lifeless types of the *ts'ai-tzu chia-jen* 才子佳人 story.

To return to the question of plot. The distinctions we drew between plot-centered and its opposite will not hold up in the later period. Even the stories with poet-heroes and the thematic stories have a concern for narrative values and for the procedures of formal realism. The rewriting of the story of Liu Yung, story No. 1, is a probable indication of the change that took place. Feng Meng-lung found the story offensive,[75] and it is not hard to see why; it is a poor

[70] *Ching-shih t'ung-yen* 32.

[71] *Hsing-shih heng-yen* 3.

[72] *Ku-chin hsiao-shuo* 1.

[73] *Ching-shih t'ung-yen* 24.

[74] *The Structure of the Novel* (new ed., London 1957) p. 23.

[75] The preface to *Ku-chin hsiao-shuo* by Lü-t'ien-kuan chu-jen 綠天館主人 describes it as such.

story, and it shows the poet in an ugly light. That it was rewritten to
show the poet in a more sympathetic light need not concern us;
what matters is that it was rewritten with a greater degree of circumstantial detail.[76]

The rise of a new kind of thematic story provides further evidence.
This is the kind of story that treats some historical or pseudo-
historical event as a matter of moral concern. Of course, concern
with political morality is evident in linked works such as the *Shui-hu
chuan* and the *San-kuo yen-yi,* but it is not found among the early short
stories. Either the stuff-material of those stories is below the level of a
public theme, or it is not treated as a public theme. (To give an
example from the drama, there is all the difference in the world
between the *Wu-t'ung yü* 梧桐雨 and the *Ch'ang-sheng tien* 長生殿,
though they have the same stuff-material: the former is a tragic play
which deeply affects two individuals only, the latter explicitly contrasts the claims of individual tragedy with those of public morality.)
This concern is evident among a number of later stories. What
distinguishes them even from the *Shui-hu* and the *San-kuo* is that they
deal, several of them, with the history of the relatively recent past.
The stories of Lu Nan 盧柟 and Shen Hsiang 沈襄, for example,[77]
deal with the Chia-ching period (1522–1566). (In the drama, the
Ming feng chi 鳴鳳記, which also deals with that period, has a
similar significance.)[78] What is noteworthy is that this new kind of
thematic story is quite unlike the earlier one. It stresses public
morality as distinct from private morality, and it is concerned with
the values of coherent plot and the procedures of formal realism.

The rise in mimetic level and the general concern for plot values
are the two main features that distinguish the later story. In fact,
most of the distinctions that were established among the early
stories have broken down. The alternative narrative methods of
"prediction" and "revelation" are no longer of much importance as
distinctions. We have seen that stress or lack of stress on plot values is
no longer a distinction either. The earlier distinctions have melted
away, and new syntheses have formed in their absence. The virtuoso
story reappears as a plot-centered story. At the same time, its social

---

[76] In *Ku-chin hsiao-shuo* 12.

[77] *Hsing-shih heng-yen* 29 and *Ku-chin hsiao-shuo* 40, respectively.

[78] Cf. article by Birch, above.

affinities are now shared with many stories, virtuoso and otherwise; this is why, in the list of types and subjects that the early story did not treat, we were continually saying "with the exception of a couple of virtuoso stories." The thematic story is now in a new guise; it has become a plot-centered story and even, in such a story as that of Lu Nan, a virtuoso story as well. Almost all of the barriers that separated the short stories seem to have gone.

In place of these distinctions, new ones will have to be drawn. That there are valuable distinctions to be made can hardly be doubted; some of the comparisons just made may indicate a little of what they are likely to be. But a fresh, comprehensive look at all of the later stories will be necessary. In such a study, considerations outside of those we have used here—for example the author's own voice as a "second voice" alongside that of the narrator, or the differences in perceived reality, the kind of social fact that is available to the writer—may have to be included. All one can be sure of is that any analysis of the later stories will appear very different from our classification so far.

Linked Stories

A.   宋四公大鬧禁魂張
     Sung Ssu-kung ta nao "Chin-hun" Chang   PWT, KC 36

B.   史弘肇龍虎君臣會
     Shih Hung-chao lung-hu chŭn-chʻen hui   PWT, KC15

C.   楊溫攔路虎傳
     Yang Wen "Lan-lu hu" chuan   PWT, CP

D.   鄭節使立功神臂弓
     Cheng Chieh-shih li kung shen-pi-kung   PWT, HY 31

E.   萬秀娘仇報山亭兒
     Wan Hsiu-niang chʻou pao shan-tʻing-erh   PWT, TY 37

F.   張古老種瓜娶文女
     Chang Ku-lao chung kua chʻŭ Wen-nŭ   PWT, KC 33

G.   董永遇仙傳
     Tung Yung yŭ hsien chuan   CP

Short Stories of the Early Period

1. 柳耆卿詩酒翫江樓記
   Liu Ch'i-ch'ing shih chiu wan Chiang-lou chi   PWT, CP

2. 風月瑞仙亭
   Feng-yüeh Jui-hsien-t'ing   PWT, CP

3. 五戒禪師私紅蓮記
   Wu-chieh Ch'an-shih ssu Hung-lien chi   PWT, CP

4. 夔關姚卞弔諸葛
   K'uei-kuan Yao Pien tiao Chu-ko   PWT, CP

5. 梅杏爭春
   Mei Hsing cheng ch'un   PWT, CP

6. 張生彩鸞燈傳
   Chang Sheng ts'ai-luan-teng chuan   PWT, Hsiung

7. 蘇長公章臺柳傳
   Su Chang-kung Chang-t'ai-liu chuan   PWT, Hsiung

8. 趙伯昇茶肆遇仁宗
   Chao Po-sheng ch'a-ssu yü Jen-tsung   PWT, KC 11

9. 宿香亭張浩遇鶯鶯
   Su-hsiang-t'ing Chang Hao yü Ying-ying   PWT, TY 29

10. 張于湖傳
    Chang Yü-hu chuan   PWT, Kuo
                                                           chüan 10

11. 錢塘夢
    Ch'ien-t'ang meng   PWT, prefaced
                                                           to 1498 edition
                                                           of *Hsi-hsiang chi*.
                                                           Facsimile edi-
                                                           tion in *Ku-pen
                                                           hsi-ch'ü ts'ung-
                                                           k'an*, First
                                                           Series, Peking,
                                                           1954.

12. 快嘴李翠蓮記
    "K'uai-tsui" Li Ts'ui-lien chi   PWT, CP

13. 花燈轎蓮女成佛記
    Hua-teng-chiao Lien-nü chʻeng fo chi   CP

14. 合同文字記
    Ho-tʻung wen-tzu chi   PWT, CP

15. 陰隲積善
    Yin-chih chi shan   PWT, CP

16. 綠珠墜樓記
    Lü-chu chui lou chi   PWT, *Yen-chü*
                                                          pi-chi, comp.
                                                          Lin Chin-yang
                                                          林近陽, *chüan* 8,
                                                          (KC 36 pro-
                                                          logue)

17. 西湖三塔記
    Hsi-hu san-tʻa chi   PWT, CP

18. 洛陽三怪記
    Lo-yang san-kuai chi   PWT, CP

19. 孔淑芳雙魚扇墜傳
    Kʻung Shu-fang shuang-yü shan-chui chuan   PWT, Hsiung

20. 崔待詔生死冤家
    Tsʻui Tai-chao sheng ssu yüan-chia   PWT, TY 8

21. 楊思溫燕山逢故人
    Yang Ssu-wen Yen-shan feng ku-jen   PWT, KC 24

22. 簡貼和尙
    Chien-tʻieh ho-shang   PWT, CP

23. 勘皮靴單證二郎神
    Kʻan pʻi-hsüeh tan cheng Erh-lang Shen   PWT, HY 13

24. 刎頸鴛鴦會
    Wen-ching yüan-yang hui   PWT, CP

25. 曹伯明錯勘贓記
    Tsʻao Po-ming tsʻo kʻan tsang chi   CP

26. 錯認屍
    Tsʻo jen shih   CP

27. 戒指兒記
    Chieh-chih-erh chi   CP

28. 沈小官一鳥害七命
    Shen Hsiao-kuan yi-niao hai ch'i-ming   PWT, KC 26

29. 任孝子烈性爲神
    Jen Hsiao-tzu lieh hsing wei shen   PWT, KC 38

30. 新橋市韓五賣春情
    Hsin-ch'iao-shih Han Wu mai ch'un-ch'ing   PWT, KC 3

31. 計押番金鰻產禍
    Chi Ya-fan chin-man ch'an huo   PWT, TY 20

32. 陸五漢硬留合色鞋
    Lu Wu-han ying liu ho-se hsieh   PWT, HY 16

33. 十五貫戲言成巧禍
    Shih-wu kuan hsi yen ch'eng ch'iao huo   PWT, HY 33

34. 陳巡檢梅嶺失妻記
    Ch'en Hsun-chien Mei-ling shih ch'i chi   PWT, CP

35. 鄭元和嫖遇李亞仙記
    Cheng Yüan-ho p'iao-yü Li Ya-hsien chi   PWT, *Yen-chü*
                                                      pi-chi, ed. Yü
                                                      Kung-jen
                                                      余公仁, *chüan* 7

Abbreviations

CP   Contained in collections published by Ch'ing-p'ing-shan-t'ang

Hsiung   Contained in *Hsiung-lung-feng ssu-chung hsiao-shuo* 熊龍峯
    四種小說

HY   Contained in *Hsing-shih heng-yen* 醒世恆言

KC   Contained in *Ku-chin hsiao-shuo* 古今小說

Kuo   Contained in *Kuo-se t'ien-hsiang* 國色天香

PWT   Mentioned in Pao-wen-t'ang catalogue

TY   Contained in *Ching-shih t'ung-yen* 警世通言 (Chien-shan-t'ang
    edition 兼善堂本)

The Military Romance: A Genre of Chinese Fiction

by C. T. Hsia

Students of traditional Chinese fiction have customarily divided historical novels into two categories: those which approximate the spirit and form of a popular chronicle and those which, despite their celebration of historical personages and events, make no pretensions to be serious history. Most, if not all, of the titles forming the latter category could be properly called military romances insofar as they tell of an individual, a family, a brotherhood, or a new dynastic team engaged in a large-scale campaign or a series of such campaigns. The popular chronicle, too, has frequent occasion to depict military engagements, but it rarely employs the language of fantasy which stylizes the battle scenes in a military romance. Nor does it concern itself with such engagements to the undue neglect of other matters of historical interest.

Even in a military romance, of course, the principal hero is given a good deal of biographical attention. We are told of his pre-military career, his friends and enemies, and his trials as a loyal servant of the throne. But sooner or later, the hero embarks upon a campaign, which tends to supplant him as the object of primary interest and beget a cluster of subsidiary themes relative to its prosecution. Preoccupation with warfare, then, is at once the principal characteristic of the military romance and the main cause for its failure to reach the status of serious fiction. It shares its fate with detective fiction, science fiction, and other such types of fiction in that its conventionalized overconcern with a special type of human activity has inevitably led to the neglect or stereotyped representation of ordinary human concerns and passions.

In the present paper I shall comment on several Yuan and Ming works of fiction essential to an understanding of the evolution of the genre and then proceed to describe its specific themes and concerns mainly with reference to romances about the T'ang-Sung periods dating from the Ming and Ch'ing. Since for most story cycles it is usually their latest versions that are most characteristic of the military romance, I shall dwell upon such works rather than their predecessors, which are as a rule more reflective of the tradition of oral storytelling or popular chronicle. Thus for the T'ang period I shall focus on *Shuo T'ang ch'ien-chuan* 說唐前傳 (hereafter abbreviated as *Shuo T'ang*), *Shuo T'ang hou-chuan* 說唐後傳 (commonly reprinted today under two consecutive titles as *Lo T'ung sao-pei* 羅通掃北 and *Hsüeh Jen-kuei cheng-tung* 薛仁貴征東), *Shuo T'ang cheng-hsi san-chuan* 說唐征西三傳 (better known as *Hsüeh Ting-shan cheng-hsi* 薛丁山征西, hereafter *Cheng-hsi*), and their sequels,[1] though, for comparative purposes, I shall have occasion to refer to such earlier works as *Ta-T'ang Ch'in-wang tz'u-hua* 大唐秦王詞話, *T'ang-shu chih-chuan* 唐書志傳, *Sui-T'ang liang-ch'ao chih-chuan* 隋唐兩朝志傳, *Sui-shih yi-wen* 隋史遺文, and the culminating title in this series of popular works characterized by their intermixture of history and legend,

[1] The direct sequel to *Cheng-hsi* is *Fan T'ang yen-yi chuan* 反唐演義傳, (cf. Sun, I, pp. 46–47), which features Hsüeh Kang 薛剛, Hsüeh Ting-shan's son, as hero. *Fen-chuang-lou ch'üan-chuan* 粉粧樓全傳 (Sun, I, p. 47; Liu, I, pp. 264–265) may also be considered a sequel as it depicts the adventures of the descendants of Lo Ch'eng 羅成 and other heroes of the early T'ang. In preparing this paper, I have consulted the popular Taiwan reprints of all the T'ang novels as well as the better Ch'ing editions available at the East Asian Library of Columbia University: *Hsiu-hsiang shuo T'ang ch'ien-chuan* 繡像說唐前傳 (如蓮居士編次, 京都文和堂藏版, 光緒戊寅新鐫); *Hsiu-hsiang shuo T'ang hou-chuan* (compiler, publisher, and date identical with those of the *Ch'ien-chuan*), comprising *Shuo T'ang hsiao-ying-hsiung chuan* 小英雄傳 and *Shuo T'ang Hsüeh-chia-fu chuan* 薛家府傳: *Shuo T'ang san-chuan* (full title: 新刻異說後唐傳三集薛丁山征西樊梨花全傳, 中都逸叟編次, 慶餘堂藏版); and *Hsiu-hsiang cheng-hsi ch'üan-chuan* 繡像征西全傳 (中都逸叟原本, 經元堂梓行, 道光庚寅年重鐫). The last item, another edition of which is described in Sun, I, pp. 45–46, is a hybrid work of forty chapters offering a condensed version of Hsüeh Ting-shan's expedition against the Hsi Liao (but differing in detail from *Cheng-hsi*) and over thirty chapters copied from *Sui T'ang yen-yi*. For bibliographic information on all these romances see Sun, I, pp. 44–47, and Liu, I, pp. 260–265. *Shuo T'ang ch'ien-chuan* was originally titled *Shuo T'ang ch'üan-chuan* 全傳; but since this title is now used to cover both the *Ch'ien-chuan* and *Hou-chuan*, I have avoided it in this paper. (A list of abbreviations used in the notes appears at the end of this chapter.)

Ch'u Jen-hu's 褚人穫 *Sui T'ang yen-yi* 隋唐演義.[2] Likewise, for the
Yüeh Fei 岳飛 saga I shall discuss Ch'ien Ts'ai 錢彩 and Chin
Feng's 金豐 *Shuo Yüeh ch'üan-chuan* 說岳全傳 (hereafter *Shuo Yüeh*)
rather than such earlier and more historic versions as *Ta-Sung
chung-hsing t'ung-su yen-yi* 大宋中興通俗演義.[3] The saga of Yang Yeh
楊業 (Yang Chi-yeh 楊繼業)[4] and his progeny, despite its continuing
popularity to the present day, has undergone no further development
as written fiction since the late Ming: accordingly, my attention will
be confined to two crude but highly influential embodiments of that
saga dating respectively from the Chia-ching (1522–66) and Wan-li
(1573–1619) periods: *Pei-Sung chih-chuan t'ung-su yen-yi* 北宋志傳
通俗演義 (hereafter *Pei-Sung chih-chuan*) and *Yang-chia-fu shih-tai*

[2] *Ta-T'ang Ch'in-wang tz'u-hua* is available in a photolithographic edition published by
Wen-hsüeh ku-chi k'an-hsing she (Peking, 1956). I have consulted on microfilm the rare
copies of *T'ang-shu chih-chuan t'ung-su yen-yi* and *T'ang-chuan yen-yi* 唐傳演義 (for data see
Sun, II, pp. 34–38) as well as *Sui-shih yi-wen*. Unfortunately, the microfilm copy of the last
title, preserved in Waseda University, contains only sixteen of its sixty chapters (ch. 1–10,
31–33, 51–52, 55). These microfilm copies were originally made by Professor James I.
Crump for the University of Michigan Library. The East Asian Library of Columbia
University now owns a duplicate set; it also owns a Xerox copy of *Sui T'ang liang-ch'ao
chih-chuan* (Sun, II, pp. 38–41), made from a Xerox copy in the possession of Professor Liu
Ts'un-yan. This work should perhaps be more appropriately known as *Sui T'ang liang-
ch'ao shih-chuan* 史傳, the title that decorates the table of contents as well as the first page of
most *chüan*. The preface by Yang Shen 楊慎 identifies the novel as *Sui T'ang shih-chuan*,
while that by Li Han 林瀚 designates it as *Sui T'ang chih-chuan*.

[3] For data on *Ta-Sung chung-hsing yen-yi*, see Sun, II, pp. 31–32. Again I have availed
myself of the microfilm copy originally prepared by Professor Crump. In addition to a
Hong Kong reprint of *Shuo Yüeh*, I have consulted a Chia-ch'ing edition of *Shuo Yüeh
ch'üan-chuan* (full title: 新鐫精忠演義說本岳王全傳) in the East Asian Library of Columbia University. This large-size edition of 1798 is definitely more valuable than the small-
size edition of 1801 described in Liu, I, p. 273. It carries the presumably identical preface
by Chin Feng, but its eighty chapters are divided into 20 *chüan*, each *chüan* consisting of
four chapters.

[4] Yang Yeh is better known as Yang Chi-yeh since he is so identified in Peking operas.
The notes appended to the biography of Yang in *Sung shih* 宋史, *chüan* 272 (*ES*, p. 5229),
cite one standard source which gives Yang's original name as Liu 劉 Chi-yeh and another
which declares it to be Yang Chung-kuei 楊重貴. Since even the standard histories are in
disagreement about Yang's name and origin, the biographical account given in *Yang-
chia-fu yen-yi* (see n. 5) may be of genuine value as history. According to this source, a
younger sister of Liu Chün 劉鈞, King of the Northern Han, was married to Hsüeh
Chao 薛釗 and had a son by name of Chi-en 繼恩. Because Liu Chün had no son of his
own, he adopted Chi-en. Later, Liu's sister married Ho Yüan-yeh 何元業 and had two
sons, Chi-yüan 繼元 and Chi-yeh 繼業, who were also adopted by Liu Chün. When Liu
Chi-en became king, Chi-yeh soon distinguished himself as a general, especially for his
repeated successes in repulsing the Sung forces sent to subdue the Northern Han. When
Chi-yeh finally surrendered, he was given the new name Yang Yeh by Emperor T'ai-
tsung. According to this account, then, the famed general was first called Ho Chi-yeh,
then Liu Chi-yeh, and finally Yang Yeh.

chung-yung t'ung-su yen-yi 楊家府世代忠勇通俗演義 (hereafter *Yang-chia-fu*), with a preface by Chi Chen-lun 紀振倫.[5] In contrast, the Ti Ch'ing 狄青 novels to be discussed in this paper, viz. *Wu-hu p'ing-hsi* 五虎平西 (hereafter *P'ing-hsi*), *Wu-hu p'ing-nan* 五虎平南 (*P'ing-nan*) and *Wan-hua lou* 萬花樓, are publications of the Chia-ch'ing period (1796–1820). It was at this time that the saga of Ti Ch'ing first received full-scale fictional treatment, although it was mentioned as a subject for storytellers in Lo Yeh's 羅燁 *Tsui-weng t'an-lu* 醉翁談錄 and subsequently embodied in drama.[6] With the exception of *Yang-chia-fu* all the above-mentioned military romances remain very

[5] Because only the front matter of *Pei-Sung chih-chuan* (Sun, II, pp. 43–46; Liu, I, pp. 268–269), including the table of contents, is available on microfilm at Columbia, I have consulted in its stead mainly the Tao-kuang edition of *Pei-Sung chin-ch'iang ch'üan-chuan* 北宋金鎗全傳, which, according to Sun, I, p. 49, is identical in text. This work survives in Taiwan in a highly corrupt, abridged version known as *Pei-Sung Yang-chia-chiang* 北宋楊家將 (Tainan, Ta-tung shu-chu, 1966). The Library of Congress has a microfilm copy of the Wan-li edition of *Yang-chia-fu* (Sun, I, p. 52; Liu, I, pp. 269–270). The title page identifies the work as *Yang-chia-chiang yen-yi* while Chi Chen-lun's preface designates it as *Yang-chia t'ung-su yen-yi*. It is uncertain whether Chi was also the editor or compiler of the work. The Wan-li edition credits him with the role of *chiao-yüeh* 校閱, while another version of *Yang-chia-chiang yen-yi* (Liu, I, p. 271) identifies him as editor (*pien-chi* 編輯). But judging by Liu Ts'un-yan's description of the work, I am positive that it is far more identifiable with *Pei-Sung chih-chuan* than with the Wan-li edition of *Yang-chia-fu*, which I have seen on microfilm. The latter is not available in reprint form in Taiwan or Hong Kong, and presumably it has been long out of print even in mainland China.

In addition to popular Taiwan reprints, I have consulted the Ching-lun-t'ang edition of *Ti Ch'ing yen-yi* 狄青演義 at Columbia's East Asian Library, comprising *Hsiu-hsiang wu-hu p'ing-hsi ch'ien-chuan* 狄青演義 征取珍珠旗、繡像五虎平西全傳. 經綸堂藏坂) and *Hsiu-hsiang wu-hu p'ing-nan hou-chuan* (狄青演義、楊文廣掛帥、繡像五虎平南後傳. 經綸堂藏版). Sun K'ai-ti has seen the Ching-lun-t'ang edition of *P'ing-hsi* but not that of *P'ing-nan*. In the Columbia set, both novels still maintain their separate prefaces and tables of contents. To my great regret, I have not been able to consult a Ch'ing edition of *Wan-hua lou* (fuller titles: 萬花樓楊包狄演義 and 後續大宋楊家將文武曲星包公狄青萬花樓初傳), but the two contemporary reprints I have used (Hong Kong, Kuang-chih shu-chü, n. d.; Tainan, Ta-tung shu-chü, 1965) are identical in text and appear not to have deviated from Ch'ing editions. For data on the Ti Ch'ing novels see Sun, I, pp. 53–54; Liu, I, p. 272; and the article "*Wan-hua lou*," in Cheng Chen-to 鄭振鐸, *Chung-kuo wen-hsüeh yen-chiu* 中國文學研究, vol. 1 (Peking, Tso-chia ch'u-pan-she, 1957).

Tsui-weng t'an-lu, ch. 2, refers to Chu-ko Liang 諸葛亮 and Ti Ch'ing in the same couplet, which would seem to indicate the popularity and magnitude of the story cycle about the Sung general: "三國志諸葛亮雄材, 收西夏說狄青大略." We know that *Shuo Ti Ch'ing* 說青狄 once existed as a *yuan-pen* 院本 play of the Chin-Yuan period. The Yuan *tsa-chü Ti Ch'ing fu-to yi-ao-ch'e* 狄青復奪衣襖車 is extant, though Wu Ch'ang-ling's 吳昌齡 play *Ti Ch'ing p'u-ma* 狄青撲馬 has been lost. *P'ing-nan chuan* 平南傳, about Ti Ch'ing's pacification of the South, was a theatrical spectacle often performed in the inner palace of Ch'ing emperors. See Ch'en Ju-heng 陳汝衡, *Shuo-shu shih-hua* 說書史話 (Peking, Tso-chia ch'u-pan-she, 1958), pp. 69–70.

popular, and they provide a double advantage for discussion in that, if we add *Shui-hu chuan* 水滸傳, the romances about the Sung generals form as much an unbroken period of history as the romances of the T'ang and that, since their dates of first publication are at least roughly ascertainable, they enable us to chart the evolution of the genre with some degree of assurance.

With the exception of *Shui-hu chuan* and *Feng-shen yen-yi* 封神演義 (though they are usually categorized under different genres),[7] the military romance has received little scholarly attention. But it is usually neglected for the wrong reasons. Ch'ing scholars have frequently called attention to the absurd distortions of history to be seen in military romances,[8] and the prejudice still prevails insofar as the more reliable chronicles are invariably regarded with greater critical respect. But in departing from history, the military romancers are not so much willfully ignorant of history (though many of them, I would gather, were not well educated) as obedient to the dictates of the genre. To judge the military romance by the standards of history is to misapprehend its character. I would maintain that the genre has suffered as a whole not because it has failed the demands of history, but because it has failed to explore fully its possibilities as fiction.

Even the popular chronicle, of course, has to be ultimately judged by the standards of fiction. Like the military romance, it draws to a significant extent upon a common heritage of hero-legends irrespective of whether these legends already existed in a written form or remained in a fluid state as oral tradition, and it has to aim at fullness of fictional detail if it is to rise above being a mere recompilation of available historical facts in more popular language. *Tung Chou lieh-kuo chih* 東周列國志, a most reliable chronicle, has been deplored precisely for its dry recital of crowded facts which leaves no room for the vivid re-creation of character and event. *San-kuo-chih yen-yi*, on the other hand, is highly praised because it

[7] Thus in *Chung-kuo hsiao-shuo shih-lüeh* 中國小說史略 Lu Hsün lists *Shui-hu* among works of *chiang-shih* 講史 and *Feng-shen yen-yi* among *shen-mo hsiao-shuo* 神魔小說 Sun K'ai-ti agrees with Lu Hsün in identifying *Feng-shen* as a *ling-kuai hsiao-shuo* 靈怪小說, but places *Shui-hu* under the *hsia-yung* 俠勇 category of *Shuo kung-an* 說公案.

[8] See comments culled from various sources on nearly all military romances in K'ung Ling-ching 孔另境, ed., *Chung-kuo hsiao-shuo shih-liao* 中國小說史料 (Taipei, Chung-hua shu-chü, 1957).

frequently meets the challenge of fiction. In narrating such events as the Battle of Red Cliff and Liu Pei's 劉備 three visits to Chu-ko Liang's 諸葛亮 retreat, Lo Kuan-chung 羅貫中 has first of all employed the arts of fiction to create an illusion of reality (and in this respect the good novelist is no different from the good biographer or historian), and secondly, he has drawn upon legend and folklore. Though logically there is no reason why the legendary material should be so favored, in nearly all good historical novels it is this material which has received the most extensive elaboration.[9] It seems that unless he had received a historical episode in a legendary form, the chronicler could not on his own initiative develop it at great length.

The tendency to elaborate upon legendary material can equally be observed in the military romance. Though their source materials differ to the extent that the chronicler relies far more upon official and anecdotal history than the military romancer, the latter is also at his best when, in his portrayal of a hero, he can draw upon a legend of human significance. The legendary hero is usually idealized: he is braver and more virtuous than his historic counterpart and he comes upon stranger adventures and suffers worse tribulations at the hands of blacker villains. But to a reader of fiction, it matters little whether a given legend agrees or disagrees with the hero's official biography; what matters is that, thanks to the rich mytho-realistic episodes provided by the legend, the hero may emerge as a real person in a real setting even though his character

[9] For many historical novels, of course, it is difficult to tell whether their authors are elaborating on a legend in their own words or merely copying an old text which had been lost or to which few scholars have access. Thus, read on its own, *Sui T'ang yen-yi* is an excellent novel, and I have accordingly lavished praise on its treatment of the legend of Ch'in Shu-pao 秦叔寶 in *The Classic Chinese Novel* (New York, Columbia University Press, 1968), p. 342. In the summer of 1970, however, Mr. Robert E. Hegel, who is completing a dissertation on *Sui T'ang yen-yi* and its sources under my supervision, alerted me to the fact that the first fifty chapters of the novel are nearly all copied from either *Sui-shih yi-wen* or *Sui Yang-ti yen-shih* 隋煬帝艷史 (see Sun, I, p. 43; Liu, I, pp. 259-260). My subsequent reading of *Sui-shih yi-wen*, which itself is an adaptation of an old source now lost, has confirmed his discovery that the whole legend of Ch'in Shu-pao contained therein has been copied, for the most part verbatim, into Ch'u Jen-hu's novel. On the evidence of such wholesale copying, *Sui-T'ang yen-yi* would seem to forfeit much of its intrinsic merit, though it will continue to be enjoyed as one of China's best novels. There can be no doubt, of course, that Ch'u Jen-hu is a most skillful adapter who was able to improve his sources beyond recognition: cf. the essay "*Yi-tse ku-shih, liang-chung hsieh-fa*" 一則故事，兩種寫法, in *Hsia Tsi-an hsüan-chi* 夏濟安選集, Taipei, Chih-wen ch'u-pan-she, 1971.

may in the process become simplified. Since the hero's official biography usually contains little information about his childhood and youth, the legend is of special service to the romancer (as to the chronicler) in investing his early years with an abundance of incident and detail. Little wonder that in most romances and chronicles the youthful adventures of the hero provide the most compelling narrative. (The military romancer was often a legend-maker in his own right. If his hero had attracted little folkloric attention, he could borrow episodes from other hero-legends and concoct a biography of his youth which, if it were not too synthetic, could in time become accepted as a legend.)

In a military romance, however, once the hero has emerged from obscurity, his career tends to be stereotyped since it is now mainly identified with military action. (In a good chronicle, a hero's historical career can be as interesting as his legendary youth.) Committed to a recital of his military exploits, the author now has to provide the details of a campaign for which neither the historical nor the legendary sources provide sufficient information. He must invent the circumstances of every battle, but usually his inventions betray a derivative character. I suppose it was the dynastic story-tellers who first conventionalized the description of warfare to be seen in Chinese fiction, though the conventional battle, insofar as it focuses attention on two warriors in a stylized combat, also betrays the influence of the stage representation of military engagements.[10] In their subsequent inventions and innovations, the military romancers have further exaggerated the conventional character of warfare in the direction of fantasy.

In a military romance, therefore, two types of material wrap around the core of historical truth: legendary and fantastic. If the hero-legend opposes good and evil in an unambiguous conflict and simplifies history in the direction of melodrama, the campaigns themselves embellish history in the spirit of fantasy. The two modes

[10] For a description of the early Chinese military opera see James I. Crump, "The Elements of Yuan Opera," *Journal of Asian Studies*, XVII, No. 3 (May 1958), pp. 431–433. Ming cognoscenti of fiction were themselves aware of the indebtedness of historical novels to the theater. Thus in his preface to *P'ing-yao chuan* 平妖傳, Chang Wu-chiu 張無咎 dismisses novels about the Seven Warring States, Han, T'ang, and Sung periods as bad plays of the Yi-yang 戈陽 school (Sun, II, p. 93). Unlike the more refined *K'un-ch'ü*, Yi-yang Opera is known among other things for its emphatic use of drums and gongs and for its acrobatics and mock representation of battle.

do not necessarily mix. If the plots hatched by a villain to trap a hero make for good melodrama, the fantasy of warfare disrupts that melodrama to the extent that the hero will be for the duration engrossed in the military business at hand. To the author of a standard military romance, the legends and intrigues prepare for, and provide a diverting respite from, the campaigns, which are regarded as the main attraction of his work; but to a modern reader less impressed by fantastic warfare, it is precisely the lengthy campaigns which prevent the author from developing to the full the melodramatic potential of the hero-legend. By the Chia-ch'ing period, when the author of *P'ing-hsi* subordinates military fantasy to melodrama in full realization that melodrama is intrinsically more exciting than the specialized kinds of interest warfare offers, he is effecting the transformation of the military romance.

I.   *The Early Romances; Magic Warfare*

If the six extant *p'ing-hua* of the Yuan dynasty are fairly representative of the oral narrators of history in their subject-matter if not in their artistry, then it would seem that the split between popular chronicle and military romance had become apparent long before any novel was compiled or printed. These *p'ing-hua* fall into at least three types of narrative. *Ch'in ping liu-kuo p'ing-hua* 秦併六國平話 is a popular chronicle with a military emphasis, but it conforms to the outline of the known facts of history with minimal stylization in the direction of a military romance. *Wu-tai-shih p'ing-hua* 五代史平話, while also a military chronicle, pays particular attention to the legendary youth of its several prominent heroes (this emphasis remains characteristic of subsequent narratives of the Five Dynasties period as witness the long recital of Chao K'uang-yin's 趙匡胤 career prior to his accession to the throne in both *Nan-Sung chih-chuan* 南宋志傳 and *Fei-lung ch'üan-chuan* 飛龍全傳).[11]   *Yüeh Yi t'u-*

---

[11] It is curious that, with the long tradition of storytellers specializing in the Five Dynasties period, there should have been no full-scale military romance about this colorful era. It would certainly seem that by the late Ming popular interest in the period had waned. The extant *Ts'an-T'ang wu-tai ch'üan-chuan* 殘唐五代全傳 (Liu, I, pp. 266–267), attributed to Lo Kuan-chung 羅貫中, is a crude chronicle containing elements of an incipient military romance. Actually, by limiting my examples to the T'ang-Sung romances and a few other works, I have not slighted any major military romances with the possible exception of the novels about the rise of the Ming. For data on the latter see Sun, I, pp. 56–58. and Liu, I, pp. 273–276.

Ch'i ch'i-kuo ch'un-ch'iu hou-chi 樂毅圖齊七國春秋後集, however, is already a pure if embryonic military romance with its emphasis on magic warfare and its total disregard of historical accuracy in its recital of the career of Sun Pin 孫臏 after his cruel mutilation by his rival in military wizardry, P'ang Chüan 龐涓 The *ch'ien-chi* 前集 of *Ch'i-kuo ch'un-ch'iu*, which must have been about their feud, is unfortunately not extant, but on the evidence of a later military romance, *Sun P'ang yen-yi* 孫龐演義 it must have been fully as fantastic as its sequel. *Wu Wang fa Chou p'ing-hua* 武王伐紂平話, too, is notable for its tendency toward military romance.[12]

Judging by the inadequate evidence of these *p'ing-hua,* then, it would seem that, whereas storytellers were relatively restrained in their embellishment of history for well-documented periods like those of the Three Kingdoms and Five Dynasties, they, like the romancers after them, tended to resort to wholesale invention of a fantastic character in their treatment of shadowy periods or celebrated figures about whom there is actually little historic information. And though we cannot be sure how much of that invention was actually folklore, the storytellers appeared especially fond of assigning fantastic deeds to characters long identified in the popular mind for their prescience and magic powers (Sun Pin, Chiang Tzu-ya 姜子牙, and, to a lesser extent, Chu-ko Liang 諸葛亮). To account for their wizardry, *Ch'i-kuo ch'un-ch'iu hou-chi* assigns to Sun Pin and P'ang Chüan a common teacher, the celestial Kuei-ku-tzu 鬼谷子. The latter thus appears to be an archetypal figure since in subsequent romances about the T'ang and Sung, many heroes would undergo a period of celestial tutelage before rising to fame on the battlefield.

To turn from *p'ing-hua* to novel-length fiction, we must first reckon with *San-kuo-chih t'ung-su yen-yi* 三國志通俗演義. It was the earliest novel to appear in print, and scholars are agreed that, of all the romances traceable to the authorship of Lo Kuan-chung 羅貫中, it bears the closest resemblance to his original version. Though a popular chronicle in form and intent, the work contains elements of the military romance and must have proved highly useful to later military romancers as the first complete manual of conventional

---

[12] Liu, II, ch. 2, gives a complete translation of the work with notes on its connections with *Feng-shen yen-yi.*

(i.e., non-supernatural) warfare. In the novel a general exchanges blows with another and may adopt certain ruses to overpower him. Aside from pitched battles, one may stealthily conduct a night attack or stage an ambush at a narrow pass where enemy troops will have little chance to escape. The military counselor (*chün-shih* 軍師) plans somewhat more advanced forms of strategy. Chu-ko Liang, the paragon of all counselors, however, at times resorts to magic or invokes supernatural aid, as do the sorcerers (leaders of the Yellow Turbans) and barbarians (Meng Huo 孟獲 and his allies). It is noteworthy that the later romancers gave the freest rein to their imagination when describing warfare involving precisely such counselors, sorcerers, and barbarian chieftains of magic power.

These romancers, however, have not enlarged the stock of conventional tricks and stratagems to be seen in *San-kuo;* nor have they advanced beyond the conventional realism of its battle scenes, though in some romances with descriptive passages in verse, especially the undeservedly neglected *Ta-T'ang Ch'in-wang tz'u-hua,* that conventional realism is decked out in pageantry and charged with considerable excitement.[13] On the whole, descriptions of battle remain stereotyped in later romances, though their authors have considerably enhanced the prowess of their warriors and diversified their weaponry.

Compared with *San-kuo, Shui-hu chuan,* another work traceable to Lo Kuan-chung, shows a far wider gap between realism and fantasy. Its early chapters detail the pre-Liangshan careers of individual heroes with realistic distinction, and if it had continued in the picaresque vein, it would not have become a military romance. But as it is, it is far more a military romance than *San-kuo* since by chapter 33 it begins to depict in earnest the Liangshan band's major military operations, at first against and then for the government. Even though two of its expeditions—against T'ien Hu 田虎 and

[13] Cf., particularly, Ch'in Shu-pao's duels with Yü-ch'ih Kung 尉遲恭 in ch. 29–30. The battle by the Mei-liang River 美良川 (美梁川 in *Ch'in-wang tz'u-hua*) which sees Ch'in desperately trying to save Li Shih-min 李世民 from Yü-ch'ih's hands is a high point in all subsequent chronicles about the Sui-T'ang period. Even Hsiung Ta-mu's *T'ang-shu chih-chuan,* usually a pedestrian narrative, gives an animated account of the battle in *chüan* 4, sections 31–33, which must have been written under the influence of the story-tellers. The author of *Shuo T'ang,* a military romance, has deliberately mocked the battle. It would be instructive to make a comparative study of the battle from the pageantry of *Ch'in-wang tz'u-hua* to the intentional parody of *Shuo T'ang.*

Wang Ch'ing 王慶 —are later additions written under the influence
of other military romances, the campaigns that take place before
chapter 71 are already none too distinguished and cater to an
audience which finds the depiction of war intrinsically satisfying even
in the absence of other types of serious interest. The novel makes use
of all the standard ruses and stratagems seen in *San-kuo* and places
greater stress on the magical element. It further widens the split
between muscle and brains (already noticeable in *San-kuo*) by
having Wu Yung 吳用 and Chu Wu 朱武, inheriting the mantle of
Chu-ko Liang, map out each battle to be fought by the brave heroes.
Among its other features copied by later military romancers are the
close bond between the suffering hero of unshaken loyalty (Sung
Chiang 宋江) and his rowdy companion of anarchic temper (Li
K'uei 李逵), and the idea that, when the government is dominated
by corrupt ministers, it is not dishonorable to occupy a mountain
and turn bandit.[14]

Both *San-kuo-chih t'ung-su yen-yi* and the Kuo Hsün 郭勳 edition of
the 100-chapter *Shui-hu chuan* were printed in the Chia-ching period.
In view of the large quantity of novels produced subsequently
during the Ming, it is understandable that modern scholars have
begun to assess individually only such famous titles as *Hsi-yu chi*
西遊記, *Chin P'ing Mei* 金瓶梅, and *Feng-shen yen-yi*. Especially, the
many works of historical fiction, with all their competing versions,
are still awaiting critical attention, despite the pioneering efforts of
such scholars as Sun K'ai-ti and Liu Ts'un-yan to straighten out
their bibliographic data. And since this body of historic fiction has
earlier appeared as topics for storytellers in *Tsui-weng t'an-lu* and
provided themes for Yuan and Ming *tsa-chü* 雜劇, the task of evaluation is rendered more difficult by the need to study it in comparative
terms with reference to an oral tradition informing both written
fiction and drama.

[14] For a study of Sung Chiang and Li K'uei as a double character cf. *The Classic Chinese
Novel*, pp. 106-114. Later in the paper I maintain that the saga of the Yang family must
have influenced the formation of the *Shui-hu* story. Perhaps even the idea of honorable
banditry had first appeared in the Yang saga. After the treacherous minister Wang Ch'in
王欽 (see n. 37) has assigned old and decrepit troops to Yang Yen-chao to guard Mt.
Chia 佳山, Yang rebuilds his strength by recruiting bandits, prominently Meng Liang
孟良 and Chiao Tsan 焦贊. Soon after, when Yang Yen-chao gets into trouble and has to
live in hiding, nearly all his lieutenants turn to banditry in the mountains. Cf. *Yang-chia-
fu, chuan* 2-4.

Nevertheless, through all this period of growth for historic fiction, we may single out for honor the name of Hsiung Ta-mu 熊大木 (Hsiung Chung-ku 熊鍾谷), an industrious author and editor of the Chia-ching period. He stood squarely in the tradition of Lo Kuan-chung and, in the absence of reliable information concerning the interim period, he must be regarded as a worthy successor responsible for a large body of historical and pseudo-historical fiction, much of it traceable in earlier form to Lo. *T'ang-shu chih-chuan, Nan-Sung chih-chuan, Pei-Sung chih-chuan,* and *Ta-Sung chung-hsing yen-yi* are all his compilations. An examination of these works on microfilm leads me to the belief that Hsiung was a popular historian who genuinely wanted to edify the less educated public (including juvenile readers) of his time. By and large he adhered to history, though legendary material that would enhance narrative interest was freely admitted. In comparison with *Shuo Yüeh,* a military romance in the ripe manner, *Ta-Sung chung-hsing yen-yi* appears a remarkably sober narrative of history, and since no precedents to this work are known, Hsiung was most probably its original author.

There is, however, one exception to my description of Hsiung's work: *Pei-Sung chih-chuan,* which has all the features of a military romance. According to Hsiung's preface, it has incorporated a work given in short title as *Yang-chia-fu,* among other unspecified romances (*chuan* 傳). Hsiung must have used this because there was no detailed historic record of the Yang family to fall back on, and the Wan-li edition of *Yang-chia-fu* must also have been an adaptation of the same old source, in all probability a more faithful one, though we cannot know whether the Taoist idea of abjuring government service to cultivate oneself, conspicuous in the new work but absent from *Pei-Sung chih-chuan,* also informs that version.[15] A full comparison of

[15] It is common knowledge that Yang Yeh's fifth son Yen-te 延德 early in his life becomes a monk on Mt. Wu-t'ai. But since *Yang-chia-fu* is a rare book, it is not generally known that, following the successful conclusion of his campaign against Nung Chih-kao, Yang Wen-kuang 楊文廣 —historically (and in *Pei-Sung chih-chuan*) the son of Yen-chao, but in most fiction (including *Yang-chia-fu*) and drama the son of Tsung-pao and therefore the grandson of Yen-chao—has a mystical experience and becomes a Taoist adept. Following the death of his father largely as a consequence of Ti Ch'ing's villainy, (see n. 72), Wen-kuang publicly performs the miracle of turning himself into a crane and disappears, even though he actually goes home to cultivate the Tao, living in total obscurity. At the age of sixty he is ordered by the emperor to lead another expedition. Upon the conclusion of this campaign his son Huai-yü 懷玉 leads the whole Yang family to live on

the two extant novels of the Yang family must await another occasion, but it may be noted that, whereas *Yang-chia-fu* gives a full account of that family, Hsiung has assigned the early career of Yang Yeh to *Nan-Sung chih-chuan* and begins its sequel with the life story of Hu-yen Tsan 呼延贊, another Northern Sung general of legendary fame, and that the later campaigns of the Yang family, ineptly narrated in *Yang-chia-fu,* are omitted altogether by Hsiung in favor of a grand expedition against the Ta-ta Kingdom 達達國 [16]

In any event, the old version of *Yang-chia-fu* must have been a seminal military romance both for its depiction of the tribulations of the Yang family despite its indispensable service to the throne and for its emphasis on magic warfare. Historically, Yang Yeh's matchless bravery has made him an object of envy, and his final defeat and suicide in a foredoomed battle against the Liao are brought about through the machinations of his commanding generals P'an Mei 潘美 (P'an Jen-mei 潘仁美 in fiction) and Wang Shen 王侁. Even his sixth son, Yang Yen-chao 楊延昭, who succeeds his father as a guardian of the frontier, is a repeated victim of calumny and imperial reprimand. [17] Out of such historical facts it is inevitable that

---

Mt. T'ai-hang in Taoist retirement. When a prince arrives at the mountain with an imperial request that he stay on in government service, Huai-yü excuses himself by reason of his father's frailty and goes on to recount the woes and indignities suffered by the family ever since Yang Yeh surrendered to the Sung.

[16] In *Pei-Sung chih-chuan,* following its total defeat signalized by the destruction of the T'ien-men chen (discussed later in the paper), the Liao Kingdom again starts trouble at the instigation of its spy at the Sung court, Wang Ch'in. Yang Yen-chao has little trouble quelling this uprising, but he dies soon afterward, grief-stricken over the deaths of his comrades Meng Liang and Chiao Tsan. Then the Ta-ta Kingdom invades China, and the novel concludes with Yang Tsung-pao's victorious expedition against the kingdom with the assistance of the twelve widows of his family. (This episode is generally known as the Expedition against the Hsi Hsia 西夏. But the term Hsi Hsia as it appears in the expression "Hsi Hsia Ta-ta kuo 西夏達達國" would seem to indicate the region in which the kingdom is situated rather than the historic Hsi Hsia Kingdom which plagued Sung China.) At that time Yang Wen-kuang is only fifteen years old. In *Yang-chia-fu* it is only when Wen-kuang has reached the age of sixty (see n. 15) that the twelve widows (not identical with those in *Pei-Sung chih-chuan*) lead a rescue operation to liberate him from his besiegement by Li Kao-ts'ai 李高材, the king of the Hsin-lo Kingdom 新羅國. Earlier in the novel, the Yang family undertook a lengthy campaign against Nung Chin-kao.

[17] The villainy of P'an Mei and Wang Shen is fully apparent from a reading of Yang Yeh's biography in *Sung shih, chüan* 272. Wang Shen is punished for not providing proper assistance to Yang, and even P'an is demoted though he is soon restored to high position. According to the biography of Yang Yen-chao in the same section of *Sung shih,* it is only because Emperor Chen-tsung appreciates his bravery and the distinguished service of his family that he is repeatedly spared more severe punishment.

storytellers should have woven a saga of outstanding generals loyal to the throne but meeting with repeated slander and punishment. The influence of this saga on the Liangshan legend must have been considerable if we assume that Yang Yeh and his sons had exercised the popular imagination at an earlier date than had Sung Chiang. This hypothesis at least explains why Sung, a minor rebel, could have been transformed into a tragic hero of outstanding military achievement leading repeated expeditions against the enemies of the state. And we may further maintain that the Hsüeh family as we know it in fiction must have been patterned after the Yang family since, historically, Hsüeh Jen-kuei's long career was sustained by imperial favor except for a few minor setbacks. The Yang saga must have also strengthened the role of villainy in the lives of Ti Ch'ing and Yüeh Fei as subsequently retold in fiction.

Judging by its subsequent adaptations, the old version of *Yang-chia-fu* must have delighted in magic warfare, especially in the form of mazes (*chen* 陣). Such *chen* already play a conspicuous role in *Ch'i-kuo ch'un-ch'iu hou-chi* so that we can be sure that narrators of certain periods of history had long capitalized on magic warfare as a regular feature of their storytelling. But still, to trace the increasing prominence of such warfare in several formative military romances is to illuminate an essential aspect of the evolving genre.

In conventional warfare *chen* refers to the formation of troops in a set manner in preparation for battle. Whereas the duel between two generals on horseback is mainly a contest of physical strength and dexterity, the kind of engagement involving the array of troops in a prescribed manner usually invites the exercise of brains rather than brawn. The preparation of *chen* and the methods of throwing them into confusion are supposedly recorded in military manuals.[18] We often read, therefore, that a general will on purpose set up a *chen* to test his opponent's military erudition. While to recognize a *chen*

[18] While the *Ching-chi chih* 經籍志 of *Chiu T'ang-shu* lists only 45 works on warfare and strategy (*ping-shu* 兵書) comprising 289 *chüan*, the *Yi-wen-chih* 藝文志 of *Sung shih*, *chüan* 207, lists 347 such works comprising 1,956 *chüan*. Many of these works deal with *chen-t'u* 陣圖 and *chen-fa* 陣法, such as 白起陣書, 女女厭陣法, 王韶熙河陣法, 韓霸水陸陣圖 九九陣圖, 五行陣圖 (two separate titles, one by 符彥卿). *ES*, pp. 3266, 5001. We may assume that the Sung storytellers' interest in things military, and not merely the *chen*, must have reflected the government's concern with national defense, as is seen in the marked increase in the production of military manuals.

is tantamount to asserting one's ability to confound it, a general really skilled in warfare will be able instantly to transform his *chen* into another one so as to confuse and trap the attacking troops. Ten numerically ordered arrays, starting with the simplest snake formation (*Yi-tzu ch'ang-she chen* 一字長蛇陣) are frequently mentioned in historical novels. But even though such formations employ only conventional soldiers, nevertheless the symbolic language used in their description suggests a utilization of esoteric lore drawn presumably from the *Book of Changes* and the *yin-yang* and Taoist schools of learning. In Chapter 36 of *San-kuo*, Ts'ao Ts'ao's 曹操 general Ts'ao Jen 曹仁 sets up a *chen* to test the military knowledge of Liu Pei 劉備 Liu Pei's counselor, Hsü Shu 徐庶, however, is learned in warfare, and tells his lord (in the somewhat free translation of C. H. Brewitt-Taylor).

> The arrangement is called "The Eight [Locked] Gates 八門金鎖陣," and each "gate" has a name. If you enter by one of the three named "Birth 生," "Bellevue 景," and "Expanse 開" you succeed; if by one of the gates "Wounds 傷," "Fear 驚" or "Annihilation 休," you sustain injuries. The other two "gates" are named "Obstacles 杜" and "Death 死," and to enter them means the end. Now, the eight "gates" are all there quite correct, the central "key-post" 主持 is lacking and the formation can be thrown into confusion by entry from the south-east and exit due west.[19]

The description is none too clear, though we are aware that the symbolic gates refer to points of varying degrees of vulnerability in the formation. In subsequent military romances what is figurative in the description here will become *literal* so that in its simplest form a magical maze is nothing but an enclosure with gates allowing for entrance and exit. Inside this enclosure usually stands a platform or elevated structure (*t'ai* 臺 or *chiang t'ai* 將臺) which serves as its keypost. A pennant or pennants of symbolic color and sinister significance rise high above the *t'ai*, visible to attackers outside the enclosure. The presiding general or sorcerer, stationed atop the *t'ai*, directs the military and magical defense of the *chen*, and he usually

[19] C. H. Brewitt-Taylor, tr., *Romance of the Three Kingdoms*, Vol. I (Rutland, Vt., Tuttle, 1959), pp. 375–376. I have amended "Docked," an obvious misprint, to read "Locked."

descends to engage in actual combat when the enemy seems to be gaining an upper hand in his struggle against the soldiery and/or magic forces in the *chen.*

Chu-ko Liang has been long celebrated in literature for his setting up of a *pa-chen-t'u* 八陣圖, which, I suppose, is something of a Maginot Line against potential invaders of his country. In *San-kuo* this is described as a formation of rocks, but these rocks are so arranged as to actuate the mysterious forces of the universe. Following his smashing victory over Liu Pei's invading forces, the Wu general Lu Sun 陸遜 leads his army into Shu territory and comes upon these rocks. He sees sinister vapors hovering above them, but he enters the maze nevertheless and would perish if he were not guided out of it by Chu-ko's kind-hearted father-in-law.[20] I suspect that the recital of this episode by Sung and Yuan specialists in the Three Kingdoms period must have stimulated their competitors to make up stories about similar mazes for their own dynastic cycles.

Shui-hu chuan has far more occasions than *San-kuo* to describe both types of *chen.* In chapter 76 Sung Chiang sets up a Nine-constellation Eight-trigram Formation (*Chiu-kung pa-kua chen* 九宮八卦陣) against the imperial army of T'ung Kuan 童貫. The verse passages descriptive of the pageantry of the array praise its utilization of the mysterious forces of nature, but actually Sung Chiang resorts to no magic because T'ung Kuan's army is easily routable even in the absence of supernatural aid. In chapters 87–88, Sung Chiang, then leading an expedition against the Liao, again prepares the Nine-constellation Formation to display his might.[21] In his turn, the king of the Liao throws in all his forces to form the *T'ai-yi hun t'ien-hsiang chen* 太乙混天像陣, which proves impregnable. The goddess Chiu-t'ien Hsüan-nü 九天玄女, who had earlier given Sung Chiang a heavenly book (*T'ien-shu* 天書) in chapter 42, now tells him how to

[20] *San-kuo yen-yi,* ch. 84. It is of interest to note that in describing the maze to Lu Sun, Chu-ko's father-in-law refers to also eight gates. These gates recur in descriptions of various *chen* in subsequent romances.

[21] In the *tsa-chü Sung Kung-ming p'ai chiu-kung pa-kua chen* 宋公明排九宮八卦陣, Sung Chiang sweeps forward to a great victory against the Liao forces by means of this *chen.* Along with many other military plays, this play is reprinted in *KYT,* III, which provides a mine of information for comparative studies in the military romance. According to Ma Tai-loi 馬泰來, "現存元代水滸雜劇考," *Ming Pao Monthly* 明報月刊, II, No. 1 (January 1967), *Chiu-kung pa-kua chen* is a Ming play written after the publication of *Shui-hu chuan.* He doesn't specify which edition, however.

destroy the *chen*. It is duly destroyed and the king of the Liao
surrenders to the Sung. In subsequent romances the foreign king or
chieftain usually sets up one or two major *chen* whose destruction
spells the grand finale of a major campaign.

Neither *Pei-Sung chih-chuan* nor *Yang-chia-fu* claims the literary
distinction of *Shui-hu chuan*, but thanks to Peking opera, the average
Chinese is far more familiar with the Seventy-two Heavenly-gate
Formation (*Ch'i-shih-erh-tso t'ien-men-chen* 七十二座天門陣)[22] set up
by the queen-dowager Hsiao 蕭太后 against the Sung forces than
with any of the formations prepared by Sung Chiang or his opponents. The Heavenly-gate Formation, to be sure, is far more
remarkable on three counts. First, the queen dowager not only
throws into the complex network of mazes all her military resources
but enlists the assistance of five neighboring states also, each sending
fifty thousand troops headed by a prince, princess, or marshal.
Second, some of the mazes forming the major *chen* are distinctly
weird or grotesque in their set-up, though in this respect they merely
confirm a trend already observable in *Ch'i-kuo ch'un-ch'iu hou-chi*. (In
one maze, for example, a princess stands in the nude, holding in her
hand a skeleton or part of a skeleton, and she is supposed to burst into
crying whenever the enemy troops enter; seven pregnant women are
buried under the ground of another maze and they are supposed to
be able to suck the souls out of the entering troops.)[23] Third, the
human battle around the Heavenly-gate Formation actually represents a feud between two of the Eight Taoist Immortals, Chung-li
Ch'üan 鍾離權 and Lü Tung-pin 呂洞賓. Chung-li once berates Lü
for his licentiousness; out of pique Lu descends to earth to help the

---

[22] For a description of this complex of mazes see *Pei Sung chin-ch'iang ch'üan-chüan*, ch. 33.
The account given in *Yang-chia-fu* is identical in detail, if not in wording. Lü Tung-pin
builds the *chen* according to a blueprint (*chen-t'u*). Seventy-two general's platforms
(*chiang-t'ai* 將臺) are erected along with five altars (*t'an* 壇) of greater strategic importance,
though the number of individual *chen* inviting attack amounts to only seven or eight. The
corresponding *T'ien-chen* 天陣 in the play *Yang Liu-lang tiao-ping p'o t'ien-chen* 楊六郎調兵
破天陣, included in *KYT*, III, comprises 142 constituent *chen*.

[23] The naked princess guarding the T'ai-yin chen 太陰陣 is Huang-ch'iung-nü 黃瓊女
daughter of the king of Hsi Hsia 西夏. She soon deserts the Liao to marry Yang Yen-chao.
The *chen* with seven buried pregnant women is known as Mi-hun chen 迷魂陣. A *chen* by
this name is frequently seen in military romances. Its earliest appearance is in *Ch'i-kuo
ch'un-ch'iu hou-chi*, chüan B. Prepared by Yüeh Yi's 樂毅 teacher Huang Po-yang 黃伯陽,
伯陽, this *chen* calls for the burial in seven places of seven foetuses ripped from the wombs of
pregnant women. Sun Pin stays captured in the *chen* for a hundred days.

queen dowager Hsiao just because Chung-li has already foretold the failure of her struggle against the Sung emperor Chen-tsung 眞宗. This feud would certainly seem to echo that between the rival wizards Sun Pin and P'ang Chüan. But far more importantly, the *T'ien-men chen* episode anticipates the involvement of a far greater number of celestials and demons in *Feng-shen yen-yi*, the first full-blown military romance of single authorship.

This episode (given identically in *Pei-Sung chih-chuan* and *Yang-chia-fu*) is of further great interest in that a more terse account of the same story is found in *Tung-yu chi* 東遊記, a book about the Eight Immortals now forming part of the omnibus volume *Ssu yu chi* 四遊記 but enjoying an independent existence during the Ming. Its earliest extant edition, its authorship attributed to Wu Yüan-t'ai 吳元泰 by the publisher Yu Hsiang-tou 余象斗, dates from the Wan-li period. But since, judging by its style and format, the work must have been composed earlier,[24] and since it has certainly drawn upon a folklore of some antiquity, it is difficult to say whether the *T'ien-men chen* episode originally belonged to the Yang saga or to the legend of Lü Tung-pin. While the altercation between the two Immortals appears very natural in *Tung-yu chi* because it is immediately preceded by an account of Lü's escapades, the same quarrel is quite arbitrarily introduced in the novels of the Yang family and the reader remains in the dark about its antecedents. On the other hand, the battle against the *T'ien-men chen* would seem to enjoy far greater relevance in the Yang saga than in the lore of the Eight Immortals. Whatever the eventual scholarly solution to this problem, it is of crucial importance to note the context of Taoist mythology for the development toward fantasy of the Yang saga, which must have begun in the Northern Sung without the palpable element of the supernatural.

The close kinship between Taoist lore and military romance is even more apparent in *Feng-shen yen-yi*. If its author is indeed Lu Hsi-hsing 陸西星, as Liu Ts'un-yan maintains,[25] then we can see why he commands incomparable freedom and the requisite erudition for

[24] Liu Ts'un-yan has examined with great care the early independent editions of what are now the four constituent parts of *Ssu yu chi*. He thinks that "they were all early story-teller's prompt-books which have probably been in circulation ever since the early Ming." Liu, I, p. 138. See also his discussion of a fragmentary Ming copy of *Tung-yu chi* on pp. 199–202.

[25] Cf. Liu, II.

the creation of this massive military romance. While Lu has adapted portions of *Lieh-kuo chih-chuan* 列國志傳, a popular chronicle, and inherited an oral tradition as represented by *Wu Wang fa Chou p'ing-hua*, at the same time he has consciously followed the tradition of *Ch'i-kuo ch'un-ch'iu hou-chi*, *Shui-hu chuan*, and the novels of the Yang family and developed the legend of the conquest of the Shang in the direction of military fantasy. With his erudition in Taoist and Buddhist lore, he would have no difficulty in making up the names and deeds of a great many of his characters, who come in all sizes and shapes, each with his distinctive magic weapons and powers. Nevertheless, with all his inventiveness, the major element of his plot—the feuding of two sects of Taoist immortals in support of the mundane struggle between the Shang and Chou—is squarely in the tradition, as is his increasing reliance on magical formations in his depiction of that struggle. The celestial and demonic friends of the Shang set up altogether three major *chen* (the Ten-exterminating Maze 十絕陣, the Celestial-slaying Maze 誅仙陣, and the Myriad-celestial Maze 萬仙陣) and two lesser ones (the Yellow River Maze 黃河陣 and the Plague Maze 瘟瘟陣). In contrast to mazes in earlier works, the majority of these *chen* are conspicuous for the absence or merely residual presence of soldiery: what counts is their magic equipment. The Celestial-slaying Maze, presided over by T'ung-t'ien Chiao-chu 通天教主, the principal deity siding with the Shang, is an enclosure bare of equipment except for four magic swords, each guarding one side of the wall. But, on the other hand, the Myriad-celestial Maze appears empty of magic paraphernalia following the routine destruction of three of its constituent *chen*: it is simply a battlefield in which the myriad gods and demons engage in mortal combat without reference to any specific formation that has to be destroyed.

All subsequent military romancers have adopted the defense and destruction of a *chen* as a standard feature of their work, but in their failure to surpass the author of *Feng-shen yen-yi* in inventiveness, their descriptions appear derivative and eventually perfunctory, and they have to exploit other sources of interest to keep the genre alive. Ironically, the only novelist who has turned this standard feature of a military romance to good literary account is Li Ju-chen 李汝珍. In

Ching-hua yüan 鏡花緣 he describes with learned humor and vivid realistic detail four allegorical mazes illustrative of the dangers of drinking, sex, greed, and anger.

II. *Heroes and Villains*

Having traced the growth of the military romance till *Feng-shen yen-yi* by reference to one of its standard attractions, we shall now examine its other features in a less chronological fashion by focusing mainly on the romances of the T'ang and Sung periods. *San-kuo, Shui-hu chuan,* and *Feng-shen yen-yi* all present a great many warriors. But if we were to single out for each work a principal hero, then the respective logical choices should be Chu-ko Liang, Sung Chiang, and Chiang Tzu-ya—all military commanders who are involved little if at all in actual fighting. Starting with *Pei-Sung chih-chuan*, however, every cycle of T'ang-Sung romance owed its rise to its fascination with a general distinguished for bravery and prowess, even though that fascination would inevitably extend to his sons and grandsons, who are in many cases entirely fictitious. The principal heroes of historical interest in these romances are, therefore, Ch'in Shu-pao 秦叔寶, Hsüeh Jen-kuei, Yang Yeh, Yang Yen-chao,[26] Ti Ch'ing, and Yüeh Fei. Each was accorded the honor of principal hero clearly because he had already become the subject of legend, but it certainly bespeaks the Chinese predilection for a definite type of hero that the man of prowess in each case should also be a loyal servant of the throne and, in some instances, a filial son as well.

The choice of a principal hero does not always abide by the verdict of history. While Yüeh Fei is without a doubt the preeminent hero of his time, Ch'in Shu-pao is but one of many flourishing during the late Sui and early T'ang. Ch'in and Yü-ch'ih Kung 尉遲恭 are equally distinguished as warriors, and judging by the evidence of Yuan drama, Yü-ch'ih certainly appeared to be a greater favorite

---

[26] The legend of Yang Yeh as retold in the novels of the Yang family is faithful to history at least in its broad outline. It is around his son Yen-chao that storytellers wove the kind of fantasy romance that later distinguished the fictional careers of Hsüeh Jen-kuei, Hsüeh Ting-shan, Yüeh Fei, and Ti Ch'ing. There can be little doubt that the original *Yang-chia-fu* as well as several Yuan-Ming plays about the Yang family depicts the fictitious career of Yen-chao in accordance with the storytellers' tradition.

with the people.[27] And in actual history, both Li Ching 李靖 and Li
Chi 李勣 (Hsü Chi 徐勣 or Hsü Shih-chi 徐世勣, better known in
fiction as Hsü Mao-kung 徐懋功, 茂功, 茂公) are statesmanlike
generals of greater stature and military achievement. Their official
biographies are fuller and they figure more frequently in the
anecdotal and fictional literature of the T'ang period.[28] But precisely
because the achievements of these men of greater intellectual powers
are more difficult for the popular mind to comprehend, Li Chi is
assigned the position of a prescient military counselor (chün-shih) in
Shuo T'ang, while Li Ching suffers an even worse fate—he becomes a
Taoist immortal only intermittently concerned with T'ang affairs.
In both cases, a comparison with Sui T'ang yen-yi and its predecessors
shows that the author of Shuo T'ang has actually pruned the available
legendary material to make these two heroes fit into certain stereo-
types of the military romance.

The principal heroes share certain basic experiences in their
youth.[29] We are usually told of their astral origin, the unusual
circumstances attending their birth and infancy, their tutelage under
a human or celestial master, their acquisition of a steed and weapons

---

[27] Of the extant Yuan tsa-chü about Sui-T'ang heroes, Yü-ch'ih Kung figures as a hero
in four: Hsiao Yü-ch'ih 小尉遲, Ching-te pu-fu-lao 敬德不伏老 Tan-pien to-shuo 單鞭奪槊, and
Yü-ch'ih Kung san-to-shuo 尉遲恭三奪槊. Ch'in Shu-pao also appears in the last two plays.
Hsü Mao-kung chih-hsiang Ch'in Shu-pao 徐懋功智降秦叔寶 (KYT, III) is most probably a
Ming play since it is not included in Yüan-ch'ü hsüan wai-pien 元曲選外編

[28] Chiu T'ang-shu, chüan 67, is devoted to the lives of Li Ching and Li Chi, whereas
Yü-ch'ih Kung and Ch'in Shu-pao share biographic attention in chüan 68 with three other
generals. Li Chi, especially, emerges from his biography as an outstanding human being
passionately devoted to his friends. His grief over the death of Li Mi 李密 and Shan
Hsiung-hsin 單雄信 is especially moving. The Ch'in Shu-pao of legend, too, is distinguished for his great friendship with Shan; there can be no doubt that storytellers had transferred this endearing trait from Li Chi to Ch'in, who is known in official history primarily
as a peerless warrior. Even in T'ang times Li Ching had become a legendary hero in
ch'uan-ch'i fiction; for other anecdotes of Li Ching and Li Chi see such works as Sui
T'ang chia-hua 隋唐嘉話, collected in T'ang-tai ts'ung-shu 唐代叢書. In the comic play of
the Yuan-Ming period, Shih-yang-chin Chu-ko lun-kung 十樣錦諸葛論功 (KYT, III),
Li Ching and Li Chi are listed among the thirteen greatest military geniuses of all time, on
a par with Chiang Tzu-ya and Chu-ko Liang. But whereas both Chiang and Chu-ko have
romances of their own, it is a quirk of fate that the two Lis should have played only
subordinate roles in the novels about Ch'in Shu-pao and Hsüeh Jen-kuei.

[29] The exception is Yang Yeh whose birth and early youth are only baldly summarized in both Nan-Sung chih-chuan and Yang-chia-fu. Had the Yang saga received further
expansion after the late Ming, Yang Yeh's early career would certainly have been
romanticized.

which will stand them in good stead in their years of military glory,
their sworn brotherhood with several lifelong friends and their
persecution by villains enjoying powerful positions at court, and
their initial participation in a public contest which attracts more than
transient attention. Thus Yüeh Fei is the Garuda (a celestial attribution suggested by his names).[30] His village is flooded soon after
his birth, causing the death of his father. He floats with his mother to
another village where he makes friends with four boys who serve him
loyally as sworn brothers and comrades-in-arms. He is taught and
adopted as a son by Chou T'ung 周侗 (since most such teachers are
celestials, the author of *Shuo Yüeh* has made the historic Chou T'ung
also the teacher of Lin Ch'ung 林冲 and Lu Chün-yi 盧俊義, among
the mightiest heroes of an earlier generation.)[31] He conquers a
wondrous serpent which turns into a lance (it is eventually reclaimed
by a monster in a river). He marries and goes to the capital with some
rowdy friends (a recurrent experience in the hero-legends, because
these friends will involve the more prudent hero in some disaster),
and receives as a gift a magic sword once owned by Hsüeh Jen-kuei.
As a candidate for the highest honors in the military examination, he
earns the patronage of an aging but loyal general (a *chung-ch'ên* 忠臣)
but at the same time contracts the hatred of three co-examiners, who
are all treacherous ministers *(chien-ch'en* 奸臣*).* At the examination
he is goaded into killing a prince, causing a riot in the capital.

As with Yüeh Fei, all principal heroes are attended by companion-
heroes. Some of these have legends of their own, but many do not.
In *Shuo T'ang*, Ch'in Shu-pao pledges brotherhood with thirty-eight

---

[30] Yüeh Fei's courtesy name is P'eng-chü 鵬舉. The Chinese name for the Garuda is
大鵬金翅明王.

[31] In *Ta-Sung chung-hsing yen-i* Hsiung Ta-mu faithfully follows the official biography
(*Sung shih, chüan* 265) in his treatment of Yüeh Fei's birth and boyhood. Thus we find that
his father did not die in the flood and that, although Yüeh Fei showed almost filial regard
for the memory of his teacher Chou T'ung 同 (*not* 侗), the latter had not been his adopted
father. That Yüeh Fei's boyhood should have been romanticized (as we have seen in
Shuo Yüeh) would seem to be inevitable in the formation of any hero-legend. It may be of
further interest to note that since the publication of this novel Chou T'ung himself
has grown in stature as a teacher of heroes. We read in Wang Shao-t'ang 王少堂, narrator,
Wu Sung 武松 (Nanking, Kiangsu wen-yi ch'u-pan-she, 1959), Vol. I, ch. 2, sec. 7, that
before Wu Sung returns home to find his elder brother murdered, he spends a month with
Chou T'ung mastering his use of the sword. Thus, according to the foremost present-day
storyteller of the Yangchow school, Wu Sung has joined Yüeh Fei, Lin Ch'ung, and Lu
Chün-yi as a disciple of Chou. Wang Shao-t'ang further depicts Chou as a man over fifty
and a sworn brother of Lu Chih-shen 魯智深.

heroes; many of these, like Hsü Mao-kung, Ch'eng Yao-chin 程咬金, and Lo Ch'eng 羅成[32] play important roles in their own right. In his humble position as a cook-soldier (*huo-t'ou chün* 火頭軍), Hsüeh Jen-kuei has eight sworn brothers of lesser ability who stay in his service. Ti Ch'ing has four sworn brothers and two attendant generals who go with him on every campaign. Among these companion heroes, the most lovable is the comic hero of bandit origin—coarse, honest, and extremely resilient. Though he is often seen in the guise of a clown, he voices the sentiment of disaffection or rebellion against an ungrateful emperor.

It is an article of faith with military romancers that though their heroes may die a tragic death, their sons and grandsons and their descendants many generations hence will carry forward the heroic spark, ready to re-emerge from the greenwood to serve the dynasty in crisis. In the novels of the Hsüeh family, the sons, the grandsons, and the great-grandsons of the founding heroes of the T'ang—Ch'in Shu-pao, Yü-ch'ih Kung, Ch'eng Yao-chin, Hsü Mao-kung, *et al.*—continue to serve the dynasty until the Wu Tse-t'ien faction is completely exterminated. It so happens that Hsu Ching-yeh 徐敬業, the grandson of Li Chi, did start an abortive rising against Empress Wu, resulting in the almost total extinction of the Hsü clan. But according to *Fan-T'ang yen-yi* 反唐演義, two of Hsü Ching-yeh's sons have escaped unharmed to continue their rebellion. *Fen-chuang lou*

---

[32] The legend of Lo Ch'eng is most interesting. According to *Ch'in-wang tz'u-hua*, Ch'eng is the given name of Lo Shih-hsin 羅士信, even though his biographies in *Chiu T'ang-shu, chüan* 187A, and *Hsin T'ang-shu, chüan* 191, make no note of this fact. This brave young warrior was born in Li-ch'eng, Ch'i-chou, and was early distinguished together with his fellow townsman Ch'in Shu-pao when serving under the Sui commander Chang Hsü-t'o 張須陀. Lo died at the age of twenty as a T'ang general captured by Liu Hei-t'a 劉黑闥 *Ch'in-wang tz'u-hua* maintains, however, that though he dies fighting against the forces of Liu, his death is actually contrived by Li Shih-min's evil brothers Chien-ch'eng 建成 and Yüan-chi 元吉, the commanders in charge of an expedition against Liu. The author of *Shuo T'ang*, who has elevated Lo Ch'eng to be the seventh mightiest hero of the Sui-T'ang era, follows this account of his tragic death. Two earlier works, *T'ang-shu chih-chuan* and *Sui-T'ang liang-ch'ao chih-chuan*, record Lo Shih-hsin's deeds and death without, however, further identifying him as Lo Ch'eng. In *Sui-shih yi-wen* the fictitious Lo Ch'eng and the historical Lo Shih-hsin have become two separate persons. Lo Ch'eng is made the son of Lo Yi 羅藝, a famous general of the Sui who eventually joined the T'ang cause and then rebelled. And since Lo Yi's wife is supposed to be an aunt of Ch'in Shu-pao, Ch'in pays her a visit and comes to know Lo Ch'eng when the latter is only a boy. In adapting *Sui-shih yi-wen*, Ch'u Jen-hu has further made Lo Ch'eng into a romantic hero while retaining Lo Shih-hsin as a historic character of minor importance. To the average Chinese it is the Lo Ch'eng of *Shuo T'ang* and Peking Opera who appears most familiar—a handsome young warrior who died tragically.

粉粧樓, a Ch'ing novel which can bear no relation to the work of the same title attributed to Lo Kuan-chung, chooses to celebrate Lo Ch'eng's descendants, Lo Ts'an 羅燦 and Lo K'un 羅焜, but sharing their honors and exploits are nearly all the scions of the founding heroes, including those of Li Ching, Ma San-pao 馬三保, and Yin K'ai-shan 殷開山.

Because *Shuo Yüeh* was in a sense written as a continuation of *Shui-hu chuan*, the roster of heroes rallying to the cause of patriotism, mostly under Yüeh Fei, is especially impressive. Fighting against the Chin invaders are the scions of Chu-ko Liang and Kuan Yü (the Three Kingdoms period), of Lo Ch'eng (the Sui-T'ang period), and of Cheng En 鄭恩, Kao Huai-te 高懷德, Yang Yeh,[33] and Ti Ch'ing (Northern Sung). In addition, Hu-yen Cho 呼延灼 Juan Hsiao-erh 阮小二, Yen Ch'ing 燕青, and An Tao-ch'üan 安道全, formerly of the Liangshan band, are still alive, and the sons of Kung-sun Sheng 公孫勝, Tung P'ing 董平, Han T'ao 韓滔, and the Vegetable Gardener Chang Ch'ing 張青 also contribute to the war effort. Little wonder that with these replicas of famed heroes assisting Yüeh Fei and his historic companions, the Chin invaders are easily routed. After the death of Yüeh Fei, the children of his followers claim our attention so that, in effect, the authors celebrate two generations of such fictitious heroes.

In reading the romances about the T'ang and Sung periods, one gets the impression that a self-perpetuating community of heroes could be called upon to meet any national emergency. In auspicious times, they indeed serve with alacrity, but very often they are hampered by villainous commanders or treacherous ministers or both, so that, even if their campaigns are successful, their loyalty and devotion to the throne are nevertheless put to trial. Unlike Chiang Tzu-ya and Chu-ko Liang, who enjoy the complete trust of their superiors, they suffer imprisonment, torture, poisoning, exile, and at times the wholesale slaughter of their families. In the long run, of course, they or their survivors are duly restored to honor, but in the short run, they are the pawns of scheming villains determined to discredit them before the emperor.

[33] Yang Tsai-hsing 楊再興 is one of the bravest generals under Yüeh Fei. According to *Shuo Yüeh*, he is a descendant of Yang Yeh, but his ancestry is not mentioned in his biography in *Sung-shih, chüan* 368.

In these romances there are few enlightened emperors. It is true that as the Prince of Ch'in, Li Shih-min 李世民 merits the love and devotion of his followers; but his father is then emperor, as easily imposed upon by his sons and concubines as any emperor in Chinese history. And after Li Shih-min has ascended the throne, he shows none of his historic brilliance and is readily deceived by his uncle Li Tao-tsung 李道宗, the determined enemy of Hsüeh Jen-kuei.[34] But for Yü-ch'ih Kung, who forfeits his life to remonstrate against the emperor, Hsüeh Jen-kuei would have been executed. He is eventually released from prison when a new crisis at the frontier requires his service. But the unmasked villain, Li Tao-tsung, is only nominally punished whereas the innocent heroes are too often maligned and suffer unmerited punishment. Both Yang Yen-chao and Ti Ch'ing rise from their supposed state of death (a ruse adopted to avoid further persecution by their enemies) only when a new invasion at the frontier makes their services indispensable.

In military romances, therefore, it is not the utterly evil and dissolute rulers that infuriate us. Few true heroes would serve a Chou-hsin 紂辛, a Yang-ti 煬帝, or an Empress Wu, and even if some are tragically caught in their web of tyranny, their plight is nevertheless understandable. It is the weak-willed, soft-eared emperor (*hun-chün* 昏君) who exasperates us with his fitful appreciation of the heroes, his forgetfulness of their past merits, and his proneness to punish them at the instance of his favorites in the harem and at court. This emperor is of course a stereotype designed to enhance our appreciation of the heroes' dogged loyalty, but the fact that this stereotype should have arisen and become accepted by readers amounts to a serious reflection on the absolute monarch. It implies that, living a life of ease surrounded by people intent on flattering and deluding him, even an emperor of good will cannot tell truth from falsehood, patriots from traitors. While the completely wicked emperors have lost their mandate of Heaven and invite their own

[34] Li Tao-tsung once provoked the wrath of Yü-ch'ih Kung at a dinner and may on this account have earned his notoriety as a villain in popular literature. This incident is related in Yü-ch'ih's biography in *Chiu T'ang-shu* (*ES*, p. 3313) and is further elaborated on in the Yuan *tsa-chü Ching-te pu-fu-lao*. Despite his distinguished record in battle, Li Tao-tsung was once imprisoned for accepting bribery, which may have further tarnished his reputation. His own biography appears in *Chiu T'ang-shu, chüan* 60.

overthrow, these blind emperors usually reign with a clear conscience. They are not openly attacked, and their acts of caprice and cruelty are to be endured by the heroes as best they can.

Sung Kao-tsung is in one sense a true emperor (*chen-ming t'ien-tzu* 眞命天子) since it is with Heaven's miraculous protection that he escapes alive from the Chin camps to serve as a rallying point for all loyalists. But once he sets up his quarters in Nanking, he lives a life of indolent hedonism and shows no interest whatever in regaining the lost territory. During the trials of Yüeh Fei, Yüeh Yün 岳雲, and Chang Hsien 張憲, the authors of *Shuo Yüeh* carefully avoid mentioning Kao-tsung's name and we do not know whether he abets or deplores Ch'in Kuei's 秦檜 treachery. But at the same time the authors make it clear that every citizen in Hangchow is burning with indignation over the shameful trials. Could it be possible that the emperor has not heard, or that if he has heard, he could let the heroes die? Later, Ch'in Kuei and his wife are hounded to death by their own consciences; they have not received a word of reprimand from the emperor. Yet precisely because the authors have shielded Kao-tsung, his crime in countenancing the heinous deeds of Ch'in Kuei appears all the more inexcusable.

On the surface, therefore, an emperor rarely turns against a hero on his own initiative unless his pride is affronted or his kinsmen are killed; the actual crime of persecution is assigned to several kinds of villains whose hatred for the hero is usually explainable in personal or supernatural terms. Hate, then, sets in motion nearly all the events in a military romance which make for melodrama. Though the principal hero (as contrasted with the comic hero) never thinks of retaliating against the emperor, he or his descendants are equally eager to clear his name and bring his enemies to justice. Hence the wheel of karma ceaselessly turns, and generations of heroes and villains are engaged in a feud. Ostensibly, the novelist laments this perpetual display of enmity. In a doggerel the author of *Lo T'ung sao-pei* records a sentiment shared by all military romancers:

Why should we keep on contracting enmity and hatred?
Vengeance begets new vengeance—when will this process ever end?
If we keep on tying these knots and make no attempt to loose
   them,

Generation after generation, the hatred will never cease.[35]

But in reality, he delights in exploiting the theme of hatred precisely for its melodramatic interest.

From Lucifer to Iago, the classic cause for hatred in Western literature is envy. To an objective observer, the envious person has little cause to harbor an undying hatred against one who surpasses him in goodness, knowledge, or beauty, but it precisely speaks for the meanness of his soul that he should do so. In military romances most villains have reasons closer to home for hating the hero, but subconsciously they are all envious. The classic case of envy in Chinese folklore is P'ang Chüan, who, as we have seen, hates the superior attainments of his fellow disciple Sun Pin. The author of *Feng-shen yen-yi* must be under the conscious influence of the legend in developing the feud between Chiang Tzu-ya and Shen Kung-pao 申公豹, both disciples of Yüan-shih T'ien-tsun 元始天尊. Out of spite, Shen supports the Shang house just because Chiang Tzu-ya is leading an expedition against it. He persuades one after another of his numerous friends in the human, demonic, and celestial worlds to block Chiang's path. By the time he meets his doom (in chapter 84), he has incited three major confrontations between opposing camps of celestials.

A comic variety of the envious person is the small-minded general acutely aware of his own limitations and determined to obstruct the advancement of any man under him possessing greater merit. Such a person is Chang Shih-kuei 張士貴, commander of the vanguard in T'ai-tsung's expedition against Korea. Serving under him is Hsüeh Jen-kuei, the young warrior in white who has earlier appeared to T'ai-tsung in a dream as his savior. In two Yüan *tsa-chü* Chang Shih-kuei has already appeared as a comic figure who suppresses Hsüeh's identity and claims all feats of valor as his own.[36] In *Cheng-tung*

---

[35] *Lo T'ung sao-pei*, ch. 12, p. 53, in *Cheng-tung, Cheng-hsi, Sao-pei* 征東, 征西, 掃北 (Taipei, Wen-hua t'u-shu kung-ssu, n. d.). This quatrain does not appear in the corresponding chapter 13 of *Shuo T'ang hsiao-ying-hsiung chuan* (see n. 1). The Taipei edition appears to be a reprint of a fuller version; in any event, verse passages of identical sentiment are not uncommon in military romances.

[36] The two plays are *Hsüeh Jen-kuei jung-kuei ku-li* 薛仁貴榮歸故里 and *Mo-li-chih fei-tao tui chien* 摩利支飛刀對箭. A comic monologue of Chang Shih-kuei from the latter play has been translated in Crump, *op. cit.*, p. 433 (see n. 10). In *Shih-yang-chin Chu-ko lun-kung* (n. 28), too, Chang appears as a boastful clown along with the brave Wei general Hsia-hou Tun 夏侯惇. Chang's brief biography in *Chiu T'ang-shu, chüan* 83, presents a praiseworthy record of his generalship, but the fact that it was he who recruited Hsüeh Jen-kuei for the Korean expedition may have led the storytellers to paint him as a buffoon or villain

Chang Shih-kuei assigns all of Hsüeh's merits to his son-in-law, Ho Tsung-hsien 何宗憲, maintaining that the latter is indeed the young warrior in the emperor's dream. His transparent deception, however, neither impedes the progress of the expedition nor deters Hsüeh from achieving mighty deeds, and until he turns traitor, Chang Shih-kuei's villainy and the attempts made by Yü-ch'ih Kung and others to expose him provide some of the breeziest comedy to be seen in a military romance.

Chang Shih-kuei, his son-in-law, and three of his four sons are all punished with death. But even if they deserve their sentences, their survivors are now committed to a course of vengeance. The surviving daughter, a concubine of Li Tao-tsung, soon implicates Hsüeh in a capital crime, and Chang Chün-tso 張君左, a descendant of Chang Shih-kuei's surviving son, serving as a high minister under Kao-tsung and Empress Wu, succeeds in bringing about the execution by imperial order of the entire Hsüeh clan. The immediate cause, however, is that Hsüeh Kang 薛剛, the unruly son of Hsüeh Ting-shan, has killed Chang's son, the bully Chang Pao 張保. Many an implacable enemy of the hero, in fact, embarks on his course of villainy primarily to avenge the death of a son or a father. In *Pei-Sung chih-chuan* P'an Jen-mei, best known for his implacable hatred of the Yang family, also plots repeatedly against Hu-yen Tsan who has killed his son in battle. Because his father was justly executed by Ti Ch'ing's grandfather, Sun Hsiu 孫秀 wreaks vengeance upon the Ti family, and with the cooperation of his father-in-law, the powerful minister P'ang Hung 龐洪, succeeds in involving Ti Ch'ing in no end of trouble.

In their determination to kill Ti Ch'ing, P'ang Hung and Sun Hsiu eventually collaborate with the foreign government at war with China. They are willing to hurt their own country in order to satisfy their private vengeance. In military romances, traitors are usually the lowest of villains. In *Pei-Sung chih-chuan*, Wang Ch'in

---

in contrast to the young warrior's shining innocence and bravery. In *T'ang-shu chih-chuan* Chang is given his due as a general. Upon the completion of the Korean expedition, however, he advises T'ai-tsung against giving Hsüeh too many honors and too high a promotion, and the emperor agrees. (Jen-kuei is duly appointed Wu-wei chiang-chün 武衛將軍). In *Sui-T'ang liang-ch'ao chih-chuan*, ch. 86, Chang is exposed by Yü-ch'ih Kung for claiming Jen-kuei's distinguished record as his own. There he appears as a villain, but not a comic one.

王欽, a Chinese in the service of the Liao government, volunteers to serve as a secret agent at the Sung court.[37] He rises to the position of a prominent minister and does everything possible to injure the Yang family and other upright servants of the throne. According to *Shuo Yüeh*, Ch'in Kuei, serving under the Chin conquerors, is sent back to the Sung capital for the express purpose of gaining total victory for his masters. It is of further interest to note that both Wang Ch'in and Ch'in Kuei are described as clever and accomplished scholars; Ch'in Kuei is a *chuang-yüan*.

As a traitor, Ch'in Kuei's hatred for Yueh Fei is perfectly explainable. But in a military romance, all such cases of deep hatred which cannot be assigned a personal motive are usually traceable to a feud existing between hero and villain in an earlier celestial or mundane existence. Thus Ch'in Kuei's crime is blamed on his wife, who is a heavenly bat (*Nü-t'u-fu* 女土蝠)[38] prior to her exile on earth. She gives forth a fart while the Buddha is expounding the Lotus Sutra, and the enraged Garuda (Yüeh Fei), also in the service of the

[37] While P'ang Hung suggests P'ang Chi 龐籍 (*Sung-shih*, *chüan* 311) on the strength of his surname and his official prominence at Jen-tsung's court, there can be no doubt that the Wang Ch'in of the Yang family saga stands for Wang Ch'in-jo 王欽若 (*Sung-shih*, *chüan* 283), the cunning and evil prime minister under Chen-tsung. He and four members of his clique were known to their contemporaries as the "Five Devils" (*wu-kuei* 五鬼). Though not a traitor, Wang was opposed to such upright ministers as K'ou Chun 寇準, who is depicted in the novels as a champion of the Yang family. In the play *Yang Liu-lang tiao-ping p'o t'ien-chen*, Act 1 (see n. 22), Yang Yen-chao gives an autobiographical monologue in which he names Wang Ch'in-jo as the *chien-ch'en* who fabricates an imperial order for his execution. In the prologue (*hsieh-tzu* 楔子) of the *tsa-chü Hsieh Chin-wu* 謝金吾 (included in *Yuan-ch'ü hsüan* 元曲選), Wang Ch'in-jo reveals himself as a Liao spy sent to the Sung court by Queen Dowager Hsiao. His real name is Ho Lu-erh 賀驢兒, and he is presumably a Liao Khitanese. Foiled in his attempt to execute Yang Yen-chao and Chiao Tsan, he is later exposed in the play as a spy and punished with lingering death. For the plot of *Hsieh Chin-wu* and a discussion of its sources see Lo Chin-t'ang 羅錦堂, *Hsien-ts'un Yuan-jen tsa-chü pen-shih k'ao* 現存元人雜劇本事考 (Taipei, Chung-kuo wen-hua shih-yeh kung-ssu, 1960), pp. 363–366.

Wang Ch'in-jo's name has been shortened to Wang Ch'in in both *Pei-Sung chih-chuan* and *Yang-chia-fu*. While the latter agrees with *Hsieh Chin-wu* in identifying Wang as a Khitanese by name of Ho Lu-erh, the former describes him as a man of Chinese origin initially serving at the Liao court. We may assume, therefore, that, while the legend of Wang Ch'in as given in *Hsieh Chin-wu* and *Yang-chia-fu* represents an older tradition, Hsiung Ta-mu must have revised it in *Pei-Sung chih-chuan* in order to restore Wang's Chinese identity and make his treachery look more heinous.

[38] Nü-t'u-fu (Female earth bat) stands for Aquarius; see *Mathews' Chinese-English Dictionary* (Cambridge, Harvard University Press, 1956), p. 1177. Many characters in Chinese fiction, not necessarily female, are supposed to be incarnations of Aquarius. Thus Li Yüan's principal wife, Empress Ch'ang-sun 長孫皇后, is described as a Nü-t'u-fu in *Ta-T'ang Ch'in-wang tz'u-hua*, vol. 1, p. 36.

Buddha, forthwith kills her. For his crime, the Garuda is exiled, while the Bat also seeks human form to avenge herself. In the same novel (chapter 73) we are shown a vision of Hell in which both Ch'in Kuei and his wife are suffering the worst possible torments along with other traitors in Chinese history. We are further informed that after three years of such torment Ch'in's wife will face the butcher's knife in endless reincarnations as a sow. Now if Ch'in's wife were really a minor celestial being with just cause against the Garuda, then her punishment would appear too severe. But since Hsiung Ta-mu had already described her suffering in Hell in *Ta-Sung Chung-hsing yen-yi*,[39] Ch'ien T'sai and Chin Feng have most probably superimposed a tale of their own invention about the celestial feud upon the older tale without seeing their inherent contradictions.

If a grievously wronged individual has left no heir to avenge his death, it is possible for him to be reborn into his enemy's family and plot its destruction. Fan Li-hua 樊梨花, a warrior of great magical prowess, detests her fiancé, the hideous Yang Fan 楊藩, and deserts her own country (the Ha-mi Kingdom 哈迷國) to marry Hsüeh Ting-shan.[40] Later, she and her adopted son, Hsüeh Ying-lung 薛應龍, kill Yang Fan in battle. In retaliation, Yang Fan is reborn as Hsüeh Kang, Li-hua's own son, who brings death and disaster upon the Hsüeh family, even though he himself lives on to exemplify the Hsüeh tradition of loyal service to the T'ang house.

[39] The scholar Hu Ti 胡迪 witnesses the torture of the Ch'in Kuei family during his guided tour through Hell in the concluding section of the novel. Hsiung Ta-mu must have adapted this episode from a storytellers' *hua-pen* which subsequently appeared in print as Tale 32 of *Ku-chin hsiao-shuo* 古今小說：遊酆都胡母迪吟詩. In both versions the hero is a native of Chin-ch'eng 錦城 (Ch'eng-tu) who waxes indignant over heavenly injustice after reading a work known as *Ch'in Kuei tung-ch'uang chuan* 秦檜東窗傳, but the independent tale further specifies that Hu-mu (or Hu-wu) Ti flourished during the reign of Shun-ti, the last Yuan emperor. In *Shuo Yüeh*, ch. 73, Hu Ti appears as a citizen of Lin-an (Hangchow) at the time of Yüeh Fei's execution and is given the additional name Meng-tieh 夢蝶.

[40] The author of *Cheng-hsi* must have named her Fan Li-hua because Hsüeh Ting-shan's father has a secondary wife called Fan Hsiu-hua 樊瀟花. Prior to his expedition to Korea in *Shuo T'ang hou-chuan*, Hsüeh Jen-kuei rescues Hsiu-hua from the hands of three bandits and promises to marry her himself. By the time he returns from the expedition he has forgotten about the girl; nevertheless, he marries her after her father has escorted her to his official residence at Chiang-chou 絳州. Having created a thoroughly colorless character in Fan Hsiu-hua, the author of *Shuo T'ang hou-chuan* nevertheless proceeded to invent in its sequel a most fascinating wife for Hsüeh Ting-shan.

Against the "soft-eared" emperor and evil ministers, the principal
hero usually has no recourse except to submit to the test of time to
vindicate his integrity and honor. In the military romance, therefore,
the forthright hero uneducated in Confucian decorum is heard as the
principal voice of protest against such authorities. A favorite with
storytellers' audiences, this savage and eventually comic hero has
been early endowed with a recognizable personality. In *San-kuo
chih p'ing-hua,* Chang Fei 張飛 appears as the dominant hero, and it is
Lo Kuan-chung's better sense of historic proportion which assigns
him a position of lesser importance in *San-kuo yen-yi.* Li K'uei appears
as the favorite character in the extant Yuan plays about the Liangshan heroes, and in *Shui-hu chuan* he is probably the most completely
individualized character. Subsequently, this archetype appears as
Cheng En in *Nan-Sung chih-chuan* and *Fei-lung ch'üan-chuan,* as Chiao
Tsan 焦贊 and Meng Liang 孟良 in the novels of the Yang family,
as Niu Kao 牛皋 in *Shuo Yüeh,* as Ch'eng Yao-chin (and Yü-ch'ih
Kung) in *Shuo T'ang* and its sequels, and as Chiao T'ing-kuei 焦廷貴
(Chiao Tsan's son) in the novels about Ti Ch'ing.

In *Shui-hu chuan,* Li K'uei repeatedly urges Sung Chiang to kill the
evil ministers and assume the throne himself. In moments of anger
and humiliation, his comic successors have similarly echoed the
sentiment. Thus Niu Kao to his friends, after the riot at the
capital: "Don't get panicky. Let's turn back and slaughter our way
into the city. Let's first kill all the treacherous ministers and capture
Pien-liang. Elder Brother Yüeh will then take over as emperor and
the four of us will become marshals. Won't that be much better?
Then we won't ever have to suffer under those rascals, and who
would still have to compete for top honors in the military examination?"[41] After Yüeh Fei's death, Niu Kao exhorts his comrades, "Our
elder brother has been treacherously put to death by evil ministers.
Let's march to Lin-an, seize the traitors, cut them into ten thousand
pieces each, and avenge our elder brother."[42] But it is the spirit of
Yüeh Fei, forever loyal, who forcibly stops them from crossing the
Yangtze River and carrying out their threat. In consequence, two of
his sworn brothers immediately commit suicide rather than live on in
shame:

[41] *Shuo Yüeh ch'üan-chuan* (see n. 3), *chüan* 4, ch. 13, pp. 2b–3a.
[42] *Ibid., chüan* 26, ch. 63, p. 35b.

They saw that Yüeh Fei was in great anger. He waved his sleeves; instantly a mighty storm overturned three or four ships, and the rest could not proceed. Yü Hua-lung 余化龍 shouted, "Since our elder brother does not allow us to carry out our task of revenge, how could I have the face to live on!" With one loud yell, he drew his sword and killed himself. Ho Yüan-ch'ing 何元慶 also cried, "Since Brother Yü has gone, I will join him." He raised his silver *ch'ui* 鎚 and smashed his own head, and he, too, was dead. Seeing that two of his comrades had committed suicide, Niu Kao burst forth into a loud fit of crying and jumped into the Yangtze River.[43]

But Niu Kao does not die. He lives on to guide the younger generation of heroes against the Chin and to intercede for the full restoration of honors due the Yüeh family. Despite his bandit origin and his anarchic temper, he is further stereotyped as a *fu-chiang* 福將 (lucky general), who can survive in the battlefield against the greatest odds. In *Shuo T'ang* the misadventures of Ch'eng Yao-chin as a *fu-chiang* are even more fully delineated for their comic value. (While suffering from a severe case of diarrhea, he faces an enemy general and beats him off with his axe. Then Ch'eng goes into the woods to relieve himself. The enemy comes upon him while the squatting hero is completely off guard. Nevertheless, trousers in hand, he manages to slay his opponent.)[44] Moreover, he is a prankster and buffoon, and dies laughing at the ripe old age of 120. To what extent the subjection of the anarchic and rebellious hero to a deliberate comic treatment is due to the storytellers' and novelists' fear of government censorship and persecution is difficult to say. But it would seem that so long as the principal hero pledges complete loyalty to the throne, the comic hero is rendered relatively harmless despite his outspoken criticism of the emperor and the government.

[43] *Ibid.*, ch. 63, pp. 36a-b. This and the two preceding quotations can more easily be found in *Shuo Yüeh ch'üan-chuan* (Hong Kong, Kuang-chih shu-chü, n. d.), *chüan shang* 卷上, p. 54; *chüan hsia* 卷下, pp. 107-108.

[44] *Shuo T'ang ch'üan-chuan*, ch. 48, pp. 122-123. This title constitutes Part I of *Ta T'ang yen-yi* 大唐演義 (Tainan, Ya-tung shu-chü, 1963). The episode appears in identical form in the Kuang-hsü edition of *Shuo T'ang ch'ien-chuan* (see n. 1), *chüan* 8, ch. 49, pp. 2a-3b. The slain general is named Wang Lung 王龍.

III. *The Romantic Element*

The sons (and daughters) of the principal heroes are a privileged lot. While their fathers suffer many hardships to reach their deserved eminence, they are early wafted to a celestial mountain to be taught military and magic arts by an immortal. Or else they have inherited a strength equal to or surpassing their fathers'. They have few adventures during their childhood, but they are all eager to prove their usefulness at the frontier, despite their mothers' apprehensions. To facilitate their rise, the heroes of an earlier generation will be conveniently besieged (usually, along with the emperor) by the enemy while a messenger, usually the *fu-chiang*, dashes to the capital with an urgent request to raise the siege. A new expeditionary force will be assembled, headed by the younger heroes. After the siege is broken, while the principal hero still exercises nominal commandership, his son usually supplants him as the military hero because of his greater command of magic. With psychological justification, therefore, the novelist often plays up the antagonism between father and son. The father (Hsüeh Jen-kuei, Yang Yen-chao, Ti Ch'ing, and even Yüeh Fei) is prepared to behead his son, sometimes over the slightest infraction of military discipline, though he will relent when other generals intercede in his son's behalf.[45] Sometimes, however, the novelist adapts or makes up a story which has true Oedipal implications. Upon returning home after twelve years at war, Hsüeh Jen-kuei, aiming his arrow at a strange beast, accidentally shoots his son Ting-shan, who is immediately succored by an immortal and wafted to his celestial quarters. Many years later, Hsüeh Jen-kuei is trapped in a mountain; Ting-shan comes to the rescue and fatally shoots a white tiger, which turns out to be his father's astral self.

The son arouses his father's anger especially over his romantic involvement with a female warrior of the opposite camp. The latter, usually a foreign king or chieftain's daughter, plays an important role in some of the later romances, and to trace her lineage is further to enhance our awareness that the military romances composed a self-

---

[45] In this connection it is of interest to read the *tsa-chü Shou-t'ing-hou nu-chan K'uan P'ing* 壽亭侯怒斬關平 (*KYT*, III), in which Kuan Yü, too, wants to execute his own son Kuan P'ing and finally relents only when other generals intercede for him. In *San-kuo yen-yi* Kuan P'ing is described as Kuan Yü's foster son.

conscious tradition. In *San-kuo* Lady Chu-yung 祝融夫人, Meng Huo's wife, is the only woman to participate in a battle, though Liu Pei's third wife is distinguished for her martial temper. The female warriors do not play a big role in *Feng-shen yen-yi* either, but there is one minor heroine who anticipates the more romantic ladies to come. Princess Lung-chi 龍吉公主, a celestial exiled on earth, captures the enemy general Hung Chin 洪錦. We know nothing of his age and appearance and there are no indications that they are enamoured of each other. When he is about to be executed, however, the Old Man in the Moon (Yüeh-ho Lao-jen 月合老人) descends and announces his predestined marriage to the princess. Lung-chi reluctantly agrees. The episode appears very crude and bears no comparison to similar episodes in later romances. The T'ien Hu episode was a late addition to the *Shui-hu chuan* and may have been composed after the publication of *Feng-shen yen-yi*. Ch'iung-ying 瓊英, the foster daughter of T'ien Hu's uncle, throws pellets with deadly precision, and so does the Featherless Arrow Chang Ch'ing 張清. Their marriage is foretold in dreams, and the two duly fall in love at first sight. With her help, Chang Ch'ing infiltrates the enemy camp as a doctor's brother, and Ch'iung-ying is only too happy to kill her evil foster father and the rebel chief. Many love episodes in later military romances show the influence of this tale.

In *Feng-shen yen-yi* we find an amatory episode of the comic variety which serves as a definite link between *Shui-hu chuan* and later romances. In *Shui-hu*, Wang Ying 王英 the Short-legged Tiger (Ai-chiao hu 矮脚虎) is short and lecherous. He is captured in battle by Hu San-niang 扈三娘 and eventually married to her. In *Feng-shen yen-yi*, T'u-hsing Sun 土行孫 is a dwarf barely over four feet tall and eager to get married to his commander's daughter, Teng Shan-yü 鄧嬋玉. Though her father has earlier granted him permission to marry her, he nevertheless has to apply force to consummate his marriage because Shan-yü finds the prospect of being married to a dwarf highly repugnant. In *Hsüeh Ting-shan cheng-hsi*, Tou I-hu 竇一虎 (One-tiger Tou), a three-foot dwarf, sees Hsüeh Chin-lien 薛金蓮 in the battlefield and instantly falls in love. Like Wang Ying, he is originally a bandit, and like T'u-hsing Sun, he can vanish and travel below ground. He, too, proves to be an unwelcome suitor. To complicate matters, a fellow dwarf, Ch'in Han 秦漢 (the grandson of

Ch'in Shu-pao) falls in love with a foreign princess while in battle. His specialty is to fight while hovering in the air. The two dwarfs eventually manage to have a double wedding. If it affords some comic diversion to have a dwarf marry a beautiful girl (the Aphro-dite-Hephaestus myth), it is even more fun to have two amorous dwarfs wooing their ladies. Many military romancers innovate in this mechanical fashion.

But the female warrior is far more often the wooer than the wooed. Judging by her best-known exemplars, she has studied under a female celestial since early childhood and is in command of greater magical power than the man she is destined to marry. As a barbarian, she is unashamed in her pursuit of love and unhindered by the kind of moral scruples that would beset a Chinese girl. While impressed by her beauty and power, the object of her love is usually too shocked to want to acknowledge his interest. The romancers consciously exploit this love situation as a clash between two ways of life.

That the female warrior should have gradually gained ascendancy appears inevitable when one realizes that each romancer, while inheriting the formulas from his predecessors, was also obliged to depart from the familiar and offer something new. Already in *Feng-shen yen-yi*, Chiang Tzu-ya warns his generals, "In battle you should exercise special caution against three types of opponents: Taoist priests, monks, and women. These three types of warriors, if they do not belong to heretical sects, usually command magic arts. Since they rely on such arts, you will certainly be injured if you are not careful."[46] In a romance where most warriors have to rely on magical arts to excel, this warning is perhaps unnecessary, but even there these three types depart from the norm of an armored male warrior who may or may not use magic. To these three categories Chiang Tzu-ya should perhaps have added the child or juvenile warrior whose small size belies his superhuman strength or magical prowess.

In point of time, the female warrior first gains prominence in the saga of the Yang family. Yang Yeh's widow, She T'ai-chün 佘太君 or Yü 余 T'ai-chün, is herself a mighty warrior and accompanies her

---

[46] *Feng-shen yen-yi,* vol. 1 (Peking, Tso-chia ch'u-pan-she, 1955), ch. 53, p. 505.

family on many expeditions during her long life.[47] By the time Yang
Yen-chao commands his first expedition against the Liao, all of
his six brothers have either died or withdrawn (although his fifth
brother occasionally leaves his monastery on Mt. Wu-t'ai to help
him) and he has to count on the female members of his family to
destroy the *T'ien-men chen.* Luckily, during this as during his second
expedition against the Liao, several ladies proficient in the martial
arts join the family (including two as his wives)[48] and the Yang
women become even more formidable as a fighting team. After the
death of Yen-chao, as we have seen, twelve widows launch a victorious campaign against the Ta-ta Kingdom. In *P'ing-nan,* when
Ti Ch'ing is beleaguered by Nung Chih-kao 儂智高, the Yang
family, composed mainly of women, twice come to his rescue. The
second expedition is led by a young girl named Yang Chin-hua
楊金花. She is assisted by Lung-nü 龍女, a hideous kitchen-maid
only three feet in height. Since female warriors are usually handsome,
this dwarf adds another twist to the formula. Upon the conclusion of
the campaign, she is ordered by the emperor to marry Wei Hua 魏化,
a nine-foot-tall retainer of the Yang family who has also distinguished
himself in battle.[49]

[47] Most Chinese call her by the title She T'ai-chün since she is usually so identified in
Peking Opera. She plays an important part in the play *Hsieh Chin-wu* and identifies herself
there as She T'ai-chün. In the Ti Ch'ing novels, too, she is known by this title. But in both
Pei Sung chih-chuan and *Yang-chia-fu* her surname is Yü 余 rather than She, though she is
commonly referred to as Yang Ling-p'o 楊令婆 (her husband is Yang Ling-kung 楊令公).
In *Pei-Sung Yang-chia chiang* (see n. 5), ch. 10, p. 19, she is unaccountably called Lü shih
呂氏 and not Yü shih, as in the corresponding chapter in *Pei Sung chin-ch'iang ch'üan-
chuan.*

[48] Yang Yen-chao's principal wife is known as Ch'ai Chün-chu 柴郡主, a descendant of
the imperial family of the Later Chou dynasty. During his first expedition against the
Liao, Yen-chao acquires his second wife Huang-ch'iung-nü (see n. 23). His third wife is
Ch'ung-yang-nü 重陽女, who joins forces with him during his second Liao expedition.
Both of these ladies are supposed to have been promised to Yen-chao during their
childhood.

[49] In *Yang-chia-fu, chüan* 6, Wei Hua commands the vanguard of Ti Ch'ing's expeditionary forces against Nung Chih-kao. When Ti Ch'ing is besieged, Wei Hua dashes through
the enemy lines to get help from the capital, and a new army led by Yang Tsung-pao and
Yang Wen-kuang is duly sent. Subsequently, in *chüan* 7, with Wen-kuang trapped by
Nung's forces and Tsung-pao immobilized by a foot injury, Wei Hua again goes to the
capital to fetch the Yang ladies, who finally quell the rebellion. Wei Hua also accompanies Wen-kuang on his mystic journey (see n. 15). It is through these connections, I
suppose, that Wei Hua is eventually reduced to the status of a retainer (*chia-chiang* 家將)
of the Yang house in *P'ing-nan.*

Thanks mainly to her colorful presence on the Chinese operatic stage, by far the most famed of the Yang women is Mu Kuei-ying 木桂英, 穆桂英.⁵⁰ But in neither *Yang-chia-fu* nor *Pei-Sung chih-chuan* is she too colorful or important, though in her determined pursuit of Yang Tsung-pao 楊宗保, the handsome son of Yang Yen-chao, she rightly appears as an archetypal figure of consequence to subsequent military romances. Early taught by a goddess (*shen-nü* 神女) in archery and in the use of flying swords, she is the daughter of a chieftain in possession of two pieces of Dragon-subduing Wood (*hsiang-lung mu* 降龍木). She instantly falls in love with Tsung-pao when he comes on a mission to obtain the wood, which is indispensable for the purpose of slaying the mighty Liao warrior Hsiao T'ien-tso (蕭天左 佐), a dragon in disguise. Tsung-pao agrees to marriage with alacrity, but when he goes back to report the news, the infuriated Yang Yen-chao orders his execution. He relents somewhat only when his own mother intercedes for the grandson's life; still Tsung-pao is put in prison. Soon after, Yen-chao faces Mu Kuei-ying in battle and is captured. Realizing the importance of obtaining the

---

In his concluding commentary to *Pei Sung chin-ch'iang ch'üan-chuan*, Yüan-hu fei-hsien chu-jen 鴛湖廢閑主人 of the Tao-kuang period says that Yang Ling-p'o will not be granted first-rank imperial honors until after the return of Yang Wen-kuang from his southern expedition, presumably against Nung Chih-kao (令婆尚未受封俟文廣征南, 班師纔得授封一品也). So presumably the commentator knows of a novel about Wen-kuang's southern expedition. While I have not seen the Kuang-hsü edition of *P'ing-Min ch'üan-chuan* 平閩全傳 (Sun, I, p. 53), which is about Yang Wen-kuang's pacification of Min, it is good to know that *P'ing-nan* itself fears an additional title, *Yang Wen-Kuang kua-shuai* (n. 6). As I suggest below, *P'ing-nan* must have drawn upon a novel about Wen-kuang's expedition against Nung. And in that work Wei Hua must also have played a part.

⁵⁰ Mu 穆 Kuei-ying is known to most Chinese as a martial lady of romantic pluck through the following series of Peking operas: *Mu-k'o-chai* 穆柯寨 *Ch'iang t'iao Mu T'ien-wang* 槍挑穆天王, *Yüan-men chan-tzu* 轅門斬子, and *Ta-p'o T'ien-men-chen* 大破天門陣. Two new operas, *Mu Kuei-ying kua-shuai* 穆桂英掛帥 and *Yang-men nü-chiang* 楊門女將, frequently seen in mainland China before the Cultural Revolution, have further enhanced her popularity. Unlike Fan Li-hua, however, she did not have an auspicious start as a fascinating character in fiction. In *Yang-chia-fu*, *chüan* 5, the home base of Mu Kuei-ying is Mu-ko-chai 木閣寨, rather than the exotic-sounding Mu-k'o-chai of Peking Opera. Her father is known by the name Mu Yü 沐羽 and the title Ting-t'ien-wang 定天王. Though the novel calls her by the name Mu 木 Kuei-ying throughout, we are initially told she is Mu Chin-hua, also named Mu Kuei-ying (名木金花 又名木桂英). In *Pei Sung chin-ch'iang ch'üan-chuan*, *chüan* 35, p. 283b, and presumably in *Pei Sung chih-chuan* as well, we are given identical information except that Chin-hua is identified as the heroine's *hsiao-ming* 小名 and Kuei-ying as her *pieh-ming* 別名. As a Tao-kuang publication, however, *Chin-ch'iang ch'üan-chuan* has printed her name as Mu 穆 Kuei-ying in the couplet heading ch. 35. The Taiwan edition of *Pei Sung Yang-chia-chiang* has consistently changed her surname to Mu 穆.

wood, he gives his consent to the marriage, and the new daughter-in-law soon distinguishes herself in the battle against the *T'ien-men chen*.

In the sequels to *Shuo T'ang* we have several instances of the infatuated foreign princess. On his expedition against a northern state, Lo T'ung encounters Princess T'u Lu 屠爐公主, daughter of its prime minister, who falls madly in love. But since she has earlier killed his younger brother, Lo T'ung hates the girl, although he swears a false oath of love (all such oaths are eventually fulfilled, as in the Indian epics, the *Mahābhārata* and the *Rāmāyana*)[51] in order to secure her help to overturn her country. T'u Lu gladly turns traitor to her own country, and upon its pacification, Emperor T'ai-tsung and the foreign king are equally happy to see the handsome warrior marry the princess. But on their wedding night, Lo T'ung denounces her not only for her murder of his brother but for her unfilial and unpatriotic behavior:

> Harlot, as a subject of your king beholden to his bounty, instead of returning his kindness, you shamelessly ran away from the battlefield to a deserted mountain in order to plight troth with me. In doing so, you have shamed your family—this is filial impiety. You opened wide the gates of the pass to let our troops trample upon your camps. You are a traitor to your country—this is the reverse of loyalty.[52]

Put to shame, the princess kills herself. As punishment for spurning the love of a selfless princess, Lo T'ung is forced to marry a demented girl of utter repulsiveness. But the author hates to carry a practical joke too far; on her wedding night, she is transformed into a beauty.

[51] In *Sao-pei*, ch. 11, Lo T'ung swears to the princess that if he is false, he will eventually die at the sharp point of a spear (*ch'iang* 鎗) held by a man in his seventies or eighties. In *Cheng-hsi*, ch. 20, he meets in battle a ninety-eight-year-old general named Wang Pu-ch'ao 王不超 With his spear (*mao* 矛) Wang slashes open his opponent's abdomen, causing his intestines to tumble out. Furious, Lo wraps them tightly with a piece of cloth, resumes battle with Wang, and decapitates him. It is not until he has reached his own tent that he drops dead. This famous episode, known as "P'an-ch'ang ta-chan 盤腸大戰," has a fuller text in *Shuo T'ang san-chuan* (see n. 1), ch. 20. The fact that, allowing for minor discrepancies of detail, Lo T'ung's death fulfills his oath provides almost certain proof that the *hou-chuan* and *san-chuan* of *Shuo T'ang* were by the same author. Lo T'ung is the son of Lo Ch'eng.

[52] *Sao-pei*, chap. 14, p. 66, in *Cheng-tung, Cheng-hsi, Sao-pei*. The corresponding passage in *Shuo T'ang hsiao-ying-hsiung chuan*, ch. 15, p. 26 b, is identical except for three characters.

Fan Li-hua, perhaps the most famous of all female warriors in Chinese fiction, is also the most determined wooer. Hsüeh Ting-shan has earlier aroused the passion of two female warriors of magic skill and married them, to the subsequent consternation of his father.[53] Now at Han-chiang Pass 寒江關, Ting-shan encounters the magic might of Fan Li-hua, who has been told by her celestial teacher that this man is her predestined husband. Already betrothed to Yang Fan, Li-hua feels all the more reason to secure her happiness and is infinitely patient with her stubborn lover. She liberates him three successive times on his false word of promise. Because they oppose her union with Ting-shan, Li-hua unintentionally kills her father in a fight and slays her two brothers in self-defense. On their wedding night, therefore, Ting-shan is even more self-righteous than Lo T'ung. He draws his sword to avenge her father and brothers. Not easily abashed, however, Li-hua fights back. Eventually Ting-shan repudiates her, and she has to pretend death to earn his love and retaliate against his repeated acts of humiliation.

Li-hua's courtship of her husband is the most interesting long episode in *Cheng-hsi*, a sequel to *Shou T'ang hou-chuan* and almost certainly by the same author. Having played several variations on the theme of a female warrior in love, he has deliberately drawn a most complicated case of courtship for the reader's enjoyment. Even in the story of Princess T'u Lu, the crude melodrama opposing instinctive passion to Confucian honor is redeemed by irony. If her determination to stake everything for love is highly repugnant to Lo T'ung's Confucian sensibility, she is at least trustful and honest whereas the Chinese hero has stooped to expediency and proved to be false. In the story of Fan Li-hua, the conflict between passion and honor is taken less seriously. There is a suggestion that Ting-shan rejects her not because of her disloyal and unfilial behavior but because she is his superior as a warrior and he finds it difficult to adjust his sense of male superiority to this reality. Whereas Hsüeh Jen-kuei has objected to his son's two earlier marriages, he is eager to have a daughter-in-law of Li-hua's unsurpassed might to facilitate his conquest of the Ha-mi. This paternal pressure Ting-shan also resents. His stubbornness is therefore quite understandable. A proud

---

[53] Hsüeh Ting-shan's first two wives are Tou Hsien-t'ung 竇仙童 and Ch'en Chin-ting 陳金定. The first is beautiful and the second ugly, but both are disciples of goddesses.

and fascinated male at first shocked by the amorality of a determined pursuer and later won over by her repeated proofs of devotion,
Ting-shan is almost the hero of a comedy of manners.

The foreign princess in love receives an even more memorable
embodiment in the novels about Ti Ch'ing. His twin sons, Ti Lung
狄龍 and Ti Hu 狄虎, both marry magical warriors of the opposite
camp, but coming as late as he does in the tradition of the military
romance, the hero Ti Ch'ing has himself become an object of romantic attention. His light of love is Princess Sai-hua 賽花公主 (or Pa-
pao Kung-chu 八寶公主). On his expedition against the Hsi Liao, Ti
Ch'ing has followed his blundering vanguard into the Shan-shan
Kingdom 單單國,[54] which is at peace with China. He must take pass
after pass until he encounters the princess. They fall in love at first
sight, and after due complications, they are married. But Ti Ch'ing
cannot long stay at a foreign court when it is his mission to pacify the
Hsi Liao. One morning, pretending to go on a hunting trip, he
escapes, but the princess, then already pregnant, soon overtakes him.
He gives her the real reasons for leaving her in precipitate haste; she
understands and lets him go. Unlike Lo T'ung and Hsüeh Ting-shan,
who denounce their wives for their betrayal of Confucian principles,
Ti Ch'ing is truly torn between love for his wife and duty to his
country. Though she possesses great magical powers and resembles
Fan Li-hua in other superficial respects, Princess Sai-hua is far more
distinguished for her humanity. In observing an old formula, the
author of *P'ing-hsi* has discovered genuine tenderness between a
Chinese general and his princess-wife.

IV. *The Transformation of a Genre*

In the preceding sections, I have dealt with the salient features of
the military romance and shown that, while these features persist
from earlier to later romances, they tend to be modified, in accordance with the felt need to vary old formulas and introduce new
sources of interest. These innovations either refine, exaggerate, or
render more comic a received plot situation. The generic structure of
the military romance remains intact, however, so long as the other

---

[54] The Shan-shan Kingdom is, of course, fictitious. I have romanized 單單 as Shan-shan
because at least once upon a time there was a Shan-shan Kingdom 鄯善國 (see *Han
shu, chüan* 96A).

elements of the plot are properly subordinate to the campaigns and do not supplant the latter as the main source of entertainment. In *Shui-hu chuan*, *Pei-Sung chih-chuan*, *Yang-chia-fu*, *Feng-shen yen-yi*, and *Shuo Yüeh* (Chin Feng's preface dated 1744), we feel that the authors are properly serious about the conventions of the military romance. Even in *Shuo Yüeh*, the comic hero is within bounds, and scenes of magic warfare are described with due seriousness. In *Shuo T'ang* (preface by Ju-lien chü-shih 如蓮居士 dated 1736) and its sequels (composed during the Ch'ien-lung period), however, we begin to detect the note of burlesque. There are scenes which unmistakably treat war as a joke, which is a different thing from comic embellishment of a battle scene. By the Chia-ch'ing period, at least in *Wan-hua lou* and *P'ing-hsi*, the legend of Ti Ch'ing is so well plotted that the campaigns themselves definitely occupy a subordinate place.

I have earlier referred to the comic treatment of certain conventions and episodes to be seen in *Shuo T'ang* and *Shuo T'ang hou-chuan*. While a certain buoyant heroism sustains the comedy of Hsüeh Jen-kuei's eastern expedition, other episodes betray intentional levity. The impression is reinforced when we compare *Shuo T'ang* and *Sui-shih yi-wen* in their treatment of Ch'in Shu-pao and his companion heroes. (For our purposes, the question of whether the author of *Shuo T'ang* also used *Sui T'ang yen-yi* as a major source is immaterial, since Ch'u Jen-hu has apparently incorporated the whole *Sui-shih yi-wen* into his novel without any attempt at serious revision.)[55] Along

---

[55] Cf. n. 9. While Sun K'ai-ti asserts that *Shuo T'ang* is a crude adaptation of *Sui T'ang yen-yi* (Sun, I, pp. 44–45), Liu Ts'un-yan agrees with Cheng Chen-to that *Shuo T'ang* appeared "after *Sui T'ang chih-chuan* had been in circulation for some time but prior to Ch'u Jen-hu's adaptation of the latter" (Liu, I, p. 261). One of the two textual proofs adduced by Cheng and Liu in support of their thesis is a passage in Chapter 8 of *Shuo T'ang*: '那叔寶的箭，是王伯當所傳，原有百步穿楊之功。若據小說上說，羅成唔助一箭，非也." Both scholars believe the novel in question (小說) to be *Sui T'ang liang-ch'ao chih-chuan*. But this is not the case since, as I have shown in n. 32, Lo Ch'eng does not appear in the novel. The author of *Shuo T'ang* must be referring to *Sui-shih yi-wen* or *Sui T'ang yen-yi* or the non-extant earlier novel of which *Sui-shih yi-wen* is itself an adaptation. In both *Sui-shih yi-wen* (chüan 3, ch. 15) and *Sui T'ang yen-yi* (ch. 14) we read that Lo Ch'eng secretly shoots down an eagle or falcon (ying 鷹) to help Ch'in Shu-pao, who is less skilled in archery. The introductory couplet for Chapter 15 of *Sui-shih yi-wen* goes as follows: 勇秦瓊簡服三軍，小羅成射鷹助一弩. Though I have not seen that chapter because the fragmentary microfilm copy of *Sui-shih yi-wen* I have examined does not include it, I am certain that for this episode as for so many episodes available for comparative study Ch'u Jen-hu has copied the earlier work. The introductory couplet for *Sui-T'ang yen-yi*, ch. 14, goes: 勇秦瓊舞鐧服三軍，賢柳氏收金匱一報. The second line differs from that of the couplet from *Sui-shih yi-wen* because it is intended to recapitulate

with the early parts of *Shui-hu chuan*, *Sui-shih yi-wen* must be ranked as one of those masterpieces of Chinese fiction that best reflect the strength of the heroic storytellers. It is *the* novel of Ch'in Shu-pao, and it has given him the most subtle and moving portrayal of any military hero in Chinese fiction. (At the same time, of course, I am aware that this kind of high praise should more justly be lavished upon the old novel of which *Sui-shih yi-wen* is itself a redaction if it were ever to be recovered.) Confronted with this moving legend of Ch'in Shu-pao as embodied in either *Sui-shih yi-wen* or *Sui T'ang yen-yi*, the author of *Shuo T'ang* shows no desire to improve it further in the direction of psychological realism; on the contrary, he appears bored by it. By Chapter 14 he drops Ch'in Shu-pao to introduce the six mightiest champions of the Sui-T'ang period who far surpass Ch'in in prowess. The first hero so introduced—Wu Yün-chao 伍雲召 - is modeled after Wu Tzu-hsü 伍子胥, and the author is still following the practice of the military romancers in importing an old legend of proven audience appeal and giving it a new setting.[56] But about the other five there is less of a story to tell: they are simply there with their unbelievable strength. The first three are especially incredible because they perform feats of wonder in the absence of magic equipment: Li Yüan-pa 李元霸, Li Shih-min's younger brother and Li Yüan's 李淵 third son by his principal wife, wields two iron hammers together weighing 800 *chin* 斤 even though he is only a puny twelve-year *(sui)*-old of sickly appearance; Yü-wen Ch'eng-tu 宇文成都, a youth of unspecified age but large size, wields a *tang* 鐋 of 320 *chin* and is the mightiest champion of the Sui empire;[57] P'ei Yüan-ch'ing 裴元慶, the twelve-year-old son of

---

chapter 16 of the earlier work: 羅元帥作書貽蔡守, 秦叔寶贈金報柳氏. There can be no doubt about the crucial importance of *Sui-shih yi-wen* as a primary source for both *Sui T'ang yen-yi* and *Shuo T'ang* in their treatment of Ch'in Shu-pao and his companion-heroes. *Sui T'ang liang-ch'ao chih-chuan*, on the other hand, is a work of much less importance in this regard.

[56] See "Wu Tzu-hsü yü Wu Yün-chao," in Cheng Chen-to, *Chung-kuo wen-hsüeh yen-chiu*, vol. I.

[57] In *Shuo T'ang ch'ien-chuan*, chüan 3, ch. 14, p. 2a, the weight of the *tang* is initially given as 200 *chin*; subsequently, it is given as 320 *chin*. This discrepancy remains uncorrected in *Ta-T'ang yen-yi* (see n. 44) as well as in Ch'en Ju-heng 陳汝衡, ed., *Shuo T'ang* (Peking, Tso-chia ch'u-pan-she, 1959).

the historical P'ei Jen-chi 裴仁基,[58] wields two hammers of 300 *chin*. (Kuan Yü 關羽, China's most revered military hero, wielded a sword with a long shaft weighing only 82 *chin*.) But Li Yüan-pa is even more deadly than the ponderosity of his weapons would suggest. Twice he routs singlehanded the combined strength of eighteen rebel kings. The second time he slaughters 1,180,000 of the 1,800,000 troops assembled against him.[59] No other hero could beat his record; he is the Hydrogen Bomb of the military romance. When an author traces the might of a hero to his possession of magical weapons, he is still appealing to a kind of logic. The devastating strength of Li Yüan-pa is beyond explanation: he is invented solely to confound the logic of the military romance.

The fact that today Li Yüan-pa remains a legendary name may lend support to the hypothesis that he had been a folklore figure even before the author of *Shuo T'ang* celebrated his deeds in his romance. But this theory is hardly tenable. None of the six mightiest champions appears in earlier works of fiction,[60] and the best proof of their being inventions of the author of *Shuo T'ang* is that by Chapter 42, these heroes are all dead, with the result that he can resume his narrative more or less in accordance with his sources. Historically, Li Yüan's third son is named Hsüan-pa 玄霸; practically no information is given of him except his early death.[61] No folklore could have gathered around him. The author of *Shuo T'ang* resurrects him partly because

---

[58] In *Shuo T'ang ch'ien-chuan*, *chüan* 5, ch. 31, p. 15b, P'ei Yüan-ch'ing is said to be ten years old. In the two popular reprints (n. 57), his age is given as twelve. But since Ch'en Ju-heng is a careful scholar and has consulted a Ch'ien-lung edition of the novel, I have followed his text with regard to P'ei's age. P'ei Jen-chi does have a son of extraordinary bravery, but his name is Hsing-yen 行儼. See Jen-chi's biography in *Sui-shu*, *chüan* 70.

[59] *Shuo T'ang ch'ien-chuan*, *chüan* 7, chap. 42. The event takes place in chapter 41 of the Tainan and Peking reprints of the novel. See postscript on p. 390.

[60] The name Li Hsüan-pa 李玄霸 the third son of Li Yüan, duly appears in the list of historic characters preceding the main narrative in *T'ang-shu chih-chuan*, *T'ang-chuan yen-yi*, and *Sui T'ang liang-ch'ao chih-chuan*. In compiling such lists, these works have followed the convention established by the Chia-ching edition of *San-kuo-chih t'ung-su yen-yi*; see *The Classic Chinese Novel*, p. 38. In these name-lists we are told that Li Hsüan-pa died at the age of sixteen *sui*. *Sui. Sui T'ang chih-chuan* further gives his *tzu* as Ta-te 大德. All this information is based on Li's biographical note in *Hsin T'ang-shu*, *chüan* 79, which further praises him for his precocity (幼辯慧). This shadowy figure, of course, bears no resemblance whatever to the Li Yüan-pa of *Shuo T'ang*.

he needs a champion for the T'ang house, since initially Ch'in Shu-pao and his sworn brothers all serve under Li Mi 李密 at Wa-kang-chai 瓦崗寨.

Among these new champions Ch'in Shu-pao is completely at a loss, although judging by the space devoted to his career, he is still the principal hero. To compensate for his mere human prowess, however, he has by Chapter 36 acquired a magic steed, and to win battles he often resorts to tricks which would have been completely unworthy of the legendary hero as he appears in *Sui-shih yi-wen* or *Sui T'ang yen-yi*. In *Hsüeh Jen-kuei cheng-tung*, Ch'in Shu-pao, now seventy, competes with Yü-ch'ih Kung for the command of the expedition against Korea. T'ai-tsung suggests that whoever can lift the gold-plated, wrought-iron lion standing by the Noon Gate and bring it before the throne will be awarded the post. Since the lion weighs a thousand *chin*, Yu-ch'ih Kung, tottering under its weight, barely manages to complete one round of the court:

> Shu-pao, addressing the emperor, sneered; "See, General Yü-ch'ih is no good any more. Though old, I will walk three rounds by your throne and make nine turns. Your Majesty please watch." Then he swept back his sleeves and tried to lift the lion as Yü-ch'ih had done, but it wouldn't move. He himself couldn't believe it, saying, "The strength of my youth, where has it gone?" Afraid of losing face he exerted his utmost strength and managed to lift it, but try as he might, how could he walk three rounds and nine turns with it! He walked one step and he saw sparks before his eyes. By the second step, blood had surged up and squirted out of his mouth. He fell flat on his face and fainted away. Poor Shu-pao, to maintain his great reputation

---

[61] Cf. n. 60. However, in the table of contents for *Chiu T'ang-shu* (*ES*, p. 3059), his name is given as Yüan-pa. In a letter sent to me after reading the draft version of the present paper, Liu Ts'un-yan speculates that *Shuo T'ang* was probably first printed in the K'ang-hsi period because of its substitution of the name Yüan-pa for Hsüan-pa. The K'ang-hsi emperor's personal name is Hsüan-yeh 玄曄; the character *hsüan* was therefore taboo during his reign. To test this theory, however, one has to find out whether there are no other characters in *Shuo T'ang* whose names contain the character *hsüan* and whether historic personages whose names contain this character bear different names in the novel. Furthermore, one has to check if the observance of this taboo applies to all other novels first published in the K'ang-hsi period. *Sui T'ang yen-yi* was definitely first published then; though I have not seen its earliest editions, all its present editions include historic characters whose names contain this character, e.g., Li Hsüan-sui 李玄邃 and Yang Hsüan-kan 楊玄感. However, I am extremely grateful to Professor Liu for this and other suggestions, many of which I have adopted.

as a hero, he had endured loss of blood and bodily injury. In his prime, he could stand this punishment: now in his age, he had been long plagued by disease and there was no more blood for him to squirt out. He had fallen unconscious.[62]

Shu-pao remains bedridden after this attempt. As early as *San-kuo*, childish warriors have competed for an assignment before Chu-ko Liang, but none has suffered such disastrous consequences. The author, who has earlier subjected his hero to an unfair comparison with Herculean champions of his own invention, now designs for him an inglorious end. Read out of context, there may appear to be a note of sympathy; but read in context the scene expresses amused contempt. It would seem that the author has deliberately exploited the absurd conventions of the military romance to mock his own hero. It should be a worthwhile task to explore whether any subsequent military romances were written in the spirit of parody.

---

[62] *Cheng-tung* ch. 3, p. 5, in *Cheng-tung, Cheng-hsi, Sao-pei*. The corresponding passage in *Shuo T'ang hou-chuan, ts'e* 3: *Shuo T'ang Hsüeh-chia-fu chuan, chüan* 1, ch. 3, pp. 7b–8b, is slightly different. The author must have got his immediate inspiration for the weight-lifting scene from *Shuo T'ang ch'ien-chuan* (probably his own composition), ch. 34 (ch. 33, in the Tainan and Peking editions), where Li Yüan-pa and Yü-wen Ch'eng-tu have a contest of strength before Sui Yang-ti. Yü-wen lifts a golden lion of 3,000 *chin* by the Noon Gate, brings it to court, and then returns it to its original position. Li Yüan-pa, however, carries two lions of equal weight to court, and before returning them he swings them up and down over a dozen times. As for the episode as a whole, however, the author of *Shuo T'ang hou-chuan* must have adapted it from *Sui T'ang liang-ch'ao chih-chuan*, ch. 82: "Ch'in Ch'iung holds a mouthful of blood and squirts it at Ching-te 秦瓊含血喋敬德." In that chapter Yü-ch'ih competes for the command of the Korean expedition by lifting a thousand-*chin* gold lion and walking three rounds with it. But T'ai-tsung misses Ch'in Shu-pao, then sick in bed, and goes with Yü-ch'ih to see him. Ch'in regrets his inability to serve in his present condition and worries that the Korean conflict will be protracted in his absence. Yü-ch'ih taunts him in kind, and Shu-pao, remembering that his disease is the direct result of having endured three lashes of Yü-ch'ih's whip years ago, holds a mouthful of blood and squirts it at him. The biography of Ch'in Shu-pao in *Chiu T'ang-shu, chüan* 68, quotes him as saying that he cannot help being sick later in his life, seeing that he has participated in over two hundred battles, repeatedly suffered severe wounds, and lost blood (*ch'u-hsüeh* 出血) altogether to the extent of several *hu* 斛. Subsequent story-tellers must have taken this statement to mean that Ch'in is a victim of hemorrhage and thus made much of his spitting or swallowing blood without, however, lessening his heroic stature. The usual explanation is that Heaven had afflicted Ch'in with this disease, for otherwise he would have been too powerful. Even during his battle with Yü-ch'ih at the Mei-liang River (n. 13), he swallows three mouthfuls of blood (*Ta-T'ang Ch'in-wang tz'u-hua, chüan* 4, ch. 30, p. 646). But the author of *Sheng-tung* deliberately makes fun of Ch'in by having him appraise his own strength in an unrealistic fashion and collapse in his attempt to compete with Yü-ch'ih.

The Ti Ch'ing novels of the Chia-ch'ing period constitute the last significant group of military romances. In time the *wu-hsia hsiao-shuo* 武俠小說, whose early titles are wedded to the conventions of detective fiction, were to replace the military romance as the main staple of adventure fiction of indigenous origin among the Chinese. The *yen-yi* novels compiled during the late Ch'ing and early Republican periods seem to have conformed more to the requirements of the popular chronicle[63] as the *wu-hsia hsiao-shuo* gradually took over the supernatural aspects of the military romance in accordance with its own evolving conventions. While in a historical study of the genre the place and influence of *Erh-nü ying-hsiung chuan* 兒女英雄傳, a work of the Hsien-feng period, must be accounted for, one can say that the actual trend toward *wu-hsia hsiao-shuo* began with the highly popular *Chung-lieh hsia-yi chuan* 忠烈俠義傳, better known as *San-hsia wu-yi* 三俠五義, first printed in 1879. That work begins with the crime-story of the substitution of a dead cat stripped of its fur for a new-born prince, the future Sung emperor Jen-tsung.[64] In diversifying the military episodes of *Wan-hua lou*, Li Yü-t'ang has earlier drawn upon another version of the same legend and narrated Pao Cheng's eventual detection of the crime with even greater dramatic power. This coincidence seems to me symbolic of the transition from one popular genre of fiction to another.

The Ti Ch'ing novels have received no attention from modern scholars beyond a few bibliographic notices and Cheng Chen-to's short essay on *Wan-hua lou*.[65] Because this novel narrates the early career of the hero, Cheng is of the opinion that *P'ing-hsi* and *P'ing-nan* were composed later as its sequels, though he is not sure whether they were by Li Yü-t'ang or not. But bibliographical

[63] See, for example, such historical novels by Wu Wo-yao 吳沃堯 as *T'ung-shih* 痛史 and *Liang-Chin yen-i* 兩晉演義. The most ambitious attempt by an early Republican author to present reliable history in the popular language of fiction is Ts'ai Tung-fan's 蔡東帆 *Li-ch'ao t'ung-su yen-i* 歷朝通俗演義 (44 vols. Reprint: Hong Kong, Wen-kuang shu-chü, 1956), which covers the whole span of Chinese history from the rise to supremacy of the Ch'in State to the early years of the Republic. The author's preface to this work is dated 1925.

[64] Hu Shih has traced the evolution of the story known as "Exchanging a tabby cat for a prince 狸貓換太子" in fiction and drama in "*San-hsia wu-i* hsü 三俠五義序," *Hu Shih wen-ts'un*, vol. 3 (Taipei, Yüan-tung t'u-shu kung-ssu, 1953). He has, however, failed to discuss Li Yü-t'ang's treatment of the story in *Wan-hua lou*.

[65] Cf. n. 6.

evidence shows quite clearly that, of the three novels, *P'ing-hsi*, dubbed the *ch'ien-chuan* 前傳 of *Ti Ch'ing yen-yi* 狄青演義 on its title page, was published first and that *P'ing-nan* was published soon afterwards as the *hou-chuan* 後傳.[66] And there can be no doubt that it was because of the popularity of these two books that a third volume tracing the earlier career of Ti Ch'ing was soon commissioned. The Ching-lun-t'ang 經綸堂 edition of *P'ing-nan* actually concludes with an announcement of the reprinting of an "old text" (*ku-pen* 古本) dealing with the birth and early career of Ti Ch'ing (plus colorful deeds by Pao Cheng and Yang Tsung-pao) which readers of the *ch'ien-chuan* and *hou-chuan* are urged to read in order to get the whole story of the great hero.[67] The commentary appended to the last chapter of *Wan-hua lou* corroborates the statement, explaining why the book had not been available earlier and why *P'ing-hsi* had to begin with Ti Ch'ing already a famous general in command of the Three Passes.[68] For this reason the full title of *Wan-hua lou* contains the phrase *ch'u-chuan* 初傳, since normally the phrase *ch'ien-chuan* would indicate the earliest title in a sequence of novels. The preface to *P'ing-hsi* is dated the sixth year of Chia-ch'ing (1801), and the preface to *Wan-hua lou* the thirteenth year of the same reign-period (1808);[69] *P'ing-nan*, then, must have been completed and published between these two dates. I have no doubt that these dates are reliable.

[66] Cf. n. 6. The full titles preceding the table of contents for the two novels are: 新鐫異說五虎平西珍珠旗演義狄青前傳 and 新鐫繡像五虎平南狄青后傳.

[67] *Wu-hu p'ing-nan hou-chuan, chüan 6*, p. 45b. It was customary, of course, for a publisher to refer to a brand-new work of fiction as a rediscovered *ku-pen*.

[68] *Wan-hua lou* (Hong Kong, Kuang-chin shu-chü), p. 278; (Tainan, Ta-tung shu-chü), p. 227. The commentary is identical in both editions, though the Hong Kong edition has divided it into three paragraphs and adopted modern punctuation. Though I have not seen any earlier editions, the very fact that both contemporary editions carry the commentary vouches for its appearance in earlier editions. Logically, it should have appeared in the first edition.

[69] The fuller titles of *Wan-hua lou* are given in n. 6. For the date of the preface to *P'ing-hsi* see Sun, I, p. 53, and for that of the preface to *Wan-hua lou*, see Cheng Chen-to, *op. cit.*, p. 308. The preface to the Ching-lun-t'ang edition of *P'ing-hsi* is not dated, but the preface to the same edition of *P'ing-nan* is signed by one Hsiao-hsiang-huai chu-jen 小鄉環主人. From the tone of the preface, however, I would rule out the possibility of his being the author of *P'ing-nan*. The editions of *P'ing-nan* seen by Sun K'ai-ti all carry a preface identical with that of *P'ing-hsi*. When the owner of Ching-lun-t'ang decided to publish *P'ing-hsi* and *P'ing-nan* as one set, he must have commissioned somebody to write a new preface for *P'ing-nan*.

The early editions of *Wan-hua lou* all carry the author's preface by
Li Yü-t'ang of Lingnan. Normally, we would have expected its
publishers to entrust its composition to the same man who wrote
P'ing-hsi and *P'ing-nan*. But while the plots of *Wan-hua lou* and *P'ing-
hsi* tally remarkably well, there still exist significant discrepancies of
the kind that would make one question the theory of single authorship.[70] Stylistically the most obvious difference is that, whereas the
reported speeches in *P'ing-hsi* and *P'ing-nan* are most often introduced by the character *shuo* 說, in *Wan-hua lou* such speeches are
commonly introduced by the more literary *yüeh* 曰, even though
expressions like *shuo, tao* 道, and *shuo-tao* are also used. Moreover, in
P'ing-hsi and *P'ing-nan,* one character often addresses another by his
name or title plus the particle *ah* 阿 (e.g., "Ti Ch'ing ah"); this
stylistic feature is rarely observed in *Wan-hua lou*. Li Yü-t'ang was by
his own admission a man of Kwangtung; the author of *P'ing-hsi* and
P'ing-nan at times uses colloquial expressions that would seem to
occur only in the Wu dialect. Even on stylistic grounds alone, therefore, there would seem to be no reason to attribute *P'ing-hsi* and
P'ing-nan to Li Yü-t'ang.

Cheng Chen-to, in giving praise to *Wan-hua lou*, fully acknowledges
its indebtedness to earlier military romances: *Fen-chuang lou, Yang-
chia-fu, Shuo T'ang, Shuo Yüeh,* and *Shui-hu chuan*. But he continues:

> Even though *Wan-hua lou* has used stereotyped plots and characters,
> we cannot say that it does not have its special distinction. Among
> Chinese hero-romances (*ying-hsiung ch'uan-ch'i* 英雄傳奇), it surely
> deserves a mention. In several parts of the book the descriptions are
> excellent. Even though the author uses the old formulas, he is able to
> vary them. Though Ti Ch'ing's deeds and companions are not unlike

---

[70] I shall mention here only a few discrepancies that can be easily grasped. In *Wan-hua
lou* Ti Ch'ing is married to the daughter of Fan Chung-yen 范仲淹; this wife is not mentioned in *P'ing-hsi*. In fact, when Princess Sai-hua tries to learn from the captive Ti Ch'ing
if he is already married, he emphatically says no (this glaring difference between the two
novels is commented on in the concluding section of *Wan-hua lou*). Shih Yü 石玉 a handsome youth and one of the "Five Tigers," is married to Kao Ch'iung's 高瓊 daughter in
Wan-hua lou; in *P'ing-hsi* his wife's maiden name is Chao 趙. Hu-yen Tsan, a general of
Yang Yeh's time who should have died long before, is still present in *P'ing-hsi*, ch. 39;
Wan-hua lou, ch. 9, describes his son Hu-yeh Hsien 呼延顯 as a man over seventy. In
Wan-hua lou Pao Cheng is said to be a man of seventy; in *P'ing-hsi* he appears as a man in
his prime.

those of Yüeh Fei, Yang Yen-chao, and Hsüeh Jen-kuei, his character absolutely differs from theirs.[71]

But Cheng Chen-to perhaps should not even have apologized for the book's derivative character since, as I have shown, it is the peculiar feature of the genre that each author builds upon the work of his precedessors and varies the formulas according to his own lights.

Cheng Chen-to, however, dismisses *P'ing-hsi* and *P'ing-nan* as routine romances of no distinction. I believe he is right about *P'ing-nan*, a short work of forty-two chapters which adds nothing to the formulas of the military romance. Though, historically, Ti Ch'ing earned his widest renown by quelling the rebellion of Nung Chih-kao in the south, the author nevertheless makes him only a nominal hero (as is Hsüeh Jen-kuei in *Cheng-hsi*) in order to glorify his sons Ti Lung 狄龍 and Ti Hu 狄虎 as warriors and lovers. Historically, Yang Wen-kuang 楊文廣, Yang Yen-chao's son, served under Ti Ch'ing in the expedition against Nung. But in the retelling of this episode in the Yang saga, the Yang family had long supplanted Ti Ch'ing as the chief architect of victory (as a matter of fact, Ti appears as a villain in *Yang-chia-fu* determined to wreak his vengeance upon Yang Tsung-pao and Yang Wen-kuang for his own failure to quell Nung).[72] The author of *P'ing-nan* has unwisely followed this tradition by emphasizing the helplessness of Ti Ch'ing, who twice must call for rescue by expeditionary forces under the command of the Yang family. The melodrama of vengeance in *P'ing-nan* also excites little interest. Since the story of Ti Ch'ing's persecution by P'ang Hung and Sun Hsiu has properly ended with their execution in *P'ing-hsi*, there is no need for the author to prolong the story by inventing the new villain Sun Chen 孫振, who, as Sun Hsiu's nephew, ineptly schemes for Ti Ch'ing's downfall. In all these

[71] Cheng Chen-to 鄭振鐸, *Chung-kuo wen-hsüeh yen-chiu* 中國文學研究, I (Peking, Tso-chia ch'u-pan-she, 1957), p. 308.

[72] Cf. n. 15 and n. 49. After surrendering his seals to Yang Tsung-pao as the new commander of the expeditionary forces against Nung Chih-kao, he swears that he will exterminate the Yang family. When Tsung-pao and Wen-kuang return victorious to the capital, Ti Ch'ing sends one of his men, Shih Chin 師金, to infiltrate the Yang mansion. He is supposed to assassinate Tsung-pao; even though he doesn't go through with the plan, Tsung-pao has reached the predestined end of his life and summons his son to his deathbed to warn him of Ti Ch'ing's enmity. And mainly because of this warning Wen-kuang decides to retire from the world. Thus in *Yang-chia-fu* Ti Ch'ing is one of a series of villains bent on injuring the Yang family.

respects, *P'ing-nan* is a derivative work that adds nothing to our appreciation of Ti Ch'ing as a hero of military romance or as a historic general of outstanding achievement.

But *P'ing-hsi* is a military romance of compelling interest, and it constitutes, with *Wan-hua lou,* a coherent legend of Ti Ch'ing from his birth to his full vindication as the supreme commander of his time. I have shown that the early careers of heroes are much more amenable to fictional treatment than their later careers as military commanders. However conventionalized, a hero's youthful adventures and tribulations tell a story of human meaning, and it is only after his emergence upon the public scene as a military commander that his career is told in terms that would suggest the basic unreality of the military romance. All the formulas and conventions described in the earlier sections are in a sense designed to disguise that unreality and diversify the routine battle. Thus *P'ing-hsi,* insofar as it has turned a conventional military romance into something of sustained narrative interest, represents a far more difficult achievement than *Wan-hua lou,* which, after all, models its hero after the Ti Ch'ing of *P'ing-hsi* and relies to a great extent upon the legends of Pao Cheng and Emperor Jen-tsung for the enrichment of his story.

Principally, the author of *Wu-hu p'ing-hsi* has refashioned the military romance by assigning predominant importance to one of its story elements—the persecution of the hero by his determined enemies—and by enhancing the hero's romantic status. The other features of the military romance are still there: the female warrior, the comic warrior, the companion heroes, magical weaponry, and the magical formations. But the author has not tried to outdo his predecessors in his handling of these elements. Though celestially tutored in magical weaponry, Princess Sai-hua is far more a domestic creature than Fan Li-hua and is seldom seen in battle. Chiao T'ing-kuei, while immensely funny in guiding the expeditionary army into the wrong country, is otherwise a rather subdued creature lacking the comic exuberance of Ch'eng Yao-chin. The magical weapons and formations are nothing to be compared with what we have seen in earlier romances. Also, the author has deliberately reduced the number of companions serving under Ti Ch'ing, and none of them is really distinguished in battle.

On the whole, therefore, the author concentrates on the continuing feud between the hero and the villains. P'ang Hung and Sun Hsiu are very cunning, but Ti Ch'ing, while a hero of uncomplaining loyalty, is no passive victim either. If P'ang Hung's daughter is Jen-tsung's favorite concubine, Ti Ch'ing's father's sister is the emperor's aunt who once nursed him. And Jen-tsung, though partial to P'ang Hung, is too soft-hearted to inflict harsh punishment upon either faction. Especially, Pao Cheng, Ti Ch'ing's civil counterpart at Jen-tsung's court, is ever ready to defend the innocent. At once a master detective and a stern judge, he corrects the power imbalance between villain and hero to be seen in most military romances and renders the course of villainy more difficult but at the same time more fascinating to watch.

With a true novelist's instinct, therefore, the author has transformed a military romance into a piece of detective fiction. Even the campaigns are instigated by the villains to get Ti Ch'ing and his companions into trouble. Ti Ch'ing does not grudge the opportunity to earn fame and glory, but each time he leads an expedition, he knows that his real enemies will watch his every move and will even collaborate with the Hsi Liao government to plot his downfall. Upon the conclusion of his second expedition, he himself brings to court a key witness to substantiate his charge of treason against P'ang Hung and Sun Hsiu. Presiding over the case, Pao Cheng not only convicts the villains of their crimes but compels the emperor himself to bring about their due punishment. At this juncture we are truly happy for Ti Ch'ing. It is the kind of happiness we feel after reading through *The Three Musketeers, The Count of Monte Cristo,* or any other well-constructed romance which has fully engaged our sympathy for the hero and our detestation for his enemies.

Measured against the tedium of *Feng-shen yen-yi* and of the Four Expeditions in *Shui-hu chuan, P'ing-hsi* has gone a long way toward making something enjoyable out of the military romance. Though the author has only written an entertaining story without pretension to literary greatness, his discovery of the well-made plot amounts to a recognition that preoccupation with the stylized presentation of warfare, however well supplied with wonders and diversified by related themes of subsidiary interest, has been a costly mistake in the development of the Chinese novel. And in composing *Wan-hua lou,*

Li Yü-t'ang has gone a step further in de-emphasizing stylized warfare for the full exploitation of the kind of human interest implicit in the tribulations of the young Ti Ch'ing and in Pao Cheng's determined attempt to bring about the reunion of Jen-tsung and his long-suffering mother. Though a full survey of the genre cannot stop with *P'ing-hsi* and *Wan-hua lou*, insofar as their authors have channeled its potential for further growth into the new genre of *wu-hsia hsiao-shuo*, they may be said to have killed the military romance.

ABBREVIATIONS

ES   *Erh-shih-wu shih* 二十五史. 9 vols. Reprint: Taipei, K'ai-ming shu-tien, preface dated 1934.

KYT, III   *Ku-pen Yüan-Ming tsa-chü* 孤本元明雜劇, vol. 3. Peking, Chung-kuo hsi-chü ch'u-pan-she, 1957.

Liu, I   Liu Ts'un-yan. *Chinese Popular Fiction in Two London Libraries.* Hong Kong, Lung Men Bookstore, 1967.

Liu, II   Liu Ts'un-yan. *Buddhist and Taoist Influences on Chinese Novels.* Vol. I: *The Authorship of the Feng Shen Yen I.* Wiesbaden, Otto Harrassowitz, 1962.

Sun, I   Sun K'ai-ti 孫楷第. *Chung-kuo t'ung-su hsiao-shuo shu-mu* 中國通俗小說書目. Reprint: Hong Kong, Shih-yung shu-chü, 1967.

Sun, II   Sun K'ai-ti. *Jih-pen Tung-ching so-chien Chung-kuo hsiao-shuo shu-mu* 日本東京所見中國小說書目. Reprint: Hong Kong, Shih-yung shu-chü, 1967.

POSTSCRIPT

The author of *Shuo T'ang* may have modeled Li Yüan-pa after Li Ts'un-hsiao 李存孝, the principal hero of *T'san-T'ang wu-tai ch'üan-chuan*. The latter, too, is a youth of slight build and sickly appearance who achieves stupendous feats on the battlefield without resorting to magic.

Index